MEDICAL LAW, ETHICS & BIOETHICS

for the HEALTH PROFESSIONS

EIGHTH EDITION

Carol D. Tamparo, PhD, CMA-A (AAMA)
Formerly Dean, Business and Allied Health
Lake Washington Institute of Technology
Kirkland, Washington
Coordinator, Medical Assistant Program
Highline College
Des Moines, Washington

F.A. DAVIS
Philadelphia

F. A. Davis Company
1915 Arch Street
Philadelphia, PA 19103
www.fadavis.com

Printed in the United States of America

Last digit indicates print number: 10 9 8 7 6 5 4 3 2 1

Editor-in-Chief: Margaret M. Biblis
Publisher: Quincy McDonald
Director of Content Development: George W. Lang
Content Project Manager: Elizabeth Stepchin
Art and Design Manager: Carolyn O'Brien

As new scientific information becomes available through basic and clinical research, recommended treatments and drug therapies undergo changes. The author(s) and publisher have done everything possible to make this book accurate, up to date, and in accord with accepted standards at the time of publication. The author(s), editors, and publisher are not responsible for errors or omissions or for consequences from application of the book, and make no warranty, expressed or implied, in regard to the contents of the book. Any practice described in this book should be applied by the reader in accordance with professional standards of care used in regard to the unique circumstances that may apply in each situation. The reader is advised always to check product information (package inserts) for changes and new information regarding dose and contraindications before administering any drug. Caution is especially urged when using new or infrequently ordered drugs.

Library of Congress Cataloging-in-Publication Data

Names: Tamparo, Carol D., 1940- author. | Preceded by (work): Lewis, Marcia
   A. Medical law, ethics, & bioethics for the health professions.
Title: Medical law, ethics, & bioethics for the health professions / Carol
   D. Tamparo.
Other titles: Medical law, ethics, and bioethics for the health professions
Description: Eighth edition. | Philadelphia : F.A. Davis, [2022] | Preceded
   by Medical law, ethics, & bioethics for the health professions / Marcia
   (Marti) Lewis, Carol D. Tamparo, Brenda M. Tatro. 7th ed. c2012. |
   Includes bibliographical references and index.
Identifiers: LCCN 2021018935 (print) | LCCN 2021018936 (ebook) | ISBN
   9781719640930 (paperback) | ISBN 9781719640954 (ebook)
Subjects: MESH: Ambulatory Care—legislation & jurisprudence | Ambulatory
   Care—ethics | Ethics, Clinical | Bioethical Issues | Legislation,
   Medical | United States
Classification: LCC KF3821 (print) | LCC KF3821 (ebook) | NLM WB 33 AA1
   | DDC 344.7304/1—dc23
LC record available at https://lccn.loc.gov/2021018935
LC ebook record available at https://lccn.loc.gov/2021018936

*"The way a book is read—which is to say,
the qualities a reader brings to a book—
can have as much to do with its worth as
anything the author puts into it."*

Norman Cousins

PREFACE

It is imperative that any health-care professional have knowledge of medical law, ethics, and bio-ethics so that clients are treated with understanding, sensitivity, and compassion. No matter what the professional's education, experience, or position, any client contact involves ethical and legal responsibility. It also is imperative that this knowledge be used to provide the best possible service for the provider and employer. Our goal is to provide the health-care professional with an adequate resource for the study of medical law, ethics, and bioethics.

Although the material is applicable to all health-care professionals in any setting, our emphasis continues to be on ambulatory health care in outpatient settings and clinics rather than on the hospital or long-term care setting. For example, we do not address such legal and bioethical issues as whether to feed an anencephalic newborn in the neonatal center of the hospital. We realize, however, that all the bioethical issues affect health-care personnel directly or indirectly. Continued enthusiastic feedback from instructors, students, and reviewers is gratifying and has resulted in many changes that will make this Eighth Edition more useful than the first seven. We are reminded of the truth, which comes from our colleagues in community and technical colleges, that no matter how many times a piece is written, it can always be improved.

The continuing evolution of health care, as well as legal and, especially, bioethical issues, neces-sitates this revision. The material has been updated throughout to reflect the latest developments and emerging ethical issues. Major changes occur in both Units III and IV where technology has advanced and changed medicine: how it is delivered and financed, often challenged by the political arena, and how those changes affect today's clients. The newest developments in stem cell research for treating disease and for creating new organs and tissue are included in the Genetic Modifi-cation chapter as the legal and ethical debate "rages." The chapter introducing the reader to the cultural perspectives of health care continues to heighten one's awareness of the importance of cultural sensitivity in health care, including sensitivity to the LGBTQIA community. The chapter on reproductive health issues has been enhanced. Abortion is still covered as an important element in reproductive health, but many new topics have been added.

The contributors to this text and their editors have made every attempt to ensure currency and pertinence of the material. However, some bioethical issues change rapidly as lawmakers and the public become actively involved and press for legislation. Even as this edition goes into production, the author struggles to be current as federal and state legislations clash, the Covid-19 Pandemic marches on, and the 2020 election played a major role. Funding and morality issues are being addressed in the political arena, sometimes bringing research and advancement in medicine to a standstill. For ease of reference, pertinent codes of ethics appear in Appendix I. Appendix II offers samples of some of the legal documents clients may use in implementing decisions about health care, life, and death.

A thought-provoking vignette appears in each chapter. The vignettes are adapted from case law or from actual situations. Learning outcomes designed for the educational setting precede each chapter. The Eighth Edition places Case Studies, Case Law, and In the News throughout the chap-ters both for reflection and chapter content. CAAHEP and ABHES competencies also appear at the beginning of each chapter to help students and faculty identify competencies necessary for accredi-tation and certification in the content area of medical law and ethics.

For students' benefit, we have included questions for review at the end of each chapter for increased learning. Classroom exercises and Internet activities will whet the appetite, stimulate discussion, and highlight the most pressing legal, ethical, and bioethical issues faced by ambulatory care employees. Last, Web resources are provided to help the reader in further research on the Internet.

F. A. Davis offers many additional resources and exercises for both the student and the instructor. Videos are available for classroom use or small-group discussions. The videos will require students to put themselves in the place of making legal and ethical decisions.

"Have a Care" has been updated. It continues to be one of the most popular pieces of this textbook. Because nearly every person has a "Have a Care" moment in his or her life and experiences with the medical community, it is our hope that it will always be a part of any upcoming edition. This is the first edition where "Have a Care" no longer is the story of Marcia (Marti) Lewis, the primary person in this story and a coauthor since the First Edition. "Have a Care" in this edition is the story of another champion for quality health care who remembers that the purpose of medical care is not only to diagnose and treat—it is to understand, to listen, and to help clients navigate a complicated system toward treatment, perhaps a cure, but always toward better health.

Two contributors to this edition, both with excellent credentials and experience, contributed six chapters each. They worked during the Covid-19 Pandemic while homeschooling children and being employed in the health-care arena. Although we never met face to face, we established a successful rapport and met the deadlines established by F. A. Davis.

We hope that from this book you will derive a great sense of pride for your professional position in health care.

Carol D. Tamparo
Christina Eliza DiStefano
Tami Kathleen Little

CONTRIBUTORS

Christina Eliza DiStefano, MSN, RN, MBA, NE-BC, CCRN-K
Nursing Administrative Coordinator, Pennsylvania Hospital
Adjunct Clinical Faculty, Holy Family University and Drexel University
Philadelphia, PA

Tami Kathleen Little, DNP, RN, CNE
Corporate Director of Nursing, Vista College
NM and TX

REVIEWERS

Brian Clinton, MA, BS, CHES
Allied Health
Quinebaug Valley Community College
Danielson, CT

Candace S. Dailey, MSN, RN, CMA(AAMA)
Health Occupations Programs
Nicolet College
Rhinelander, WI

Christina G. Lee, MSAH, RT(R)(CT)(MR)(QM)
Math, Science, & Health Technologies
Southwest Virginia Community College
Richlands, VA

Candice Spaulding, CMA (AAMA)
Allied Health
Manchester Community College
Manchester, NH

Michael P. Waide, MPhil, MDiv
Health Sciences
Pierpont Community & Technical College
Fairmont, WV

ACKNOWLEDGMENTS

It is never possible to acknowledge all the people who make contributions to the authors of a book. Completing a book requires assistance from so many individuals and sources. We wish to thank, however, a few who were especially helpful. Without them, the book would have been impossible to create.

F. A. Davis has a fine cadre of individuals who make a writing project pleasant. Each individual's desire for excellence and thoroughness helps to create the final product. Margaret Biblis, Editor-in-Chief, and Quincy McDonald, Publisher, refresh our thoughts and goals with new ideas and discerning eyes. Elizabeth Stepchin, Content Project Manager, monitors our budget and provides direction and support as necessary. All these people have been positive, encouraging, and helpful to us in all matters. Our relationship with F. A. Davis for over 40 years has always been one of high professionalism and integrity.

Students continually offer critical thought and information on legal, ethical, and bioethical issues and act as a sounding board for all ideas. Their input and comments have influenced this product. Students continue to be our inspiration and the reason for this book!

The support of families and friends has been an essential ingredient from the inception of the First Edition to the completion of this Eighth Edition. Thanks to Tom Tamparo, Jayne Bloomberg, and Duuana Warden and their families. They relinquished their time with us so we could write.

Carol D. Tamparo

My family provided time and space for me to accomplish my chapter assignments during the pandemic while homeschooling children, my spouse working from home, and maintaining my own employment. Working with Carol Tamparo in the revision of this text was extremely rewarding. Carol's desire for excellence was intoxicating and led to many long days of research, reflection, and writing. I appreciated all her support and guidance. I hope our students are inspired and learn as much as I have.

Tami Kathleen Little

What would we ever do without family when such a task is undertaken? Much appreciation is given to Anthony DiStefano, Anthony DiStefano, Jr., and Michael DiStefano for your unending support during this process. Thank you, thank you.

Christina Eliza DiStefano

CONTENTS IN BRIEF

DETAILED TABLE OF CONTENTS

UNIT I

Understanding the Basics

CHAPTER 1

Medical Law, Ethics, and Bioethics

"The aim of education is the knowledge, not of facts, but of values."—William Ralph Inge (1860–1954); Church of England clergyman, scholar, and critic

KEY TERMS

hospitalist Individual who assumes the care of hospitalized individuals in place of their primary health-care provider.

pluralistic Referring to numerous distinct ethnic, religious, and cultural groups that coexist in society.

LEARNING OUTCOMES

Upon successful completion of this chapter, you should be able to:

1.1 Define key terms.
1.2 Compare medical law, ethics, and bioethics.
1.3 Discuss some bioethical issues in medicine.
1.4 Explain the importance of medical law, ethics, and bioethics in the practice of medicine.
1.5 List and discuss at least three ethical codes.
1.6 Describe the American Association of Medical Assistants (AAMA) Code of Ethics.
1.7 Interpret the AAMA Creed.
1.8 Compare/contrast the AAMA and the American Medical Association (AMA) codes of ethics.
1.9 Describe the Patient Bill of Rights.
1.10 Explain the Ethics Check questions.
1.11 Describe characteristics that are important for a professional health-care employee.

COMPETENCIES

COMMISSION ON ACCREDITATION OF ALLIED HEALTH EDUCATION PROGRAMS (CAAHEP)

• Summarize the Patient Bill of Rights. (CAAHEP X.C.4)
• Define ethics and morals. (CAAHEP XI.C.1)
• Differentiate between personal and professional ethics. (CAAHEP XI.C.2)
• Identify the effect of personal morals on professional performance. (CAAHEP XI.C.3)
• Apply the Patient's Bill of Rights as it relates to choice of treatment, consent of treatment, and refusal of treatment. (CAAHEP X.P.4)

- Demonstrate sensitivity to patient rights. (CAAHEP X.A.1)
- Develop a plan for separation of personal and professional ethics. (CAAHEP XI.P.1)
- Demonstrate appropriate response(s) to ethical issues. (CAAHEP XI.P.2)
- Recognize the impact personal ethics and morals have on the delivery of healthcare. (CAAHEP XI.A.1)

ACCREDITING BUREAU OF HEALTH EDUCATION SCHOOLS (ABHES)

- Display compliance with the Code of Ethics of the profession (ABHES 4.g)
- Analyze the effect of hereditary, cultural and environmental influences. (ABHES 5.g)

VIGNETTE

Are You Professional?

A certified medical assistant (CMA) employed by an obstetrician/gynecologist calls her former medical assistant instructor to inform her of an opening for a clinical assistant in the obstetrics and gynecology (OB-GYN) clinic. After describing the position and its responsibilities, the CMA says, "We really need another person in the clinical area. I'm the doctor's only nurse."

Surprised by the comment, the instructor inquires, "When did you go back to school to become a nurse?"

She replies, "Oh, I didn't, but everyone thinks I am his nurse. I do everything a nurse does."

The title of this text, *Medical Law, Ethics, and Bioethics for the Health Professions,* presents three distinct topics: medical law, ethics, and bioethics. Such distinction, however, is for the sake of clarity. Discussion of any one of these topics will include the others. Any study of health law will surface themes of ethics and bioethics. Conversely, discussing ethics and bioethics without considering the law is futile.

LAW

Laws are societal rules or regulations that are prudent or obligatory to observe. Failure to observe the law is punishable by the government and/or law enforcement agencies. Laws are designed to protect the welfare and safety of society and to resolve conflicts in an orderly and nonviolent manner. They constantly evolve in accordance with an increasingly **pluralistic** society. Laws have governed humankind and the practice of medicine for thousands of years. Today federal and state governments have constitutional authority to create and enforce laws. A brief look at these laws, their sources, and their definitions appears in subsequent chapters.

Medical law is essential in regulating licensure of health-care professionals and institutions, providing for client safety, protecting the client-provider relationship, and identifying liability for health-care professionals and institutions. Health law also regulates insurance and managed care as well as federal public health programs. It also has established standards for reproduction and birth issues as well as life-and-death decisions.

ETHICS

Ethics is a set of moral standards or a code for behavior to govern an individual's interactions with other individuals and within society. Joseph Fletcher (1905–1991), an American professor who pioneered in the field of bioethics, differentiates *morals* from ethics, stating, "'morality' is what people do in fact believe to be right and good, while 'ethics' is a critical reflection about morality and the rational analysis of it." According to Fletcher, for example, "Should I terminate pregnancy?" is a moral question, whereas "How should I go about deciding?" is an ethical concern.

Although laws are more apt to be rules applied to and observed by all, different cultures have different moral codes. Cultural differences exist relative to age, gender, sexual orientation, ethnic heritage, educational preparation, life experiences, spiritual influences, economics, values, and health and illness. Every standard for ethics is culture-bound. Ethical standards also evolve through time. Therefore, there are few if any universal truths in ethics because it is difficult to identify customs as being either correct or incorrect. It is also true that one person's moral code has no special status relative to another person's moral code; it is only one among many. See Chapter 12, A Cultural Perspective for Health Professionals, for further discussion on the influence of culture.

Ethical standards can be personal, organizational, institutional, or worldwide. Ethics refers to the various codes of conduct that have been established through the years by members of many professional organizations, including the medical profession. A number of medical codes appear in the appendices and at http://FADavis.com, keyword *Tamparo*.

 ## BIOETHICS

Bioethics refers to the ethical implications of biomedical technology and its practices. *Bio* refers to life, and issues in bioethics are often life-and-death issues. Edmund D. Pellegrino, Professor Emeritus of Medicine and Medical Ethics at Georgetown University, states that "bioethics, still in its infancy, is routinely called on by the government to provide political cover for controversial public health decisions involving the life and death of Americans." In other words, political leaders often look to bioethical discussions to guide them in making decisions regarding controversial public health issues. Specialists in the field of bioethics provide the platform for this decision making.

Bioethics commissions have provided valuable guidance to U.S. presidents for the past 45 years. The first was established by President Richard Nixon in 1974 as the National Commission for the Protection of Human Subjects of Biomedical and Behavioral Research. Subsequent presidents, including Presidents Jimmy Carter, Ronald Reagan, Bill Clinton, George W. Bush, and Barack Obama, have established their own commissions that provided input to national leaders on issues of bioethics. President Donald Trump did not establish a bioethical commission, but these commissions have traditionally played a key role in keeping presidents informed about bioethical issues. President Joseph Biden is expected to establish his commission.

The challenge to bioethics created by modern medicine and research in the past few decades is staggering. Rapid changes in medicine and technology offer unique and sometimes overwhelming choices to clients and their families. Consumers today are more actively involved in their health care and have greater access to information related to health-care options and available medical technology. These informed consumers ask more questions of medical professionals and carefully scrutinize medical technology and how it relates to their daily lives. Thus, the application of bioethics in everyday life provides opportunities, challenges, enthusiasm, and sometimes difficult choices.

 ## COMPARING MEDICAL LAW, ETHICS, AND BIOETHICS

Law, ethics, and bioethics are different yet related concepts. Laws are mandatory rules to which all citizens must adhere. Ethics often relate to morals and set forth universal goals to try to meet. There is no risk of civil or criminal liability for failing to meet ethical goals, but there is when a citizen breaks the law. Although law and ethics are very different, law in the United States has been and continues to be a driving force in shaping ethics.

Confusion over the interpretation of law, ethics, and bioethics is understandable. They sometimes conflict. Consider the following example for further clarification:

The U.S. Supreme Court addressed the issue of abortion in *Roe v Wade*, 410 U.S. 113, 1973. The *law* states that during the first trimester, pregnant women have a constitutional right to abortions, and the state has no vested interest in regulating them at this time. During the second trimester, the state may regulate abortions and insist on reasonable standards of medical practice if an abortion is to be performed. During the third trimester, the state's interests override pregnant women's rights to abortions, and the state may deny abortion except when necessary to preserve the health or life of the mother.

The personal *ethics* of a provider or health-care professional may dictate participation or non-participation in an abortion or any abortion-related activities. *Bioethics* and the allocation of scarce resources are evidenced by some state statutes that have denied the use of state funds for an abortion or strive to make abortions less available, if at all. As demonstrated by this example, sometimes law, ethics, and bioethics conflict.

IN THE NEWS

As a result of two U.S. Supreme Court rulings that prohibit parents from having absolute veto over their daughters' decision to have an abortion, many state legislatures rushed to tighten controls on abortions. As of July 2020, 11 states and the District of Columbia (Washington, D.C.) had no parental notification or consent laws related to minors seeking abortion (Fig. 1-1). Thirty-seven states require some involvement in a minor's decision. Thirty-four states permit a minor to obtain an abortion in a medical emergency; 15 states permit a minor to obtain an abortion in cases of abuse, assault, incest, or neglect. This information changes yearly as state legislative bodies struggle to exercise control over abortions in their state. Sometimes, such legislation is later overturned by the U.S. Supreme Court. Legal attempts continue the move to rescind *Roe v Wade*.

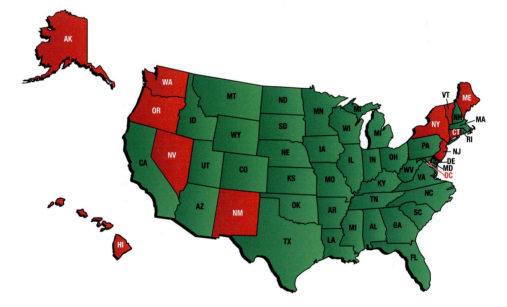

Figure 1-1. U.S. map showing states requiring no parent notification and/or consent for a minor's abortion.

THE IMPORTANCE OF MEDICAL LAW, ETHICS, AND BIOETHICS

Medical law, ethics, and bioethics are important concepts for health-care professionals. It is necessary to follow health-care laws and to examine one's actions in both laws and ethics. It is helpful to learn more from the bioethical issues that clients face and to appreciate differences in moral reasoning among individuals and various cultures. Also, there is always the need to confront personal biases and bigotry.

In addition, there are political and economic factors that are relevant and often shape medical law, ethics, and bioethics. They include the following:

- Demands of society for quality health care at minimal personal cost
- The debate over whether health care is a right or a privilege
- The equality of the distribution of and access to emerging medical technology

- The controversy among the political arena, national health-care reform, and the consumer over who pays for health care and how it is paid
- The powerful role of medical insurance and managed care

Thoughtful consideration of the reasons identified here, as well as the political and economic factors, fosters mature decision making and quality health care for clients.

 ## TODAY'S HEALTH-CARE CLIMATE

There is much in today's health-care environment to challenge any health-care professional's ethics, values, and practices. Just a few are identified here for reflection.

- *Consumers are bombarded with medical information.* The media, both printed and electronic, report on many aspects of health care. This immediate access of information empowers consumers to ask more questions of medical professionals, allowing them to be better informed about choices.
- *Hospitals and ambulatory care centers have established ethics committees and/or institutional review boards (IRBs)* that enable community resource persons, educators, and providers to grapple with ethical dilemmas both before and after they occur in the clinical setting. Laws and ethical standards designed to protect clients and establish guidelines for the medical community represent an effort to create a climate for an equitable exchange between client and provider. The primary goal of an ethics committee is to have a plan in place before a crisis occurs. IRBs have been empowered by the U.S. Food and Drug Administration (FDA) and the Department of Health and Human Services (DHHS) to monitor, review, and oversee any medical research involving human subjects. An IRB is required if there is either direct or indirect support from the DHHS.
- *Medical technology is advancing at a more rapid rate than legal and ethical standards can address.* Consider the time without antibiotics, when premature infants died due to lack of neonatal intensive care and when invasive surgery rather than a computed tomography scan was the only method to reveal problems with internal organs. There are numerous medical advances likely to occur in the next decade. Many may come with a flurry of ethical and bioethical implications that will create debate in the medical community. These medical advances may include the following:
  - Restoring irreversibly damaged hearts by replacing dead heart muscle with new laboratory-grown muscle and creating artificial organs such as pancreas and synthetic ovaries
  - Using harvested skin cells obtained through a small biopsy, suspended in a solution, and sprayed directly onto a major burn area to rapidly divide and cover the wound up to 80 times larger than the donor site
  - Precision medicine that allows professionals to select medicine or therapy based on a person's genetic makeup
  - Using high-technology brain scans to detect the earliest signs of both plaques and tangles found in Alzheimer disease and using a vaccine to stimulate the body's own immune response to wipe out the plaques once identified
  - The use of 3-D printing to create prosthetics and joints that are matched to an individual's measurements down to the millimeter
  - Robotic surgery that enables very complex procedures that otherwise would be very difficult or impossible to perform
- *Increasing numbers of specialists in medicine make it more difficult to coordinate client care.* It is conceivable that a client has a primary health-care provider, a neurologist, a nephrologist, and an oncologist all providing care. If hospitalization is necessary, is the primary health-care provider or a **hospitalist** in charge? Who coordinates, and who approves care? Who decides the appropriate course of action in the case of conflicting medical opinions? Although specialization may enhance quality health care, it demands greater coordination for clients to benefit, and it increases the cost of medical care.
- *Costs of medical care have risen exponentially.* In 1940, a normal infant delivery cost $35 for 10 days of inpatient hospital care, and the delivering physician received an additional $35. In 2005, hospitalization for normal delivery and a 1- to 2-day hospital stay was $5,200. In 2010, the

typical cost of a vaginal delivery ranged from about $9,000 to $17,000 and the typical cost for a cesarean delivery ranged from $14,000 to $25,000. In 2019, the average price charged for a vaginal delivery was around $30,000 and for a cesarean delivery around $50,000. The cost of pregnancy, birth, and newborn care differs based on region of the country and whether the facility is in a rural or urban setting. Additional factors affecting the cost include whether it is a vaginal or cesarean delivery, whether there are complications, and the length of the hospital stay. It is interesting to note that a normal delivery in Finland is only $45.

The importance of these issues is further evidenced by ongoing debates over national health-care programs. In 2010, two health-care reforms were passed: the Patient Protection and Affordable Care Act and the Health Care and Education Reconciliation Act. Future reforms of the U.S. health care system continue to be proposed, including a single-payer system, a reduction in fee-for-service program, and a Medicare plan with greater consumer access. Changing a health-care system is complex, political, and often contentious, and health-care professionals will want to remain apprised of medical laws and bioethical controversies around medical technology, health-care advances, and access to quality health care.

ETHICAL ISSUES IN MODERN MEDICINE

Many situations arise in the practice of medicine and in medical research that present problems requiring moral decisions. A few of these can be illustrated by the following questions:

Should a parent be able to refuse a mandated immunization for his or her child? Does public safety supersede an individual's right? Is basic health care a right or a privilege—a topic much debated in the current political arena? Who dictates client care—the client, the provider, or the health insurance company? Who pays for the care of children with serious and life-threatening birth defects? Should more medical attention be paid to a "cure" or for "prevention?" How should legal abortions be funded? Is it important that everyone receive equal treatment in medical care? What are the issues related to prolonging life or assisted death for individuals with terminal illnesses? What criteria determine who receives donor organs? Should stem cell research be limited or advanced?

None of these questions has an easy answer, and most individuals do not even think about them unless suddenly and personally faced with one or more of them. These questions and other possibilities are the reason for entering into a discussion of pertinent bioethical issues. For some, answers can be found in ethical codes.

CODES OF ETHICS

For generations ethical codes have been written to further clarify medical law and ethics. Nearly every health profession has its own code of ethics. Many codes have become law. Professional codes have evolved throughout history as practitioners grappled with various ethical and bioethical issues. Increasingly, groups of medical professionals have defined how members of their profession ought to behave. Following are a few examples.

The *Hippocratic Oath* (see Appendix 1), although not prominent in medical schools today, still carries significant weight among the medical community. The oath, which was first written in the fifth century B.C., was Christianized in the 10th or 11th century A.D. to eliminate reference to pagan gods. The Hippocratic Oath protected the rights of clients and appealed to the inner and finer instincts of the physician without imposing penalties.

The *Geneva Convention Code of Medical Ethics,* established by the World Medical Association in 1949, is similar to the Hippocratic Oath. This code refers to colleagues as brothers and states that religion, race, and other such factors are not a consideration for care of the total person. This code reflects the fact that medicine was becoming available to all during this era.

The *Nuremberg Code* was established between 1946 and 1949 following the trials of war criminals after World War II. This code suggests guidelines for human experimentation and is directed to the world. The writers hoped that the code would ensure the safety of humans in the years to come.

The *Declaration of Helsinki,* written between 1964 and 1975, is an update on human experimentation. Much more detailed than the Nuremberg Code, it includes guidelines for both therapeutic and scientific clinical research. Unlike the Nuremberg Code, the Declaration of Helsinki is directed to the world of medicine rather than the world at large.

The American Medical Association (AMA) established the *Principles of Medical Ethics* in 1847 and updated it in 1957, 1980, 2001, and 2016 (see Appendix 1). The preamble and nine principles have served as guidelines for physicians for many years. The document "Current Opinions of the Judicial Council of the American Medical Association" is intended as an adjunct to the revised Principles of Medical Ethics. Both documents are pertinent to physicians and their assistants today.

The number of professional medical organizations with written ethics codes is numerous. The codes are available on the Internet by searching the particular association and then for its code of ethics. A few are identified here:

- American Academy of Professional Coders (AAPC)
- International Medical Informatics Association (IMIA)
- National Association of Emergency Medical Technicians (NAEMT)
- American Osteopathic Association (AOA)
- American Association of Naturopathic Physicians (AANP)
- American Chiropractic Association (ACA)
- National Certification Commission for Acupuncture and Oriental Medicine (NCCAOM)
- National Medical Association (NMA)
- American Nurses Association (ANA)

An important code directed to persons employed in medical clinics and outpatient care is the *AAMA Medical Assistant Code of Ethics* and AAMA Medical Assisting Creed directed to the medical assistant (MA) (see Appendix 1). The code was adopted by the American Association of Medical Assistants and appears in its constitution and bylaws. It provides guidelines to assist MAs in serving their profession in an ethical and professional manner. This code, as well as most other ethical codes, identifies to society at large what the standards are for the profession.

A number of codes have appeared that deal more with the rights of clients than the responsibilities and guidelines for health-care providers. They include numerous patient bills of rights established by the American Hospital Association (AHA) and federal and state governments as well as individual hospitals and institutions. Contact the hospital nearest you for a sample of a patient bill of rights or go to http://FADavis.com, keyword *Tamparo,* for the sample from the AHA; they are all quite similar in content.

Increasing in popularity are patient bills of rights specific for outpatient care. They are usually written by specific clinics and generally include patients' right to be respected, right to access to their medical record, right to receive a second opinion, right to participate in their health care, and right to have their privacy protected at all times. Check for samples on the Internet by searching for entities such as the Cleveland Clinic and the Mayo Clinic.

The 2010 Healthcare Reform Bill included a Patient Bill of Rights that has an entirely different scope. This portion of the bill was designed to ensure that there is affordable health care for everyone; it is designed to put consumers back in charge of their health coverage and prevent insurance carriers from certain practices to ban clients from coverage. The purpose of any patient bill of rights is to make certain clients know their rights. It can be helpful to recognize that in some cases clients always had these rights but were not aware of them.

The most challenging aspect of any ethical code is its personal application. Many books have been written on the subject, and decades of scholarly debate have sought effective criteria for making ethical decisions. There is not one method that is appropriate in all situations or for all individuals. Ethical decisions are very personal to each individual involved. The following Ethics Check questions may be helpful as you begin to think about medical law, ethics, and bioethics as a health-care professional.

ETHICS CHECK

Blanchard and Peale, in *The Power of Ethical Management,* developed a set of questions to serve as an "ethics check" that is a useful tool for a person facing an ethical dilemma. These questions suggest that ethics is a very personal concept and a personal decision. Consider Blanchard and Peale's three questions to include in a personal code of ethics:

1. Is it legal or in accordance with institutional or company policy?
2. Does it promote a win–win situation with as many individuals (client/employee/employer) as possible?
3. How would I feel about myself if I read about my decision or action in the daily newspaper (Fig. 1-2)? How would my family feel? Could I look myself in the mirror?

According to Blanchard and Peale, if the answer to any one of the three questions is no, consider the action unethical. If the answer to all three questions is yes, the action is ethical. The identification of such a simple personal code of ethics can help to clarify actions, and these Ethics Check questions may provide further guidelines on how to act when in a difficult situation.

An individual will have greater difficulties remaining ethical in an organization in which the highest leaders are not ethical in their actions. It helps if the leader of a group is ethical, setting the standard and making it easier for everyone else to be ethical. However, ethical actions may and should come from anyone, regardless of status.

Figure 1-2. Ethics Check question: How do I feel seeing my decision in the newspaper?

Case Study

You are the clinic manager in a large multiprovider medical center. There is no upward mobility in this center, and you relish a new challenge. It is a rather slow day, and you use your office computer to access the Internet to do a job search. You find four jobs that are exciting, and you send your resume via the Internet. As you disconnect from the Internet, you recall that it is easy to trace access to sites on the Internet that you have just used for personal business.

Apply the Ethics Check to this case study.
What is your conclusion?

APPLYING MEDICAL LAW, ETHICS, AND BIOETHICS AS A PROFESSIONAL HEALTH-CARE EMPLOYEE

The significant conflict that often arises among medical law, ethics, and bioethics mandates that individuals choosing to be health-care professionals be people of high moral standards. They should be clear, open, and knowledgeable about their personal choices and beliefs and be able to recognize vast diversity in a pluralistic society. Health-care professionals must feel comfortable in a "servant" role while maintaining their own integrity and the respect of their clients.

Individuals employed in a service-oriented industry such as health care are expected to have certain characteristics. The health professional must always be tactful and should know instinctively when speaking is wise and when listening is better. The health-care employee is an important communication link between the client and the provider.

Anyone in a health-care profession is in a nonreciprocal relationship with clients. The professional serves the client and gives the client full respect even when the client is disrespectful. Health-care professionals will want to act and speak nonjudgmentally of their clients and their activities, offering information rather than personal opinions. Clients expect to be treated with courtesy and understanding. Only the most caring and sensitive of employees can handle day after day of sick, hurting, and complaining clients and remain objective, compassionate, and positive.

Physician- and provider-employers require that their employees be diligent and knowledgeable in every detail of the job. Such knowledge and training can come only through professional preparation that is demanding and continues throughout employment. Professionals who are flexible and take initiative will be an asset to their employers.

Honesty and integrity are traits required of the employee. Health-care professionals must always remember to practice only within the scope of their professional training and never misrepresent themselves. Confidentiality must be tenaciously protected, and both the clients' and the providers' best interests must be guarded.

Wise and prudent health-care employees will select employers for whom they have respect and to whom they can remain loyal. Matching one's personal understanding of how to care for clients to that of the employer avoids conflicts later. The majority of health-care professionals have a concern for quality health care, and that concern is often reflected in community efforts and contributions.

Refer to the following Case Law that illustrates a disregard of personal and professional ethics on the part of a medical provider.

Case Law

A physician in Lehi, Utah, was accused in August 2009 of the following:
1. Fondling his female medical assistant (MA) while pretending to teach her how to diagnose heart murmurs (Civil Suit)
2. Two counts of forcible sex abuse (Criminal Case)
3. Two counts of voyeurism (Criminal Case)
4. One count of obstruction of justice (Criminal Case)

Dr. Steven Pack also faces an investigation by the Division of Occupational and Professional Licensing.

Dr. Pack allegedly called his 18-year-old MA to an examination room to teach her how to diagnose heart murmurs. He asked her to lie on an examination table, lifted her shirt and bra, and fondled her breasts as he told her he was "feeling" for heart murmurs. Pack allegedly again inappropriately touched the woman while teaching her how to use a heart monitor and electrocardiograph machine. The MA became upset and told a nurse practitioner at the office what happened. This civil lawsuit comes 1 day after Lehi police arrested Pack for allegedly recording with a concealed digital camera his female patients undressing in an examination room. In August 2010, Judge Samuel McVey sentenced Steven Pack to 1 year in jail without any early release and a second year with global positioning system (GPS) monitoring. Pack's license to practice was suspended by the Utah Division of Occupational and Professional Licensing.

Civil suits brought by the victims were settled before the sentencing, but the civil remedies were not made public.

There are a number of ethical and legal issues in this case. Identify them.
Describe the action you might take in a similar situation.

YOU MUST DECIDE

There is no attempt in this book to determine right or wrong for any of the ethical issues in modern medicine. The purpose is to present the law and the facts that are pertinent in the health-care setting and to raise some questions for consideration. Most everyone has decided what is right or wrong on the majority of moral issues, but the same distinction in ethics and bioethics is more complex and not so easily identified. This is partly because of lack of accurate knowledge or information on an issue, but accuracy, knowledge, and information are imperative. It is also important to know how and why those opinions have been formed and to look at what is acceptable according to the legal and ethical standards of today.

As health-care professionals, the challenge is to live and act out of respect for oneself and others and to encourage others to do the same. It is important to know what we are to become and how we can become better than we are. Even when opinions differ from those of the clients served, our clients always deserve respect and dignity from us. The hope is that the forthcoming chapter discussions on "Allocation of Scarce Medical Resources," "Genetic Modification," "Reproductive Issues," "End-of-Life Issues," and "Have a Care" will offer a better understanding of what *is* and what may become.

In reading the following chapters and considering their effect on you personally as well as your role as a health-care professional, you may find the following lines from a poem by F. A. Russel (1849–1914) helpful.

REMEMBER ... *Seek the right, perform the true,*
Raise the work and life anew.
Hearts around you sink with care;
You can help their load to bear.
You can bring inspiring light,
Arm their faltering will to fight.

SUMMARY

Knowledge of law, ethics, and bioethics is essential for all health-care professionals. The Ethics Check questions offer one approach to address these issues on a personal level. Professional codes of ethics are further guides to performance as a health-care professional. Those who have the professional traits identified in this chapter will be successful health-care employees and will find their profession rewarding and fulfilling. There is no opportunity for boredom in such a fast-paced and rapidly changing field as health care.

Watch It Now! Why study law and ethics? at http://FADavis.com, keyword *Tamparo*.

Questions for Review

SELECT THE BEST ANSWER

1. Medical law, ethics, and bioethics are necessary to understand
   a. Health law.
   b. Differences in moral reasoning among individuals and groups.
   c. The need to confront biases and bigotry.
   d. All of the above.
   e. Only a and b above.

2. A Patient Bill of Rights usually includes
    a. The right to participate in health-care decisions.
    b. The right to receive a second opinion.
    c. The right to access personal health information.
    d. All of the above.
    e. Only a and c above.

3. The Hippocratic Oath
    a. Was written as a result of trials of war criminals.
    b. Protected the rights of clients and appealed to the finer instincts of the physician.
    c. Is an update on human experimentation.
    d. Is very similar to the Nuremberg Code.
    e. Only a and c above.

4. The most important code of ethics for the ambulatory care professional is the
    a. AMA Principles of Medical Ethics.
    b. AAPC Code of Ethics.
    c. AAMA Code of Ethics and AAMA Creed.
    d. Personal Ethics Check questions.
    e. Only c and d above.

5. Making an ethical and/or bioethical decision is based on
    a. An individual's religious belief for the most part.
    b. The direction of the provider-employer.
    c. State and federal law.
    d. The cost effectiveness of the particular decision to be made.
    e. Accuracy, knowledge, and information of the particular issue.

SHORT ANSWER QUESTIONS

1. What is the difference between law and ethics? Can a law be unethical? Can an ethic be unlawful? Justify your response.

_____

_____

_____

2. List characteristics that are important for a professional health-care employee.

_____

_____

_____

3. Identify three changes in today's health-care environment that make professional ethics more challenging.

_____

_____

_____

4. How does bioethics affect law?

_____

_____

_____

5. What questions do Blanchard and Peale suggest answering when faced with an ethical dilemma?

_____

_____

_____

CLASSROOM EXERCISES

1. State in your own words what medical law, ethics, and bioethics mean to you.

2. What would you do if your personal morals and code of ethics do not agree with those of your employer?

3. Do the Medical Assistant Code of Ethics and the AMA Principles of Medical Ethics have any conflicting views? Explain.

4. In a small group discussion, tell how you as a health-care professional can show respect for a client who is rude and disrespectful to you.

5. What will you do if your opinions differ from your clients? For instance, a mother refuses inoculations for her child, and you believe they are necessary.

INTERNET ACTIVITIES

1. Using your favorite Internet search engine, key in the words "world medical ethics codes." Identify the results.

2. Research the Judicial Council of the AMA on the Internet. What is the Council's function? List two or three standards identified by this group as ethical/legal guidelines for physicians.

3. Research the current status of the 2010 Healthcare Reform Bill to determine whether the Patient Bill of Rights has been implemented, eliminated, or modified. Report your findings and identify any ethical concerns.

4. Research "patient bill of rights" for clinics for a number of samples. Compare with the hospital patient bill of rights. Identify the similarities and the differences.

REFERENCES

Blanchard, K., & Peale, N. V.: _The Power of Ethical Management_. New York: William Morrow, 1988.

Fletcher, J. _The Ethics of Genetic Control Ending Reproductive Roulette_. Buffalo, NY: Prometheus Books, 1988.

For additional resources please visit
http://FADavis.com, keyword _Tamparo_.

CHAPTER 2

Medical Practice Management

"The best career advice to give to the young is, 'Find out what you like doing best and get someone to pay you for doing it.'"—Katherine Whitehorn; English journalist and writer

KEY TERMS

bond An insurance contract by which a bonding agency guarantees payment of a specified sum to an employer in the event of a financial loss to the employer caused by the act of a specified employee; a legal obligation to pay specific sums.

capitation Health-care providers are paid a fixed monthly compensation for a range of services for each health maintenance organization (HMO) member in their care.

complementary medicine The practice of medicine that complements traditional medicine with alternative medicine.

conglomerate A corporation of a number of different companies operating in a number of different fields.

co-payment A medical expense that is a member's responsibility; usually a fixed amount of $25 or higher.

deductible A cost-sharing arrangement in which the member pays a set amount toward covered services before the insurance carrier begins to make any payments.

fee-for-service Pays providers for each service performed.

gatekeeper A term referring to managed care primary care providers responsible for referring members to specialists (usually within the same plan) with the intent of matching the client's needs and preferences with the appropriate and cost-effective use of those specialists' services.

group practice Type of business management in which three or more individuals organize to render professional service and share the same equipment and personnel.

health maintenance organization (HMO) A type of managed care plan offering health-care services from participating physicians and providers to an enrolled group of persons for a predetermined fee per member.

integrative medicine The practice of medicine that accounts for the whole person (body, mind, spirit, and lifestyle) using all appropriate therapies, both traditional and alternative.

joint venture A type of business management formed by hospitals, physicians and other providers, and clinics to offer client care.

managed care A type of health-care plan; generally one of two types, namely HMO or preferred provider organization (PPO).

opt-out option Members or clients can seek treatment from providers outside the health-care plan but pay more to do so.

partnership Type of business management involving the association of two or more individuals who are co-owners of their business.

pay for performance (P4P) A type of managed care that encourages providers to improve the quality of their clients' care; reimburses them for their progress toward a fixed goal.

preferred provider organization (PPO) A type of business agreement between a medical service provider and an insurer organization in which the fees for specific services are predetermined for an already established group of clients assigned to or selected by the provider.

professional service corporation Specific type of corporation in which licensed individuals organize to render a professional service to the public. Such licensed individuals include physicians, medical providers, lawyers, and dentists.

sole proprietorship Type of business management owned by a single individual.

LEARNING OUTCOMES

Upon successful completion of this chapter, you should be able to:

2.1 Define key terms.
2.2 Compare/contrast types of medical practice management.
2.3 List two advantages and two disadvantages of each of the types of practice management for both the provider and the employee.
2.4 Compare personnel needs in each of the types of practice management.
2.5 Discuss the role of managed care.
2.6 Describe health maintenance organizations (HMOs).
2.7 Discuss joint ventures and preferred provider organizations (PPOs).
2.8 Define the concept of general liability for providers.
2.9 Identify providers' responsibilities to employees in medical practice management.

COMPETENCIES

CAAHEP

• Define the concept of general liability for providers. (CAAHEP X.C.8.a)

VIGNETTE

How Did This Happen?

It is 9:00 p.m. Thursday, and Geralyn is sitting at her desk in the Midway Medical Clinic. Everyone else has gone home. Her work is not yet done; she sits back to reflect on the past 30 years. She started as a medical assistant when the clinic was a two-physician partnership. The practice grew, and many changes were made. Soon there were five providers and multiple staff and specialists, and a corporation had been formed. Because of tenure and willingness to expand her education and responsibilities, Geralyn became the clinic manager. She really likes this job, her staff, and her employers. She is, however, continually frustrated by the fact that she has less time to do what she really enjoys as a clinic manager. Instead, she finds herself managing the practice and its finances for her employers. It is more than a full-time job just to keep track of all the insurance contracts, including federal and state reimbursement programs. As manager she wants to make sure that her employers and the clinics' clients are well served.

Graduates of today's medical schools have numerous choices to make before entering practice. Increasing numbers of graduates seek advanced education and training opportunities in a specialty area. Fewer graduates are choosing to specialize in family practices than are actually needed by society, and the last two decades have seen many changes in the delivery of health care. Before that time, most graduates chose to function in private practice with a partner or a small group. Ultimately, their goal was to "fly solo" because that was where the most money could be made. Today that model has changed. Less than one 1% of graduates enter into solo practice unless it is in a rural part of the country where the federal government, in cooperation with some medical schools, has set forth incentives for graduates to pay their college loans if they commit to practice in a rural area for a set amount of time. Most graduates will enter one of any number of different group forms of management.

Providers may function as partners with other providers, as members of **health maintenance organizations (HMOs)**, and as shareholder/employees in **professional service corporations**. Increasingly, however, many providers practice in a complicated combination of more than one type of medical practice management. Some serve as salaried employees in clinics sponsored by hospitals. Although fewer physicians may be practicing as sole proprietors, other providers of health care are picking up the model for their practices. Naturopaths, podiatrists, chiropractors, and acupuncturists often practice as sole proprietors. The type of business management to select is an early decision when entering practice but likely changes throughout one's career.

The type of organization for the medical practice is important to health-care employees and their duties. Differences will be seen in the medical records, billing and accounting procedures, payroll, number and duties of employees, and benefits. The type of business organization will determine, in part, how health-care employees do their jobs. A brief overview of the most common medical management models is provided here, beginning with the most simple and easiest to establish.

 ## SOLE PROPRIETORS

A **sole proprietorship**, or single proprietorship, is a business owned by a single individual who receives all the profits and takes all the risks (Fig. 2-1). It is the oldest form of business and is the easiest to start, operate, and dissolve. It can be the most expensive to establish. Even sole proprietors, however, are likely to provide services under the umbrella of one or more managed care health insurance programs as preferred providers and in other types of business management. Sole proprietorships are a common management choice for the increasing number of providers in **complementary medicine** and **integrative medicine**. There are advantages and disadvantages to this form of business management.

Figure 2-1. Sole proprietor is a practice owned by a single individual.

ADVANTAGES OF SOLE PROPRIETORSHIPS

The advantages of a sole proprietorship include having simplicity of organization; being one's own boss; being the sole receiver of all profits that may generally be larger than any other forms of business management; and having lower organizational costs, greater flexibility in operation, and fewer government regulations than other forms of business management.

In addition, a sole proprietorship allows the provider to establish a practice in a community through the purchase or rent/lease of a facility, to make all the decisions without having to consult with any partners or other business colleagues, and to incur minimal organizational costs. This provider also will not have to divide the profits with any other person and will be able to run the practice exactly as desired. When the provider participates as a preferred provider in a **managed care** system, the provider must follow the guidelines of the system but is free to choose whether to participate.

DISADVANTAGES OF SOLE PROPRIETORSHIPS

The sole proprietorship does have disadvantages. For instance, providers may have difficulties raising sufficient capital to begin their business. Medical equipment is among the most expensive of any type of equipment in a new business. The sole proprietor typically performs all or most of the managerial functions in the business and works more than a standard 40-hour workweek. The profits of the business may be insufficient later to allow for expansion. In addition, providers must know that if the business fails in a sole proprietorship or if a liability claim surpasses their insurance protection, their personal property may be attached, and they may lose virtually all personal savings and possessions.

Again, consider a provider who has sufficient capital when entering practice to establish business as a sole proprietorship. Initially, the system works well while the client load is light. However, the provider soon finds that time is at a premium if working 70 to 80 hours a week carrying a full client load, managing the business aspects of the practice, and having no other provider to cover weekends or vacations. Also, no one is available when the provider is ill or a family crisis must be attended to.

CONSIDERATIONS FOR THE HEALTH-CARE EMPLOYEE

The sole proprietor probably begins with just one assistant. This person needs education and training in *all* areas of administrative and clinical tasks to be performed in the health-care setting and will have variety in the work. Although some assistants enjoy the opportunity to use all their skills in the entire operation, others may find this situation less attractive and prefer that the provider have certain tasks sent outside the clinic for completion. These tasks may include laboratory work, transcription, correspondence, or billing and coding. The sole proprietorship often uses the services of an accountant for payroll and quarterly and yearly tax reports.

The sole proprietorship offers little if any opportunity for advancement for its employees. Therefore, providers will want to select employees carefully based on their education, training, credentialing and experience; reward them sufficiently for their work; and encourage them to stay a long time with the practice. Some medical assistants will prefer the sole proprietorship because of the opportunity they have to make decisions and assume leadership responsibilities.

Case Study

The 64-year-old sole proprietor, a family practitioner, is the only physician in a rural community with a population of 3,500. He has one medical assistant who has been with him for several years. The physician works 70 hours a week and many weekends. His assistant is feeling overworked also and complains of less time with family. The physician wants very much to ease into retirement or to lessen his load.

What might the physician and the assistant do?
Identify how the plan you suggest might be implemented.

PARTNERSHIPS

A **partnership** is an association of two or more persons who are co-owners of a business for profit (Fig. 2-2). Partnerships may have only two or three members, but there is no maximum number of individuals who may enter into a partnership. The organization may take many forms and should be defined in a partnership agreement.

The partnership agreement should be written and reviewed by an attorney. It should include such items as the type of business to be conducted or services to be performed, the type of partnership being established, authority held by each partner, length of the partnership agreement, and capital invested by each partner. The agreement should also include a description of how profits and losses are to be shared, how each partner is to be compensated, limitations on monetary withdrawals by a partner, accounting procedures to be followed, procedures for admitting new partners, dissolution of the partnership, and, of course, the signatures of the partners involved in the agreement.

ADVANTAGES OF PARTNERSHIPS

Some advantages of partnerships are easily recognized. Generally, a partnership has more financial strength than a sole proprietorship. Partners are likely to bring additional managerial skills and share the workload. The organization of a partnership remains relatively simple, although somewhat more complicated than a sole proprietorship.

When a provider is deciding how to establish a practice, the partnership may be desirable. If the practice is already established, only a small capital investment may be required in the beginning. This investment can be increased as the provider becomes more financially secure. A sole proprietor often will turn to a partnership when the workload of the practice requires a second person to share the work.

DISADVANTAGES OF PARTNERSHIPS

A disadvantage of a partnership is that two or more people make the decisions, depending on the partnership contractual agreement. In addition, each partner is responsible for the business. If one partner lacks the personal finances to assume a full share of any loss, the other partners are required to make up for the deficit. If the partnership fails, usually one partner can be liable for all the partnership debts, regardless of the size of the investment.

Figure 2-2. Partnership is a business agreement between two or more individuals.

Personality differences should be considered because compatibility is important in any partnership. A trial period that allows a partner to withdraw from the association or be asked to withdraw after a given period may be advantageous. If the provider does not wish to enter a partnership agreement but needs additional help, another provider may be hired strictly on a salary basis. Although this arrangement does not constitute a partnership, a contract is desirable for the protection of each party.

CONSIDERATIONS FOR THE HEALTH-CARE EMPLOYEE

A partnership should consider hiring more than one assistant in the health-care setting because of the increased workload. Each partner may desire an assistant, but many tasks will be common to each and are best performed by one person. Assistants must understand the partnership relationship and the line of authority. Open communication on the part of all members of the staff is essential. Otherwise, each provider may expect an assistant to function as a member of the staff but may not provide input as to how this function should be performed.

In addition, with more than one employee, both job advancement and job specialization are possible. For example, the newly formed partnership hiring a second assistant may want to name the first assistant clinic manager with a specific set of duties or to assign one assistant to administrative tasks while the other performs clinical duties.

PROFESSIONAL SERVICE CORPORATIONS

A corporation is a legal entity that is granted many of the same rights enjoyed by individuals. These include the right to own, mortgage, and dispose of property; the right to manage its own affairs; and the right to sue and be sued (Fig. 2-3). Providers in a professional service corporation (PSC) remain personally liable for their acts of medical malpractice; however, they are not liable for the professional acts of their colleagues. Corporations are costly to establish, are more formal than either the proprietorship or partnership, and require a legal document for formation and operation.

Professional service associations or professional corporations are designed for such professional persons as medical providers, lawyers, dentists, and accountants. These corporations can be identified by the letters SC (service corporation), PC (professional corporation), PSC, Inc. (professional service corporation, incorporated), and PA (professional association), depending on each state's

Figure 2-3. Medical providers often form professional service corporations.

law. The PSC is the most intricate of all forms of medical practice and can be formed by one or more individuals.

ADVANTAGES OF PROFESSIONAL SERVICE CORPORATIONS

Advantages of PSCs include the fact that contributions to pension or profit-sharing plans can be made for all employees as well as the provider. Such funds are deducted by the corporation from its taxable income, are invested, and accumulate in tax-free trusts until a future time of disbursement. Taxes are not paid on the funds until the time of their disbursement, usually at retirement, when the individual is in a lower tax bracket.

Another advantage of a PSC is the corporate medical reimbursement plan. Medical and dental expenses are deductible to the corporation and nontaxable to the employee. This plan can result in substantial savings to both corporation and employee. Group term life insurance on a deductible premium basis is another advantage of a professional corporation. The professional corporation also may pay the professional liability premiums for providers and their employees. Furthermore, in a corporation, providers' personal assets are protected and cannot be attached to satisfy a debt as they can be in a sole proprietorship or partnership.

DISADVANTAGES OF PROFESSIONAL SERVICE CORPORATIONS

When PSCs first became legal, many providers eagerly incorporated, only to discover the disadvantages. The complexity of the PSC and its detailed requirements call for reliable, well-informed attorneys and accountants to advise the corporation. The PSC may be more expensive to operate than other forms of organizations.

Regular meetings and agreement on organization, investments, pensions, and profit-sharing plans are important and legally required. Because more individuals generally are involved than in a sole proprietorship or most partnerships, decision making is more complicated. Providers often have problems finding the time to perform the business functions required to run a corporation.

Although a PSC usually involves two or more providers functioning in a group setting, a sole proprietor can incorporate as a PSC. The income of a single individual who incorporates needs to be sufficient to allow full participation in the benefits granted to the PSC, or such an arrangement is financially ineffective.

CONSIDERATIONS FOR THE HEALTH-CARE EMPLOYEE

The PSC generally employs more assistants than a partnership or sole proprietorship. The possibility of having medical expenses covered by the corporation is an attractive inducement to prospective employees. This form of practice usually provides ample opportunity for advancement and specialization. One person should be responsible for all personnel matters to enable a smooth-running organization.

GROUP PRACTICES

Another option of medical practice available to providers is joining a **group practice**. Group practice in medicine is defined as a group of medical providers who formally organize and agree to provide medical care, consultation, diagnosis, and treatment to clients. Equipment and personnel are used jointly. The income from the group is distributed according to a predetermined agreement of the members.

The provider in a group practice will either be a partner, an officer of the corporation, or an employee of the practice. Most group practices are also professional corporations or partnerships, but as the workload increases, new providers may be hired as employees.

There are four main types of group practice:

1. *Single specialty* group practices provide services in only one field of practice or major specialty; for example, a group of pediatricians joining together in practice.
2. *Multispecialty* group practices provide services in two or more fields of practice or major specialties; for example, a group of obstetricians/gynecologists and pediatricians joining together in practice.

3. *Primary care* group practices provide services by obstetricians/gynecologists, pediatricians, family practitioners, and internists.
4. *Hospital-managed medical groups* provide all the services of a group practice, but are owned by a hospital. Group practices formerly managed by providers are being sold in increasing numbers to hospitals when the members realize that the challenges of running a group are simply too costly and take too much time. Figure 2-4 illustrates this trend toward medical practices owned by hospitals.

Group medical practices operate on some form of **fee-for-service** basis, through insurance coverage, preferred provider arrangements, or even private pay with the same type of business arrangement as a sole proprietorship, a partnership, or a professional service corporation. A few of the largest groups are Kaiser Permanente Medical, Veterans Health Administration, Mayo Clinic, Ascension Health, and Fresenius Medical Care.

Case Law

In 2017 Dr. Tullio Emanuele, an employee of Medicor Associates—a large group practice in Pennsylvania—blew the whistle on his associates. While Emanuele was employed by Medicor, he became aware of providers knowingly submitting claims to Medicare and Medicaid involving the UPMC Hamot hospital in order to receive Medicor referrals. Hamot allegedly had no legitimate need for the contracted services that were sometimes duplicated or not performed, but Hamot paid up to $2 million per year under physician and administrative service arrangements to secure these referrals.

Acting Assistant Attorney General Chad A. Reader said, "The Department of Justice is committed to preventing illegal financial relationships that undermine the integrity of our public health programs." On March 15, 2017, the U.S. District Court of the Western District of Pennsylvania ruled that two of Hamot's arrangements with Medicor violated the Stark law.* The case was set for trial when the United States helped to facilitate a settlement. Dr. Emanuele was awarded $6,107,500 for his actions.

United States ex rel. Emanuele v. Medicor Associates, Inc. et al. Civil Action No. 10-cv-00245-JFC (W.D. Pa.)

Would you have the same courage as Dr. Emanuele? What risks do you take in reporting? In not reporting?

*The Stark law is a health-care fraud and abuse law that prohibits providers from referrals for certain designated health services paid for by Medicare to any entity with which they have a "financial relationship."

ADVANTAGES OF GROUP PRACTICE

Advantages to providers in group practice include a shared financial investment for diagnostic and therapeutic equipment, the opportunity for consultation with other providers, little administrative responsibility for the practice (groups often employ medical managers for the business side of the operation), and more family and recreation time because providers in the group cover for one another. In addition, group practice may offer informal consultations as well as the intellectual and social stimulation desired by many practitioners.

DISADVANTAGES OF GROUP PRACTICES

The disadvantages of group practices are easily identified. Not every individual has the personality to function well in a group setting. A provider cannot act totally independent of the group and may feel a loss of freedom in such a situation. Although the working hours may not be as long as in sole practice, the income, although guaranteed, also may not be as high. Working in a close relationship with colleagues daily may lead to personality clashes and differences of opinion.

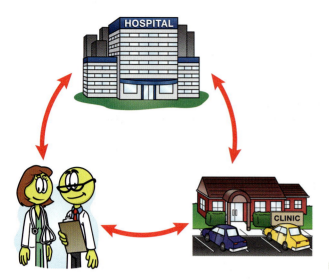

Figure 2-4. A hospital-managed medical group.

CONSIDERATIONS FOR THE HEALTH-CARE EMPLOYEE

A group practice will have more employees than the other forms of medical organizations simply because of the larger staff of physicians and providers. Providers may have less responsibility for hiring and selecting personnel, which may be an advantage or a disadvantage, depending on the provider's personal preferences. An employee may choose employment in a group for many of the same reasons as those in the corporation. Depending on the number of employees, a larger group may be less personalized.

HEALTH MAINTENANCE ORGANIZATIONS

The health maintenance organization (HMO) is a familiar form of medical practice management in today's society. Kaiser Foundation Health Plan is one of the largest, not-for-profit HMOs in the country. In this form of management, groups contract with clients to provide comprehensive health care and preventive medicine for premiums paid that entitle the subscriber to service during the duration of the contract.

The staff-model HMO owns and operates health-care centers staffed by providers contractually employed directly by the plan. These health-care centers provide a broad range of services "under one roof," although perhaps in many locations.

The advantage to providers who practice in a staff-model HMO is that the working hours will be regular and allow for more personal time. Practitioners will not have to provide the building or equipment necessary for starting a practice. Also, providers have the additional advantage of collaboration with other professional colleagues regarding clients' care.

Another form of HMO allows providers to maintain their private practices, charge their fee-for-service clients, and be reimbursed for their HMO clients by the central HMO organization. This type of HMO is not a medical practice management model. The providers involved in this form of HMO may have clients who have prepaid for their services to any number of HMO organizations that will, in turn, pay the provider. The HMO may make use of the concept of a primary care provider (PCP) (often referred to as a **gatekeeper**) as a method of controlling costs. In a gatekeeper situation, all medical care sought by a client must be channeled through the PCP, and any referrals are made within the HMO provider list.

Generally speaking, client and provider satisfaction with managed care services is based on personal experience. Some clients feel more satisfied; others feel less satisfied. Providers, forced to pay more attention to the management of their practice, are generally frustrated by this additional organizational burden.

MANAGED CARE

Managed care is any arrangement for health care in which an organization, such as an insurance company, an HMO, or another type of provider–hospital network, acts as an intermediary between the person seeking care and the provider (Fig. 2-5). Although it is not a form of business management in the strictest sense of the word, managed care has dramatically restructured the delivery and financial aspects of health care. No provider can practice without feeling the effects of this system. In managed care, clients, too, have experienced a radical change in the delivery of their health care. Some question the managed care corporation's financial interest in client care. To fully understand managed care, a brief history of insurance coverage is warranted.

In the early 1900s, consumers expected to pay for all health care from their own pockets. During the Depression, many health-care providers received little or no pay for their services. Blue Cross first provided insurance for hospital costs in the early 1930s. Blue Shield was introduced soon afterward to cover office and physician costs. Both were driven by union contracts in the automobile industry.

Soon employees expected that a part of their employment benefit package would include health insurance to cover all but a few incidental and minor expenses. Increased specialization, advancing technology, and little or no emphasis on preventive care drove health-care costs to a new all-time high. Employers began to struggle with the increased costs of offering health insurance to an all-demanding workforce. HMOs were introduced to emphasize preventive health care, assure providers they would receive payment for their services, and ultimately begin to contain costs. It was not long before nearly every health insurance carrier was offering some form of HMO to employers as one of the available health-care plans.

Not all providers and health-care consumers were excited about HMOs, however. In some cases, consumers lost the right to choose their PCP. The choice had to be made from a list of participating providers. A common complaint from providers was their loss of control in the provider–client relationship because they felt the HMO dictated the kind and type of care to give clients. While providing basic health care to all persons was being hotly debated in Congress and across the country, HMOs

Figure 2-5. Managed care serves all its subscribers with an umbrella policy.

continued to grow in popularity by paying close attention to preventive care, standardizing many medical practices, and eliminating unnecessary tests and procedures. Today, the largest HMOs in the country have become billion-dollar businesses; they still dictate how many medical decisions related to client care are made, and consumers are paying more for their medical coverage.

The method of payment for professional services has changed from only the fee-for-service method of payment, in which a provider is paid for each service rendered, to payment that may include a **co-payment**, a **deductible**, and/or **capitation**.

Co-payments, a specific dollar amount paid by the client or member (usually $25 to $50 or a percentage of the total bill), were established. The co-payment helps clients to realize their responsibility toward payment, but the amount is not considered exorbitant. It adds a cash flow to the provider receiving deductible amounts and the percentage paid by insurers for remaining services.

The deductible requires policyholders to pay a set amount toward covered services on a fee-for-service or preferred provider basis before the insurer begins to pay claims. Providers, however, often receive only a percentage of the cost of their services once the insurer's responsibility begins.

Another method of payment, much less popular with providers, and little known and understood by clients, is capitation. Capitation gives health-care providers a fixed monthly compensation for a range of services for each managed care or HMO member under their care rather than a fee for each service performed. The capitation models have not been particularly successful and are decreasing in popularity.

Another form of managed care is **pay for performance (P4P)**. P4P is a plan to encourage providers to improve the quality of their clients' care and reimburses providers for their progress toward a fixed goal. Payment is dependent on how well providers adhere to practice standards, especially in the arenas of preventive care and management of chronic illness. The plan took a beating and has proven to be costly and ineffective. Research has shown that the plan did not improve the health of its participants, often harmed the sicker and the poorer clients, and encouraged providers and hospitals to avoid those who needed increased time and care because they dragged down the providers' quality score.

One can readily see the complexity of the problem faced by both providers and consumers in understanding the payment process and the cost of health care. What were seemingly subtle changes in the managed care contracts have had a great impact on providers and clients. Many found themselves in a form of managed care in which profit rather than health was the motive. Increasingly, providers must contact a third party for permission to perform certain procedures or make a referral to a specialist. Likewise, a client's health-care services are covered when obtained from a preferred provider chosen by the insurance carrier but only partially covered or not covered at all if obtained from an unaffiliated provider. Further, some managed care plans allow members to seek treatment outside the network but charge the members more to do so. This is called an **opt-out option**.

The problems of a "business-first, client care–second" system are found not only in managed care insurance. Covered fee-for-service plans have similar problems. The increased power of insurance carriers, which no longer simply collect premiums from subscribers and process claims, continues to take decision making away from providers and clients. Political influences at the state and national levels cannot be ignored either. The U.S. Congress struggled for years to create a Patient Bill of Rights legislation that would return some control, choice, and power to clients and their providers. The Affordable Care Act of 2010 finally got it accomplished.

Case Study

Medicare clients find themselves in a bind. Because of continuing reduction in Medicare reimbursements since 2010, increasing numbers of providers are opting *not* to provide medical care to the senior population. They simply cannot cover the loss incurred. This means that individuals with Medicare insurance can find it difficult to select a PCP if they move to another area (perhaps to be closer to family members) or they just wish to choose another provider. Many providers will continue to carry their current clients on Medicare, but take no new clients.

As an employee in a practice that chooses to limit its Medicare clients to the current number, how will you respond to requests from individuals with Medicare seeking a PCP?
Does the 2010 Affordable Care Act address this issue? Explain your findings.

Some form of managed care or managed competition seems destined to play a role in the health-care delivery system for some time to come. Good and bad managed care plans are no different from good and bad health-care providers. Change will most likely come from informed clients, who will benefit most from their health-care providers. Information available through the Internet, television, public service programs, and print media will empower clients by giving them the information and vocabulary necessary to make themselves true partners in the client–provider relationship. Ideally, the federally mandated Healthcare Reform Bill will provide options.

 ## OTHER BUSINESS ARRANGEMENTS

Today's ambulatory health-care setting as a form of business management for medical practice continues to evolve. Larger clinics, PSCs, and **conglomerates** are increasingly popular.

JOINT VENTURES

Competition, marketing, and escalating costs have encouraged hospitals and providers to enter into **joint ventures** that may be profitable and advantageous to both entities. For example, hospitals are building ambulatory health-care settings within their service area to entice providers to rent office space and in turn refer their clients to the hospital. Hospitals may purchase a practice and staff it with one or more of their providers. Such ventures offer providers improved marketing capabilities and fewer start-up costs.

Case Law

The Sarah Bush Lincoln Health Center employed Richard Berlin, Jr., MD, in 1992 to practice medicine at the Health Center for 5 years. They entered into a written agreement whereby Dr. Berlin could terminate his employment arrangement for any reason during the 5-year period by giving 180-day advance written notice. The agreement also stipulated that he could not compete with the hospital by providing health services within a 50-mile radius of the Health Center for 2 years after the end of his employment.

On February 4, 1994, Dr. Berlin terminated his employment with the hospital (effective February 7, 1994) and immediately began employment with the Carle Clinic Association located approximately 1 mile from the Health Center.

The Health Center brought an injunction against the doctor to prohibit him from practicing so close to the hospital.

What problems surface here?
Did Dr. Berlin satisfy all elements of his agreement? Explain.

Summary Judgment: Richard Berlin, Jr., MD, filed a complaint seeking to have the restrictive covenant of his employment agreement with Sarah Bush Lincoln Health Center declared unenforceable.

The Circuit Court found in favor of Dr. Berlin on the basis that the entire employment agreement was unenforceable. A divided appellate court affirmed the district court's decision. On appeal, however, the Supreme Court of Illinois reversed the decision, stating that the central issue was that the "corporate practice doctrine" is inapplicable to licensed hospitals.

Supreme Court of Illinois, 1997. 179 Ill.2d 1, 227 Ill. Dec. 769, 688 N.E.2d 106.

Note: Since the time of this case, many states have enacted legislation that permits licensed hospital corporations to utilize physicians as independent contractors and/or employees.

An unusual twist to the joint venture is the establishment of in-store medical clinics in chain-store markets, large and small, across the country. These chains seek such ventures to increase their customer base. The in-store clinics are providing limited medical care at decreased costs and added convenience to customers. A unique example of this is seen in over 1,000 "Minute Clinics" common in CVS pharmacies that provide basic and very quick medical attention to clients. They are staffed by physician assistants (PAs) and nurse practitioners (NPs) and accept most insurance plans. Today, it is common to go to the pharmacy within a grocery conglomerate to receive flu vaccinations.

Physician–hospital organizations (PHOs) combine hospital and group medical practices in order to offer clients a "one-stop shopping approach." A primary reason for forming a PHO is the concept that combined services are more attractive than individual services would be. In addition, both providers and hospitals benefit one another. Clients receive more services, sometimes at a lower cost. This concept is becoming increasingly popular.

Case Study

In a joint venture arrangement, the hospital manages three satellite clinics. In one of the clinics, there is concern that a PA is spending too much time with clients. The PA is asked to log time in and time out for clients seen during a 3-week period. The PA's profitability is in question.

What do you think?
Identify circumstances that may contribute to longer periods of time with clients.

The *multiple service organization (MSO)* can be owned by providers, hospitals, a totally separate party, or any combination of the three. This organization is developed to perform office management services. For example, the MSO often provides secretarial and office services, billing and collections, group purchasing, and computer servicing. An MSO allows providers to focus on client care and permits the management service to run the business side of the organization.

PREFERRED PROVIDER ORGANIZATIONS

A provider may be a sole proprietor, a partner, or a member of a professional service corporation as well as a preferred provider for an organization. A **preferred provider organization (PPO)** creates a contractual agreement between an insurance carrier organization and the provider to supply medical care to an already established number of clients. For example, a provider may contract with Blue Cross's preferred provider plan to give medical care to a certain number of individuals who have subscribed to the Blue Cross preferred provider plan.

Providers considering a move into any of the integrated organizations should be certain that the business arrangement does not violate antitrust laws. Antitrust laws exist to preserve free-market competition. Consequently, under antitrust laws any activities that restrict competition are unfavorable. Providers must ensure that the business arrangement does not oppose Medicare's fee-for-service reimbursement rules or violate any Medicare or Medicaid fraud and abuse laws. Because Medicare seeks a direct relationship with its providers, it may not recognize some business organizations as being eligible for Medicare reimbursement. Medicare and Medicaid laws further prohibit kickbacks and some referrals. For example, providers cannot refer Medicare or Medicaid clients to any entity in which they have any financial interest.

More and more physicians and providers are entering into a variety of business management arrangements, and they most likely will want to seek the appropriate legal advice to ensure that they are within the legal bounds of medical practice.

Case Study

The large medical conglomerate provides services to health-care providers in rural areas that would otherwise not have access to medical specialists. Telemedicine has enabled residents in rural areas to access specialized care quickly and efficiently. For instance, a practitioner in a rural area can send a troubling electrocardiogram via telephone and have it read by a cardiac specialist, resulting in state-of-the-art, immediate response, diagnosis, and possible treatment.

Can you think of another example in which medical care can benefit from new technologies?

IN THE NEWS

Response to the Covid-19 Pandemic of 2020 has caused an increase in the use of telemedicine/telehealth. Some providers were already embracing the technique of seeing their clients via a media platform where provider and client could see one another and discuss concerns and possible treatment. The Covid-10 Pandemic caused the Centers for Medicare & Medicaid Services (CMS) to loosen the regulations for telemedicine. Telehealth services are now available to Medicare and most Medicaid beneficiaries so long as video capability is available. Beginning March 6, 2020, CMS began paying providers on a temporary basis for telehealth services for beneficiaries residing across the entire country.

Do you think telemedicine/telehealth will continue after the pandemic? Discuss the advantages and disadvantages.

GENERAL LIABILITY

Physicians and providers engaged in business must be aware of their general liability. Unlike professional liability that relates to clients' medical treatment (see Chapter 5, Professional Liability), general liability regards business matters. These matters include liability for the building, any automobiles, theft, burglary, fire, and employees' safety. Clinic employees will be involved in payments of these liability insurance premiums and submission of claims. Also, they likely assist their employers in practice when making applications for business licenses.

BUSINESS LICENSE

Some communities require a business or occupational license before allowing a clinic to be opened for the practice of medicine. Providers should check with county and city clerks to determine whether a license is required and what procedures are to be followed. An annual renewal fee may be necessary; payment of the annual fees generally becomes the responsibility of an employee responsible for monitoring the activities of the business side of the practice.

BUILDING

The provider or the organization that owns the building is responsible for the building and grounds where business is conducted. If a person is injured on those premises, providers may be held legally responsible. Therefore, providers and managing organizations will carry liability insurance for the premises.

AUTOMOBILE

Aside from personal car insurance, providers may want to consider nonowner liability insurance. Such a plan protects the provider-employer if an employee has an automobile accident while performing some duty related to the business. For providers who commonly ask their employees to make a bank deposit on their drive home or to deliver the monthly statements to the post office, such protection is wise. Whose car an employee drives makes no difference.

FIRE, THEFT, AND BURGLARY

Providers should have protection against fire, theft, and burglary on the building as well as on equipment and furniture. Two types of fire insurance are most common. A coinsurance plan dictates that the owner is responsible for payment of a certain percentage of the loss, such as 20% or 30%. A second plan covers not only the loss but also the replacement costs. The replacement costs are, of course, more expensive, but more beneficial in the case of loss.

Cost of protection from burglary and theft depends on location and the amount of money or valuables kept on the premises. Large amounts of money should not be kept on the premises, even though most burglary attempts are made for the purpose of stealing opioids. A discussion with insurance agents will identify proper protection.

Some providers may also insure their accounts receivable, which would be nearly impossible to recover in case of fire or loss. These items belong in a fireproof cabinet or safe after working hours to prevent their loss, even if insured.

EMPLOYEE SAFETY

Providers are expected to provide a safe place of employment for their employees. Safety requirements include federally mandated regulations as well as rules that vary from state to state. Some of the variables include the number of employees, the type of employment, and the safety record of the business. Check with the state agency administering such safety regulations, with workers' compensation statutes, and with the state medical association to determine responsibility in this area. Refer to Chapter 11, Employment Practices, for a discussion of Occupational Safety and Health Administration (OSHA) and other regulations to further protect employee safety.

BONDING

Providers may wish to **bond** employees who are handling financial records and money in their clinics. Bonding is an insurance contract with a bonding agency. The purchase of a bond for a certain amount in an employee's name ensures that providers will recover the amount of the loss, up to the amount of the bond, in case the employee embezzles funds. This precaution is especially important when providers do not have the time to spot-check financial transactions made by employees. Careful employers ask prospective employees if they are bondable. It is also an advantage to an employee of a medical clinic to be bonded. Many providers may even check the credit ratings of potential employees who will be managing financial transactions if this is not included as part of the bonding process. This step is legal if the potential employee is informed in advance.

RESPONSIBILITIES TO EMPLOYEES

Whatever the style of operation in which providers choose to practice, employers have certain business responsibilities to employees. These include federal, state, and local requirements for Social Security compensation protection and workers' compensation for all employees. Benefits can include a uniform allowance, paid parking, medical benefits, retirement benefits, profit-sharing plans, vacations, sick leave, paid holidays and personal leave time, professional improvement allowances, and professional liability insurance.

As stated previously in this chapter, providers must realize the value of appropriately qualified and educated employees and encourage them to remain with the organization as long as possible. Specific information about providers' responsibilities to employees can be obtained from an accountant or attorney. County, state, or national medical associations have information about requirements for establishing a practice and have guidelines for employees.

SUMMARY

Physicians and providers can open new practices, function as sole proprietors, be employed by others on a straight salary basis, establish partnerships, become part of PSCs, and practice alone or in groups. Most also will be related to some form of managed care and may participate in at least one HMO. All forms of medical practice have advantages and disadvantages. The choice depends on the individual personality and preference of the provider. None should be entered into without advice and consideration from people knowledgeable in the field.

The overriding factor for providers to consider is what type of business organization will best permit them to serve their clients. Providers must remember that the type of practice chosen will dictate their responsibilities in all areas of general liability. To be less than meticulous in this area of business can potentially mar a provider's professional reputation.

 Watch It Now! Where will you choose to work? at http://FADavis.com, keyword *Tamparo*.

Questions for Review

SELECT THE BEST ANSWER

1. The sole proprietor
   a. Is owned by two or more individuals.
   b. Is the oldest form of business.
   c. Will have at least two medical assistants.
   d. Works a standard 40-hour workweek.
   e. None of the above.

2. A partnership
   a. Is an agreement that should be in writing.
   b. Has more financial strength than a sole proprietorship.
   c. Usually only has one medical assistant.
   d. Does not protect personal financial loss.
   e. Only a, b, and d are correct.

3. Professional service corporations
   a. Allow deductions from taxable income to make contributions to pension plans.
   b. Are relatively inexpensive to establish.
   c. Can only be formed with at least three providers.
   d. Are only established for multispecialty practices.
   e. Only a and c are correct.

4. A health maintenance organization
   a. Is one type of managed care.
   b. Often identifies a gatekeeper for each member.
   c. Always provides services under one roof.
   d. Only a and b are correct.
   e. None are correct.

5. Joint ventures are created
   a. To provide better insurance coverage for clients.
   b. To avoid paying taxes on shared income.
   c. To be profitable and advantageous to both entities.
   d. To perform clinic management services for providers.
   e. As a preferred provider organization.

SHORT ANSWER

1. As a clinic manager, describe your possible responsibilities in keeping your providers'/employers' general liability up to date and current.

_____

_____

_____

2. The Veterans Health Administration is identified as one of the largest group practices, but it has been in the public eye for not providing adequate and/or efficient and timely care to its members. What issues have been identified? How has the agency attempted to change the public's perception? What if anything might you do as an employee of the agency?

_____

_____

_____

3. When conflict arises among partners in the medical clinic, how might the conflict be resolved? If it is personal? If it is related to their clients' care?

_____

_____

_____

4. With increasing demands on the business aspect of medical care, what can you do as an employee to protect your clients' personal medical care and their integrity? Consider the role of their medical insurance in their care, your providers' approach to their clients, and that you are often the first and last person they see in the clinic.

_____

_____

_____

5. From the client's perspective, compare the advantages/disadvantages of a managed care organization to that of a proprietorship.

_____

_____

_____

CLASSROOM EXERCISES

1. What kind of business management exists in the clinic setting where you are employed or where you would be most interested in seeking employment? Justify your response.

2. The clinic's neighborhood is changing and includes more low-income residents. The practice already has a high percentage of Medicare and Medicaid clients. The providers are considering "closing the doors" to any new clients in this category. As a receptionist, you know you will be the one to turn people away. Describe your feelings. What can you do?

3. If the number of primary care providers in family practice continues to decrease, what might medical care begin to look like?

4. Why would an employer in a clinic have the bookkeeper bonded?

5. In the vignette "How Did This Happen?" what options does Geralyn have? What advantages does either the partnership or corporation offer her? Personally, what gains has she made as the practice has grown, and what has she lost?

INTERNET ACTIVITIES

1. Research the Internet for "concierge medical practice." Describe your findings. Would you like to be employed in such a practice? Explain your response.

2. Visit the website for the Medical Group Management Association (MGMA). Browse the site to determine resources available. What do you find to add to your knowledge base related to this chapter's topics? Would it be beneficial for a member of a clinic's practice to be a member of the MGMA? Justify your response.

For additional resources please visit
http://FADavis.com, keyword *Tamparo.*

CHAPTER 3

The Professional Health-Care Team

"The idea behind the tiny flower is that it really doesn't matter how small you are, whether in size or numbers. It doesn't matter how much you know, or how skilled you are. It doesn't matter how much education or how many credentials you have. What really matters is how you affect the world around you."—Serge Kahili King; Author, Humanitarian, Shaman of the Hawaiian Tradition

KEY TERMS

certification Documentation usually from a professional organization that an individual has met certain requirements and standards set forth by that organization.

clinic manager Person who has additional education and experience in the health-care field to manage a facility.

continuing education units (CEUs) These are awarded to professionals within a particular field after gaining additional knowledge at a workshop or seminar.

credential Evidence of having achieved a certain level of knowledge through education and experience.

endorsement An agreement in which one state recognizes the licensing procedure of another state, considers it valid, and grants a license to practice; sometimes referred to as *reciprocity.*

licensed practical nurse (LPN) or licensed vocational nurse (LVN) A graduate from an approved practical nurse vocational or college program who has passed the national examination for practical nurses and is licensed by a state board of nursing.

licensure Legal permission, granted by state statutes, to perform specific acts; for instance, a physician is licensed to practice medicine.

medical assistant (MA) Person who assists the provider in both administrative and clinical duties; education varies from on-the-job instruction to 2 years in an accredited program for medical assisting.

medical/professional coder Person who has had education and experience in *Current Procedural Terminology and International Classification of Diseases* (ICD-10) coding; responsible for the correct application of codes for procedures, supplies, and diagnoses used for billing professional medical services. (Note: ICD-11 goes into effect in 2022.)

medical laboratory technician (MLT) A graduate from a certificate or associate degree program who works under the supervision of a provider or medical technologist in a laboratory preparing specimens and operating automated analyzers.

medical technologist (MT) A graduate from a 4-year college or university program in medical technology that includes 1 year of clinical experience in the laboratory. MTs perform complex tests and analyses, ensure accuracy of testing, and may supervise medical laboratory technicians.

medical transcriptionist Person who may or may not have formal education; will have superior medical terminology knowledge as well as keyboarding and grammar skills; transcribes medical dictation.

nurse practitioner (NP) A registered nurse who has a graduate degree and advanced knowledge to diagnose illnesses and prescribe treatments and medications. Nurse practitioners may work independently in some states, in collaboration with a physician, or under a physician's supervision.

physician A provider who is identified by law as a doctor of medicine (MD) or a doctor of osteopathic medicine (DO).

physician assistant (PA) A graduate of a master's level, accredited PA program who has passed the Physician Assistant National Certifying Exam (PANCE). PAs are able to diagnose, prescribe, but work under the supervision of a physician.

provider Any health-care professional who examines, diagnoses, and treats individuals (includes MDs, DOs, NPs, and PAs).

reciprocity An agreement by which two states recognize the licensing procedures of each other, consider them valid, and grant licenses to practice based on the other state's licensure. In some states, it is referred to as *endorsement*.

registered nurse (RN) A graduate from an approved associate degree, diploma, or bachelor's degree professional nurse program who has passed the national examination for RNs and is licensed by a state board of nursing.

registration An entry in an official record listing names of persons satisfying certain requirements and level of education.

scope of practice Terminology used by state licensing boards that defines the procedures, actions, and processes that are permitted for a professional depending on their education, experience, and demonstrated competency.

tickler file A chronological file used as a reminder to do specific tasks on schedule; usually daily, weekly, or monthly.

LEARNING OUTCOMES

Upon successful completion of this chapter, you should be able to:

3.1 Define key terms.
3.2 Discuss licensure, certification, and registration of health-care professionals.
3.3 Identify the role of the medical assistant (administrative and/or clinical) in ambulatory care.
3.4 Provide at least three examples of nonlicensed personnel in the health-care setting.
3.5 List and define the three categories of nurses found in health-care settings and compare their education and their scope of practice.
3.6 List two similarities and dissimilarities between a physician assistant and a nurse practitioner.
3.7 Describe scope of practice for health-care personnel.

COMPETENCIES

CAAHEP
- Differentiate between scope of practice and standards of care for medical assistants. (CAAHEP X.C.1)
- Discuss licensure and certification as they apply to healthcare providers. (CAAHEP X.C.5)
- Locate a state's legal scope of practice for medical assistants. (CAAHEP X.P.1)

ABHES
- Compare and contrast the allied health professions and understand their relation to medical assisting. (ABHES 1.b)

- List the general responsibilities and skills of the medial assistant. (ABHES 1.d)
- Describe and comprehend medical assistant credentialing requirements, the process to obtain the credential and the importance of credentialing. (ABHES 1.c)
- Define scope of practice for the medical assistant within the state that the medical assistant is employed. (ABHES 4.f.1)

VIGNETTE

What Would You Do?

The receptionist in a pediatrician's clinic answers the phone and immediately hears a baby crying in the background. The caller states that her baby seems to be in pain and is pulling at her ears. The receptionist states, "Oh, she probably has an ear infection. Why don't you come right in and the doctor will see you." Discuss the issues raised by this conversation.

In any type of health-care setting there is a "team" of people who provide care to a client. The leader of the team is the provider, but the team includes every individual employed in the facility. Each member has a very important responsibility and many assigned tasks, some of which can be performed only by that individual. Even the custodian contributes to the client's care by helping to provide a safe and clean environment. All employees need to work in cooperation and collaboration as a team to provide the client with quality health care. The number and types of employees in the health-care setting will vary with the size and type of the practice. Each employee has specific skills and education level.

THE HEALTH-CARE TEAM

Employees in the health-care setting may fall into the following categories: (1) those that are certified, (2) those that are registered, and (3) those that are licensed. Some employees may be none of the three, and some more than one. The classifications of certification, registration, or licensure establish that the employee has met a minimum standard required by law or a national organization.

Certification is the most common form of regulation. It occurs when a professional organization administers a national examination to assess the knowledge and skill of its applicants. With passage of this examination, applicants have demonstrated that they have met the minimum standards set forth by the organization. This certification of health-care professionals usually exceeds the standards required by any governmental agency. There is a fee associated with the examination and a membership fee for the organization. There is a process set forth for recertification that takes place every 2 to 5 years depending on the organization. Certification is a self-regulating, credentialing process that is fully voluntary. However, this does not prevent anyone without certification from practicing. Increasingly, employers seek individuals who are appropriately credentialed.

Registration is a process by which individuals in a particular health field are listed in a registry. This list is then available to health-care providers. The state has little or no power over the registration process. There are two methods of registration. One occurs when individuals list their names in an official registry of a health area in which they work. The second form of registration requires a predetermined level of education. Professional associations interested in recognizing qualified health-care professionals administer examinations that must be passed before the appropriate **credential** can be conferred. This formal registry is most likely seen in ambulatory care. There is a fee associated with the examination and a membership fee for the organization.

Licensure is the strongest form of regulation. It requires passing a licensing examination and paying a licensing fee as well as a fee associated with the examination. A license establishes that the employee has met minimum standards required by law. Licensure laws protect the public from unqualified practitioners, and limit and control admission to different health-care occupations. When licensure is a requirement to practice, it is illegal to practice without one. Licensed employees must obtain their licenses from the state authority in which they wish to be employed. Most licensed personnel also hold memberships in professional organizations.

Certified, registered, and licensed individuals may use appropriate abbreviations after their names to verify their credentials. Examples include certified medical assistant, CMA (AAMA); registered medical assistant, RMA; and licensed practical nurse, LPN. Both certification and registration are voluntary. Licensure is mandatory (Fig. 3-1). Renewal of certification, registration, and/or licensure usually involves a fee and proof of **continuing education units (CEUs)** over a certain period of time, usually 2 or 5 years.

There are a number of members of the health-care team serving in either administrative and/or clinical areas that fit within the models of certification, registration, and licensure.

IN THE NEWS

Research indicates that there are presently over 80 different health-care professions in the United States. In 2020, there were 18 million individuals employed in health care for a total of about 15% of the nation's economy. Health professionals are almost always the part of a team where each has a specific responsibility. An effective team has been described as one where the team members, including their clients and patients, openly communicate with each other. The effective team will merge their observations, expertise, and decision-making to provide the best care for those in need.

During the Covid-19 Pandemic, many health professionals were called on to expand their expertise to another area of health care to provide relief for overloaded staff in hospitals. This may be one of the best examples of the team response.

ADMINISTRATIVE TEAM MEMBERS

The administrative staff is most likely to schedule appointments, tend to the client flow through the clinic, and complete all the clinic's clerical work. These team members may include receptionists or administrative assistants, insurance specialists, coders, billers, and file clerks. Most of these health professionals have additional education and experience beyond high school. Such educational experiences include community and technical colleges, private schools, and/or online course preparation. These courses include medical terminology, anatomy and physiology, medical office procedures, medical records, coding and billing, and other pertinent classes. Such courses may lead to a Medical Office Certificate, a Medical Receptionist/Secretary Certificate, or a Medical Support

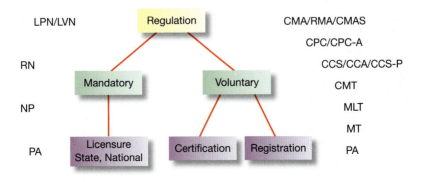

Figure 3-1. Not all professions follow the same regulations.

Certificate conferred by the educational institution and not to be confused with professional certification. It is this additional education that gives a prospective employee an advantage in the job market or helps an employee gain additional compensation in pay.

Among the administrative team members there are those who are apt to be certified. There are a variety of certifications offered by professional organizations to administrative team members. For example, a medical assistant (MA) can be a graduate medical assistant, MA; certified medical assistant, CMA (AAMA); registered medical assistant, RMA; or certified medical administrative specialist, CMAS (Fig. 3-2).

The **medical assistant (MA)** works closely with providers in outpatient and ambulatory care facilities and is cross trained to perform both administrative and clinical duties. The MA's versatility provides for efficient management of the entire ambulatory health-care setting. Although the MA is a generalist, the role may be highly specific, depending on the duties assigned, location, specialty, and size of practice.

Educational programs for the MA include academic courses and clinical experiences, and are usually 1 or 2 years in a postsecondary vocational/technical, community, junior, or senior college awarding a certificate, diploma, or associate's degree. The Commission on Accreditation of Allied

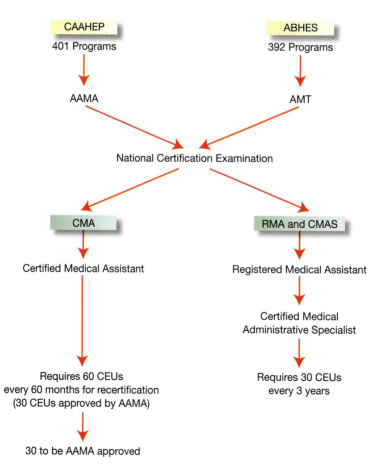

Figure 3-2. Education and credentialing of medical assistants.

Health Education Programs (CAAHEP) awards or denies accreditation to MA programs (in addition to many other allied health programs). The American Association of Medical Assistants (AAMA), working in conjunction with the American Medical Association (AMA), defines the essential components and standards of quality that educational institutions must follow in educating MAs.

The Accrediting Bureau of Health Education Schools (ABHES) also awards and denies accreditation to MA programs in private and public postsecondary institutions. The American Medical Technologists (AMT), in cooperation with ABHES, defines the curriculum for the programs that prepare students for the medical assisting profession. ABHES and CAAHEP are both recognized by the U.S. Department of Education.

Only graduates of accredited MA programs are eligible to sit for the national certification examination. The AAMA believes that this safeguards the quality of care to the consumer, ensures the CMA's role in a rapidly evolving health-care delivery system, and continues to promote the identity and stature of the profession. There is a fee for each examination. With successful passage of the examination, the individual becomes either a certified medical assistant (CMA) through the AAMA or a registered medical assistant (RMA) through the American Medical Technologists (AMT). The RMA recertification requires 30 CEUs every 3 years. The CMA (AAMA) must renew the credential every 60 months, requiring a total of 60 CEUs, 30 of which are AAMA approved. Current certified status is required to use the CMA (AAMA) credential in connection with employment.

Another certification is that of a certified medical administrative specialist (CMAS). This certification is offered by the AMT organization. A CMAS is familiar with clinical and technical concepts required to coordinate administrative functions throughout the entire clinic. This credential is often held by a **clinic manager** or practice manager. This person oversees the daily operation of the clinic, including all the staff, whereas medical-related issues are managed by the providers. Clinic managers will have procedures in place to monitor the certifications, registrations, and licenses of all employees. Practice-specific certifications and compliances, such as Clinical Laboratory Improvement Amendments (CLIA) and Occupational Safety and Health Administration (OSHA), and other legal requirements may also be overseen by the clinic manager.

Medical/professional coders are responsible for the correct application of procedures, supplies, and diagnostic codes used for billing professional medical services. Without accurate medical documentation and the correct coding, reimbursement will be lessened or even denied. There are approximately 92,000 professional coders in the country. Two associations credential professional coders:

1. American Academy of Professional Coders (AAPC), which includes certified professional coder apprentice (CPC-A) and certified professional coder (CPC) for those who work in an ambulatory setting, and certified professional coder—hospital apprentice (CPC-HA) and certified professional coder—hospital (CPC-H) for those working in a hospital.
2. American Health Information Management Association (AHIMA), which includes certified coding associate (CCA), certified coding specialist (CCS), certified coding specialist—physician based (CCS-P).

These various levels of certification can be attained with additional education and experience.

Case Study

Margie is the billing clerk at Lake Family Practice. She is working on Dr. Dillon's forms and notices that Linda Young is being billed for a complete physical examination. Margie remembers seeing Linda, a friend from the gym, and thought she had spent only a little time in the clinic with Dr. Dillon. Margie decides that she must have been mistaken.

As Margie progresses through the forms, she sees a form for Robert Brown. Mr. Brown is being charged for an expanded focus examination. Margie remembers Mr. Brown commented on his way out that he had never been in and out of the office so fast. He was happy to have had a quick appointment.

Margie becomes suspicious of Dr. Dillon's billing and checks closely the encounter forms for today, comparing them to his chart documentation. She finds more contradictions.

Is the billing clerk qualified to question the provider's billing practices?
What is your responsibility in this situation?
What legal ramifications does this situation present?

Medical transcriptionists may be part of the administrative team. These team members have knowledge and experience in the transcription of the provider's clinic notes, medical reports, and correspondence. Much of this work is currently outsourced to private companies, often overseas. Whether located in-house or offsite, these individuals remain an important part of the health-care team. The certified medical transcriptionist (CMT) is a transcriptionist who has passed the national certifying examination offered by the Association for Healthcare Documentation Integrity (AHDI) (formerly the American Association of Medical Transcription [AAMT]).

Medical scribes have come on the scene since the adoption of electronic health records (EHR). Documentation in the EHRs led many providers to employ medical scribes whose primary goals is to enter into the record the important conversation and examination results during the client/provider visit. All this is under the supervision of the provider and permission of the client.

There are additional certifications available to the administrative staff. These can be found at the websites of various organizations.

Case Law

A medical assistant had a phone conversation with a client in which the client told the assistant that "she was experiencing pain radiating from her flank and back, bleeding, and changes in her bowel movement." The medical assistant determined that the symptoms were related to a urinary tract infection and did not report the symptoms to a doctor, nurse practitioner, or physician assistant. The result is that the client was denied needed medical attention, later developed a life-threatening complication, and died. The medical assistant violated state law by practicing outside of the established scope of practice and was found guilty of negligence.

Wong v Chappell, 773 s.E.2d 496 (2015)

CLINICAL SUPPORT TEAM MEMBERS

The clinical support staff will include members with a variety of educational experiences. In this area you will find a CMA (AAMA) or RMA performing clinical duties as assigned by the physician or provider. Among their duties are assisting with examinations and minor surgeries, checking vital signs, and taking electrocardiograms. Providers see the value of these professionals because CMAs (AAMA) or RMAs have been educated and specifically prepared for ambulatory care settings. An MA or any other health professional must never attempt to go beyond their education and experience. Some states limit an MA's **scope of practice**. For example, in some states a CMA (AAMA) is not allowed to administer vaccinations even though they have been trained to do so. MAs must be aware of the laws in the state in which they wish to practice.

If there is a laboratory onsite at a health-care facility, **medical laboratory technicians (MLTs)** may be employed. MLTs have graduated from a certificate or associate degree program. They work under the supervision of a physician or medical technologist in a laboratory preparing specimens and operating automated analyzers, among other tasks. Most MLTs become certified by the AMT.

Also employed in a laboratory is a **medical technologist (MT)** who has graduated from a 4-year college program. This education includes 1 year of clinical experience. MTs are certified through the American Society of Clinical Pathologists (ASCP). The job of an MT encompasses a wide variety of responsibilities. Most MTs work in clinical pathology laboratories where they run blood and tissue tests and analyze biological samples. Whether employed in a large independent laboratory, a hospital laboratory, or ambulatory care, this individual offers a critical piece to a client's care.

Nurses may be employed in clinics (especially those clinics where surgery is performed) because of their technical expertise in clinical areas. Few nurses, however, have skills relating to the business aspect of the ambulatory health-care setting or have the desire to function in that capacity. There are three distinctions for nurses and each must be licensed to use the nurse title (LPN, LVN, or RN). Nurses also must practice only within their legal scope of practice as established by the state board of nursing. The scope of practice is different for each category of nurse and varies among states.

A **licensed practical nurse (LPN)** or a **licensed vocational nurse (LVN)** is educated to provide health care for diverse clients in a variety of settings but most work in skilled nursing homes and long-term care facilities. The terms LPN and LVN are interchangeable, depending on the geographic region of the country. These team members have completed educational coursework at an approved vocational/technical school or a junior, community, or senior college and are licensed through the state in which they work. They must meet all regulatory standards, pay a fee, and pass the National Council Licensure Examination for Practical Nurses (NCLEX-PN) to be licensed. The LPN/LVN scope of practice requires care to be provided at the direction of and under the supervision of qualified health professionals including providers and registered nurses (RNs).

A **registered nurse (RN)** is an individual who has graduated from a state-approved school of professional nursing, passed the National Council Licensure Examination for Registered Nurses (NCLEX-RN), and is licensed by a state board of nursing to provide patient care. The scope of practice for an RN is different than that of an LPN or LVN. RNs are educated to provide health care in acute care, ambulatory care, community-based, and public health settings. They are educated in hospital-based diploma programs, associate's degree programs, and bachelor's degree programs.

A nurse's license is renewed as mandated by state law. Most states require a renewal fee; some states require CEUs for license renewal. All nurses need to know their state's requirements and recommendations for license renewal. Nurses wishing to practice in another state may seek **reciprocity** or **endorsement** in that state. Reciprocity or endorsement occurs when one state recognizes the licensing procedure of another, considers it valid, and grants a license to practice based on the other's licensure. If there is no reciprocity process, the nurse must satisfy the state's licensure requirement.

Case Study

An MA and an RN work side by side in a large medical setting. A recent downsizing has required assignments to be shifted. The RN is angered by the MA's appointment to an expansion of duties. There is a significant pay difference between the two salaries, with the nurse's salary being higher.

Discuss the ramifications of this situation as they apply to both the RN and the MA.

HEALTH-CARE PROVIDERS

This portion of the health-care team includes those who provide the examination, diagnosis, and treatment plan for each client. There are a variety of caregivers in this area, all with varying degrees of education.

Within the category of health-care providers is a **physician assistant (PA)**. A PA can fit into all three models of certification, registration, and licensure. The typical PA program is 24 to 32 months and requires at least 4 years of college and some health-care experience before admission. There are more than 240 PA programs that are accredited by the Accreditation Review Commission on Education for the Physician Assistant (ARC-PA). More than 55% of PAs work in group practices or solo physician clinics, and more than one quarter are found in hospitals. The remaining PAs are in outpatient care centers, community health centers, freestanding surgical facilities, skilled nursing homes, school- or college-based facilities, industrial settings, and correctional systems. These individuals perform tasks usually done by physicians and work under the direction of a supervising physician. All states require PAs to pass the certification examination of the National Commission on Certification of Physician Assistants (NCCPA), the Physician Assistant National Certifying Exam (PANCE). Following certification, PA-Cs must meet the requirements of the state in which they wish to practice. All states require state licensing; most include CEUs and recertification through the NCCPA. Recertification requires 100 hours of continuing medical education (CME) every 2 years and a recertification examination every 10 years. PAs are credentialed by their state medical board and fall under the medical practice act provisions. With more than 125,000 PAs in practice, these health-care providers serve a significant role in the health-care field. PAs may supervise MAs.

The **nurse practitioner (NP)** is a licensed RN who has successfully completed additional education in an NP program at the master's or doctoral level. Graduates are prepared for primary and acute care practice in family medicine, women's health, neonatology, pediatrics, geriatrics, mental health, and emergency services. NPs are licensed in all states. They practice under the rules and regulations of the state in which they are licensed. Most NPs are nationally certified in their specialty area and are recognized as expert health-care providers. National certification requires written and/or oral examination. NPs may examine, diagnose, and treat clients—acts formerly performed solely by physicians.

The employment field for NPs varies. For instance, they may be found in isolated areas of the country managing a clinic and providing total client care, or they may be found in public health in charge of family planning clinics. NPs also may be found in medical clinics and hospitals. They work independently and collaboratively on the health-care team. One third of all NPs work in family practice. There are more than 300,000 NPs practicing in the United States. Recertification requires 1,000 direct patient-contact hours and 100 CEUs every 5 years. No examination is required.

NPs practice under their basic RN license and fall under the Nurse Practice Act. In most states they may supervise MAs but this may not be true for all NPs as the Nurse Practice Act is unique to each state. This fact illustrates the point that no matter what the position is in the health-care field, the rules and regulations for the geographic area in which employment is held must be known and fully understood.

Case Study

Edna Johnson came into the office for nasal congestion, cough, and a fever of 2 days. She was given one of the only available appointments open for the day with the NP. After taking Edna's vital signs, the MA told her that the NP would be in shortly. Edna became agitated and demanded to see the doctor, stating, "I want to see someone who can diagnose my condition and prescribe an antibiotic."

What is your response to Edna?
How can you reassure Ms. Johnson regarding the experience and preparation of the NP?

Also in the clinical setting is the doctor. Among these individuals are **physicians** (MDs), osteopaths (DOs), and naturopaths (NDs). The doctor oversees some health-care professionals directly (PA, LPN, LVN, RN, MA); for others they provide clinical guidance and/or advice (clinic manager and administrative staff). The doctor is the one who sets the standard and is responsible for maintaining the medical and ethical standards within a clinic. These providers are ultimately responsible for everyone on staff. The education of MDs and DOs includes a 4-year bachelor's

IN THE NEWS

According to the Association of American Colleges (AAMC), the United States will have a shortage of nearly 122,000 physicians by 2032. The demand for physicians is due, in part, to an aging population that continues to grow. An additional factor has been the reduction of smoking, obesity, and advances in medicine that translates into Americans living longer. Although rural and underserved areas may experience this shortage more acutely, the need for more providers will be felt everywhere. The current increase in the supply of physician assistants (PAs) and advanced practice registered nurses (APRNs) will help to fill the gap in medical care.

degree, a 4-year medical degree, and then a 2- to 8-year residency program, depending on the type of doctor and the specialty involved. Doctors are also licensed by a state medical board. (See Chapter 4, State and Federal Regulations.) Physicians may go on to take a certification examination in their specialty area offered by their professional organization. They gain the distinction of being "board certified." This board certification is then renewed every 2 to 7 years depending on the specialty.

An ND attends a 4-year graduate-level naturopathic medical school and is educated in all of the same basic sciences as an MD, but also studies holistic and nontoxic approaches to therapy with a strong emphasis on disease prevention and optimizing wellness. NDs take professional board examinations so that they may be licensed by a state as primary care general practice physicians.

 ## CONSIDERATIONS FOR HEALTH-CARE EMPLOYEES

It is important for health-care employees to remember that, because of the ever-changing field of medicine, they need to continue their education. Obviously, continuing education benefits not just the individual and the employer but also, and more important, the welfare of the clients they serve. Many health-care professions require continuing education to maintain their certification, registration, or licensure. Employers should have a procedure for making certain all employees are up to date in their credentialing. This task is often assigned to the clinic manager, who perhaps will maintain a **tickler file** of all important dates to recall. These include due dates for license renewals, insurance premiums, and narcotic registrations. Established patterns must be maintained for drug inventory and accurate records. Detailed descriptions and examples of such activities in the clinic's procedure manual are most helpful. All employees, administrative and clinical, are to be encouraged to belong to and be active in a professional organization that pertains to their area of expertise. Many employers will give incentives to employees who seek certification in their area, if available. Some employers will pay membership fees as part of a benefit package. This is a win–win situation for all parties. Employees can keep up to date and network within their field; the employer has a well-informed and educated employee; and the quality of care to the client is improved.

SCOPE OF PRACTICE

State regulations vary from state to state and will continue to change as medicine becomes more specialized. These state regulations are addressed in medical practice acts. These are state laws written for the express purpose of governing the practice of medicine that delineates the scope of practice for health-care professionals. "Scope of practice" is terminology used by state licensing boards to define the procedures, actions, and processes that are permitted for a professional depending on education, experience, and demonstrated competency. The scope of practice varies from one health-care professional category to the next. Even within one specific category, the scope of practice can vary from state to state. There is one constant, however, from state to state within each category: the requirement to have certain providers oversee all other health-care professionals.

Case Law

East Missouri Action Agency is a federally tax-exempt, not-for-profit corporation that maintains several clinics in Missouri. The agency, specializing in family planning, obstetrics, and gynecology, services the low-income population.

Among the many staff members that the agency employs are two nurses who are licensed and have postgraduate education in the field of obstetrics and gynecology. They take histories, provide and give information about birth control, perform breast and pelvic examinations, dispense certain designated medications, and provide counseling services and community education. All acts of the nurses are performed under written standing orders and protocols signed by the physicians of the agency.

The Missouri Board of Registration threatened to order the nurses and physicians to show why the nurses should not be found guilty of the unauthorized practice of medicine and the physicians guilty of aiding and abetting such practices.

The two nurses and five physicians petitioned the court for a declaratory judgment and injunction stating that the agency nurses are authorized under the nursing law of Missouri and that such practices do not constitute the unauthorized practice of medicine.

The court found that the nurses' acts were authorized and within their scope of practice to provide these services.

Sermchief v Gonzales, Supreme Court of Missouri, 1983

As stated previously, the **provider** is responsible for overseeing the medical and ethical standards of the health-care staff. It is the provider's responsibility to see that the staff are assigned tasks within their scope of practice. Ultimately, however, each staff member is responsible for his or her actions. In some states, MAs cannot perform venipuncture or give injections. Some states also regulate who can practice radiography and who can administer medications. All states regulate laboratory procedures and protocol. An employer must understand regulations pertinent to those individuals in his or her employ. Employees also have the professional responsibility to abide by the regulations pertaining to their jobs. Practicing within the law is essential for the protection of all concerned. Employers must recognize that hiring employees with appropriate qualifications and credentials helps ensure that clients receive the optimal level of quality care and reduce risk for liability.

Case Study

The Medical Board of California in their October 2002 Action Report responded to physicians' interests about who may perform what type of cosmetic procedures. In response to who may use lasers or intense pulse light devices to remove hair, spider veins, and tattoos, they state: "Physicians may use lasers or intense pulse light devices. In addition, physician assistants and registered nurses (not licensed vocational nurses) may perform these treatments under a physician's supervision. Unlicensed medical assistants, licensed vocational nurses, cosmetologists, electrologists, or estheticians may not legally perform these treatments under any circumstances, nor may registered nurses or physician assistants perform them independently, without supervision."

In response to who may inject Botox, they state: "Physicians may inject Botox, or they may direct licensed registered nurses, licensed vocational nurses, or physician assistants to perform the injection under their supervision. No unlicensed persons such as medical assistants may inject Botox."

What are the regulations in your state?
As a medical assistant, what role and responsibilities do you have related to cosmetic procedures?
Watch for action in other states regarding these issues.

SUMMARY

When considering the education of various health-care professionals, one must remember that each is a vital link in the chain to quality health care. No one functions independently of any other. Each health professional has skills and responsibilities to complement every other health professional. When competition and territoriality cause conflict between professionals, quality health care is diminished. The education, knowledge, and scope of practice for each health-care professional are specifically and purposely designed to complement rather than to conflict. Because health-care delivery is changing every day, it is vital that the health-care team's abilities keep changing with it.

 Watch It Now! Can you be a member of the "team" in health care? at http://FADavis.com, keyword *Tamparo*.

Questions for Review

SELECT THE BEST ANSWER

1. When two states recognize the licensing procedures of each other, consider them valid, and grant licenses to practice based on the other state's licensure, this is called
   a. Reciprocity.
   b. Endorsement.
   c. Certification.
   d. Only a and b above.
   e. None of the above.

2. Which of the following are specifically prepared to work in a medical clinic/practice?
   a. LPN/LVN
   b. RN
   c. MA
   d. Only a and c above
   e. None of the above

3. A medical transcriptionist may become certified by passing a certifying examination offered by the
   a. AAMA.
   b. AHDI.
   c. AMA.
   d. AMT.
   e. NCCPA.

4. Which certifications are available for medical assistants (MAs)?
    a. CMAS (certified medial administrative specialist)
    b. RMA (registered medical assistant)
    c. LMA (licensed medical assistant)
    d. Only a and b above
    e. None of the above

5. Once an MD has achieved the designation of "Board Certified," he or she
    a. is certified for life.
    b. must recertify every 2 to 7 years.
    c. must recertify every 15 years.
    d. is certified in all specialties.
    e. must register the certification yearly.

SHORT ANSWER QUESTIONS

1. What is the difference between licensure, certification, and registration of health-care professionals?

_____

_____

_____

2. What is the role of the medical assistant (MA) in ambulatory care?

_____

_____

_____

3. List three examples of nonlicensed personnel in the health-care setting.

_____

_____

_____

4. What are two similarities and two differences between a physician assistant (PA) and a nurse practitioner (NP)?

_____

_____

_____

5. What does scope of practice mean?

_____

_____

_____

CLASSROOM EXERCISES

1. *Case A:* A solo family practitioner is setting up a practice in a small, rural community.
   Case B: Six providers are entering a group practice in a city of 40,000. Specialties include obstetrics/gynecology, family practice, internal medicine, and pediatrics.
   What number and kinds of employees would you recommend in case A? In case B? Explain your choices.

2. Identify the kind of medical practice most likely to employ a
   a. PA.
   b. MA.
   c. Nurse practitioner.

3. Discuss the difference between a CMA (AAMA) and an RMA in their certification requirements.

4. Discuss the advantages of belonging to and being active in a professional organization.

5. Consider the AAMA definition of a medical assistant. Change that definition to include any state regulations particular to your area.

6. Increasingly, large health facilities are asking health-care professionals to do more with less. Some are approached about becoming a specialist in an area with or without additional education. For example, a CMA may be asked to become an emergency department (ED) technician with specialized, in-house education. Or the same person may be asked to be a surgical technician with the appropriate education. What are the legal and ethical implications of such requests? Discuss.

INTERNET ACTIVITIES

1. As we have learned, the scope of practice for MAs is different in each state. Search the Internet and research the scope of practice for MAs in your state. Compare what you find with the education that you have received. Will you be able to do everything that you have learned?

2. Visit the website for the AAMA. List the advantages of becoming a member as a student and the advantages of continuing your membership once you have graduated.

REFERENCES

Furrow, B., Greaney, T., Johnson, S., Jost, T., & Schwartz, R.: *Health Law: Cases, Materials and Problems, 7th Edition*. St. Paul, MN: Thomson West, 2013.

For more resources, visit
http://FADavis.com, keyword *Tamparo*.

UNIT II

Law, Liability, and Duties

CHAPTER 4

State and Federal Regulations

"When you get right down to the root of the meaning of the word 'succeed,' you find it simply means to follow through." —F. W. Nichol; Author

KEY TERMS

administer a drug To introduce a drug into the body of a client.

Controlled Substances Act Federal law that regulates the administration, dispensing, and prescribing of particular substances that are categorized into five schedules.

dispense a drug To deliver controlled substances in a bottle, box, or some other container to a client; under the Controlled Substances Act, definition also includes the administering of controlled substances.

Drug Enforcement Administration (DEA) Branch of the Department of Justice that enforces drug laws.

drug formulary An insurance carrier's list of preferred drugs.

Health Insurance Portability and Accountability Act (HIPAA) National standards to protect health information.

medical practice acts State statutes that define the practice of medicine, describe methods of licensure, and set guidelines for suspension or revocation of a license.

National Provider Identification (NPI) A 10-digit unique number given to a health-care provider for identification purposes under HIPAA regulations.

prescribe a drug To issue a drug order for a client.

Privacy Rule A portion of HIPAA that regulates the confidentiality of a client's health record while still allowing that information to flow properly and effectively in order to treat the client.

protected health information (PHI) All the past, present, and future physical and mental conditions of an individual's health care.

LEARNING OUTCOMES

Upon successful completion of this chapter, you should be able to:

4.1 Define key terms.

4.2 Identify four common requirements for a physician to be licensed.

4.3 Identify three conditions under which a physician's license may be revoked.

4.4 Explain the purposes of the DEA and its regulations.

4.5 Identify the five controlled substances drug schedules, giving an example of each.

4.6 Discuss the role of the health professional in preventing and treating substance abuse.

4.7 Summarize the key points of HIPAA related to health care.

4.8 Explain the key points that should be provided in a clinic's Notice of Privacy.

4.9 Explain the main points of the Health Care and Education Reconciliation Act of 2010.

COMPETENCIES

CAAHEP
- Describe components of the Health Insurance Portability & Accountability Act (HIPAA). (CAAHEP X.C.3)
- Summarize the Patient Bill of Rights. (CAAHEP X.C.4)
- Apply HIPAA rules in regard to privacy and release of information. (CAAHEP X.P.2)
- Apply the Patient's Bill of Rights as it relates to choice of treatment, consent for treatment and refusal of treatment. (CAAHEP X.P.4)
- Demonstrate sensitivity to patient rights. (CAAHEP X.A.1)

ABHES
- Comply with federal, state, and local health laws and regulations as they relate to health care settings. (ABHES 4.f)
- Comply with legal aspects of writing prescriptions, including federal and state laws. (ABHES 6.c.3)
- Demonstrate compliance with HIPAA guidelines. (ABHES 4.h)

VIGNETTE

Who Has a Right to Know?

Kelly, a first-year medical assistant (MA) student, tells her instructor that she thinks she may be pregnant and wonders what she should do. The instructor recommends that Kelly go to the campus health center for a pregnancy test. When Kelly's test is positive, she again discusses her case with her instructor. As a single woman, Kelly decides she cannot support a child now but is not sure whether to have the baby and put it up for adoption or to have an abortion. After a few days and a discussion with the father of the child, their decision is to have an abortion.

Kelly returns to the campus health clinic for her test results so that she can take them to the abortion clinic. The nurse refuses to give Kelly the test results, saying, "You'll have to talk to the nurse practitioner. I don't believe in abortion." The nurse practitioner gives Kelly the laboratory results.

As you read in the last chapter, licensure offers some benefits, but it also brings many regulations. The rules and regulations for physicians and some other health-care providers can be found in the **medical practice acts** passed by each state. These are state statutes that define the practice of medicine, describe methods of licensure, and set guidelines for suspension or revocation of a license. All 50 states have such statutes to protect their citizens from harm by unqualified health-care professionals.

LICENSURE (MDs AND DOs)

Physicians (doctors of medicine [MDs] and doctors of osteopathic medicine [DOs]) must be licensed to practice medicine in the United States. States differ in their licensing requirements. The more common requirements include a 4-year undergraduate degree, graduation from an accredited medical school, completion of an internship, and successful completion of the United States Medical Licensing Examination (USMLE), which was implemented in 1994. Physicians must then meet the requirements for the state in which they wish to practice. This process usually involves completing an application, providing proof of required education and training, and paying an application fee.

Physicians who choose to practice in more than one state must satisfy the license requirements of each state. This process may require a physician to meet each state's reciprocity requirements. Not all states have reciprocity or endorsement, so rules for each individual state need to be researched. Each state also differs on its requirements for non–U.S.-trained and non–U.S.-educated health-care providers. Most of the state regulations include additional education and/or internships. All states require the individual to pass the USMLE before being allowed to practice in the United States.

Many states require a complete and unrestricted license to provide medical services. The Department of Defense requires full licensure of its military personnel even when they are currently only serving in military medical services. Health-care providers engaging strictly in research and not practicing medicine need not always have a license but most likely will need postdoctorate training to qualify.

LICENSE RENEWAL

Physicians periodically renew their licenses to practice, usually every 2 years. Once a physician receives notice at the time of renewal, he or she is required to complete a renewal application form and pay a fee. Documentation of continuing medical education (CME) is a common requirement for license renewal in most states; however, some states require only payment of a fee. Specific state requirements differ, but CME credits may include (1) reading books, papers, and publications; (2) teaching health professionals; (3) attending approved courses, workshops, and seminars; and (4) self-instruction.

A clinic manager may be responsible for keeping records of the physician's CME activities and will want to have the state's requirements on file in order to verify the appropriate credits.

LICENSE REVOCATION AND SUSPENSION

A physician's license to practice may be revoked or suspended as a result of (1) conviction of a crime, (2) unprofessional conduct, and (3) personal or professional incapacity. Each of these conditions is defined by state statute.

Conviction of a crime is a more obvious reason for license revocation than is unprofessional conduct or personal or professional incapacity. Examples of crimes that would result in revocation would include conviction of child abuse or sexual assault against a client.

Unprofessional conduct of physicians and other licensed health-care professionals is defined by law. Although unprofessional conduct may not be considered a crime, such conduct is unacceptable according to state law and therefore is punishable. Examples of unprofessional conduct include falsifying any records regarding licensing, being dishonest, and impersonating another practitioner. Personal or professional incapacity includes chronic substance misuse, continuing to practice when severe physical limitations prevent adequate care, and practicing outside the scope of training.

Usually charges against physicians are made by the state's licensing board in all three conditions, necessitating the suspension or revocation of their license. In all states, the basic procedure for disciplinary action is similar. Most boards are required to give the physician licensee sufficient notice of the charges and allow the physician legal counsel and a hearing. The board then investigates, prosecutes, makes a judgment, and sentences the physician. Some states have empowered their licensing boards to suspend a license to practice on a temporary basis without a hearing (i.e., due process) when the physician poses an immediate threat.

Case Study

On a cold, icy, winter day, Dr. Roberts was severely injured in a motor vehicle crash on his way to the hospital. He was listed in critical condition for several days, lapsing in and out of a coma. Dr. Roberts finally stabilized and was released home after 2 weeks. With lots of hard work and rehabilitation, Dr. Roberts went back to work after 5 months. Within 2 weeks, his support staff and the hospital personnel started noticing his forgetfulness. He forgot to document that he had ordered an x-ray. He argued with an MA regarding his request that an opioid medication be called in for a client. The answering service called the hospital on a weekend when they could not find Dr. Roberts, who was on call. Dr. Roberts forgot he was on call and left town unexpectedly. The hospital's board of trustees is about to take action that rarely occurs. They feel the need to deem Dr. Roberts incompetent to practice medicine and have his license revoked.

If you are a member of Dr. Roberts' staff, what might you do in this situation?
Does this situation fall under ethics or law? Explain your response.
Is there any other action that might be taken by the hospital's board of trustees?

PRESCRIPTIONS

Note: *Throughout this section, the terms* nonnarcotic *and* narcotic *are used because they are referenced in the Controlled Substances Act. However, the majority of health-care providers now use the terms* nonopioid *and* opioid *to refer to medications.*

A prescription is an order for medication that is dispensed to or for a client. To prescribe a medication for a clients, health-care providers must be licensed in the state in which they practice medicine and possess a **National Provider Identification (NPI)**. An NPI is a 10-digit number that can be obtained from the Centers for Medicare and Medicaid Services (CMS). This number is used for various reasons, including prescribing medications and submitting claims for services to insurance carriers.

TRANSMISSION OF PRESCRIPTIONS

Prescriptions can be supplied in a variety of ways. They may be handwritten, electronically printed, e-scripted (sent electronically directly to the pharmacy), and phoned or faxed to a pharmacy. For years, the usual transmission method has been the handwritten prescription. The handwritten method proved to be problematic and is used much less frequently today because of the illegible handwriting of many health-care providers that caused many prescription medication errors.

In 2004, the first electronic-prescribing tools appeared in clinics and were offered first by insurance carriers. These tools were stand-alone devices, similar to a large cellular phone, into which the insurance carriers input their **drug formulary,** hoping to coax the health-care provider to prescribe only their approved medications. The health-care provider then created a database of clients on the device, making refills relatively simple. Electronic prescriptions were printed or sent electronically to the pharmacy.

E-prescribing has improved health care and reduced costs by increasing compliance with formularies and the use of generic medications. E-prescribing tools are now readily available and embedded in electronic medical records (EMRs) software. Since the passage of the American Recovery and Reinvestment Act of 2009, most health-care providers have adopted EMRs with assistance from the federal government's Medicare and Medicaid programs that provided incentive payments to health-care providers to encourage e-prescribing.

UNDERSTANDING NARCOTIC AND NON/NARCOTIC PRESCRIPTIONS

Medications fall into one of two categories—narcotics and nonnarcotics. Note that the terms *nonopioid* and *opioid* are increasingly being used. Prescriptions for nonnarcotics are identified first.

NONNARCOTIC PRESCRIPTIONS

A nonnarcotic prescription can be transmitted to a pharmacy by any of the manners mentioned previously. Valid prescriptions can be filled any time within a 6-month period. The health-care provider may order up to a year's worth of refills for such medications as birth control and some chronic conditions. However, in order to ensure that the client is evaluated on a regular basis, the health-care provider usually prescribes only five refills, requiring the client to be reevaluated before additional refills are given. Insurance carriers, who partially or totally pay for their subscriber's medications, usually limit the quantity dispensed to 1 month's worth at a time. The only exception is when the client mails a prescription to an insurance carrier's approved pharmacy, at which time they will allow a quantity of up to 3 months' worth to be sent to the client.

The health-care provider is responsible for ensuring that the prescription conforms to all requirements of both federal and state laws and regulations. A nonnarcotic prescription issued by a health-care provider may be communicated to the pharmacist by health-care employees.

Drug Sample Closets

There are health-care providers across the country that choose to maintain drug samples of the most commonly prescribed nonnarcotic medications for the convenience of their clients. Most of these sample drugs are provided by pharmaceutical companies to promote new medications. A health-care provider may choose to have samples available for several reasons, among which is having medications on hand so that when starting a client on a new medication, the client can try samples before purchasing a whole prescription. This cost savings for clients is beneficial, especially if there is uncertainty about the medication's success for a client. Medication samples also help clients who do not have health insurance or cannot afford their medications.

Under the direction of the health-care provider, MAs may be responsible for many of the requirements related to record-keeping, inventory, and security of the drug samples. All distribution of samples must be logged on an inventory sheet with the following information:

- Date and time of dispensing
- Client's name and date of birth
- Name of medication
- Dosage
- Lot number
- Expiration date
- Prescriber (health-care provider)

And, as always, documentation in the client's record is *vital*.

Drug sample records must be kept for 2 years and are subject to **Drug Enforcement Administration (DEA)** inspection. An inventory of drug samples should be done every 8 to 12 weeks to ensure that any outdated medications are removed. Any added medications must also be logged. Security is necessary for all medications; therefore, sample drugs must be kept in a locked closet or cabinet that is substantially constructed.

There are health-care providers who oppose keeping drug samples within the medical office or clinic. These health-care providers believe that they are being encouraged to prescribe new, more expensive brand-name medications supplied by pharmaceutical company representatives. These health-care providers strive to help keep health-care costs down by prescribing generic drugs as often as possible.

Another method to acquire needed medications for a client is for the health-care provider or the MA to contact the pharmaceutical company directly. Many pharmaceutical companies have what is known as an *indigent program*. Working with the health-care provider, the client provides income verification so that the pharmaceutical company can determine his or her needs and if he or she qualifies for the medication free of charge. If the client is eligible, the drugs are mailed to and dispensed by the health-care provider.

NARCOTICS

Drug Enforcement Administration Registration

Federal law requires that a health-care provider has a separate registration to *prescribe* narcotic drugs. Registration is made with the DEA, a subdivision of the Department of Justice. An application or renewal can be completed by paper or online (providing a credit card for the application fee) at the DEA website, www.deadiversion.usdoj.gov. The current registration fee (for initial and renewal applications) is $731. On receipt of the application or renewal form and payment of the fee, a DEA registration number is assigned to each legitimate health-care provider, and registration is renewed every 3 years. Updating a health-care provider profile (e.g., address change), if needed, can also be accomplished through the website.

Health-care providers must know the narcotic-related laws of their state. The health-care provider is required to follow the strictest regulations, whether federal or state. The renewal date of a health-care provider's DEA certificate should be part of a tickler file for the office clinic manager to ensure timely renewal and proper compliance.

 ## CONTROLLED SUBSTANCES ACT

The Comprehensive Drug Abuse Prevention and Control Act of 1970, more commonly known as the **Controlled Substances Act,** is administered by the DEA. Narcotics are controlled because of their potential for abuse and dependence. The DEA has divided potentially abusive drugs into different categories or schedules. See Figure 4-1 for definitions and examples of each schedule.

DRUG SCHEDULES

The Controlled Substances Act lists controlled drugs in five schedules (I, II, III, IV, and V). This act and the *U.S. Code of Federal Regulations* are important to all health-care providers but are especially pertinent to anyone who will **administer a drug**, **prescribe a drug**, or **dispense a drug** that is listed in one of the five schedules. The majority of practitioners only *prescribe* controlled substances. A few may *administer* or *dispense* controlled substances. A listing of drugs in each of the five categories is available on the U.S. Department of Justice Drug Enforcement Administration Diversion Control Division website.

Electronic prescribing of narcotics is legal in all 50 states with strict regulations mandated by the DEA. In some states electronic prescribing will not be in place until 2021 or 2022. Prescriptions for a controlled substance must include the following information:

- Patient's full name, date of birth, and address
- The practitioner's full name, address, and DEA registration number
- Drug name
- Drug strength
- Dosage form (liquid, pill, or capsule)
- Directions for use
- Quantity prescribed
- Number of refills (if any) authorized
- Date and signature when issued

Although the guidelines are voluntary, most states have implemented regulations that limit narcotic prescriptions to a supply ranging from 3 days to 14 days. The current opioid epidemic has resulted in additional regulations to improve the way narcotics are prescribed, enhance client access to safer more effective chronic pain treatment, and reduce the risk of substance use disorder, overdose, and death.

Any health-care provider who practices medicine or opens a medical office or clinic must be familiar with controlled substance laws. The *U.S. Code of Federal Regulations* can be obtained either through the Internet or from the nearest federal government bookstore and must be studied carefully before controlled substances are managed in the health-care setting.

The majority of health-care providers do not keep narcotics or any controlled substances in their clinics. The threat of theft and mandatory record-keeping are the driving forces for this decision. However, health-care providers who perform in-clinic surgical procedures may have narcotics in the clinic and must implement strict protocols to minimize liability associated with keeping narcotics on site. Health-care providers *dispensing* controlled substances also must comply with their state's Prescription Drug Monitoring Program (PDMP). This is an electronic database collecting information

SCHEDULE	DEFINITIONS	EXAMPLES
The Federal Controlled Substances Act Primer for Providers* **Drug Schedules**		
SCHEDULE I	No accepted medical use with a lack of accepted safety and high misuse potential; may not be prescribed, dispensed, or administered	Heroin, peyote, ecstasy, lysergic acid diethylamide (LSD), marijuana
SCHEDULE II	High misuse potential with severe psychological or physical dependence; have acceptable medical use; may be prescribed, dispensed, or administered	Morphine, codeine, Vicodin, hydromorphone, methadone, oxycodone, fentanyl, amphetamine, pentobarbital
SCHEDULE III	Misuse potential less than Schedules I and II but more than Schedule IV medications; misuse may lead to moderate or low physical dependence or high psychological dependence	Products with < 90 mg of codeine per dosage unit (Tylenol with codeine), dronabinol, anabolic steroids, ketamine
SCHEDULE IV	Misuse potential less than Schedules III but more than Schedule V medications	Propoxyphene, various benzodiazepines, sibutramine
SCHEDULE V	Medications with least potential for misuse among controlled substances	Robitussin AC, Phenergan with codeine, pregabalin

For a prescription of a controlled substance to be valid, it must include: Issue Date; Name and Address of Client; Name, address, and DEA Registration Number of Practitioner; Drug Name; Strength of Drug, Dosage and Quantity Prescribed; Directions for Use; Any Refills; Signature of Prescriber.

Schedule II drugs may not be refilled and can be phoned into a pharmacy only in the case of an emergency, in which case the prescriber must provide a written order within 7 days. Schedule III and IV drugs may be refilled up to 5 times within a 6-month period. Schedule V drugs may be refilled as authorized by the prescriber.

Electronic Prescribing became effective in June, 2010 and still must include all the items identified in the first paragraph above.

Figure 4-1. Controlled substances schedules for providers. *(Summarized and adapted by Carol D. Tamparo from Michael Gabay, PharmD, JD, BCPS, November 20, 2019.)*

on dispensing controlled substances. Loss of any narcotic is to be reported to the regional DEA office and local law enforcement.

 ## SUBSTANCE MISUSE

Substance misuse is found in every sector of society. No group is exempt. It is commonplace in all professions, schools, and industries. The most commonly misused substances are drugs and alcohol. The Controlled Substances Act is driven, in part, by the fear of drug misuse.

DRUG MISUSE

Health-care providers must be particularly mindful of persons who misuse drugs and are seeking controlled substances for their personal use or for resale on the street. Pharmacists must also be mindful of fake prescription requests on the telephone and forged written prescriptions in their stores. Health professionals themselves are particularly vulnerable to drug and alcohol misuse due to the availability of opioids in the workplace. Health-care providers and their employees have a public duty to be alert to all forms of substance misuse and to do everything possible to prevent its increase, even when the misuse is by a coworker.

A common problem in the health-care setting is a person who misuses drugs and secures the same prescription drug from more than one health-care provider and pharmacy in a geographic area. Often these individuals go from door to door at medical clinics with a convincing tale of woe or a set of symptoms they hope warrants a prescription for narcotics. A person who misuses narcotics may be a well-established, well-liked client who for medical reasons has developed a need for excessive drugs. The client may be seeing a specialist for the same complaint and receive several prescriptions. Quite often, the client also makes excuses for missing prescriptions, such as "they fell in the sink," "I left them in my hotel room on vacation," or "someone stole my purse." Health-care providers and staff who are alert will start to notice patterns among clients that point to drug addiction.

Another problem occurs when a health-care provider becomes known as a "script doctor," one who freely and excessively prescribes potentially dangerous drugs. People who misuse drugs quickly learn who these health-care providers are and become their regular clients.

The misuse of prescription medications is common among young adults. Teens may steal their parents' medications, take them to school, and sell them for more potent and illicit drugs, or take the medications themselves. Young adults have learned that street drugs may be laced with very dangerous and poisonous substances and are very costly, and they often consider stolen prescription medications as free and safe.

The market for prescription drugs on the street is a lucrative one. The street price of prescription drugs varies according to the drug and the location. When compared, the current street value of commonly misused drugs is significantly higher than the legal price without insurance from a pharmacy. Examples include the following:

- Oxycodone (street name: *Kicker*), costs $1.26 per tablet and sells for approximately $5.00 on the street.
- Fentanyl (street names: *Apace, China white, Dance fever*), costs $9.40 per 25 mcg/hr patch and sells for approximately $40.00 on the street.
- Ritalin (street name: *Vitamin R*), costs less than 50 cents per pill and sells for approximately $10 on the street.

Case Law

In August 2019, a judge in Oklahoma ruled that Johnson & Johnson intentionally minimized the dangers and oversold the benefits of opioids in order to increase the sale of their prescription painkillers. Judge Balkman was harsh in his assessment of the company and wrote in his ruling that Johnson & Johnson used "false, misleading, and dangerous marketing campaigns" that "caused exponentially increasing rates of addiction, overdose deaths and neonatal abstinence syndrome" (babies born exposed to opioids). The state of Oklahoma sought judgment to pay for addiction treatment, drug courts, and other services necessary to care for citizens who have been affected by the opioid epidemic. Johnson & Johnson was ordered to pay the state $572 million.

Oklahoma's trial was the first opioid lawsuit against a drug manufacturer for damages caused by prescription painkillers. There are more than 2,000 additional opioid lawsuits pending across the country against dozens of opioid makers, distributors, and retailers. Opioid-related battles will continue in courtrooms as well as health-care clinics to provide necessary services to those who need them.

Oklahoma v. Johnson & Johnson, August 26, 2019.

ALCOHOL MISUSE

Another substance that is greatly misused is alcohol. Much of the information related to drug misuse is the same for alcohol misuse. It knows no socioeconomic boundaries and afflicts individuals of all ages and genders. One major difference between drug misuse and alcohol misuse is that alcohol is more readily available to most anyone at any time. The World Health Organization estimates 237 million men and 46 million women throughout the world suffer from alcohol-related disorders. According to the Centers for Disease Control and Prevention's Behavioral Risk Factor Surveillance System survey, "in 2018 more than half of the US adult population drank alcohol in the past 30 days. About 16% of the adult population reported binge drinking (consuming 4 or more drinks for a woman and 5 or more drinks for a man in about 2 hours) and 7% reported heavy drinking (consuming weekly at least 8 drinks for women and 15 drinks for men)."

Alcohol misuse can cause multiple problems at any age, but youths are more at risk because the alcohol can interrupt the progression of their normal development. Problems seen in teens misusing alcohol include the following:

- Disruption of normal growth and sexual development
- Memory problems
- Changes in brain development that may have life-long effects
- Social and school problems

PREVENTION OF SUBSTANCE MISUSE

Clinic policies can aid greatly in the control of narcotics misuse. The following stipulations should be part of every clinic's policy and procedure manual:

- When checking in for the first time, a client may be asked to produce picture identification to verify the correct name and match the name to the face.
- The health-care provider will authorize no controlled substance prescriptions without first seeing the client.
- The health-care provider needs to see the client on a regular basis before any refills will be authorized.
- A picture ID is needed to pick up a narcotic prescription.

Health-care providers and clinic staff who are still using handwritten prescriptions must keep prescription pads in a secure place. They should be carried in the health-care provider's pocket and should not be kept in the examination room, on counters, or in drawers, where clients have access to them while waiting for the health-care provider. Electronic prescriptions have helped to minimize risks of stolen prescription pads.

Whether the drug of choice is alcohol, prescription medications, or illicit street drugs, the approach is the same. Substance misuse of any kind is injurious to the health and well-being of clients. Health-care providers and health professionals must establish firm and clear procedures to curb the increase of substance misuse. Health-care professionals who have the most success with such clients are those who honestly discuss the misuse issues and possible treatment plans without judgment or condemnation.

A frank, honest discussion must be conducted with all clients, especially young adults, which encourages saying "no" to alcohol and drugs; however, health-care professionals must be careful to keep an open dialog so that their clients are comfortable in admitting any substance misuse problems. In the case of young adults, this kind of discussion is best held when parents or guardians are not present.

All health-care professionals should take a comprehensive substance misuse history from their clients. This history taking is often administered as a self-assessment questionnaire. Clients may present with a current substance misuse condition in addition to another disease or illness, so both must be addressed. It is imperative for health-care professionals to be knowledgeable of signs and symptoms of substance misuse and report them to the health-care provider.

If health-care professionals misuse substances, their ability to function safely will be impaired, and the problem needs to be addressed in a quick and efficient manner to avoid errors. Such misuse and impairment are cause for loss of the health-care professional's license.

Author's Note: Health-care providers have been acutely aware of the increase of alcohol and drug misuse during the Covid-19 pandemic. Sales of hard liquor were up 33% in 2020, and mental health providers reported an increased demand for services related to misuse of all substances during the pandemic.

Case Law

A Florida physician, David W. Webb, MD, was sentenced to life imprisonment for distribution of and conspiracy to distribute controlled substances resulting in death. He was convicted of 36 counts of health-care fraud, 90 counts of illegal distribution of controlled substances, 2 counts of conspiracy to commit those offenses, and 2 counts of identity theft. He was also found responsible for the deaths of three of his clients who overdosed on drugs that he had prescribed. Dr. Webb had been prescribing controlled narcotics, sedatives, and stimulants in quantities and dosages that caused clients to abuse, misuse, and become addicted to these drugs.

Even after his clients suffered overdoses, he continued to prescribe the same prescriptions to them. During the trial, the evidence showed that the defendant failed to monitor his clients' use of drugs and failed to document the clients' files with sufficient medical justification for prescribing the drugs. In the cases of more than 100 of the clients to whom the defendant prescribed controlled substances, agents were able to find no evidence that the defendant kept any file. Dr. Webb was found to be prescribing controlled substances over the Internet to individuals he had never seen. Once Dr. Webb's DEA certificate had been suspended, he continued to prescribe controlled drugs under another physician's number.

U.S. Department of Justice, Northern District of Florida v David W. Webb, Pensacola, Florida, January 28, 2010.

HEALTH INSURANCE PORTABILITY AND ACCOUNTABILITY ACT

Another federal regulation, the **Health Insurance Portability and Accountability Act (HIPAA)**, was passed by Congress in 1996 and became effective in April 2003. HIPAA requires (1) standardization of electronic client health data, administrative data, and financial data; (2) unique health identifiers for individuals, employees, health plans, and health-care providers; and (3) security standards to protect the confidentiality and integrity of the individually identifiable health information, past, present, or future (Privacy Rule).

HIPAA established for the first time a set of national standards for the protection of health information. According to the U.S. Department of Health and Human Services, the major goal of the **Privacy Rule** is to "assure that individuals' health information is properly protected while allowing the flow of health information needed to provide and promote high quality health care and to protect the public's health and well-being." The Privacy Rule protects "all individually identifiable health information," which is called **protected health information (PHI)**.

Under HIPAA, clients must grant written consent or permission to provide or disclose their PHI for any reason. Health-care providers must provide clients with a notice of their privacy practices, which include the following:

1. Right to restrict use of PHI
2. Right to request confidential communication
3. Right to inspect and obtain a copy of the PHI
4. Right to request any amendment to the PHI
5. Right to receive an accounting of PHI disclosures

Clients acknowledge these rights and sign a form stating they have received the privacy statement.

Because HIPAA is a federal regulation, failing to comply with privacy and security standards equates to breaking the law. Criminal penalties for noncompliance with HIPAA standards include fines that range from $100 to $50,000 per person for all identified violations in a calendar year. Depending on the circumstances of the breach of confidentiality, fines can reach up to $1.5 million and imprisonment of 1 year can be levied against offenders.

IN THE NEWS

Congress passed the CARES Act on March 27, 2020, to ensure every American access to health care needed during the Covid-19 pandemic and to address the economic fallout resulting from the pandemic. Individuals with a substance use disorder (SUD) will have access to treatment during the pandemic and their confidentiality protected. This provision is an important part of the federal response to the opioid epidemic while maintaining confidentiality protections. The CARES Act required a change made in a portion of the HIPAA regulations, namely 42 CFR Part 2.

CONFIDENTIALITY

One of the main purposes of HIPAA is to ensure and protect a client's privacy related to health-care issues. Unless otherwise required by law, health-care providers must keep confidential any communication necessary to treatment of the client.

The client's privacy must be protected. Health-care providers and their employees must be extremely careful that all information gained through the care of the client is kept confidential and given only to those health professionals who have a medical need to know. Care should also be taken that any information communicated about a client cannot be overheard by others (Fig. 4-2). Confidentiality also applies to any form of media that might be involved in the client's care.

In many cases, HIPAA regulations have meant that clinics reconsidered how clients are greeted, how basic personal information is viewed, how billing is discussed, and how clients are addressed in the reception area and any other areas when personal information may be seen or heard. For example, a clinic with a very open reception area created a cubicle at one side of the reception area for the exchange of private information. Another clinic chose to enclose the reception area in glass. Even this glass enclosure does not guarantee privacy. The receptionist needs to keep his or her voice lowered to maintain confidentiality. No telephone calls are made to remind clients of appointments

Figure 4-2. An example of a breach of confidentiality.

or to discuss bills or laboratory results where any other party can hear. It is imperative that clients' charts and any personal information be out of view of others.

Another area of concern within the physical setup of the clinic is the use and placement of computers. Placement should be where only the employee can view the computer screen. Additionally, the computer should have a screen protector that fits over the monitor so that any information is distorted to anyone except the employee who is looking straight at the monitor. Health-care professionals should be directed to log off any time they leave the computer. The confidentiality of the client is of utmost concern, and all physical areas and policies should be constantly monitored to ensure that privacy.

Case Study

In your podiatrist's office, there is a sign-in sheet at the reception desk requesting your name, phone number, insurance number, and Social Security number.

What do you do?

VIGNETTE

Can't I Tell My Friend?

To continue with the dilemma of Kelly's pregnancy in the vignette, "Who Has a Right To Know?" consider the following information.

Several days later in the MA's clinical class, another MA instructor overhears Nancy, a student who is receiving work experience in the campus health center, breach a confidence and tell other students in the class about Kelly's pregnancy and abortion.

The program's coordinator privately speaks with Nancy about the breach of confidentiality. Nancy responds, "I didn't tell the whole class. I only told my friend."

Is this situation HIPAA compliant? How would you respond if you were the coordinator?

HEALTH CARE AND EDUCATION RECONCILIATION ACT OF 2010

The Health Care and Education Reconciliation Act of 2010, comprehensive health-care reform law, was enacted in March 2010. This Act is also commonly known as the Affordable Care Act (ACA) or "Obamacare." Primary goals of this law are to make affordable health insurance available to more people, expand the Medicaid program to cover all adults with income below 138% of the federal poverty level, and support innovative medical care delivery methods designed to lower the costs of health care. Although the bill has endured many political and legal challenges, its passage is considered one of the most historic domestic policy achievements since the creation of Medicare in 1965.

The Health Care and Education Reconciliation Act was implemented in stages and has grown over the past 10 years. As of April 2020, thirty-eight states participated in the federal health-care exchange and over 11.4 million Americans had health insurance from these state programs. Meeting the health-care needs of all inhabitants within a country is challenging. The United States and its state governments continue to evaluate and revise health-care services to accommodate for the dynamic health environment of the country. Recent revisions to health-care services include the expansion of Medicare telehealth services, legal ruling to allow appeals for hospital-mandated status changes that increase out-of-pocket costs, and adjustment of enrollment periods to provide additional opportunities for health insurance.

SUMMARY

Health-care providers must be aware of all state and federal rules and regulations to practice medicine. Among those regulations are licenses to practice and DEA certificates of registration. Another federal regulation is HIPAA, which helps to protect the confidentiality of the client. Health-care reform will continually be updated and changed depending on the political climate. Health-care professionals have a responsibility, as public servants, to both prevent substance misuse and treat those who misuse either drugs or alcohol. Any health-care professional must also understand that there are numerous changes taking place not only with treatments and research but also with the organization and the methods of delivery of health care that may affect both federal and state regulations.

 Watch It Now! When do you find time for CEUs? at http://FADavis.com, keyword *Tamparo.*

Questions for Review

SELECT THE BEST ANSWER

1. When a drug is introduced into a client's body, it is known as
   a. Dispensing a drug.
   b. Prescribing a drug.
   c. Administering a drug.
   d. All of the above.
   e. None of the above.

2. The controlled substances act divides narcotics into how many schedules?
   a. Two (2)
   b. Three (3)
   c. Four (4)
   d. Five (5)
   e. Six (6)

3. The Affordable Care Act and the Patient Bill of Rights provide which of the following benefits for clients?
   a. No rescinding of insurance coverage
   b. Limit on the amount of co-pay
   c. No preexisting condition exclusions for all clients
   d. Protects the client's choice of doctors
   e. Only a and d above

4. A health-care provider's license may be revoked for which of the following reasons?
   a. Conviction of a crime
   b. Professional incapacity
   c. Personal incapacity
   d. All of the above
   e. Only a and b above

5. The acronym DEA stands for
   a. Department of Environmental Agency.
   b. Department of Drug Agency.
   c. Drug Enforcement Administration.
   d. Drug Education Agency.
   e. Drug Enforcement Agency.

SHORT ANSWER

1. What is the purpose of the DEA and its regulations?

   _____

   _____

   _____

2. Using the Internet, identify the controlled substances drug schedules and give an example of a substance for each schedule.

   _____

   _____

   _____

3. Describe actions to be taken to safely keep sample drugs in a clinic.

   _____

   _____

   _____

4. What is your role as a health-care professional in preventing and treating substance misuse?

   _____

   _____

   _____

5. What privacy rights must be shared in writing with all clients as part of the clinic's Notice of Privacy?

   _____

   _____

   _____

CLASSROOM EXERCISES

1. Ben LaPaglia, your health-care provider's client, who is a practicing attorney, is being weighed on the scale in the hallway. He looks up and sees the daily client's schedule posted by the health-care provider's office door. He says to you, "Is that where you always post the schedule?" Discuss.

2. What might constitute license revocation?

3. In the vignette "Who Has a Right to Know?" could the program coordinator do anything more than speak with Nancy about her breach of confidentiality? Discuss.

4. Identify medical specialty clinics that might dispense as well as prescribe controlled substances and discuss their uses.

INTERNET ACTIVITIES

1. Assume that you are the clinic manager for a family practice. You are responsible for keeping track of your health-care provider's license renewal and CMEs. Go to your particular state's board of registration in medicine. Research the requirements for health-care provider license renewal and the regulations regarding CMEs and what activities constitute CMEs.

2. Research the *U.S. Code of Federal Regulations*. Who and what do they regulate? What topics do they cover when it comes to drugs and medications?

3. Research the Health Care and Education Reconciliation Act of 2010 to see what changes have been made to the Act since its passage. What reforms have been put into place already?

4. Research the pros and cons of keeping a "drug sample closet" in a health-care provider's clinic. Decide where you would stand on this topic. Debate a fellow classmate who holds a different opinion than yours.

5. Explore your state's Board of Registration in Medicine. What helpful information can you find there that would aid you in your career as a medical assistant? Describe.

For more resources, visit
http://FADavis.com, keyword *Tamparo*.

CHAPTER 5

Professional Liability

"Character is much easier kept than recovered."

—Thomas Paine (1737–1809); controversial revolutionary propagandist

KEY TERMS

agent Person (the health-care employee) appointed by a principal party (the physician or provider) to perform authorized acts in the name of and under the control and direction of the principal.

alternative dispute resolution (ADR) Methods outside the judicial system used to solve potential malpractice actions; methods include arbitration, mediation, and negotiation.

assault A threat to inflict injury with an apparent ability to do so.

battery The unlawful touching, beating, or laying hold of persons or their clothing without consent.

breach of contract Failure to comply with the terms of a valid contract.

civil liability Identifies conflicts between individuals, corporations, government bodies, and other organizations.

compliance plan Guidelines established to protect a clinic or health-care facility from fraud and litigation charges.

contract A voluntary agreement between parties.

criminal liability When an individual commits an act that is considered to be an offense against society as a whole and can be held legally responsible.

defamation Spoken or written words concerning someone that tend to injure that person's reputation and for which damages can be recovered. Two types of defamation are *libel* and *slander:*

libel False, defamatory writing, such as published material, effigies, or pictures.

slander False, malicious, or defamatory spoken words.

fiduciary Holding in confidence or trust.

malfeasance Commission of an unlawful act.

medical malpractice Professional negligence of physicians or providers.

misfeasance Improper performance of an act resulting in injury to another.

negligence (medical) Doing a certain act that a reasonable and prudent provider would not do or failing to do a certain act that a reasonable and prudent provider would do.

nonfeasance Failure to perform an act when there is a duty to do so.

res ipsa loquitur A Latin phrase meaning "the thing speaks for itself"; a doctrine of negligence law.

respondeat superior A Latin phrase meaning "let the master answer"; that is, the provider is responsible for employee acts.

tort Wrongful act committed by one person against another person or against property; distinguished from a breach of contract.

vicarious liability Legal doctrine assigns liability for injury to a person or institution who did not cause the injury but who has a particular legal relationship to the person who did act negligently.

LEARNING OUTCOMES

Upon successful completion of this chapter, you should be able to:

5.1   Define key terms.
5.2   List three elements necessary for a contract to be valid.
5.3   Describe how a contract may be breached.
5.4   Discuss the meaning of standard of care.
5.5   Explain professional liability for providers and their employees.
5.6   Identify the four Ds of medical negligence.
5.7   Compare and contrast intentional and unintentional torts.
5.8   Restate, in your own words, the importance of professional liability insurance.
5.9   Name three alternative methods to litigation.
5.10   Recall 10 guidelines for risk management.

COMPETENCIES

CAAHEP

- Describe liability, professional, and personal injury insurance. (CAAHEP X.C.8.a.b.c)
- Compare and contrast physician or provider and medical assistant roles in terms of the standard of care. (CAAHEP X.C.2)
- Differentiate between scope of practice and standards of care for medical assistants. (CAAHEP X.C.1)
- Explain how the following impact the medical assistant's practice and give examples:
  - Negligence (CAAHEP X.C.7.a)
  - Malpractice (CAAHEP X.C.7.b)
- Describe the process to follow in compliance reporting errors in patient care. (CAAHEP X.C.11.b)

ABHES

- Follow established policies when initiating or terminating medical treatment. (ABHES 4.c)
- Distinguish between employer and personal liability coverage. (ABHES 4.d)
- Perform risk management procedures. (ABHES 4.e)

VIGNETTE

Is There Professional Responsibility?

Nicole, an Arkansas resident, calls the office of the obstetrician who delivered her first child 2 years ago. She reports to the receptionist that she is having minor cramping and discomfort and believes she also may be pregnant due to a missed period. The receptionist tells Nicole "not to worry at this stage." She also informs Nicole that her obstetrician is not taking new patients. Later that night Nicole is admitted to the hospital as a result of shock due to blood loss from a ruptured ectopic pregnancy. As a result of the rupture and complications, Nicole required a hysterectomy.

 Once physicians and certain providers become licensed, they become legally liable for their actions as physicians and providers. They are responsible, accountable, obligated, and legally bound by law; this is known as *professional liability.* ●

 ### PROFESSIONAL LIABILITY

Professional liability can be criminal or civil, or both, but criminal liability is less common in health care than civil liability. **Criminal liability** results when an individual commits an act that is considered to be an offense against society as a whole. The legal term **malfeasance** reflects this liability. Malfeasance is the commission or performance of an unlawful act.

Examples of criminal liability for providers and their employees include fraud in insurance billing, client abuse, the evasion or breach of the Controlled Substances Act, or aiding in the death of a client in a state that does not allow physician-assisted death. Physicians or providers found to be grossly negligent or reckless in the injury or death of a client also may be held criminally responsible. Any health-care professional who breaks the law or aids a provider in a criminal act becomes liable for a criminal act as well.

Civil liability identifies conflicts between individuals, corporations, government bodies, and other organizations. Most of the time, examples of civil liability for health professionals include a breach of contract or commission of a tort. A **contract** is a voluntary agreement between parties. A **tort** is a wrongful act or injury committed by one person against another person that is not dependent on a contract. **Misfeasance** is another term that is used in tort law to describe an act that is legal but performed improperly. Contract law and tort law related to medical care are identified here.

CONTRACTS

Health-care professionals are liable for professional negligence issues that often arise related to contract principles. A contract or a provider–client relationship is normally a prerequisite for any professional negligence on the part of the provider before any litigation can occur. This is known as *contract law*. Health-care employees and their providers are parties to contracts on a daily basis. When a provider accepts a client, a contract has been made. When the provider's assistant calls an office supply company to reorder office stationery, the assistant acts as the provider's **agent** in making a contract.

For a contract to be valid, it must be (1) an agreement between two or more competent people, (2) an agreement to do or not to do a certain task for payment or for the rendering of a benefit, and (3) a lawful agreement. An example of a contract in health care occurs when a client calls the clinic to make an appointment for an annual physical examination. Assuming that the provider is legally able and capable to practice medicine and the client is a competent adult, the first two parts of the contract exist and are valid. The performance of a physical examination is a lawful act, so part three of the contract exists and is valid. The client is given a statement of the charges, and the fee is paid. Hence, the contract is valid in all respects.

A contract can be expressed or implied. An *expressed contract* can be written or oral, but all facets of the contract must still be specifically stated and understood (Fig. 5-1). An *oral contract* is as legally binding as a written one; however, it may be more difficult to prove. Providers' telephone contacts with clients are examples of oral contracts, especially when medical advice is given. A *written contract* requires that all necessary aspects of the agreement be in writing and signed by each party. Each state, in its statute of frauds, identifies those contracts that must be in writing. Usually included in this list are deeds and mortgages. Most states' statutes of frauds include a section that is pertinent to health care, that is, an agreement made by a third party to pay for the medical expenses of another. Such an agreement must be in writing to be valid. For example, if Joel tells the medical receptionist that he will pay the medical expenses for his partner, Dwayne, the receptionist should have Joel fill out a form to that effect and affix his signature to it. If not properly executed, it may be impossible to collect payment for the bill.

Implied contracts are the most common form of contracts occurring in health care. Such contracts occur every time the provider and client discuss what course of treatment to take and an agreement is reached. An implied agreement does not require a specific expression of the parties involved but is still valid if all points of the contract exist. An implied contract may be implied from the facts or circumstances of the situation or by the law. For example, when a client complains of a serious sore throat and fever and the provider does a throat culture to diagnose and treat the ailment, a contract is implied by the circumstances of the situation. Another example of an implied contract would be a provider who administers epinephrine after a client goes into anaphylactic shock. In this example, the law will say that the provider did what the client would have requested had there been an expressed agreement.

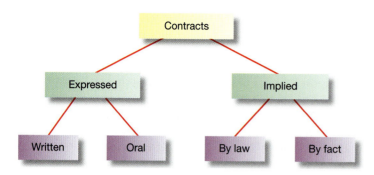

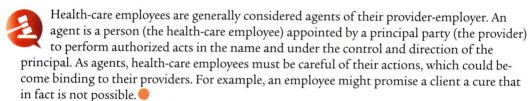

Figure 5-1. Contracts, either expressed or implied, can be legally binding.

Other contractual agreements determine obligations for providers. Providers who practice in institutions, such as hospitals or long-term care facilities, must provide health care to whomever comes into the facility within the limits of their employment contracts with the institution. Similarly, providers who are a part of a health maintenance organization (HMO) have a duty to treat plan members as a result of their written contractual obligation to the HMO.

Contracts made by the mentally incompetent, the legally insane, those under heavy influence of drugs or alcohol, infants, and some minors are not valid. Such persons are not considered by law to be competent to enter into binding contracts.

Health-care employees are generally considered agents of their provider-employer. An agent is a person (the health-care employee) appointed by a principal party (the provider) to perform authorized acts in the name and under the control and direction of the principal. As agents, health-care employees must be careful of their actions, which could become binding to their providers. For example, an employee might promise a client a cure that in fact is not possible. ●

BREACH OF CONTRACT

A **breach of contract** arises when one of the parties involved fails to meet the contractual components. For example, the contract may be violated when the client does not pay the bill or refuses to follow medical advice. The contract can be breached when the provider fails to use the treatment promised, promises to perform a procedure and then allows someone else to do the procedure, or promises a cure and no cure results. Such breaches of contract are cause for litigation in which the court will attempt to reward reimbursement to the offended party. Usually this reimbursement is in the form of a monetary reward to offset any incurred losses.

ABANDONMENT

Providers' **fiduciary** or trusted obligation, posed by their professional ethics, causes the law to look outside the parameters of contract law when determining providers' obligation to treat a client. Health-care professionals are constrained in their ability to withdraw from contractual relationships by judicial case law, which has set rules against abandonment.

Once the provider–client relationship has been established, providers can be found liable if they abandon their clients. Abandonment seems like a harsh term, but in this context, it refers to the provider's action or desire to no longer serve a client. To avoid charges of abandonment, it is recommended that a provider withdraw formally from a case or formally discharge a client. This withdrawal or discharge requires giving reasonable notice to the client with the recommendation for the client to seek further medical care. The written notice should be sent so that the client has ample time to secure another provider.

A point to remember is that some managed care contracts limit a provider's ability to terminate a provider–client relationship. A provider should carefully read the contract to determine whether termination is possible and how to give notice to the managed care plan. If a provider leaves a managed care plan for some reason, even though the managed care plan will give notice to its clients, it is a good idea for the provider to send his or her own written communication (i.e., letter) advising clients what arrangements have been made for the continuation of their care.

Additionally, a provider may wish to withdraw from a case if a client fails to follow instructions, take the prescribed medications, disclose information pertinent to the care, or return for recommended appointments. Almost any nondiscriminatory reason is valid as long as proper written notice is given. To withdraw formally from a case, a provider should notify the client in writing, state the reasons for the dismissal, and indicate a future date when the provider is no longer responsible. Such a letter should be sent by certified mail with restricted delivery only to the person specified and a return receipt requested providing that individual's signature. Figure 5-2 shows an example of a letter of withdrawal. A copy of the letter and the returned receipt are kept in the client's record. To further protect a provider from abandonment charges, any canceled or missed appointments should be noted in the client's record.

Clients, too, may wish to terminate the contractual relationship with a provider at any time and for any reason. Most of the time clients simply stop making appointments rather than officially withdrawing from the provider's care. It is important, however, for the provider to acknowledge in writing even this kind of termination, when known, if the client still needs medical care. Knowledge of such a termination may happen when clients request that their records be sent to another provider. The clinic staff should never respond to such a request without their provider-employer's knowledge and instructions.

STANDARD OF CARE

One cannot fully understand professional liability without some knowledge of "standard of care" principles. Acceptable *standard* of care requires that providers use the ordinary and reasonable skill that would be commonly used by other reputable practitioners when caring for individuals. They are expected to perform those acts that a reasonable and prudent provider would perform in a similar situation. Failure to perform an act when there is a duty to do so is known as **nonfeasance**. Standard of care also dictates that providers must not perform any acts that a reasonable and prudent provider would not perform in a similar situation. Providers should always practice in the realm of safety and obtain all necessary data on which to base a sound judgment. This practice includes obtaining a thorough medical history, a complete physical examination, necessary laboratory tests, and procedures. Providers are expected to know what new therapeutic developments might benefit those in their care and still not subject them to undue risk.

Employees in health care also must adhere to a standard of care. The standard a health-care employee will be measured against depends on the task the employee is undertaking; the education, training, credentialing, and experience of the employee; and the responsibility the provider has given to the employee. For example, if an MA makes a diagnosis or treats a client, the MA can be held to the same standard of care as the provider. Any time MAs act outside their level of competency (i.e., diagnosing and treating) and the client is injured as a result, the MAs are negligent. An MA will be expected to use the same standard skill and reasonable judgment that would be commonly used by other reputable MAs in the same area when assisting with clients. Health-care employees often act in a variety of roles, and they must understand the standard to which they can be held. If, on the other hand, the health-care employee is mopping the floor, the reasonable standard is that of a custodial person rather than the standard of a specific health-care professional.

Unfortunately, errors can be made. By the very nature of today's health-care environment, where clients with multiple illnesses are being cared for, providers are seeing more clients for shorter periods of time and may be processing as many as 900 laboratory results in any given week; serious but preventable errors can be made. A study made by Coverys, a nationally recognized medical professional liability insurer, reports that diagnostic errors are implicated in about 33% of malpractice claims, followed by errors in treatment at 20%.

RECOMMENDED TERMINATION LETTER

Letter of Withdrawal to a Client

Dear_____:

You may recall from your most recent visit that we discussed the possibility that it may be better for you to seek medical attention from a different provider.

After further consideration of that discussion, I find it necessary to withdraw my professional services as your primary care provider. This action is necessary because you have not followed the instructions in my personal treatment plan for you. Please place yourself in the care of another provider as soon as possible, but no later than 14 days from the time you receive this letter.

Upon receipt of a written request from your chosen provider, your case history with my diagnostic and treatment recommendations will be promptly supplied. Since your condition requires medical attention, please do not delay in finding another provider among the many competent providers in this area.

I regret the need to take this action, but believe it is best for your continuing medical care. Thank you for your cooperation in making this change as quickly as possible.

Sincerely yours,

Provider's Name and Credentials

SEND BY CERTIFIED MAIL WITH RESTRICTED DELIVERY AND RETURN RECEIPT

Figure 5-2. Recommended withdrawal letter.

Errors made by MAs require immediate reporting to the provider or supervisor, admitting the error, making corrections when possible, and helping to plan procedures to prevent a recurrence.

IN THE NEWS

A July 10, 2018, article in *Medscape* notes that the clinic's support staff is the "first line of defense against malpractice risk." Support staff can either introduce or prevent errors by their actions. They also can frustrate and anger clients when there is an uncomfortable experience. Support staff may expose the practice to litigation with medication errors, transcribing mistakes, entering incorrect information into the electronic health record (EHR), or exceeding their scope of practice.

Providers are advised to periodically discuss protocols with staff, to be open to suggestions from staff, and to recognize when additional support is necessary. For example, helping receptionists understand that they are the "face of the practice" who are to be viewed as the person providing *access* rather than a *barrier* to the provider is a place to begin.

PROFESSIONAL NEGLIGENCE OR MALPRACTICE

Failure to perform professional duties according to the accepted standard of care is called negligence. More specifically, **negligence** occurs when a reasonable and prudent provider performs an act that he or she would not perform or fails to perform an act that he or she would perform according to acceptable guidelines in the standard of care. Professional negligence has the same meaning as malpractice, and malpractice may be referred to as professional negligence.

Professional negligence is more easily prevented than defended. Obviously, providers and their employees do not wish to be found negligent or become involved in a malpractice suit of any kind. However, consumers are quite aware of their rights in today's society. Therefore, all health professionals must protect the provider–client relationship at all times and be above reproach in the performance of their duties.

THE FOUR Ds OF MEDICAL NEGLIGENCE

To more clearly understand professional negligence, the four Ds of medical negligence are often used as guidelines. The four Ds are duty, derelict, direct cause, and damages:

1. *Duty* exists when the provider–client relationship has been established. For example, the client calls the office to make an appointment, keeps the appointment, and makes another to return for further treatment.
2. *Derelict* is more difficult to define. The client must prove that the provider failed to comply with the standards required and dictated by the profession.
3. *Direct cause* implies that any damage or injuries that resulted from the provider's breach of duty were directly related to that breach and that no intermittent circumstances or intervening acts could have caused the damages.
4. *Damages* refer to the compensation provided for injuries suffered by the client. The most common in medical professional liability cases is monetary compensation, which may be actual, or compensatory damages and exemplary or punitive damages. *Actual damages* are those that compensate the client for injuries sustained and nothing more. These include past medical care, loss of wages, and future medical care. *Exemplary* or *punitive* damages are compensation that punishes the defendant and awards the client for pain, suffering, and mental anguish. Punitive damages may be limited by law in some states.

TORTS

Tort law is an area of law that health-care professionals are most likely to be involved in because the law identifies negligence and **medical malpractice**. Health-care employees or providers may commit a tort that can result in litigation.

A tort is a wrongful act committed by one person against another person or property that causes harm to that person or property. A tort results if there is damage or injury to the client directly or indirectly caused by the conduct of the provider or the health-care employee that does not meet the standard of care governing either the provider or the health-care employee (see the Four Ds of Medical Negligence). If a provider commits a wrongful act against a client with no resultant client harm, a tort has not been committed.

The two main classifications of torts are *intentional* and *unintentional/negligent* acts. Intentional torts or wrongs involve the intentional commission or a violation of another person's rights. Unintentional or negligent wrongs may be the result of the omission or the commission of an act. Malpractice is an unintentional tort (Fig. 5-3). It is a specific type of negligence that occurs when the standard of care commonly expected from a health-care professional is not met. It is also known as *professional negligence*.

INTENTIONAL TORTS

Intentional torts are intentional acts that violate another person's rights or property. The ethical obligation to "do no harm" to a client *(nonfeasance)* is the basis for any intentional tort action. If the principle of nonfeasance was never violated and there was no harm to the client, there could be no grounds for litigation based on intentional tort.

Some of the more common intentional torts that may occur in a health-care setting are assault and battery, defamation, and invasion of privacy. *Assault* and *battery* are terms often used together; however, assault rarely occurs in the medical setting. **Assault** refers to a threat to inflict injury with an apparent ability to do so. **Battery**, in the medical context, occurs when a client receives treatment without having given consent to do so; it is the unlawful touching, beating, or laying hold of persons or their clothing without consent. Some intentional torts such as assault and battery may also violate criminal laws and can become complaints in both criminal court and civil court. In this situation, separate trials will be held, one criminal and one civil. In a civil case the plaintiff must show, by a preponderance of evidence, that a tort has been committed, whereas in a criminal case the prosecution must prove its case beyond a reasonable doubt.

When battery occurs, an individual's right has been invaded. Individuals have the right to be free from invasion of their persons. Regardless of whether the procedure constituting the battery improves the client's health, the client must consent to the treatment.

Case Law

"Jane Doe," a San Francisco woman in her 30s, went to the Union City Kaiser on June 25, 2017, to see a provider. While in the examining room a medical assistant, Efrain Castanon, entered the room. Instead of doing preliminary intake for the doctor, Castanon grabbed the woman, put his arm around her throat and pushed her up against the examination table. He said, "I have something for you," and forced her to touch his bare penis. Fearing rape and his arm around her throat, she did not call out and soon he left the room. When the doctor arrived, police were called. The doctor told police that Kaiser had earlier complaints about this medical assistant.

Castanon was later arrested and charged with four felonies including assault with intent to commit a sex crime, sexual battery by restraint, false imprisonment by violence, and dissuading a witness from reporting a crime.

On April 20, 2018, Castanon was sentenced to 3 years in prison. A civil lawsuit against Kaiser, Kaiser Foundation Hospitals, and Kaiser Foundation Health Plan is not yet settled. Kaiser reports that Castanon is no longer an employee.

Defamation is spoken or written words that tend to injure a person's reputation and for which damages can be recovered. One type of defamation is **libel**, which is false, malicious, defamatory writing, such as published material, effigies, and pictures. Another type of defamation is **slander**, which is the false and malicious defamatory spoken word. For defamation to be a tort, a third person must hear or see the slander or libel and understand it.

Invasion of privacy is the unauthorized publicity of client information. Medical records and treatments cannot be released without the client's knowledge and permission. Clients have the right to be left alone and the right to be free from unwanted publicity and exposure to public view (i.e., Health Insurance Portability and Accountability Act [HIPAA]).

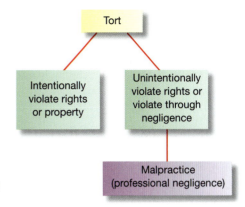

Figure 5-3. Torts are violations, either intentional or unintentional.

UNINTENTIONAL TORTS OR MALPRACTICE

An example of an unintentional tort occurs in the medical profession when a provider prescribes a pain medication over the phone for a client with a migraine-like headache, not recalling that this client is recovering from hepatitis. Because the pain medication is contraindicated in hepatitis, the client becomes violently ill and suffers liver damage. Although the provider did not intentionally prescribe an inappropriate medication, negligence did cause injury to the client for which the provider is liable.

Unintentional torts are the basis for the majority of civil lawsuits against health-care professionals. When the standard of care is not very carefully adhered to, errors can be made, and the client suffers the consequences.

Torts are best prevented by practicing legally and ethically. The standard of care in the health-care setting needs to be excellent. The privacy of clients must be guarded, their bodies and possessions are to be respected, and their reputations are to be protected. The rights of clients must be protected by all who come in contact with them. All health professionals must perform only within their scope of training, education, and credentialing, and recognize the standard of care required for each action taken.

DOCTRINE OF *RES IPSA LOQUITUR*

Another rule of the law of negligence is the doctrine of *res ipsa loquitur*, "the thing speaks for itself." It relates chiefly to cases of foreign bodies being left in clients, instruments slipping during surgical procedures, burns from heating modalities, and injury to a portion of the client's body outside the field of treatment. In other words, the negligence is obvious; the result was such that it could not have occurred without someone being negligent.

Case Law

Mrs. Farley had a tubal ligation. She was informed of the risks and signed consent forms before surgery. Five months later she returned to the same provider, who determined that she was pregnant. After the birth of Mrs. Farley's baby, the attending provider examined both of her fallopian tubes and found that one was ligated, but the other appeared normal. Mrs. Farley sued the provider who performed the tubal ligation on the basis of *res ipsa loquitur*.

Outcome: The court held that Mrs. Farley could not rely on the doctrine of *res ipsa loquitur* to establish the medical malpractice claim against the provider. The court held that "the doctrine of *res ipsa loquitur* cannot be invoked where the existence of negligence is wholly a matter of conjecture and the circumstances are not proved, but must themselves be presumed, or when it may be inferred that there was no negligence on the part of the defendant." The doctrine only holds in cases in which the defendant's negligence is the only inference that can reasonably and legitimately be drawn from the circumstances. This was not the case here. The court stated that this was probably one of those cases in which the sterilization procedure failed; the ligation was performed, but the ligation band came off soon thereafter.

Farley v Meadows, 404 SE2D 537 (1991)

DOCTRINE OF RESPONDEAT SUPERIOR

As stated earlier, professional liability exists for both employer and employee. Physicians and providers are responsible not only for their own actions of negligence but also for the negligent actions of their employees under the doctrine of **respondeat superior**. This Latin phrase means "let the master answer." For example, consider an MA who administers an allergy shot, dismisses the client, and hastens on to the next task without keeping the client under observation for 20 minutes. The client collapses in the parking lot a few minutes later as a result of anaphylactic shock from the injection. The provider-employer is responsible for the negligence of the MA; however, the MA is also liable for not following the proper standard of care.

The doctrine of *respondeat superior* may extend to a hospital or HMO that employs providers and their assistants, thus making the institution liable for negligent acts of their employees or agents when they are performing within the scope of their employment, even if the organization was not at fault in any way. The legal term used in this situation is **vicarious liability**. You learned in Chapter 2, Medical Practice Management, that increasing numbers of providers are becoming employees of hospitals and HMOs; therefore, it becomes important for many reasons to be able to identify the legal relationship between the organization and the provider.

Case Study

A woman in her 80s, recovering from hip surgery, returns to her surgeon's clinic for a checkup. The MA is cautious to make certain the woman's walker is carefully placed over the scale. With chart and pen in hand, the MA stands to the right of the client on the scale. While the MA is recording the weight, the woman steps back and falls backward off the scale. Her hip is reinjured, and there are other injuries as well. The instant the MA turned to enter data in the chart, the fall occurred. The client and her family are suing both the surgeon and the MA.

The provider-employer is responsible for ensuring that all employees perform only those tasks within the scope of their knowledge and training. However, the employer's responsibility does not diminish employees' responsibility to perform any acts within the scope of their knowledge and training. In this case study, both the provider and the employee can be found liable when injury occurs to the client as a result of the employee's actions.

The provider's employee also has a responsibility to question an order if there is good reason, and a prudent employee in such a position would do so. If the order is not questioned and negligence occurs as a result, both the provider and the employee may be liable. For example, an MA tells the provider that the client he saw two days ago for a cold now is coughing up yellow sputum. The provider orders penicillin to be added to the treatment regimen. Before calling the pharmacy, the MA notices that the patient is allergic to penicillin and so questions the provider.

Professional liability is a concern of all health professionals, but providers are most concerned because they are in a position of higher authority and responsibility.

PROFESSIONAL LIABILITY/MALPRACTICE INSURANCE

The need for providers to carry professional liability insurance is obvious for numerous reasons. The most important, perhaps, is financial protection. Some states mandate the minimum amount of professional liability insurance that a provider must carry.

Providers need liability insurance protection whether they are employees or employers. For example, employment in a corporation, an HMO, or a hospital does not guarantee professional liability coverage. Many employers or institutions carry professional liability insurance merely on themselves or the institution, not on their employees. Some hospitals require a minimum amount of professional liability insurance before hospital privileges are granted. In some cases, clients sue both the employer and the employee.

One of the reasons employers will carry professional liability insurance is the doctrine of *respondeat superior*. Providers may not be directly negligent, but they are liable for the acts of their employees, even while the employees are liable for their own actions.

Employees will want to remember that the only way in which they can be covered under an employer's liability insurance policy is by being specifically named in that policy—something that is very rare. Employees are advised to carry their own professional liability insurance. For example, MAs who are members of the American Association of Medical Assistants may purchase professional and personal liability insurance through the organization.

Many providers carry professional liability insurance because they are often asked for medical advice or assistance from friends or neighbors in a "casual setting." For example, at an outdoor barbecue, a neighbor asks the provider, "My back is killing me. What can I do?" In the case of strangers when medical care may be emergent and the provider is the only one available to provide the care, an employer's or institution's policy probably will not extend coverage in this situation. The Good Samaritan Law, which may be applied in such an emergency, is discussed in Chapter 7, Public Duties.

COST OF PROFESSIONAL LIABILITY INSURANCE

The kind and amount of liability coverage to carry vary according to the type of practice, the community economic level, the level of risk of the specialty, and the claims-consciousness of the clients. Most professional liability policies, however, should address (1) what the insurer will pay, (2) effective policy dates, (3) the power of the insurer in obtaining legal counsel, (4) the power of the insurer in seeking settlement, (5) what costs are covered, and (6) how payment is to be made. The professional liability insurance policy will specify monetary limits for each claim and is issued in increments of $1 million. For example, a policy may have professional medical liability of $1 million for each claim and $3 million aggregate as a total amount.

Some providers are limiting their practice and their professional liability insurance coverage because of the high cost of premiums. This can be seen when a family practitioner chooses not to perform surgeries or deliver babies, thus reducing the cost of professional liability insurance.

States have been diligent in writing legislation that would limit or control the monetary amounts awarded to plaintiffs (i.e., clients) in malpractice claims, but have not been fully successful. Even in states that have been successful in tort reform legislation, the cost of professional liability insurance has decreased only a little. Therefore, insurance costs will vary by state and by specialty. Insurance premiums for an internist, for example, may range from $10,000 a year in states with a "low-end" rate to as much as $56,000 per year in states with a "high-end" insurance rate. An obstetrics/gynecology specialist may pay as much as $50,000 per year in a state with low-end insurance premiums and as much as $215,000 in a state with high-end insurance rates. Why is there a difference? Providers say the high cost of malpractice insurance is not about lawsuits, but rather is about insurance companies making up for investment losses. Insurance companies generally decline to reveal how premiums are established but insist that skyrocketing rates are related to the increasing costs of health care and clients' litigious nature to sue.

ALTERNATIVES TO LITIGATION

Some providers and institutions have tried solving the malpractice dilemma with **alternative dispute resolution (ADR)** methods, such as arbitration, mediation, and negotiation. These methods eliminate the use of the court system. The client voluntarily agrees, sometimes in advance, with the provider or institution to permit a neutral person or persons to arbitrate the dispute. The parties involved generally select the impartial third party, who is an expert in the area of controversy. In most instances, the decision of the arbitrator is binding, and there is limited judicial review of the process. In mediation, there is no third party; rather, the mediator is selected by both parties and attempts to facilitate negotiation between them.

A number of states have statutes addressing the use of arbitration and mediation. Some states have established ADR centers, often with the state bar association, for such alternatives to litigation. Generally, the cost of arbitration, mediation, and negotiation is less than a court-litigated solution and saves time for both parties. Such arbitration, mediation, and negotiation cases also may remain more private.

RISK MANAGEMENT AND COMPLIANCE PLANS

Generally, if a healthy provider–client relationship exists, litigation is less likely to occur. Also, the clinic that has taken the time to develop a **compliance plan** is further protected because steps have been taken to ensure that precautions are in place.

The Office of the Inspector General (OIG) suggests that a medical practice's focus on quality client care is enhanced with the adoption of a voluntary compliance program. Compliance plans are an aid to avoid litigation, to help prevent problems from arising in the delivery of health care, and to remind employees of the importance of every aspect of the practice. A fully effective compliance plan has seven basic components as identified by the OIG:

- Establishes written policies, procedures, and standards for major areas of the clinic/practice
- Names a compliance officer (often the clinic manager or supervisor) to monitor and enforce the compliance plan
- Educates all employees so that the compliance plan is well understood
- Develops open lines of communication so that employees feel comfortable reporting any unsafe activities or potentially fraudulent areas and to continually update employees on the status of the plan
- Audits and monitors all aspects of the plan on a regular basis
- Enforces disciplinary standards through well-publicized guidelines
- Corrects action for detected offenses appropriately and promptly

There is not just one compliance plan for a medical practice; there are several. High-risk areas that will benefit from a compliance plan include confidentiality, documentation, coding and billing, and employee and client safety. When a compliance plan is in place and appropriately followed, areas of concern can be noted and corrected before they become major problems. Fraud cases are determined on "intentional fraud." A clinic with a plan in place can show that compliance is strived for, helping to refute any fraud charges.

RISK MANAGEMENT WITHIN THE AMBULATORY HEALTH-CARE SETTING

All employees can help to manage risks. This can be accomplished in their work habits and in their dealings with clients.

Risk Management with Good Work Habits

1. Perform within the scope of training, education, and credentialing.
2. Comply with all state and federal regulations and statutes, including HIPAA.
3. Keep the clinic safe and equipment in readiness.
4. Diligently practice standard precautions.
5. Log telephone calls. Return all calls to clients within a reasonable time.

6. Have all diagnostic test results viewed and initialed by the provider before filing.
7. Select employees carefully, and encourage a team approach.
8. Keep all matters related to client care confidential.
9. Follow up on missed or canceled appointments and incomplete documents.
10. Continue to grow professionally.
11. Formally document (a) withdrawing from a case and/or (b) discharging clients.
12. Keep accurate and meticulous records.
13. Limit practice to scope of training and to a manageable number of clients.
14. Document when clients are called with test results.
15. Document all canceled appointments and no-shows.
16. Always retain original records or radiographs.
17. Pay meticulous attention to coding and billing.
18. Have provider review accounts before sending any to a collection agency.
19. Consider turning the reception area into an education area.
20. Continue to build on your knowledge base in all areas of the practice.
21. Maintain professional certification, registration, and/or licensure.
22. Document, document, document.

Risk Management with Clients

1. Practice uninterrupted listening during the critical first 60 seconds of any conversation with a client.
2. Provide an opportunity for clients to ask questions.
3. Provide time- and action-specific instructions at the close of client contact and indicate the expected time for follow-up or recovery.
4. Put verbal instructions in writing, and give a copy to the client.
5. Do not criticize other practitioners.
6. Explain any appointment delays. Do not keep clients waiting more than 20 minutes. Offer another appointment if feasible.
7. Discuss fees before treatment.
8. Treat all persons equally.
9. Never guarantee a cure.
10. Secure informed consent.
11. Listen to clients, and always tell your provider-employer when a complaint occurs.
12. Call clients at home the day after outpatient surgery to check on their progress. Document the follow-up in the client's chart.
13. Tell clients how to get care on nights and weekends.
14. Regularly survey clients for satisfaction and follow suggestions for improvement.

In addition to the risk management guidelines discussed previously, the Bayer Institute for Health Care recommends the four Es of client interaction to help health professionals prevent malpractice. They are (1) engage, (2) empathize, (3) educate, and (4) enlist clients in management of their health care. These suggestions can further help in risk management.

Case Study

As clinic manager, you want to find ways to improve your clients' satisfaction in your large clinic. You know of a company that "infiltrates" your clinic and actually "pretends" to be some of your clients. The company's "clients" call to make appointments, come in to see your providers, use your laboratories, and use other ancillary services. A report is made to the employers. It becomes an ongoing practice to help you identify areas for improvement. You use the report to educate your staff.

If you are a staff person, what do you think of this practice?
Should the results regarding a particular individual be used in the employee evaluations?

SUMMARY

Once physicians and certain providers become licensed, they become professionally liable for themselves and their employees. Well-established compliance plans and employees who are conscientious with regard to risk management will aid the provider in managing the clinic's risks. If litigation becomes a reality, however, it is advisable to seek professional legal advice promptly.

 Watch It Now! How do you manage unpleasant situations? At http://FADavis.com, keyword *Tamparo*.

Questions for Review

SELECT THE BEST ANSWER

1. Professional negligence
   a. Is more easily prevented than defended.
   b. May be referred to as malpractice.
   c. Can be the result of either a provider or an employee error.
   d. All of the above.
   e. Only a and b above.

2. *Res ipsa loquitur* means
   a. Let the master answer.
   b. Let the buyer beware.
   c. The thing speaks for itself.
   d. Defamation has occurred.
   e. A name has been slandered.

3. A contract may be
   a. Expressed or implied.
   b. Written or oral.
   c. Invalid if the agreement is unlawful.
   d. All of the above.
   e. Only b and c above.

4. Tort
   a. Is a French dessert.
   b. Identifies negligence and medical malpractice.
   c. Is a lawful act committed by one person against another.
   d. Is a wrongful act against another with no resultant harm.
   e. Is an action not covered in professional liability insurance.

5. Alternatives to litigation may include
   a. Alternative dispute resolution.
   b. Arbitration, mediation, and negotiation.
   c. An impartial third party.
   d. A heavy fee for the service.
   e. Only a, b, and c above.

SHORT ANSWER

1. What might be done to prevent some providers from limiting their practice due to the high cost of professional liability insurance?

_____

_____

_____

2. Compare/contrast defamation, libel, and slander.

_____

_____

_____

3. Briefly describe the four Ds of negligence.

_____

_____

_____

4. How can risk management and compliance plans reduce litigation?

_____

_____

_____

5. Name two classifications of torts and give an example of each.

_____

_____

_____

CLASSROOM EXERCISES

1. It has been reported that because providers fear litigation, they often order testing on clients that is not actually necessary just to be certain that "no stone is left unturned." Discuss the implications of this practice for the provider, the client, and health care in general.

2. List and describe medical practices that are deemed "higher risk" and are apt to require larger fees for malpractice insurance. Justify your choices.

3. Describe the standard of care for the MA in the health-care setting.

4. Identify steps to be taken if you make an error while attending to a client's needs.

5. If you do all the coding for insurance in the clinic in which you are employed, but you are not a professional coder, is it possible you could be held to the same standard as a professional coder? Explain your answer.

6. In the vignette at the beginning of the chapter, identify the errors that were made by the obstetrician's office. What action might have prevented this scenario? Do you think Nicole might have basis for a lawsuit? Justify your response.

INTERNET ACTIVITIES

1. Search the Internet for recent legal cases in your area's district court related to medical malpractice. Describe your findings.

2. Research tort reform in your state. Describe your findings.

REFERENCES

Furrow, B. R., Greaney, T. L., Johnson, S. H., Jost, T. S., Schwartz, R. L., Clark, B., Fuse Brown, E. C., Gatter, R., King, J. S., & Pendo, E.: *Health Law: Cases, Materials and Problems, Abridged Eighth Edition*. St. Paul, MN: Thomson West, 2018.

Harris, D. M.: *Contemporary Issues in Healthcare Law and Ethics, 4th Edition*. Chicago: Health Administration Press, 2014.

For additional resources please visit
http://FADavis.com, keyword *Tamparo*.

CHAPTER 6

Law for Health Professionals

"The virtue of a man ought to be measured, not by his extraordinary exertions, but by his everyday conduct."—Pascal (1623–1662); French mathematician, physicist, inventor, and writer

KEY TERMS

appellant One who appeals a court decision to a higher court.

arraignment The court procedure of formally listing criminal charges against defendants, which they are expected to answer.

civil case Court action between private parties, corporations, government bodies, or other organizations. Compensation is usually monetary. Recovery of private rights is sought.

closing arguments Summary and last statements made by opposing attorneys at a hearing or trial.

Congress The law-making body of the federal government. It is made up of two separate groups, the House of Representatives and the Senate.

court of appeals Court that reviews decisions made by a lower court; may reverse, remand, modify, or affirm lower court decision.

court order An order issued by a judge to appear or to request certain records. The release of any records requested in a court order does not require the client's permission or violate HIPAA.

criminal case Court action brought by the state against individuals or groups of people accused of committing a crime; punishment is usually imprisonment and/or a fine; includes recovery of rights of society.

cross-examination Examination of a witness by an opposing attorney at a hearing or trial.

defendant The person or group accused in a court action.

deliberation The process whereby a jury considers the evidence presented in a case.

deposition A written record of oral testimony made before a public officer and/or both attorneys. It is for use in either a criminal or a civil case and is completed outside of court before the trial begins.

direct examination Examination of a witness by the attorney calling the witness at a hearing or trial.

examination of witness Questioning of a witness by attorneys during a court action.

expert witness (medical) Person trained in medicine, usually a specialty, who can testify in a court of law as to what the professional standard of care is in the same or similar circumstances.

felony A serious crime, such as murder, larceny, assault, or rape. The punishment is usually severe.

higher (superior) court The court to which appeals of trial court decisions can be made; a court with broader judicial authority than a lower or inferior court.

judge A public official who directs court proceedings, instructs the jury on the law governing the case, and pronounces sentence.

jurisdiction The limits or territory within which authority may be exercised.

jury Six to twelve individuals, usually randomly selected, who are administered an oath and serve in court proceedings to reach a fair verdict on the basis of the evidence presented.

law Rule or regulation that is obligatory to observe.

litigation A lawsuit; a contest in court.

lower (inferior) court Usually, the court in which a case is first presented to the trial court; a court with limited judicial authority.

misdemeanor Type of crime less serious than a felony; examples include property theft or damage.

opening statements Statements made by opposing attorneys at the beginning of a court action to outline what they hope to establish in the trial.

plaintiff The person or group initiating the action in litigation.

probate (estate) court State court that manages wills and settles estates.

sentencing Imposition of punishment in a criminal proceeding.

small claims court Special court intended to simplify and expedite the handling of small claims or debts. Individuals represent themselves; attorneys are not required in small claims court.

subpoena An order to appear in court under penalty for failure to do so.

subpoena duces tecum A court order requiring a witness to appear and bring certain records or tangible items to a trial or deposition.

summons An order, in a civil case, from the court directing the sheriff or other appropriate official to notify the defendant where and when to appear to answer charges against him or her.

verdict Findings or decision of a jury.

LEARNING OUTCOMES

Upon successful completion of this chapter, you should be able to:

6.1   Define key terms.

6.2   Explain in a brief paragraph why knowledge of the law is necessary for health professionals.

6.3   Describe the source of law.

6.4   List the three branches of government in the United States.

6.5   Give an example of each of the following terms: (a) constitutional law, (b) common law, (c) statutory law, (d) administrative law, (e) plaintiff, (f) defendant, (g) felony, and (h) misdemeanor.

6.6   List two similarities and two dissimilarities between criminal and civil law.

6.7   Review, in diagram form, the process for (a) a civil case, (b) a misdemeanor case, and (c) a felony case.

6.8   Diagram the federal court system and state court system.

6.9   List two factors that determine in which court a case is heard.

6.10   Discuss the use of probate and small claims courts.

6.11   List two similarities and two dissimilarities among a subpoena, a *subpoena duces tecum,* and a court order.

6.12   Explain, in your own words, the trial process.

6.13   Name two circumstances that might require the services of an expert witness.

COMPETENCIES

CAAHEP
- Compare criminal and civil law as it applies to the practicing medical assistant. (CAAHEP X.C.6)
- Explain how the following impacts the medical assistant's practice and give examples:
  - Statute of limitations (CAAHEP X.C.7.c)

ABHES
- Comply with federal, state, and local health laws and regulations. (ABHES IV.D.1)

Can She Be an Expert Witness?

As a medical assistant educator with several years of experience in the administrative area and a recognized authority on medical records, you have been asked to testify as an expert witness regarding protocol for making corrections in a medical record. You agree.

When you are interviewed by the attorney and given the records to review, you recognize that the person responsible for the data entered in the record is a former student and a practicing certified medical assistant. It appears obvious that the records have been altered after the fact.

The U.S. legal system is complex and multifaceted. It can confuse even the most astute citizen. Basically, there is one federal legal system that governs the entire United States in federal matters and 50 different and unique state legal systems, all created by federal and state constitutions. The District of Columbia (Washington, DC) is governed by Congress but allows local officials to govern in many instances. Most legal actions pertinent to health care occur within the state and local systems.

SOURCES OF LAW

Law encompasses rules derived from several sources. The Constitution of the United States provides the highest judicial authority. Adopted in 1787, it provides the framework for our government. The Constitution, federal law, and treaties take precedence over the constitutional law of the states. The Constitution of the United States is a legal document that defines the structure and function of federal, state, and local government. There are 27 amendments to the Constitution of the United States.

The federal government has three branches: (1) the legislative branch is the lawmaking body, called the **Congress**; (2) the executive branch is the administrator of the law and includes the president; and (3) the judicial branch is the judges and courts, including the Supreme Court. Each branch provides a system of checks and balances for the other two. For example, the power of lawmaking belongs to Congress, but the president can veto its legislation, and the judiciary is empowered to review legislation. Congress, in turn, can investigate the president and control the appellate jurisdiction of the federal courts. No one branch has absolute authority. In addition to the federal government, each state has a constitution defining its own specific governing bodies. All powers not conferred specifically on the federal government are retained by the state, yet states vary widely in their assumption of that power.

TYPES OF LAW

The two basic types of law are common law and statutory law. *Common law* was developed by judges in England and France over many centuries. It emerged from customs, the ways things were done over time in England and in France. Common law was brought to the United States with the early settlers. Common law, views decided by judges, is always evolving as established principles are tested and adapted in new case situations. Many of the legal doctrines applied by the courts in the United States are products of common law. Common law is a body of law based on judicial decisions that attempts to apply general principles to specific situations that arise. It has the force of statutory law, although common law is not enacted by the legislature. Common law is also called *judge-made law* or *case law*. Case law from past legal decisions is used in legal proceedings to solidify the positions of parties in a case. When a situation presents itself during a legal proceeding, case law will be used to emphasize a position. Case law is extremely helpful for vague or uncommon situations. Legal proceedings are closely watched if the outcome could result in the development of new case law.

Congressional and state legislative bodies enact rules (laws) known as legislative or *statutory law*. These laws make up the bulk of our laws as they exist today. Publications containing these statutes are known as *codes*. An example of a statute pertaining to health care is a medical practice act, which defines and outlines the practice of medicine in a given state. (See Chapter 4, State and Federal Regulations.) A federal law will be uniformly applied throughout the country. A state law applies only in that given state.

FEDERAL AND STATE LEGAL CONFLICT

If there is a conflict between a federal and state law, the Constitution mandates that the federal law governs. This mandate comes into question for states that have legalized the use of marijuana for medical or recreational purposes. Under the Controlled Substances Act (CSA), marijuana is listed as a Schedule I controlled substance. Individual states may have legalized the use of marijuana while it remains illegal under federal law. Federal agencies have been reluctant to lodge criminal charges, however. In *Coats v. Dish Network* (2015), the Supreme Court upheld that a Nevada employer might fire an employee for testing positive for marijuana even though its use is legal in the state. Businesses that touch the marijuana industry also violate the CSA. They may include banking, housing, security, and cleaning service firms. In 2014, Congress approved a budget amendment, the Rohrabach-Farr amendment, which prohibits the Department of Justice for using funds that would prevent states from implementing their state marijuana laws. This amendment must be renewed each year. President Donald Trump signed a bill on December 20, 2018, that descheduled hemp from a Schedule I to a Schedule II drug. This made cannabis containing under 0.3% THC legal.

 Health-care workers must take heed of *Coats v. Dish Network* (2015). Individuals who work in health care, even in states that have legalized the use of medical and/or recreational marijuana, cannot test positive for marijuana and expect to remain employed. Spas that use THC products in massages have clients sign waivers because even though the chance is small, the client may test positive for marijuana. ●

ADMINISTRATIVE LAW

Legislative bodies, however, do not have the time or knowledge to enact all laws necessary for the smooth functioning of the government. Thus administrative agencies are given the power to enact regulations that also have the force of law. This type of law is called *administrative law*. The Internal Revenue Service and Federal Trade Commission are examples of administrative agencies. Both implement extensive rules in their areas of concern.

Administrative law, an extension of statutory law, affects the health-care employee. The state health department, the state board of medical examiners, and the state board of nurse examiners are administrative agencies that dictate rules and regulations for health care. Further, licensing and accrediting bodies, as well as such federal government programs as Medicare and Medicaid, directly influence many policies, procedures, and functions of health care and fall under the category of administrative law. The Drug Enforcement Agency, an administrative agency of the Department of Justice, enforces the Controlled Substances Act.

CIVIL AND CRIMINAL LAW

Law may also be classified as civil, criminal, international, and military. International and military law are not considered here. This book concentrates on civil and criminal law because of their importance in the health-care setting. Figure 6-1 provides a brief overview of the trial process.

The Trial Process

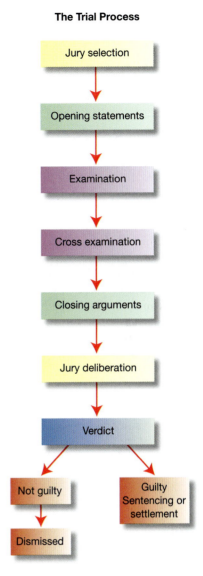

Figure 6-1. A general example of the trial process.

CIVIL LAW

Civil law affects relations between individuals, corporations, government bodies, and other organizations. Restitution for a civil wrong is usually monetary in nature. The bulk of law dealt with in health care is civil in nature.

In a **civil case**, the party bringing the action (**plaintiff**) must prove the case by presenting evidence that is more convincing to the **judge** or **jury** than the opposing evidence, a preponderance of evidence. The procedure for a civil case is shown in Figure 6-2. The plaintiff's complaint is filed in the proper court, usually by an attorney for the plaintiff. The **defendant** is formally summoned, prepares an answer, and files it in the court. If the defendant fails to answer the **summons** within the prescribed time, the plaintiff will win the case by default, and judgment will be entered against the defendant.

The case may be disposed of without a trial. For example, the complaint may be dismissed because of a technical error, the summons may have been improperly served, or the complaint may not have set forth a claim recognized by law. The parties also may decide to settle out of court. In some medical cases, a defendant will offer a plaintiff a small, or nuisance, settlement. The malpractice legal firm

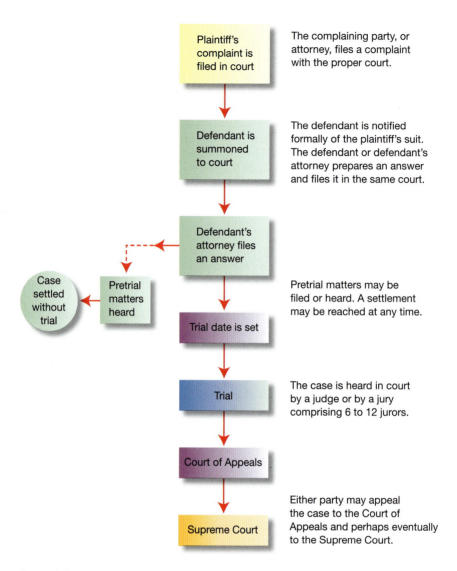

The complaining party, or attorney, files a complaint with the proper court.

The defendant is notified formally of the plaintiff's suit. The defendant or defendant's attorney prepares an answer and files it in the same court.

Pretrial matters may be filed or heard. A settlement may be reached at any time.

The case is heard in court by a judge or by a jury comprising 6 to 12 jurors.

Either party may appeal the case to the Court of Appeals and perhaps eventually to the Supreme Court.

Figure 6-2. Chart explaining the procedure for a civil trial. Each state has a similar process. Compare with your state's civil trial process.

along with the insurance company and defendant may determine that it would cost more to defend the case than to offer a small settlement in the range of $5,000 to $10,000. The defendant does not admit guilt or causation in these instances.

Case Study

Consider, for example, a "slip and fall" case. Fran enters her provider's office and slips and falls as she approaches the reception desk. She suffers a simple fracture of the left femur. When the receptionist comes to her aid, they discover that a snag from the rug caught the heel of Fran's shoe. Fran later takes civil action and sues her provider for medical fees and loss of employment wages for the time she was unable to work as a result of her injuries. As the plaintiff, she must prove that her provider (the defendant) was negligent.

How might this case be settled in a civil suit?

CRIMINAL LAW

Criminal law pertains to crimes and punishment of persons violating the law. Criminal law affects relations between individuals and government. Criminal wrongs are acts against the welfare and safety of the public or society as a whole. Criminal acts usually result in a punishment of imprisonment and/or a fine.

A **criminal case** is brought by the state against individuals or groups of people accused of committing a crime. The prosecuting, district, or state attorney brings the charge against the accused person (defendant) on behalf of the state (plaintiff). The prosecution must prove that the defendant is guilty beyond a reasonable doubt. In other words, the prosecution must be able to prove to the satisfaction of the court that a criminal act was committed by the accused beyond reasonable doubt. Criminal case outcomes may include dismissal, not guilty, plea agreement, and guilty.

A crime is a **felony** or **misdemeanor** that is statutorily defined. Felonies are more serious crimes and include murder, larceny (thefts of large amounts of money), assault, and rape. Misdemeanors are considered lesser offenses. These include disorderly conduct, thefts of small amounts of property, and breaking into an automobile. Certain traffic violations can be misdemeanors or felonies depending on the severity of the infraction.

In a misdemeanor case (Fig. 6-3), the prosecuting attorney is made aware of violations of the law either by traffic or police citations, by police arrest, or by citizen information. When the prosecutor determines that enough evidence is present, the court arraigns the person on the prosecutor's charge. The charged person may plead guilty and consequently face **sentencing**. The guilty person may be put on probation, may serve a jail term and/or pay a fine, or may go through the appeal or appellate process. If the charged person pleads not guilty, a trial date is set. At the end of the trial, a **verdict** is given of either guilty or not guilty. If the person is found not guilty, the charge is dismissed. If found guilty, the person faces a jail term, probation, and/or must pay a fine. The guilty person (**appellant**) may also use the appeal process.

The felony case process is shown in Figure 6-4. When evidence exists that a crime may have been committed, the police begin their investigation. The information is either filed by the prosecuting attorney or given to a grand jury, depending on the practice of the particular jurisdiction and severity of the charge. If the evidence is sufficient, the individual is charged. Pretrial proceedings, to plan the manner in which cases will proceed, are generally informal in nature, and many cases are settled at this point.

If the accused pleads guilty, he or she is sentenced to imprisonment, probation, and/or a fine. The appellate process then may be available. If the person pleads not guilty, the trial is set, the facts of the case are determined, the principles of law relating to those facts are applied, and a conclusion as to guilt or innocence is reached. If the verdict and judgment are guilty, the individual goes through the same sentencing process as in the guilty plea. If the verdict is not guilty, the person is acquitted, and the charges are dismissed.

Case Study

To illustrate both civil and criminal law, consider the following situation. Drunk driver Shawn is involved in an automobile crash that causes the death of a stay-at-home mother of two children. Law enforcement officials charge Shawn with involuntary manslaughter and reckless driving while speeding and intoxicated. The courts later find Shawn guilty. This is criminal law protecting society. Taking this situation a step further, the husband then sues Shawn for the wrongful death of his wife. There is not a one-size-fits-all monetary amount for every wrongful death lawsuit. Placing a monetary amount on the worth of a person's life is very difficult. Attorneys will need to consult with economics and financial professionals to assist with placing a value on the decedent's life. Many things are considered in the determination of a

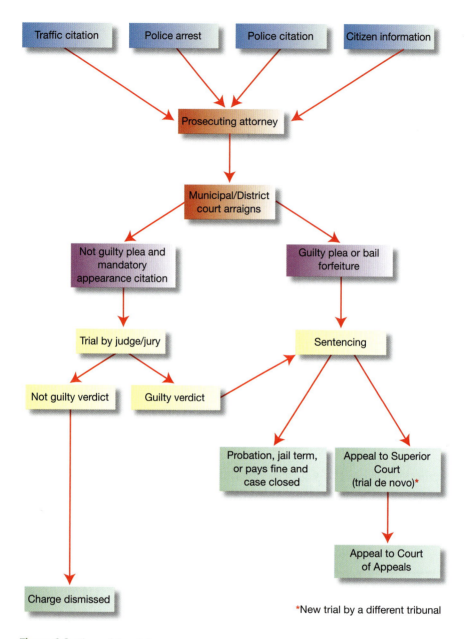

Figure 6-3. Chart of the misdemeanor case process.

monetary award, including age, health, education, and wages. On the basis of the facts of the case, the court may grant a monetary award. This is civil law.

Identify similar actions that you are aware of in your locale. What amount would you place on the lost life of a young woman with a master's-level education who put her career on hold to raise her two children?

 In a criminal case the proof is beyond a reasonable doubt. In a civil case there only needs to be a preponderance of evidence. So, a person can be found not guilty in a criminal case but then found guilty in a civil case. ●

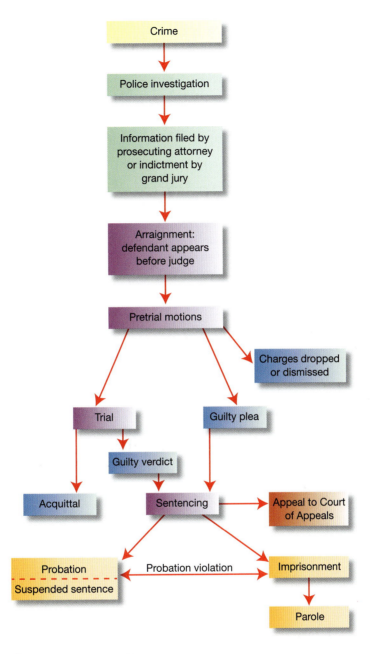

Figure 6-4. Chart of the felony case process.

TYPES OF COURT

As indicated earlier, the type of court that hears a particular case depends on the offense or complaint. In criminal cases, the type of court depends on the nature of the offense and where it occurs. In civil cases, it depends on the amount of money involved and where the parties reside. The jury and judge are neutral arbitrators of the evidence.

Courts also are classified as lower or higher, inferior or superior. A **lower or inferior court** has less authority than a **higher or superior court**.

FEDERAL COURT

Three **jurisdictions** belong only to federal courts: federal crimes, such as racketeering and bank robbery; constitutional issues; and civil action involving parties not living in the same state.

The U.S. Supreme Court is the highest court in the federal court system. Directly under the jurisdiction of the U.S. Supreme Court are the U.S. Court of Claims, the U.S. Court of Customs and Patent Office, and the U.S. Court of Appeals. The U.S. Supreme Court directs the actions of all courts: federal, state, trial, and appellate.

The circuit courts are below the Supreme Court, and they direct the actions of the U.S. Federal District Courts and Tax Courts.

IN THE NEWS

During the 1990s, drug manufacturers assured everyone (including providers) that opioids were not addictive and that medical professionals were undertreating chronic pain. Increased prescriptions led to extensive misuse. The country's opioid crisis saw a slight decline in 2018, but still is alarmingly high. In 2020, opioid overdoses resulted in over 81,000 deaths, the largest number ever recorded in one year by the CDC, likely due to the disruption of daily life caused by the Covid-19 pandemic.

Case Law

In 2017, the State of Oklahoma filed suit against several defendants, including Johnson & Johnson, for their part in the state's opioid crisis. The State of Oklahoma, in Case No. CJ-2017-816, accused Johnson & Johnson et al. of fueling the opioid crisis by conducting deceptive marketing and sales efforts.

Judge Thad Balkman presided over the case where the State presented its sole claim for relief against the defendants for causing a public nuisance pursuant to Okla. Stat. tit. 50, §1 et seq. Other defendants settled before the trial; Johnson & Johnson decided to defend the case. The 2019 decision was against Johnson & Johnson for $572 million. Johnson & Johnson plans to appeal the decision as it works toward settling over 2,000 additional lawsuits, many of which have consolidated into a multidistrict litigation proceeding. The proposed multidistrict settlement with the other defendants is in the billions. Part of the settlement would include funding for addiction treatment programs. The Oklahoma appeal is expected to continue into 2021.

STATE COURT

The pattern for state courts is similar to the pattern for federal courts. There are inferior or lower courts and a process of appeals. Figure 6-5 illustrates the state court system. The lower courts (district or municipal court) hear cases involving civil matters, small claims, housing, traffic, and some misdemeanors. The State Superior Court has general jurisdiction in all types of civil and criminal cases. The **court of appeals** has power to review decisions of this court. The court of appeals may reverse, remand, modify, or affirm a decision of a lower court. The final route of appeal is to the State Supreme Court, the determination of which becomes the law of the state.

Each state defines by statute the types of cases a particular court will hear and the maximum money value of the cases over which it has jurisdiction. In the event **litigation** does arise in a civil matter, providers and their health-care employees will most likely find themselves in a state court. Other civil matters may also take place in probate court and small claims court.

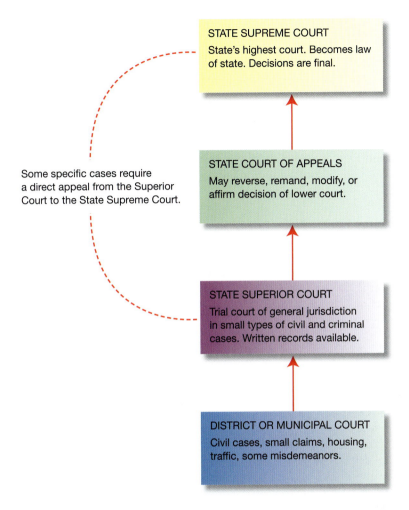

Figure 6-5. Titles of courts vary from state to state, but this diagram illustrates the overall structure of the court system in most states.

PROBATE COURT

Probate law oversees the distribution of a person's estate after the person's death. In **probate court** (sometimes called **estate court**), a provider may decide to initiate action on the collection of a bill owed by a deceased client if all other options have been unsuccessful. Generally, a health-care employee represents the interests of the provider and attempts to locate the responsible person or party for the debt, whose name can be obtained from the deceased client's family or lawyer, or from the mortuary. If unable to obtain a name from these sources, the health-care employee must write or call the county seat in which the estate is being settled. The county probate court recorder will provide information concerning the filing of the claim (in court, to the executor of the estate, or elsewhere), the proper forms to file, and when the claim must be submitted (Fig. 6-6). Quick action is required because most states have a file period from 4 to 12 months after the publication of notice in a newspaper by the administrator or executor.

Once the probate forms are ready to be mailed, the health-care employee sends them by certified mail, return receipt requested. This step establishes that the documents were received and by whom. The administrator will either accept or reject the claim. If it is accepted, payment will follow, but it may be delayed for months in the courts. If it is rejected and the provider believes the bill is justified, a lawsuit may be filed against the administrator within a designated

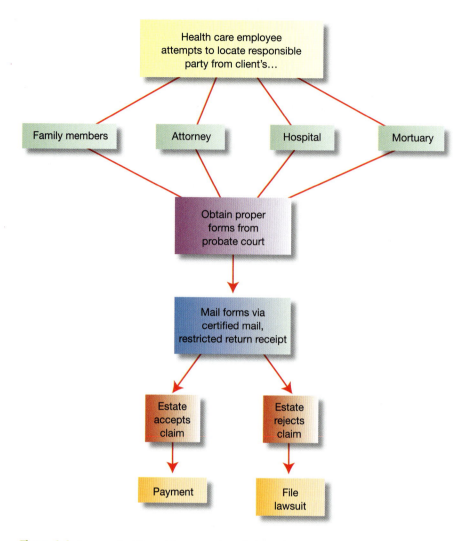

Figure 6-6. An example of financial recovery through the probate process.

amount of time, depending on the state. Health-care employees should be aware of their particular state's time limits.

 Keep in mind that even though you may be hesitant to collect a deceased client's bill, the provider rendered services for the client and deserves payment. Failure to file a claim may be construed by others as an admission of poor medical care on the part of the provider. ●

SMALL CLAIMS COURT

Small claims court allows the provider or the provider's representative to file action against a client for an unpaid or delinquent account. In the state of Virginia, for example, small claims court has jurisdiction over cases when the plaintiff seeks monetary judgment up to $5,000. The maximum monetary limit sought in small claims court in the United States ranges from $2,500 in Kentucky to $25,000 in Tennessee. In addition to the judgment of the amount owed, the provider plaintiff may also recover the costs of the litigation. There is no representation by an attorney. The plaintiff bringing the action files a preprinted form identifying facts in the account to be collected. A summons is issued on the complaint requesting the appearance of the defendant before the judge.

The defendant is given time to file a cross-complaint against the plaintiff for any possible grievance the defendant may have. A date is set for delivery and decision.

The plaintiff presents the facts in the case, and the defendant responds to the allegations or charges. Both parties may **subpoena** witnesses to testify on their behalf. After all information is heard, the matter goes to the judge for a decision. If judgment is in favor of the defendant, there is no right to appeal. However, if judgment is in favor of the plaintiff, the defendant may appeal the decision to a higher court.

The prudent health-care employee will contact the clerk of the small claims court for instructions and information regarding the procedures to follow. This is in direct contrast to lawsuits in higher courts, where court clerks cannot assist the parties in completing forms.

SUBPOENAS

Providers may find themselves in court even though they and their employees have practiced good preventive measures. No matter what the dispute or reason for litigation, providers need to be adequately prepared. The reasons for court appearances are numerous, but most commonly the provider will be a defendant, a witness, or an **expert witness (medical)** in civil or criminal trials; insanity and probate contests; in personal injury actions; or in cases arising under insurance policies including life, health, or accident.

In any of these cases, providers may appear with or without a subpoena. A subpoena is an order commanding attendance in a specific court or office, at a specific time, under penalty for failure to do so unless a protective order from the court invalidates the requirement. The subpoena may be signed by the clerk of the court, a notary public, or an attorney. The subpoena may require a **deposition** to be taken rather than an actual appearance in court.

The attendance requested in a subpoena may be of a person (provider or health-care employee) or of data (medical record). The summons is referred to as a *subpoena duces tecum* when the witness is required to appear and to bring certain records. The provider most likely would not need to appear to identify a record; proper identification usually can be done by an employee. The provider would be required to appear, however, if the record needed to be interpreted. The health-care employee should verify with the court magistrate whether his or her appearance is necessary or if just a copy of the medical record would suffice. In most cases, it is a copy of the medical record that is needed.

A **court order** is an order issued only by a judge to appear or to request certain records. The release of any records requested in a court order does not require the client's permission. However, out of courtesy to clients, the provider will notify them of the request. Any records related to substance misuse, mental health, or dangerous communicable diseases also require a court order. State laws differ on rules related to court orders, but generally these orders have stronger force of the law than a summons, a subpoena, or a *subpoena duces tecum*.

Whether a subpoena or a court order, it should authorize witness fees, photocopying fees, or mileage fees. If fees are not authorized, they are to be requested when the subpoena is served. If the provider is being subpoenaed, the subpoena must be hand-delivered to the provider. However, because so many subpoenas are served and there are so few officers to serve them, some subpoenas may be served to the provider's employee instead of to the provider. In such cases, the provider, out of courtesy, appears in court as though the subpoena was served by an officer to him or her. If the medical record is subpoenaed, the subpoena may be served to an employee. Legal advice should be sought for any questions about a subpoena or its circumstances. Any questions can be answered by the provider's malpractice insurance company or by the risk management department at the affiliated hospital.

THE TRIAL PROCESS

A case may be tried before a judge or a judge and jury. Usually, trial courts have a jury, but the parties to a trial may waive (voluntarily give up) their right to a jury trial.

First, the jury, consisting of 6 to 12 people, must be selected. A pool of potential jurors is chosen at random from voter registration lists and auto license records in the area. How the actual jurors are picked from this pool depends on the level of court, the type of case being tried, and local court rules. Once the jurors are selected, they are given the oath by a clerk or judge.

The trial procedure (**arraignment**) then begins. **Opening statements** usually are made by each attorney, first for the plaintiff and then for the defendant. Such statements outline the facts each party hopes to establish during the trial. The plaintiff's attorney calls the first witness and asks questions with the purpose of providing evidence to support the case being made (**examination of witness**). This part of the process is called **direct examination**. The defendant's attorney then questions the witness (**cross-examination**). This procedure continues until the plaintiff's entire case has been presented. The case for the defense is presented in the same manner. The direct examinations and cross-examinations recur. The witnesses have previously testified under oath, usually in a deposition. The opposing attorney attempts to point out inconsistencies to discredit the witness's knowledge and testimony. In a criminal case, the state must prove guilt "beyond a reasonable doubt," whereas in a civil case it is by "a preponderance of evidence." Then both attorneys rest their cases, that is, indicate that no further evidence or testimony is to be given.

If it is a jury trial, the judge then instructs the jury on the law governing the case. The attorney for each party is allowed **closing arguments**, after which the judge charges the jury to reach a fair verdict based on the evidence presented. Then the jury is ushered from the courtroom to consider the case (**deliberation**) and reach a verdict.

In civil court, the judge or jury finds for the plaintiff or for the defendant. If the verdict is found in favor of the defendant, the case is dismissed. If the plaintiff wins the case, a monetary settlement usually is awarded, the amount determined by the judge or jury.

In a criminal trial, if the defendant is found guilty, the judge imposes sentence. At sentencing, the court can commit the defendant to an institution or allow probation. At the end of the trial, the judge informs the defendant of all rights to appeal. If the defendant is found not guilty, the case is dismissed.

 ## EXPERT WITNESS

In medical cases, an expert witness is a person specifically qualified in medicine, usually a specialty, who can testify in court as to what the professional standard of care is in the same or a similar situation. An expert witness is necessary if the subject of the court action is beyond the general understanding of the average layperson or if the knowledge of the expert witness will aid in discovering the truth. Expert witness will have examined all relevant evidence in the matter, including medical records and deposition testimony, to provide their opinions.

As expert witnesses, providers testify as to what they see, hear, know to be fact, and know is the recognized standard of care. Opinions not based on their experience or expertise, certain out-of-court statements, and conclusions are not admissible in most cases. Expert witnesses in medical cases are usually skilled in the art, science, or profession of medicine and may be practicing medicine or teaching in a school of medicine. In litigation, attorneys may have difficulty obtaining an expert witness who is geographically close because experts are often hesitant to testify about a situation that may appear to contradict their own peers.

Expert witnesses are expected to be reputable, honest, and impartial. The attorney who has called the witness will try to establish the witness's training, experience, intelligence, and accuracy. Witnesses should talk in lay terms rather than medical language and bear in mind that their dress and appearance may influence the judge and jury. Attorneys cannot prompt or cue witnesses.

Expert witnesses may wish to illustrate or clarify their testimony by employing such visual aids as electronic media, photographs, diagrams, charts, radiographs, skeletons, and human-type models. In some instances, sketch artists or illustrators may be employed. During cross-examination, witnesses may face difficulties. The cross-examining attorney may try to intimidate the witness or create confusion. Witnesses should take their time and answer truthfully. They should not be afraid to say, "I don't know," if that is the case.

Expert witnesses are entitled to a fee commensurate with their time away from their practice or teaching for the case, their preparation for the case, and their participation in the case. If questioned during cross-examination regarding a fee for witnessing, they should answer truthfully. A fee should be established before serving as an expert witness rather than on a contingency basis.

If a health-care employee or a provider is subpoenaed to be an expert witness, legal counsel should be sought. Ethically such testimony should not be seen as adversarial to peers. An attorney will guide, advise, and take whatever legal action is indicated.

 ## STATUTE OF LIMITATIONS

State legislatures have established statutes of limitations that restrict the time allowed for individuals to initiate any type of legal action. The length of time allowed for starting a lawsuit varies greatly from state to state. For example, in the case of personal injury, the statute of limitations ranges from 1 year in Louisiana to 6 years in Maine.

The statute of limitations most commonly begins at the time when the negligent act was allegedly committed or when the client discovered or should have discovered the alleged negligence. Health-care professionals should understand their state's law on the subject as well as how the law has been interpreted in case law. Tort actions and contracts usually have separate statutes of limitations. The statute of limitations is typically longer for contracts than for torts.

Circumstances that may alter the statute of limitations occur with a person who is legally insane or when an individual has not yet reached the age of maturity. Therefore, a person declared legally insane will not come under the statute of limitations until the period of insanity has ended. In the case of minors, the statute of limitations may not apply until the child has reached the age of maturity, usually 18 years. Thus, it does not matter what age a child was when a situation occurred; the statute of limitations does not begin until the 18th birthday. This fact is of special concern to pediatricians and obstetricians.

Providers and their employees must concern themselves with the statute of limitations when considering the retention of their medical records as well as when they could be involved in a malpractice suit (refer to Chapter 9, Medical Records). Legal counsel should be sought for interpretations and advice.

Case Study

On a winter morning in Oklahoma, Lisa Boudreau, a 40-year-old mother of two, started to sweat profusely even though she was outdoors building snowmen with her children. She also was dizzy. Lisa was frightened and extremely concerned because her mother had suffered from the same symptoms 4 years earlier and died from unknown causes. Lisa called her neighbor, Barb, who rushed over. Barb called 911. By the time Lisa reached the hospital, she was unresponsive. Tests determined that Lisa was diabetic. With aggressive treatment, Lisa recovered and was released from the hospital. In discussing the situation with her neighbor, Lisa realized that her mother probably had diabetes also and just was not diagnosed. Lisa ponders on whether to sue the doctor and the hospital where her mother died for not diagnosing her condition properly.

What additional information would Lisa need before approaching an attorney? What is the statute of limitations in Oklahoma? Do you think Lisa's case went to court? Justify your response.

It cannot be stressed enough how important legal counsel is in the case of any questions or doubts. Providers often seek consultation on difficult medical problems and should do no less for themselves and their employees if faced with litigation.

SUMMARY

This introduction to law does not attempt to provide all the necessary information the health-care employee may need. It provides basic information, not legal advice. However, health-care employees must be knowledgeable of the law and aware of their professional responsibilities so that they can act responsibly. Many activities in health care require this knowledge of the law to prevent illegal acts; however, when in doubt always seek legal counsel.

Watch It Now! Why is law important in health care? at http://FADavis.com, keyword *Tamparo.*

Questions for Review

SELECT THE BEST ANSWER

1. A court order calling someone to court to answer a charge is a
   a. Subpoena.
   b. Summons.
   c. *Subpoena duces tecum.*
   d. Misdemeanor.
   e. Felony.

2. A court that manages wills and settles estates is a
   a. Probate court.
   b. District court.
   c. Superior court.
   d. Supreme court.
   e. Appellate court.

3. A public official who directs court proceedings is a
   a. Plaintiff.
   b. Jury.
   c. District attorney.
   d. Judge.
   e. Defense lawyer.

4. A person who brings a claim against another individual is a
   a. Plaintiff.
   b. Jury.
   c. District attorney.
   d. Defendant.
   e. Judge.

5. A person who must appear in court to answer charges against them is a
   a. Plaintiff.
   b. Jury.
   c. District attorney.
   d. Defendant.
   e. Judge.

SHORT ANSWER QUESTIONS

1. Who can act as an expert witness? What are the necessary qualifications?

_____

_____

_____

2. Your state has legalized recreational marijuana. You attended a weekend party and ate brownies made with THC from marijuana; your friend said it was now legal. If tested positive, can you lose your job as a Certified Nurse Assistant in a hospital? Why or why not?

_____

_____

_____

3. Describe a situation that would overlap both the criminal and civil courts.

_____

_____

_____

4. An infant is without oxygen for a prolonged period of time during delivery, causing serious injuries to the brain. How long would the parents have to file a lawsuit?

_____

_____

_____

5. Which is more serious, a misdemeanor or a felony? Why?

_____

_____

_____

CLASSROOM EXERCISES

1. State laws cannot override federal laws, yet states may enact a statute that does just that (i.e., states legalizing marijuana for medicinal and/or recreational use). What happens when that occurs? Discuss the "checks and balances" that exist in the United States.

2. Describe a situation in which an understanding of the law is important to a medical receptionist.

3. If you were involved in a civil case, describe the process the case would follow and identify the factors that would determine the appropriate court.

4. Compare and contrast a summons, a subpoena, and a court order. Give an example of the use of each.

5. In the vignette at the beginning of the chapter, "Can She Be an Expert Witness?" what issues does the medical assistant educator consider?

6. Although probate court and small claims court are avenues to collect a client's account, discuss the disadvantages of doing so.

INTERNET ACTIVITIES

1. Research and identify the statute of limitations for malpractice in your state.

2. Go to the website for your state judicial system and describe how your state's court system is organized.

For additional resources please visit http://FADavis.com, keyword *Tamparo*.

CHAPTER 7

Public Duties

"The return from your work must be the satisfaction which that work brings you and the world's need of that work. With this, life is heaven, or as near heaven as you can get. Without this—with work which you despise, which bores you, and which the world does not need—this life is hell."—William Edward Burghardt Du Bois

(1868–1963); Sociologist, author, and civil rights leader

KEY TERMS

autopsy Examination by specially trained medical personnel of a body after death to determine cause of death or pathological conditions.

coroner An official, usually elected, who investigates death from sudden, unknown, or violent causes; may or may not be a physician.

intimate partner violence (IPV) Intimate partner violence refers to violence/abuse between a spouse or former spouse; boyfriend, girlfriend, or former boyfriend/girlfriend; same-sex or opposite-sex intimate partner; or former same-sex or opposite-sex intimate partner.

LGBTQIA Acronym for lesbian, gay, bisexual, transgender, queer, intersex, and asexual.

mandatory reporter A person mandated by law to report abuse or neglect to the proper authorities.

notifiable or reportable disease A disease that concerns the public welfare and requires reporting to the proper authority; a potentially pathological condition that may be transmitted directly or indirectly from one individual to another.

notifiable or reportable injury An injury that concerns the public welfare and requires reporting to the proper authority; for example, injuries resulting from gun or knife wounds.

LEARNING OUTCOMES

Upon successful completion of this chapter, you should be able to:

7.1 Define key terms.

7.2 List at least five areas of public duties for physicians and providers.

7.3 Discuss the importance of completing birth and death certificates.

7.4 Identify three circumstances in which a county coroner or medical examiner would be called to investigate a death.

7.5 Discuss the importance of prompt reporting of the death of a client.

7.6 Describe the process necessary for reporting communicable and notifiable diseases.

7.7   Restate the protocol to use for reporting adverse events of vaccines and toxoids.

7.8   List at least four injuries that are reportable.

7.9   Discuss child and elder abuse laws.

7.10   Identify professionals who are required to report suspected child abuse.

7.11   Summarize the five main types of intimate partner violence.

7.12   Describe the process used in gathering and securing evidence in the health-care setting.

7.13   Discuss Good Samaritan laws.

COMPETENCIES

CAAHEP

- Recognize the role of patient navigator in the practice of medical assisting. (CAAHEP V.C.12)
- Explain how the following impacts the medical assistant's practice and give examples:
  - Good Samaritan Act (CAAHEP X.C.13.n)
- Describe the process in compliance reporting unsafe activities (CAAHEP X.C.11.a)
- Report illegal and/or unsafe activities and behaviors that affect health, safety, and welfare of others to proper authorities. (CAAHEP X.P.6)

ABHES

- Comply with federal, state, and local health laws and regulations. (ABHES 4.f)
- Demonstrate an understanding of the core competencies for Interprofessional Collaborative Practice i.e. values/ethics; roles/responsibilities; interprofessional communication; teamwork. (ABHES 5.f)

VIGNETTE

What Would You Do?

Jose Gonzalez, a long-time client who owns a popular Mexican restaurant where you have often eaten, comes into the clinic not feeling well and looking sick. The provider assesses Jose and orders laboratory work. The test results reveal hepatitis A. Jose is called and asked to return to the clinic immediately. The provider discusses the diagnosis with Jose, his need to rest and take his prescriptions to cure the hepatitis A. The provider also informs Jose that he cannot return to his restaurant until the medications are completed and he is cured. Jose is also informed that his diagnosis must be reported to the county health department. Jose is devastated. When he leaves, he tells you there is no way he can stay away from the restaurant because it cannot run without him.
What is your responsibility in this situation?

 ## REPORTING REQUIREMENTS

Physicians, as licensed professionals, and many other health-care professionals have a duty to protect the health of their clients but also have a responsibility to protect the health of the community as a whole. They must follow certain statutory and regulatory requirements. Reports of births, communicable diseases, and abuse are a just a few examples. Reporting requirements vary among states and can be found at each state's Department of Health (DOH). There are a number of similarities among the states. Health-care employees will want to be familiar with the statutes, regulations, and reporting requirements for the state in which they are employed.

Good Samaritan laws are discussed in this chapter so that health-care professionals realize when their professional responsibility goes beyond the health-care setting.

Reporting statistical data and information gathered by health professionals may become an impersonal task, but it is important to remember that these data represent individuals. Therefore, the task is a personal matter. Deaths, rapes, and abuse are sensitive issues. Individuals involved need special attention and care.

BIRTHS AND DEATHS

The recording of births and deaths is an important function of the provider. These certificates are legal documents and require truthfulness and prompt and proper completion. In some states, a criminal penalty will result if birth or death certificates are not properly completed. Some states refuse to accept certificates completed in inks other than black; others refuse to accept a certificate with any blanks.

BIRTH CERTIFICATES

A birth certificate will be used throughout a person's life to prove age, parentage, and citizenship. A child will need a birth certificate when entering school. Adults will need a birth certificate to register to vote or to obtain a driver's license, a marriage license, a passport, veteran's benefits, welfare aid, and Social Security benefits.

Birth certificate requirements vary from state to state. A stillbirth or fetal death, in which the fetus has not reached the 20th week of gestation, may require neither a birth nor a death certificate. In some states, however, a special stillbirth form is used; in others, it is necessary to file both a birth and death certificate. Pennsylvania requires both birth and death certificates for a fetal demise at 16 weeks' gestation or older. If the birth is considered a live birth and then the infant dies, both a standard birth and death certificate are to be completed. In the event of a nonhospital birth, the person in attendance is responsible for initiating the birth certificate. In such a delivery, a parent should verify that the process is completed according to state regulations.

Check with your state's public health or vital statistics department, which offers information regarding reporting of birth and death certificates. This agency provides detailed information for completing the standard forms.

DEATH CERTIFICATES

Generally speaking, physicians (MDs and DOs) sign a certificate giving the cause of death of the deceased upon whom they have been in professional attendance. Some states allow nurse practitioners and physician assistants to sign if they were providing care to the deceased. In some circumstances, someone of greater authority, such as the county health officer or **coroner**, will assume the responsibility. A death may need to be reported to the coroner or medical examiner in the following instances: a death occurring within 24 hours after a client is admitted to a hospital or licensed health-care facility, postsurgical procedure deaths, nonattendance by a physician during the 3 days before death, or death of an individual outside a hospital or licensed health-care facility. The rules vary by state. For example, in Massachusetts, any death needs to be reported to the coroner unless the client is in hospice. In that case, the hospice nurse calls the physician to discuss the death and then completes a pronouncement form. Within 24 hours the physician will complete a death certificate.

The top two thirds of the death certificate is completed by the funeral home, and the bottom one third is completed by the physician. It is then turned in to the city or town hall for recording.

In some states, a physician is forbidden by law to sign certain death certificates. Examples include, but are not limited to, a death caused by criminal activity, a death from an undetermined cause, and a death that is the result of an accident or an occupational or environmental hazard. In these cases, the police, who are likely the first responders, immediately call the coroner, medical examiner, or equivalent official for investigation. The police will ensure that the bodily remains are not disturbed, and evidence will be collected by both the police and the coroner and his or her team. This is particularly significant if an investigation or **autopsy** is to be performed. An investigation may result in prosecution of criminals and alteration of survivors' rights or other benefits. The client's provider may also be consulted with regard to the deceased client's medical record and his or her most recent condition.

Once the cause of death has been determined, a death certificate is issued. At this time a consultation with the next of kin or person financially responsible for the burial will take place, and the body can then be released to a mortician.

As a courtesy to the deceased's family, it is imperative that the death certificate be completed and signed as quickly as possible so that funeral and financial arrangements can begin. Many states have a requirement that the death certificate be filed within 24 to 72 hours.

Health-care professionals should understand the rules for completion of death certificates, and some blank certificates may be kept on hand for quick completion. They should realize that no arrangements can be made until the death certificate is signed. As a courtesy, many morticians will complete the death certificate for a physician and bring it to the clinic where the physician will review and sign the certificate. Electronic medical records in many hospital settings are used to print death certificates. The provider who pronounces a person's death will enter the information into the electronic chart and then sign the death certificate when printed. A dedicated printer with a specific type of paper is usually maintained to print death certificates.

The death certificate proves a person has died. A certified copy of a death certificate is generally necessary in obtaining access to insurance policies, bank accounts, safe-deposit boxes, dispersal of estates, real estate transactions, tax base information, Internal Revenue Service information, and Social Security and veteran's benefits.

NOTIFIABLE DISEASES

A **notifiable or reportable disease** concerns the public welfare and is a potentially pathological condition that may be transmitted directly or indirectly from one individual to another. In Georgia, the DOH states that the purposes of reportable disease surveillance are as follows:

1. To conduct active and passive surveillance to detect diseases and adverse health conditions
2. To investigate reports of acute diseases or outbreaks
3. To recommend appropriate prevention measures, treatment, and control
4. To monitor and investigate reports of unusual health conditions
5. To conduct data analyses and disseminate information from surveillance systems
6. To provide guidance to health-care professionals, facilities, and other agencies and organizations regarding disease prevention and control
7. To respond to disease-related inquiries from residents, health-care providers, and others

Statistics and records on reportable diseases began in the 19th century, but in 1961, the Centers for Disease Control and Prevention (CDC) assumed responsibility for the collection and publication of data concerning nationally notifiable diseases.

 According to the CDC website: "The list of nationally notifiable infectious diseases is revised periodically. For example, a disease may be added to the list as a new pathogen emerges, or a disease may be deleted as its incidence declines. Public health officials in state health departments and the CDC continue to collaborate in determining which diseases should be notifiable at the national level; however, reporting of nationally notifiable diseases to the CDC by the states is voluntary. Reporting is currently mandated (i.e., by state legisla therefore, varies slightly by state. All states generally report the internationally quarantinable diseases (i.e., Ebola, cholera, plague, SARS, Covid-19, and yellow fever) in compliance with the World Health Organization's International Health Regulations." Some reporting occurs via telephone; others require a specific format. ●

The current list of notifiable diseases is available at the CDC website, listed by years: wwwn.cdc.gov/nndss/conditions/notifiable/2020. Each state publishes a list of 30 or more notifiable diseases and their required reporting format.

Providers have a duty to report notifiable diseases according to the state's requirements. Reports are usually made by the medical assistant, who telephones the local health department and furnishes the following information that may require a written follow-up:

1. Disease (or suspected disease)
2. Name, address, age, and occupation of person with suspected disease
3. Date of onset of disease
4. Name of person reporting

To report by mail, the appropriate forms furnished by the health department are used. A check with the local health department may reveal 20 or more specific forms for diseases. Some states encourage reporting by phone, with the statistical data being collected by the health department. Other states require that the initial paperwork be completed at the time the notifiable disease is detected. Whatever method of reporting is used, it should be prompt, consistent, factual, and complete. A copy of the report is kept for the files. The health department's responsibility is to determine the source of infection and mode of transmission so that public health will be protected. The list in Figure 7-1 is not exhaustive; however, it identifies those communicable diseases that most threaten public safety.

CHILDHOOD AND ADOLESCENT VACCINATIONS

For more than two centuries humans have benefited from vaccines. Vaccine discovery started with Edward Jenner, who in 1790 developed a vaccine for smallpox. Until Jenner's time, such contagious diseases as smallpox, measles, diphtheria, and pertussis topped the list for childhood killers. Since Jenner's discovery, many more vaccines have been identified for diseases. Through widespread distribution of effective, safe, and affordable vaccines, industrialized nations have been able to contain these devastating diseases.

Health-care providers have a duty to the public to immunize children. The CDC publishes a schedule each year listing at what age the immunizations should be administered. The American Academy of Family Physicians and the American Academy of Pediatrics follow these same recommendations (Fig. 7-2).

Before any immunizations are given, the parent or guardian is to receive a Vaccine Information Statement (VIS). The VIS is given before each vaccination, regardless of whether it is the first or third in a series. The VIS is a pamphlet published by the CDC that contains the following topics:

- Why the child should be vaccinated
- Description of the specific vaccine
- Who should get the vaccine
- Who should not get the vaccine
- Identified risks
- What to do if there is a severe reaction
- The National Vaccine Injury Compensation Program phone number and website address
- How to learn more

 After the parent or guardian has read the pertinent VIS, the health-care professional should have a consent form signed stating that they have received the VIS, have had their questions answered, and have agreed to the vaccination for the child.

Providers who administer certain childhood vaccines and toxoids are required by law to record the following information in each person's medical or health record:

- Type of vaccine
- Date of the vaccine's administration

2020 NATIONAL NOTIFIABLE CONDITIONS AND DISEASES

Anthrax

Arboviral Diseases

Botulism

Brucellosis

Cancer

Chlamydia trachomatis infection

Cholera

Coccidioidomycosis

Coronavirus Disease 2019 (Covid-19)

Diphtheria

Foodborne Disease Outbreak

Gonorrhea

Hantavirus Infection

Hepatitis A, B, C, acute

HIV Infection (AIDS or HIV Stage III)

Lyme Disease

Malaria

Measles

Meningococcal Disease

Mumps

Pertussis

Plague

Poliomyelitis

Rabies

Rubella

Salmonella Infections

SARS

Smallpox

Syphilis

Tetanus

Tuberculosis

Tularemia

Vancomycin *Staphylococcus aureus*

Varicella

Vibriosis

Viral Hemorrhagic Fevers

Waterborne Disease Outbreak

Yellow Fever

Zika Virus Diseases and Infections

Red denotes infectious diseases as potential weapons

www.cdc.gov/nndss/conditions/notifiable/2020

Figure 7-1. Communicable and infectious conditions commonly reported immediately by telephone. Laboratory confirmation is not necessary before report being filed. Diseases in red are potential agents of bioterrorism.

- Dose
- Route
- Site
- Manufacturer and lot number of the vaccine
- Date on the VIS and date given
- Vaccine administrator's initials

This information aids the clinic or providers' facility if an adverse reaction or a vaccine recall occurs.

According to the American Academy of Pediatrics (AAP) and the American Academy of Family Physicians (AAFP), the recommended childhood immunizations as of 2020 are as follows:

Diphtheria, tetanus, and pertussis (DTaP)

Hepatitis A

Hepatitis B

Haemophilus influenzae type b (Hib)

Human papillomavirus (HPV)

Influenza

Measles, mumps, and rubella (MMR)

Meningococcal

Pneumococcal

Poliovirus, inactivated (IPV)

Rotavirus

Varicella

For more detailed information visit the Centers for Disease Control and Prevention (CDC) Website at https://www.cdc.gov/vaccines/schedules/hcp/imz/child-adolescent.html

Figure 7-2. Recommended childhood immunizations.

The path of vaccine administration has not been straight or easy. There have been many bumps in the road, including adverse reactions, supply shortages, and litigation. Providers must also report any adverse events following administration. In 1986, Congress passed the National Childhood Vaccine Injury Act (NCVIA) to address concerns about vaccine supply, safety, and liability. The primary purpose of NCVIA was to create the National Vaccine Injury Compensation Program (NVICP) to compensate those injured by vaccine on a no-fault basis. The program covers all routinely recommended childhood vaccinations.

A Vaccine Injury table was created to identify those injured by vaccines and due compensation. The table is updated as information becomes available from research on vaccine adverse effects. Qualification for compensation occurs in three ways: (1) by showing that an injury found on the Vaccine Injury table occurred in the appropriate time interval following immunization; (2) by proving that the vaccine caused the condition; or (3) by proving that the vaccine aggravated a preexisting condition. Initially awards were paid from taxpayer funds, but since October 1, 1988, awards are paid from the Vaccine Injury Compensation Trust Fund. The funds come from an excise tax on every dose of covered vaccine that is purchased.

The Vaccine Adverse Event Reporting System (VAERS) was created in 1990 to provide a computerized database management system for the collection and analysis of these reports. It is operated jointly by the CDC and the U.S. Food and Drug Administration (FDA). These agencies monitor VAERS data to detect previously unknown adverse events or increases in known adverse events.

Not only do health-care providers have a responsibility for appropriate immunizations, but also school districts in all states have immunization requirements for children before they can be admitted to school. Individuals (regardless of age) must produce a record of vaccination dates or blood work proving the establishment of antibodies to the diseases. Most states follow the recommendations of the CDC. The fear of adverse effects of several of the vaccines has caused many individuals to oppose immunizations for themselves and their children. Most schools will grant exemptions for individuals with medical or religious reasons.

IN THE NEWS

In December of 2019, New Jersey proposed to remove religious reasons as an acceptable rejection to receiving the influenza vaccine. A last-minute amendment was added to allow private schools and day care centers to accept students without proper immunizations. The bill did not have the required votes and was not passed on January 13, 2020. Lawmakers in New Jersey plan to rework the bill in 2020. In Seattle in 2020, unvaccinated children were not permitted to attend classes without proper vaccination verifications.

The CDC constantly monitors vaccines and any adverse reactions. The CDC makes recommendations regarding what vaccines should be given, on what schedule, and when any recalls of vaccines occur. Local Boards of Health will alert clinics and providers in their area of any changes. Vaccine package inserts will assist a medical assistant on the proper storage of the vaccine. Health-care professionals must understand the rules, regulations, and schedules for vaccines and immunizations.

NOTIFIABLE OR REPORTABLE INJURY

A **notifiable or reportable injury** is identified when it concerns the public welfare and reporting is required to the proper authority; for example, injuries resulting from gun or knife wounds. Most states have detailed requirements for reporting injuries. Check with the local or state medical associations and law enforcement agencies for specific requirements.

Generally, however, injuries caused by lethal weapons, such as guns and knives, are treated in emergency or hospital facilities and are always reported. When persons who have been raped or battered seek and receive treatment from clinic health-care providers, they can be treated in the clinic or may be referred to the emergency department of a local hospital.

Questions may surface concerning reporting requirements. For example, if an adult survivor reports for medical care in the clinic health-care facility after a spousal rape, must it be reported? What if the client begs the provider not to report the incident? If the physician suspects abuse, must it be reported? To whom and how? At least 50 state variances govern the reporting of such incidents. In some states, marital rape laws may mandate reporting of spousal abuse; others do not. In the states where reporting is required, failure to report child, elder, and spousal abuse may be specifically considered a misdemeanor. Information that follows is important for the health professional in identifying and recognizing abuse and violence.

ABUSE

The responsibilities and tasks performed in the health-care setting can sometimes be very stressful. Abuse is one of the most serious of those stressors. Emotions are especially charged when there is evidence of child or elder abuse but are equally as difficult to hold in check when there is abuse in family or close personal relationships. The most difficult task may not be in treating the individual abused but rather in remaining calm and nonjudgmental about the circumstances that bring the abused and/or the abuser to the health-care setting.

CHILD ABUSE

Culturally, the issue is complex because there is the belief in a majority of cultures that parents are best able to provide for the care and discipline of their children. There may be the belief that parents have a moral obligation to correct a child's misbehavior. The idea of "spare the rod, spoil the child" is a paraphrase from a Bible verse. The Mother Goose rhymes some learned as children express the frustration of the old woman in a shoe who did not know what to do with all her children, so she "whipped them all soundly and put them to bed."

Incidents of child abuse and neglect may be seen in a hospital or a clinic when a child displays fractures, burns, severe bruises, and questionable injuries. Not so obvious injuries may include dislocations, cerebrospinal trauma, and internal injuries resulting from blows to the abdomen. Malnutrition, lower than expected growth rate, poor hygiene, gross dental problems, and unattended medical needs also may indicate neglect or abuse.

Definitions of child abuse are essential for understanding what is to be reported.

- *Neglect:* Failure to provide for basic care, including food, clothing, shelter, or medical attention that endangers the health of the child.
- *Physical injury:* Burns, severe bruising, lacerations, fractures, injuries to internal organs, or serious bodily injury. Injury is often obvious, but many abusers will harm a child in places that are not obvious so that the casual observer will not notice.
- *Mental injury:* Harm to a child's well-being that damages his or her psychological or intellectual development. The child may be emotionally withdrawn, depressed, anxious, or aggressive, but injury is not obvious.
- *Sexual abuse:* Using a child to engage in sexual activity of any sort, including rape, molestation, incest, prostitution, or sexual exploitation. Physical evidence may be present.
- *Sexually explicit conduct:* Actual or simulated sexual intercourse with a child (same sex or opposite sex), masturbation, exhibition of genitalia, or sadistic or masochistic abuse; likely is not obvious to health-care professionals.
- *Child molestation:* Oral-genital contact or viewing and fondling of genitals; likely is not obvious to health-care professionals.
- *Sexual exploitation:* Child pornography, child prostitution, or sexually explicit use of child's image in electronic media; likely is not obvious to health-care professionals.
- *Incest:* Sexual relations between children or parents or siblings in the same family; may be recognized by health-care professionals.

All 50 states and the District of Columbia have laws that mandate the reporting of child abuse and neglect. The report is made to an agency named in the state statute. Certain individuals are required to report suspected abuse and neglect. These **mandatory reporters** include health professionals, social service personnel, law enforcement personnel, educators, and any professional person working with children. Many states require education and training related to child abuse. For example, the Pennsylvania State Board of Nursing requires 2 hours of continuing education in child abuse recognition and reporting as a condition of license renewal every 2 years. Some states also allow a hospital administrator or a physician to detain a child legally without a guardian's consent in such instances. Individuals making the report are protected from civil and criminal liability if the report is found to be false. Failure to report is a misdemeanor in some states. The function of reporting is to identify incidents of suspected abuse and neglect, not to prove abuse or neglect. The report may be oral, written, or both. Immediate reporting is paramount so that a proper investigation can be initiated. Information required in the report may include the following:

1. Name, address, and age of child
2. Name and address of child's parents (or guardians)
3. Nature and extent of the injury, neglect, or abuse
4. Any evidence of previous incidents of abuse or neglect, including their nature and extent
5. Any other information that may be helpful in establishing the cause of the child's injuries, neglect, or death and the identity of the perpetrator

If a crime has been committed, law enforcement must be notified.

Case Study

Mrs. Dobbs is a substitute teacher for a busy first-grade classroom. She met Jade when teaching first grade in September. Jade had several scratches on her arm and face she said were from her new cat. When Mrs. Dobbs returned to teach in December, she noticed that Jade was not using her arm to full range of motion. When questioned, Jade stated that she hit it on the car door. When Mrs. Dobbs returned to teach again in February, she was told that Jade had been "out sick" for over a week. She decided to call the main classroom instructor to follow up regarding Jade.

Should Mrs. Dobbs be concerned? What are her options? Discuss and decide what you would do if you were Mrs. Dobbs, who is concerned about repercussions to reporting potential child abuse if the claim turns out to be false. What would you tell Mrs. Dobbs?

IN THE NEWS

On February 14, 2019, New York State enacted the Child Victims Act (L. 2019 c.11) ("CVA") which (1) extended the statute of limitations on criminal cases involving certain sex offenses against children under 18; (2) extended the time which civil actions based on such criminal conduct may be brought until the child victim reaches 55 years old; and (3) opened a 1-year window reviving civil actions for which the statute of limitations has already run (even in cases that were litigated and dismissed on limitations grounds), commencing August 14, 2019.

INTIMATE PARTNER VIOLENCE

For many years, the terms *spousal abuse* and *domestic violence* have been used. Today **intimate partner violence (IPV)** more accurately describes the problem. IPV refers to violence or abuse between a spouse or former spouse; boyfriend, girlfriend, or former boyfriend or girlfriend; same-sex or opposite-sex intimate partner, or former same-sex or opposite-sex intimate partner. The phrase *teen date violence* also falls into this category. IPV refers to actual or threatened physical, sexual, or psychological harm to another individual. The term *survivor* rather than *victim* is used because survivor is believed to be a more appropriate and empowering term.

Four main types of IPV are identified:

1. Physical violence is the intent to do harm or cause disability, injury, or death. Some examples include hitting, pushing, grabbing, biting, punching, slapping, restraining, burning, or using a weapon and one's strength to hurt another person.
2. Sexual violence is forcing another to commit a sex act against their will; having sex with someone who is unable to understand, decline participation, or say "no" because they are disabled or under the influence of alcohol or drugs; or having abusive sexual contact. Date rape falls under this category.
3. Threats of physical or sexual violence occur when gestures, words, or weapons are used to cause harm, injury, disability, or death.
4. Psychological or emotional violence refers to trauma that includes humiliation, control, and any acts to embarrass or diminish a partner; isolating a partner from family and friends; and denying access to monetary funds or basic resources.

A fifth form of IPV has been added, called *stalking*. Stalking is the act of following, spying on, making repeated calls or contacts after being asked not to, appearing at one's home or place of employment, and making threats, with or without a weapon.

No one knows for certain how much IPV occurs because not all incidences are reported. Men as well as women may be abusers; however, more women than men are abused. IPV is a criminal offense in some states. Not all states require IPV to be reported; often it depends on whether a weapon is used. In many states, there is no criminal action unless the abused individual wishes to file a claim. Any form of IPV that is acknowledged in the health-care setting will have to be reported when required to do so. All attempts should be made to keep the survivor as safe as possible. Referral and resources should be made available to survivors who seek protection.

It is important to note that within the **LGBTQIA** (lesbian, gay, bisexual, transgender, queer, intersex, asexual) community, IPV is equal to or higher than in the heterosexual community. Often survivors do not report out of fear of being denied services because of homophobia, transphobia, and biphobia. Many domestic violence shelters, which are typically for women, do not permit transgender individuals entrance due to their gender/genital/legal status.

RAPE

Rape, a crime of violence, is forced sexual intercourse or penetration of a bodily orifice by a penis or some other object. If a weapon is used, aggravated criminal assault has occurred. One or more persons may commit rape against an individual, and gang rape can involve several individuals. Rape is a reportable criminal act.

Rape is a serious crisis for survivors, who are likely to react to the experience in four phases.

1. *Disorganization:* phase of fear, shock, denial, and a feeling of loss of control
2. *Denial:* phase when the survivor outwardly appears normal, but inwardly has suppressed the incident; gradually begins to gain control
3. *Reorganization:* phase when the survivor is no longer in denial, but often becomes depressed; may feel a need to talk about the rape
4. *Recovery:* phase when survivors realize they are not to blame for the rape

It helps if survivors are able to vent their feelings of anger, guilt, and shame during the recovery process. Women and girls are more often raped than men. Men and boys, however, are more likely to be gang-raped, especially in jail and prison. Male rapes and those of the LGBTQIA community are often underreported due to the stigma associated with this type of assault and the discrimination against LGBTQIA individuals.

ELDER ABUSE

Intentional or unintentional harm, physical or psychological, to someone 60 years of age or older is termed *elder abuse*. Elderly persons may be more vulnerable than others because of their social isolation and mental impairment. Elderly abuse can be difficult to assess because of cultural implications as well. Their abusers may include professional caregivers, family members, partners, doctors, lawyers, bankers, accountants, or strangers. Elder abuse may occur anywhere but is more commonly found in the home, a nursing home, or other institution.

The types of elder abuse are as follows:

- *Physical abuse:* Violence that results in bodily harm or severe mental stress. Assault, beating, whipping, hitting, punching, pushing, shoving, pinching, force-feeding, shaking, or rough handling during caregiving are some of the examples of physical abuse.
- *Financial abuse:* Financial or material exploitation of an elder's resources. The improper use of money, assets, or property is financial abuse. Examples include withdrawing cash from accounts without permission, cashing checks received (e.g., pension and Social Security) and denying those funds to the elder person, forcing an elderly person to alter a will, and forging a senior's signature. A January 2015 True Link report suggests that financial abuse involving the elderly results in the loss of more than $36 billion per year. In 2016, 33 states, the District of Columbia, and Puerto Rico addressed financial exploitation of vulnerable adults during the legislative session. States adopted different ways to address this growing issue from instituting reporting requirements to developing task forces.
- *Emotional/psychological abuse:* Actions that dehumanize an elderly person, including social isolation, name-calling, harassment, humiliating, insulting, threatening to punish, treating

an elderly person like a child, and yelling or screaming. This form of abuse usually accompanies one of the other forms.

- *Sexual abuse:* Any sexual contact with an elderly person without his or her permission, including fondling, touching, kissing; forcing the elder to observe sexual acts, rape, or sodomy; spying on the elder in the bathroom or bedroom; and coerced nudity.
- *Neglect:* Careless lack of attention that results in harm. Neglect may be emotional or physical. Examples include withholding medication or necessary medical attention, personal care, food and water, or any basic necessities of life. Abandonment, lack of assistance with mobility, failure to provide adequate diaper changes, and insufficient help with hygiene or bathing also constitute neglect.

Case Law

Judy Quesenberry was an incapacitated 75-year-old female who was being taken care of in her home by her daughter, 42-year-old Peggy Nanette Quesenberry. Judy's sister, Jean Hawks, was concerned for her sister's well-being and notified Adult Protective Services twice. Both times, Adult Protective Services stated that Judy was able to answer their questions appropriately.

Peggy called 911 for her mother in March of 2018 to request help for her mother's shortness of breath. When emergency workers arrived, the conditions were deplorable in the home. Judy was fused to her blanket with urine and feces and her head was stuck to her arm. Judy Quesenberry was admitted to the hospital with dehydration, severe sepsis, pneumonia, respiratory failure, and skin breakdown. Jean was told not to come to the hospital because she should not have to see her sister in that condition. Judy died several days later. An autopsy confirmed the cause of death as neglect and sepsis.

Peggy Quesenberry was arrested and given a psychiatric evaluation. She was sentenced to 10 years in jail for fatally neglecting her mother by Kanawha Circuit Court Judge Tod Kaufman.

The majority of states have enacted legislation addressing elder abuse or abuse of vulnerable adults. The laws generally name a health-care professional as one who reports the abuse, and in some states, it is a requirement to report the suspected abuse. States may protect the reporter of suspected elder abuse from civil and criminal liability. The reporting agency varies in each state but generally is a social or welfare agency, a long-term care facility, or police. Risk factors for elder abuse include advanced age, female gender, dependence on a caregiver, social isolation, behavior problems, and increased physical and mental impairment.

 ETHICS CHECK

Basic considerations when dealing with the abused survivor include the following:

1. Consider the vulnerability to future assault. Providers may feel an ethical obligation and choose to intervene. Such intervention might include questioning the possibility of abuse, discussing safety options, providing a list of community referrals and resources, giving therapeutic support, and documenting the situation for future reference.
2. Respect the survivor's right not to report abuse if this is permissible by law.
3. Remember that both the survivor and the abuser need professional care and have rights protected by law.

Caring for individuals who have been abused is emotionally difficult; requirements for reporting abuse will vary by state. Urban areas have community service agencies, such as rape relief and sexual assault centers. The provider may refer the survivor to such an agency for additional, specialized services. However, if these services are unavailable or the survivor chooses to be treated by the provider alone, information is needed from law enforcement agencies regarding reporting the incident and obtaining, securing, and handling medicolegal evidence.

The survivor should be treated as soon as possible after the injury or assault, not only for the survivor's welfare but also to preserve evidence of possible criminal acts. Rape survivors need to feel supported and cared for and to feel that the violent act will make no difference in how they are treated by people. In certain areas of the country, specially trained nurses called SANE nurses (sexual assault nurse examiner) assess, collect evidence, and assist the victim of a sexual assault.

EVIDENCE

Gathering of evidence is more likely to occur in the emergency department or hospital setting. Situations will arise in the clinic health-care setting, however, in which employees and providers need to be knowledgeable about the methods of proper collection and preservation of evidence. (See Chapter 6, Law for Health Professionals, for an explanation of the trial process.) When in doubt, seek professional guidance from attorneys and the proper authorities.

In the health-care setting, providers may gather legal evidence knowingly or unknowingly. Later they may be asked to offer the evidence or may be subpoenaed to give the evidence. Office and clinic situations in which evidence will be collected include the female child's urinalysis showing sperm, the young boy receiving medical treatment who reveals he has been gang raped, or a client entering with a superficial knife wound. The circumstances just described may involve providers as witnesses in litigation; therefore, proper examination and documentation are essential.

One of the first sources of evidence is documentation in medical records. Malpractice lawsuits are commonly lost because of improper documentation. Specifically, providers must record the time of client arrival; a complete explanation of the client's condition, both physical and emotional; and what was done for the client. Obviously, treatment and care of the client is primary, but documentation in the client's medical record must follow. The written documentation must be clear, concise, complete, and in order.

Evidence may be in the form of a complete written description, x-rays, photographs, clothing, samples for laboratory testing, or samples of foreign objects. Photographs and x-rays are to be dated and labeled with the client's name. Photographs may need a brief description relaying what is pictured. Both x-rays and photographs should be stored in envelopes to protect them when not digitized into the client's medical record. Any objects and clothing must be properly and carefully removed, labeled, and stored. Clothing should not be cut unless necessary and then along seams. Clothing should not be rinsed or washed. In fact, wearing gloves and not handling clothing any more than necessary will avoid changing or damaging evidence. Any body fluids, such as vomitus or gastric washing, should be saved, especially in poisoning cases, for future analysis.

You may be requested by law enforcement to take such client samples as blood; semen; vaginal, oral, or rectal smears; or skin, fingernail, or hair clippings. Samples must be properly labeled and preserved. Every piece of evidence is to be preserved as much as possible and securely stored in a locked place to avoid tampering or loss.

Having only one employee handle all evidence can prevent it from becoming inadmissible because it cannot be properly traced or verified. When giving evidence to the proper authorities, providers should ask for a receipt for their files. They should know to whom they are giving the evidence.

Providers should cooperate with law enforcement authorities who need to talk to the client. The provider and clinic staff should not be overprotective of the client, nor should the client be jeopardized. The authorities need to receive information on the client so that they can begin their investigation immediately.

If a client dies in the health-care facility or arrives deceased, the medical examiner or coroner should be called immediately, and the body should not be touched or removed. Health-care employees should not touch, tamper with, or remove any tubes or paraphernalia from the client. The deceased client should be left as is; otherwise, evidence may be useless to authorities.

GOOD SAMARITAN LAWS

 Good Samaritan laws are laws or acts protecting from liability those who choose to aid others who are injured or ill. Good Samaritan statutes exist in all 50 states, yet their content varies widely with regard to who is protected, the standard of care required, and the circumstances under which protection is provided. The statute itself is a legal doctrine meant to encourage physicians and health-care professionals to render emergency first-aid treatment to accident victims without liability for negligence. In some states, statutes encourage bystanders to get involved in providing potentially life-saving assistance to someone in need without fear of liability for negligence, so long as they act within the scope of their capabilities. The statutes may not apply to an emergency arising in a clinic, hospital, or office where the client–physician relationship exists. However, the scene of an emergency may include the emergency department of the hospital in the event of a medical disaster. Most Good Samaritan laws state that the person administering the aid cannot benefit financially or receive any rewards. In most states, no one, including physicians and health-care professionals, has the legal obligation to render first aid in a life-threatening situation.

Most Good Samaritan statutes merely attempt to protect the physician or health-care professional who gives first aid and acts "in good faith" and "without gross negligence." In some states you must be a Good Samaritan or face a penalty, whereas in others legislation states that physicians must administer emergency treatment to the best of their ability. In most states a professional should not leave an individual during an emergency (1) unless it is to call for assistance, (2) until an equally competent professional is available, or (3) unless it is unsafe to continue.

The majority of Good Samaritan statutes are poorly written and leave many unanswered questions. Not many define the following: What is an emergency? What is care rendered gratuitously? Where and to what extent can care be given and be covered by the statute?

Many health-care professionals are reluctant to render aid in an emergency. Reasons for this attitude may include the laws that are vague, the legal and professional advice to be cautious, and the fear that the situation may require skills outside of one's training and education. The health professional may be as anxious to avoid getting involved as the layperson. The risk for liability, however, has been grossly exaggerated. In some states such as Vermont there is a fine for those who fail to offer such assistance.

Case Law

A patient underwent elective surgery for a total hip replacement. Early during the surgery, the assistant surgeon became so ill he had to lie down on the operating room floor. The hospital called another physician (Dr. Howard), who had his office across the street from the hospital. He canceled his office appointments, came to the hospital, and completed the surgery with the surgeon. After the surgery, the patient suffered complications and sued Dr. Howard.

Outcome: Under the Good Samaritan law in California, the court ruled that Dr. Howard "did not commit any willful act or omission" while assisting the surgeon. Dr. Howard was rendering emergency care in "good faith," which addresses the quality of the intentions and not the quality of the care delivered. Also, Dr. Howard had no preexisting duty of professional care to this patient; the patient was not an established patient of his. This is another requirement of the Good Samaritan law. Further, the court stated that, as a matter of public policy, the Good Samaritan law encourages physicians to respond to emergency requests.

Perkins v Howard, 283 Cal Rptr 764 (1991)

Note: Although this case involves physicians working in a hospital, the legal implications are strong for health-care professionals as well.

Case Law

In *Guerrero v. Copper Queen Hosp.*, *Steffey v. King*, and *Jackson v. Mercy Health Ctr., Inc.* (Georgia, Illinois, and Utah, respectively), the courts have interpreted their state's Good Samaritan statutes as protecting physicians who render emergency medical care in a hospital setting. However, a March 30, 2014, Supreme Court ruling has weakened the protections in Illinois, especially for emergency providers, when an emergency department physician responded to a code in the intensive care unit (ICU) and was accused of negligence for airway management issues when the patient suffered brain damage. The physician's contract stated that he was not to care for non–emergency department patients although he could in "dire" circumstances. He attempted to claim the Good Samaritan defense because his physician group did not bill the patient for services rendered. The Illinois Supreme Court ruled that his response to the code was a part of his expected duties.

Homestar Bank and Financial Services v. Emergency Care Health Organizations, et al. 2014 IL 115526.

All health-care professionals and their employees ought to know their Good Samaritan laws and specifically what and whom they address. Certainly, the legal and ethical ramifications of rendering aid in an emergency should be considered before an emergency presents itself. Although the health-care professional may feel inadequate and unprotected in an emergency, the general public considers such a professional to be far more qualified than any layperson appearing on the scene.

Health-care professionals who do render aid in an emergency must remember to treat within the scope of their training and to give adequate care in light of the circumstances. They also should take comfort in the fact that the chance of a lawsuit is slim.

 For protection from possible liability for performing under the Good Samaritan law, always act on behalf of the victim. Continue to update cardiopulmonary resuscitation (CPR) and first aid classes. Follow your scope of practice (see Chapter 3, The Professional Health-Care Team) and use common sense. Do not do anything you are not trained, educated, or credentialed to do. Do not, under any circumstances, accept gifts or rewards. ●

SUMMARY

The health-care climate of today indicates that hospitals are often full, and emergency departments are overcrowded and understaffed. The result is that many clients turn toward their primary care provider in the health-care setting for treatment that might otherwise be given in the hospital or emergency department. Many births take place in the home or birthing center, placing emphasis on the attending physician or midwife to file the information for the birth certificate. Clients with communicable and reportable diseases are likely first seen in clinic health-care settings. Increasingly, some individuals who are abused or harmed in an abusive situation are less comfortable in the hospital emergency environment than they are with their personal primary care provider. Health-care professionals must be prepared and have the appropriate knowledge and education to provide the best medical care. They must function within legal and ethical guidelines.

Establish policies regarding public duties including the inquiry and reporting process in your clinic. Each employee should know what kind of inquiry to make, how reporting is done, who is responsible, what information is required, and when and where the report is filed. A copy should always be kept for the facility. Be knowledgeable of any community agencies that are available to provide information for the clinic and to provide valuable services for the clients.

 Watch It Now! How do you manage your public responsibilities? At http://FADavis.com, keyword *Tamparo*.

Questions for Review

SELECT THE BEST ANSWER

1. An individual who is required by law to report child abuse is a
   a. Medical reporter.
   b. Good Samaritan.
   c. Mandatory reporter.
   d. Only a and b above.
   e. None of the above.

2. Child abuse includes which of the following?
   a. Physical injury
   b. Sexual exploitation
   c. Psychological harm
   d. Neglect
   e. All of the above

3. All of the following are phases that a rape survivor may experience except
   a. Denial.
   b. Disorganization.
   c. Neglect.
   d. Reorganization.
   e. Recovery.

4. The list of notifiable diseases comes from
   a. The CDC.
   b. Hospitals and medical providers.
   c. VAERS.
   d. American Medical Association.
   e. Only a and b above.

5. Death certificates are
   a. Mandated by law.
   b. Signed by provider in attendance at time of death.
   c. Required before release of body to mortician.
   d. Filed within 24 to 72 hours of death.
   e. All the above.

SHORT ANSWER QUESTIONS

1. Give examples of the five types of IPV.

   _____

   _____

   _____

2. Discuss who may complete and sign a death certificate.

   _____

   _____

   _____

3. Identify where to report an adverse effect from a vaccination.

_____

_____

_____

4. Describe how to report a suspected case of child abuse.

_____

_____

_____

5. An adult client presents with multiple old and new injuries and asks for help. Where would you direct this individual?

_____

_____

_____

CLASSROOM EXERCISES

1. What problems occur when a death certificate remains unsigned?

2. What are the future implications if a birth is not reported?

3. Discuss the premise that global/world vaccinations help to stop the spread of disease into industrialized nations. Are any difficulties associated with global/world vaccinations? With vaccinations in the United States? Explain.

4. Explore agencies in your community for the referral of abused persons and share your findings.

5. The provider gives you an envelope of x-rays and a sealed bag of clothing items and asks you to keep them safe until law enforcement officials arrive. How do you keep them safe? Why is this important?

6. Identify cultures in which abuse (child, intimate partner, adult, elder) is defined differently. For example, consider the following:
   • The use of a belt to spank a child
   • A cultural attitude that recommends circumcision of young girls (removal of clitoris and suturing of the vaginal opening)
   • A culture that severely punishes a rapist but financially and emotionally supports the female survivor or a child born of that rape
   • A culture that kills its infants if they are infirm and there is not enough food and shelter available

7. Under what circumstances might a provider decide not to render emergency aid?

8. Intimate partner violence is a relatively new term. Discuss its relevance with a close friend.

9. Identify advantages and disadvantages of using the term _survivor_ rather than _victim_. Which would you use? Justify your response.

INTERNET ACTIVITIES

1. Visit the website for your state's public health department and find the list of notifiable diseases. Print it for your future reference.

2. Visit the website for two additional states in different regions of the country. Find the list of notifiable diseases. Compare these lists with the list found for your own state. How are they the same or how do they differ?

3. Go to the CDC website and find the VIS for the current year's influenza vaccine.

4. Find the school entry requirements for vaccinations for your state: www.cdc.gov/phlp/publications/topic/vaccinations.html

5. Explore the Internet for the Good Samaritan statutes for your state. What do they provide for? Would you as a medical assistant be covered under this statute?

For additional resources please visit
http://FADavis.com, keyword *Tamparo*.

CHAPTER 8

Consent

"Realize that you always have choices. It's up to you."—Leo Buscaglia (1924–1998); Author, lecturer

KEY TERMS

consent Permission by a client to allow touching, examination, or treatment by medically authorized personnel.

expressed consent Written consent that is signed by the client, provider, and a witness; it is usually for invasive procedures.

implied consent An expression of consent to something through conduct; usually used for routine services.

informed consent Specific guidelines for consent; usually identified by medical practice acts at the state level.

minor A person who has not reached the age of maturity—18 years in most jurisdictions.

    emancipated minor A person younger than 18 years of age who is free of parental care and is financially responsible for himself or herself.

    mature minor A person, usually younger than 18 years of age, who possesses sufficient understanding and appreciation of the nature and consequences of treatment despite chronological age.

uninformed consent Client gives permission to allow touching, examination, or treatment by medically authorized personnel but does not understand what has been consented to.

LEARNING OUTCOMES

Upon successful completion of this chapter, you should be able to:

8.1 Define key terms.

8.2 Explain the legalities of consent.

8.3 Give an example of verbal consent, nonverbal consent, and written consent.

8.4 Compare informed and uninformed consent.

8.5 List the four elements of the doctrine of informed consent.

8.6 Identify the following special situations in consent: minors, spouses and domestic partners, language barriers, clinical research, and when consent is not necessary.

8.7 Discuss the role of the health-care employee in the consent process.

COMPETENCIES

CAAHEP

- Recognize the elements of oral communication using a sender-receiver process. (CAAHEP V.C.5)
- Discuss applications of electronic technology in effective communication. (CAAHEP V.C.8)

ABHES
- Perform risk management procedures. (ABHES 4.e)
- Understand the health-employee's role in records management. (ABHES 8.a)

When Is Informed Consent Really Informed?

A client comes in for a consultation with his surgeon regarding a complicated surgical procedure. After the consultation, the medical assistant asks the client to read and sign the lengthy informed consent. The client states, "Here, just give me that thing to sign. I am *not* going to read all of this."

What are the implications of this action?

In the health-care field, clients have the right to manage their care and treatment. To make the best decisions, clients should be thoroughly informed. Once informed and clients' understanding of the procedure or treatment is determined, they are able to consent for or refuse the treatment or choose other options.

Consent is the voluntary affirmation by clients to allow touching, examination, or treatment by medically authorized personnel. Consent allows clients to determine what will be done with their bodies. For consent to be more than a formality, providers must communicate in a manner that encourages shared decision-making with their clients.

All health-care employees are involved in the consent process with the clients they serve. Although the health-care provider has the primary responsibility to inform clients of proposed treatment and to obtain consent for a procedure, employees are often responsible for having the consent form signed, and clients commonly ask questions of those health-care employees. Consequently, everyone must understand all aspects of consent.

IMPLIED AND EXPRESSED CONSENT

There are two types of consent: implied consent and expressed consent.

Implied consent (sometimes referred to as *general consent*) usually occurs at the time of routine treatment but can also cover emergency circumstances. Consider the following examples:

1. A client calls complaining of a persistent, productive cough. When the receptionist makes the appointment with the provider, the client has given implied consent for examination, which may include throat examination and culture.
2. When a provider requires a blood test for diagnosis and the client comes to the laboratory with a rolled-up shirt sleeve, implied consent is being given.
3. If a client who comes to the clinic suddenly stops breathing during the provider's examination, the provider will take immediate action to restore breathing and preserve life. Consent is implied by law in an emergency situation when a client is unable to give consent. An emergency is said to exist when the client is in immediate danger and action is necessary to save a life or prevent further damage.

Expressed consent is made in writing and usually reserved for surgical or invasive treatments. Consider the following examples:

1. A client is scheduled for a clinic surgical procedure and signs an informed consent form. This action constitutes a medical contract between the client and the provider.
2. A mother signs the consent form to authorize a vaccination for her son.

Expressed consent has been obtained in both circumstances. See Figure 8-1.

CONSENT

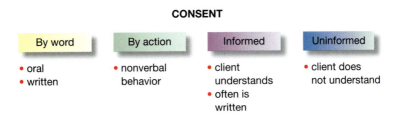

Figure 8-1. The four forms of consent.

INFORMED AND UNINFORMED CONSENT

Because of the many occasions arising in health care involving complicated medical procedures that are often difficult for clients to understand, informed consent is important to give the provider permission to act. To ensure that proper consent is obtained, it usually is put in writing (known as expressed consent).

Informed consent is the communication process between a client and a provider that results in the client's agreement to undergo a particular medical procedure or treatment.

Two underlying reasons for obtaining informed consent are to ensure individual autonomy (the right to be left alone or the right to privacy) and to encourage rational decision-making. Written consent also aids in protecting the provider in cases of malpractice.

Regardless of the type of consent, the ideal is that all consents should be informed where the client understands all facets of the consent including risks and expected outcomes of the medical treatment and/or procedures.

Uninformed consent occurs when clients give permission but do not understand or comprehend what they have consented to.

 Consent is a process, not a mere piece of paper or form to sign. The process implies a two-way communication between client and health-care provider that will maximize the client's participation and ensure full knowledge and understanding of any procedure. Without consent, intentional touching can be considered a criminal offense, such as battery. ●

Integral to consent is the client's belief that the health-care professional to whom consent is given has the knowledge, skill, and ability to perform such tasks. The client has a right to expect that the provider has the ability to determine the need for a throat culture, perform the required surgery, or administer emergency treatment. Likewise, the client can expect the laboratory technician to know proper venipuncture technique.

Case Law

In November of 2007, Megan Shinal met with Dr. Toms to discuss the removal of a benign pituitary tumor. The procedure, risks, and alternatives were discussed. Mrs. Shinal called back later and further discussed the surgery with Dr. Toms' physician assistant. A month later, she met with Dr. Toms' physician assistant for a preoperative workup and signed the informed consent.

Mrs. Shinal had an open craniotomy with total resection of the tumor 2 weeks later. The surgery was complicated by bleeding that resulted in stroke and partial blindness. Ms. Shinal and her husband sued Dr. Toms for malpractice. A claim for lack of informed consent was included in the lawsuit in that Dr. Toms failed to obtain informed consent from Ms. Shinal secondary to the physician assistant obtaining the informed consent. The Court found in favor of Dr. Toms. The case was appealed and included the inability to excuse from the jury anyone insured by or employed by the hospital named in the original complaint.

The Superior Court also found in favor of Dr. Toms. In June of 2017, however, the Supreme Court of Pennsylvania decided that Dr. Toms should have received informed consent as the provider and the Court also allowed for a change in venue and remanded the case back to the lower courts for a retrial.

Shinal v. Toms, No. 31, MAP 2016 (June 20, 2017).

THE DOCTRINE OF INFORMED CONSENT

Informed consent is a client's right to know and understand, before agreeing to, a procedure. It is the provider's sole responsibility to obtain consent from the client, even if other staff members assist in the process. Consent should be obtained in writing because written consent implies an intentional and deliberate decision. Health-care employees must understand their state's doctrine of informed consent laws.

States vary in their consent laws. The American Medical Association recommends the following topics to be included and discussed for informed consent:

1. The client's diagnosis, if known
2. The nature and purpose of a proposed treatment or procedure
3. The risks and benefits of a proposed treatment or procedure
4. Alternatives (regardless of their cost or the extent to which the treatment options are covered by health insurance)
5. The risks and benefits of the alternative treatment or procedure
6. The risks and benefits of not receiving or undergoing a treatment or procedure
7. The expected recovery time for the treatment or procedure

Case Study

To further illustrate the necessary elements of informed consent, consider Viennina, age 75. She speaks primarily Italian and English with a limited understanding of medicine. Viennina suffered a heart attack 1 year ago and is on several medications. She recently had an echocardiogram, which showed a weakened heart muscle. Viennina called her daughter-in-law and informed her that her cardiologist stated that she needed a pacemaker and to bring someone who speaks English with her to her next appointment. Her daughter-in-law, a critical care nurse, immediately started asking questions. Viennina could not answer anything about the recent appointment.

At the second appointment with the cardiologist, the doctor started the visit by speaking above Viennina's comprehension level about her echocardiogram results, laboratory values, and the "pacemaker" procedure. The cardiologist was actually identifying a defibrillator to automatically shock Viennina's heart back to normal should a lethal rhythm be experienced. When Viennina's daughter-in-law questioned the physician, he asked, "Are you a physician?" After discovering she was a nurse, he spoke at an even a higher level of comprehension. When Viennina's lack of comprehension was pointed out to the physician, he replied, "I'm talking to you not her." Viennina looked scared and started to shake. The daughter-in-law did not want to argue with the physician and let the visit end with the full intention of finding a new cardiologist for Viennina.

Have all the points of informed consent for the "pacemaker" been satisfied? Explain your response. How do you rate the shared communication of the doctor and client?

In Viennina's situation (see the previous Case Study), as with most others, all health-care professionals must be sensitive to the impact of such a conversation. For consent to be meaningful, clients may need time to comprehend the essential elements of the consent. This may include talking with family members, seeking a second opinion, considering financial implications, seeking further explanations, or just time to process the circumstances.

Staff members also need to be prepared to clarify, further explain (if possible), or direct additional questions to the provider if the client so indicates. Not until a later time will written consent be obtained and the provider able to proceed. The written consent must reflect each of the elements previously described and should also contain the client's signature, the provider's signature, and the signature of a witness.

It is suggested that providers ask their clients to explain in their own words what they believe is happening. Any language barrier presents special challenges. If a family member is not available to translate, a translator service must be used. The translator service is preferred to ensure true informed consent.

IN THE NEWS
Informed Choice: A Needed Paradigm Shift

In a *Health Affairs* blog in 2019, Sharon Brownlee lamented how frequently individuals agree to treatments that they know little about. She reported that 30% of adults report that they do not always understand their providers, and 70% relay that their providers often do not check their understanding or instructions.

Don Berwick, the lead for health literacy at the Agency for Healthcare Research and Quality, states, "I believe that if we are to overcome the inherent power differential between clinicians and their patients/clients, we need a paradigm shift." Thus, the wording *informed choice* vs. *informed consent*.

Some issues in consent present complicated circumstances for providers. Such an example occurs when Jehovah Witnesses refuse blood transfusions due to their religious belief. All clients and patients have a right to manage their care, but providers can then be faced with life-death circumstances if the only way to save a life during surgery is with a blood transfusion. Consider both the Case Law and the Case Study that follows it.

Case Law

Cindy Werth was expecting twins. Because she was a Jehovah's Witness and had a firm belief in the religion's teaching "that it is a sin to receive blood transfusions," Cindy signed a "Refusal to Permit Blood Transfusion" form as part of her hospital preregistration.

After delivery, Cindy had complications and was experiencing uterine bleeding. She was advised to undergo a dilation and curettage and agreed. Again, she discussed her refusal to allow a blood transfusion with her obstetrician/gynecologist. After being placed under anesthesia and despite the specialist's efforts during surgery, Cindy continued to bleed and was experiencing, among other things, premature ventricular activity and a significant decrease in blood pressure. The anesthesiologist (Dr. Michael Taylor) determined that Cindy needed a blood transfusion to sustain her life. Cindy's obstetrician/gynecologist (OB/GYN) expressed Cindy's refusal of blood transfusions, but the anesthesiologist proceeded anyway stating that it was medically necessary.

The Werths filed a malpractice action, alleging that Dr. Taylor committed battery by performing the transfusion without Cindy's consent. Dr. Taylor moved for summary disposition "because Cindy's refusal was not conscious, competent, contemporaneous, and fully informed."

The trial court found that Cindy's refusals of a transfusion were made when she contemplated "merely routine elective surgery" and not life-threatening circumstances, and that "it could not be said that she made the decision to refuse a blood transfusion while in a competent state and while fully aware that death would result from such refusal." The record apparently reflected "the unexpected development of a medical emergency requiring blood transfusion to prevent death or serious compromise of the patient's well-being." The trial court therefore granted summary disposition in favor of Dr. Taylor.

The Michigan Court of Appeals affirmed the trial court's decision.

Werth v Taylor, 475 N.W.2d 426, 427 (Mich. Ct. App. 1991).

Case Study

A 19-year-old Jehovah's Witness was admitted to the hospital with a gastrointestinal (GI) bleed. Her hemoglobin was 6.6 g/dL; normal hemoglobin for a female is between 12.3 and 15.3 g/dL. She refused to consent for blood products because of religious beliefs. The GI bleed could not be stopped and the patient continued to bleed. The patient's mother was with her and agreed with her refusal to accept blood. When the patient's hemoglobin fell below 4 g/dL, she lost her vision and consented to receive blood. The patient's mother stepped in and refused to allow her daughter to receive blood. The patient again requested blood before she became unresponsive. The patient's mother continued to refuse blood on behalf of her daughter stating that if she was in her right mind, she would never go against her religion.

The hospital sent attorneys to court to plead the patient's case and have a court-appointed legal guardian assigned to make decisions. However, the patient died while the attorneys were still in court.

Should the medical staff have given the patient blood when she first requested it? Explain your response. Are there other religions or cultures that do not allow blood transfusions?

PROBLEMS IN CONSENT

There are other issues to be considered in consent. Consent may be difficult to obtain in the treatment of a **minor**, a person who has not reached the age of maturity, which is 18 years old in most states. In some states, courts recognize two types of minors as being capable of informed consent. **Mature minors** are considered to possess sufficient understanding of treatment they are to receive and its consequences despite their chronological age. **Emancipated minors** have the legal capacity of an adult as indicated by age, maturity, intelligence, training, experience, economic independence, and/or freedom from parental control. In some states, someone who is married or in the military is an emancipated minor. Legal questions of capacity to consent related to both the mature minor and the emancipated minor are considered on a case-by-case basis because not all states recognize mature or emancipated minors.

In most states, minors are unable to give consent for medical care except as described previously or in special cases when minors are pregnant, request birth control or an abortion, have suspected sexually transmitted diseases, have possible problems with substance misuse, or are in need of psychiatric care. In all other situations, the provider or staff should attempt to reach the parents or legal guardians for consent.

Legal implications to consider when treating a minor are as follows:

1. A minor has the right to confidentiality. A 16-year-old who seeks a prescription for birth control pills has the right for that information to be kept confidential.

2. A minor who may legally consent to treatment may not be financially responsible. If the 16-year-old in the first example does not pay when services are given, collecting from parents who have not given their consent may be difficult and breaches confidentiality.
3. A minor's legal guardian may have to be determined—a special problem in the case of divorce and remarriage. If the father of a child is financially responsible, but the child resides with the mother, who may properly give consent for treatment?

Knowledge regarding your particular state's laws regarding minors is important. Also, seek an attorney's recommendations when questions occur regarding a minor's rights.

The law that governs consent is not well defined for minors, and it may be vague or even non-existent with respect to spouses and/or domestic partners. Increased awareness of the rights of women and domestic partners has had a significant impact on the legal system. More advances can be expected in the future. A spouse has the legal right to consent to and receive medical care and treatment without a spouse's approval. Domestic partners also may consent without the other partner's approval.

Case Law

Historically, the father of an unborn child has not had a say in the decisions of a pregnant woman with regard to her unborn child. Author Armin Brott described a father's rights with the following statement: "A woman can legally deprive a man of his right to become a parent or force him to become one against his will." A recently filed lawsuit in Alabama seeks to change this long-held conception about men's reproductive rights.

In 2017, Ryan Magers was informed by his then 16-year-old girlfriend that she was 6 weeks pregnant and wanted an abortion. Ryan Magers failed to convince her to keep the pregnancy and she followed through with the procedure.

The state constitution of Alabama was amended, unrelated to this case, in November of 2018 to recognize a fetus as a legal person from conception.

On February 6, 2019, Ryan Magers filed a wrongful death lawsuit against the women's clinic, clinic staff, and the pharmaceutical company that provided the abortifacient drug. Madison County Probate Judge Frank Barger recognized "Baby Roe" as a person with rights paving the way for the case to be filed. Ryan Magers was named as the representative of "Baby Roe's" estate.

On August 30, 2019, Alabama Madison County Circuit Court Judge Chris Comer dismissed Magers' case, stating that he could not bring a wrongful death claim because it was a "legal abortion." Magers' attorney, J. Brent Helms, anticipated dismissal and is contemplating an appeal stating that "the case may gain traction in the appellate court."

Magers v. Alabama Women's Center for Reproductive Alternatives, LLC., et al., Madison County Circuit Court Case No. 47-2019-900259.00

This case has excited parties on both sides of the abortion debate. Pro-choice groups fear the ramifications of future changes to *Roe v. Wade,* and pro-life parties eagerly await the establishment of a new legal precedent.

Other problems in consent may arise in the case of foster children, stroke clients who cannot communicate, persons who are mentally incompetent (including those in shock and trauma), demented clients, and those temporarily or permanently under the influence of drugs or alcohol. A legal guardian who can give consent may have to be appointed by the courts. The health-care staff must determine who is legally responsible in each case. When there is immediate danger to life and limb, however, the law implies consent for treatment for these individuals without consent from the responsible party.

Language can become a barrier to informed consent. An interpreter may be necessary so that information for consent can be given in a client's native tongue to ensure comprehension. If an interpreter is used, this should be documented on the consent form, and there should be a place for the interpreter's signature.

A number of exceptions to informed consent are particular to each state. Examples include the following:

1. The provider may not need to disclose commonly known risks.
2. The provider may not be responsible for failing to disclose risks when the knowledge might be detrimental to the client's best interest.
3. A provider may not need to disclose risks if the client requests to remain ignorant.

A client has the right to refuse treatment. In some situations, the court appoints a guardian, who then may give consent for the client. This is especially true in the case of minors. Check your state's doctrine of informed consent for specific exceptions and information. Local medical associations also may offer information.

A unique problem surfaces for consent when the client is going to be part of any clinical trial, experimental treatment, or human research. The federal Office for Human Research Protections (OHRP), a branch of the National Institutes of Health, oversees the safety of participants in federally funded research. Each major institution that conducts research also must perform its own audit of client safety and report its results. Audits of "human subject laws," however, reveal a number of problems:

1. Serious adverse reactions to experimental drugs often are not recorded or reported to clients.
2. Clients are coerced into waiving their rights to sue in case of malpractice or serious problems.
3. Clients are placed in trials that are medically inappropriate but that need research subjects.
4. Informed consent is rushed because of the "desperate" nature of a participant's condition.
5. Researchers are allowed to have financial interests in the procedures or drugs that are used, which is in direct violation of federal regulations.
6. Not all benefits, risks, and possible alternatives are adequately explained.

OHRP records and U.S. Food and Drug Administration (FDA) sources say the biggest problems surface at high-volume institutions where the pressure to do research is intense. Both agencies have the power to shut down clinical trials and do so; however, both agencies have limited budgets. Participation in any research places a burden on clients and their families to conduct their own investigation of the research in which they are involved.

 ## IMPLEMENTING CONSENT

Consent forms are prepared for the client's signature. The staff may be responsible for the preparation of specifically designed forms or the procurement of preprinted consent forms. In either case, the form must be understandable, protect the rights of the client, and be broad enough to cover anything contemplated but specific enough to create informed consent. A so-called blanket consent form, which seeks to cover all aspects of client care and is not specific, must be avoided.

Many providers use electronic consent forms (available in more than 3,500 procedures and treatments) that allow them to tailor the form to a specific procedure and a specific client. Some provide space for clients to explain in their own words what they are consenting to.

Care should be given to be certain that all elements of informed consent have been understood by the client before a signature is affixed. The consent form should include an expiration date. In some states, 90 days is the maximum. Another consideration may be allowing a waiting period between consent and administration of the procedure or treatment.

The consent process ought to be concisely documented in the medical record. Some providers tape-record the informed consent process and save the tapes or have a staff member present who signs the consent form also. Others have a checklist for the informed consent interview. Whatever procedures are followed, informed consent should be sought as soon as possible after the need is identified (Fig. 8-2).

A health-care employee may be asked to witness a signature in order to verify that the signature is indeed that of the client. The provider is responsible for the explanation of medical treatment to the client, even though the employee may provide reinforcement through clarification. If the client has any further questions about the treatment or difficulties with the consent form, let the provider know. If the client signs with an X, two witnesses are required. Younger staff members should witness consent forms; this helps ensure the longevity of the witnesses should there be any problems in later years. At least three copies of the signed consent form are necessary—one for the client, one for the medical record, and one for the hospital, if necessary.

INADEQUACY OF CONVENTIONAL CONSENT FORMS

The typical preprinted consent form is often incomplete in that it does not contain all of the topics required. Most of these preprinted forms are fairly generic and vague in order to cover all situations. This inadequacy makes the provider liable for litigation. Increasingly common is the ability in most consent forms to provide a section for write-in comments for the provider to add any additional information or specific items discussed during the consent process.

Also, these forms may be missing some of the required signatures and are easily misplaced or lost. The electronic medical record has decreased this concern today as the paperwork is scanned into the system as soon as it is signed.

 ## IMPROVING THE CONSENT PROCESS

With the growing number of lawsuits due to miscommunication, providers and hospitals are doing more to ensure that the client has been fully informed regarding the proposed procedure. They are now presenting the client with videos and diagrams to ensure that the client is well informed. Providers and hospitals are increasingly using electronic consent forms in the hope that they will more fully meet the requirements for clear, informed consent forms.

These electronic consent forms can be tailored individually for each client. These software programs offer the following options:

1. A comprehensive library of education materials that describe different medical conditions and treatments so that the provider can choose which options meet the diagnosis of each client.
2. Detailed informed consent materials that facilitate a discussion of the given procedure or treatment, including the following:
   a. Description of the procedure for that particular client and their unique condition. These include risks, benefits, treatments, and likely outcomes if there is no treatment.
   b. An expansive collection of anatomical diagrams and images that facilitate the provider's ability to describe the nuances associated with a given condition or procedure.
   c. A wide range of postprocedural care instructions.
   d. A comprehensive library of drug information documents.

Therefore, an individualized consent form tailored directly to that client and his or her specific diagnosis and treatment plan will be developed by the provider and presented to the client. Once discussed and totally understood, the client signs the consent form on a digital pad, and this comprehensive, signed document is printed and saved electronically and automatically noted in the client's electronic medical record.

The Veterans Health Administration has been using these electronic consent forms for several years. When initiating them, Secretary of Veterans Affairs Anthony J. Principi said, "We owe it to our veterans to do all we can to ensure that they understand the care they receive and to make sure

BOTULINUM TOXIN TYPE A
(Botox Cosmetic)

Botox is made from the Botulinum Toxin Type A, a protein produced by the bacteria Clostridium botulinum. For the purpose of improving the appearance of wrinkles, small doses of the toxin are injected into the affected muscles blocking the release of a chemical that would otherwise signal the muscle to contract. The toxin thus paralyzes or weakens the injected muscle. The treatment usually begins to work within 24 to 48 hours and can last up to four months. The Food and Drug Administration (FDA) approved the cosmetic use of Botulinum Toxin Type A for the temporary relief of moderate to severe frown lines between the brow and recommends that the procedure be performed no more frequently than once every three months.

It is not known whether Botulinum Toxin Type A can cause fetal harm when administered to pregnant women or can affect reproduction capabilities. It is also not known if Botulinum Toxin Type A is excreted in human milk. For these reasons, Botulinum Toxin Type A should not be used on pregnant or lactating women for cosmetic purposes.

Patient's
Initials

_____ The details of the procedure have been explained to me in terms I understand.
_____ Alternative methods and their benefits and disadvantages have been explained to me.
_____ I understand that the FDA has only approved the cosmetic use of Botulinum Toxin Type A
for frown lines between the brow. Any other cosmetic use is considered "off-label".
_____ I understand and accept the most likely risks and complications of Botulinum Toxin Type A
injection(s) that include but are not limited to:

- *abnormal and/or lack of facial expression*
- *allergic reaction/violent allergic reaction*
- *disorientation, double vision, and/or past pointing*
- *facial pain*
- *headache, nausea, and/or flu-like symptoms*
- *inability to smile when injected in the lower face*
- *local numbness*

- *paralysis of a nearby muscle, which could interfere with opening the eye(s)*
- *product ineffective*
- *temporary asymmetrical appearance*
- *swallowing, speech, and/or respiratory disorders*
- *swelling, bruising, and/or redness at injection site*

_____ I understand and accept that the long-term effects of repeated use of Botox Cosmetic are as yet
unknown. Possible risk and complications that have been identified include but are not limited to:

- *muscle atrophy*
- *nerve irritability*

- *production of antibodies with unknown effect to general health*

_____ I understand and accept that there are complications, including the remote risk of death or
serious disability, that exist with this procedure.
_____ I have informed the doctor of all my known allergies.
_____ I have informed the doctor of all medications I am currently taking, including prescriptions,
over-the-counter remedies, herbal therapies and supplements, aspirin, and any other
recreational drug or alcohol use.
_____ I have been advised whether I should take any or all of these medications on the days
surrounding the procedure.
_____ I am aware and accept that no guarantees about the results of the procedure have been made
or implied.
_____ I have been informed of what to expect post treatment, including but not limited to:
estimated recovery time, anticipated activity level, and the necessity of additional
procedures if I wish to maintain the appearance this procedure provides me.
_____ I am not currently pregnant or nursing, and I understand that should I become pregnant while
using this drug, there are potential risks, including fetal malformation.
_____ If pre- and postoperative photos and/or videos are taken of the treatment for record purposes, I
understand that these photos will be the property of the attending physician.
_____ I understand that these photos may only be used for scientific or record keeping purposes.
_____ I have been advised to seek immediate medical attention if swallowing, speech, or respiratory
disorders arise.
_____ The doctor has answered all of my questions regarding this procedure.

I certify that I have read and understand this treatment agreement and that all blanks were filled in
prior to my signature.

I authorize and direct _____ , M.D., with associates or assistants of his or her choice,
to perform the following procedure of Botulinum Toxin Type A injection(s) on _____
for the treatment of _____ .   (patient name)
                        (i.e., brow, forehead, "crow's feet," etc.)

_____   _____
Patient or Legal Representative Signature/Date   Relationship to Patient

_____   _____
Print Patient or Legal Representative Name   Witness Signature/Date

I certify that I have explained the nature, purpose, benefits, risks, complications, and alternatives to the
proposed procedure to the patient. I have answered all questions fully, and I believe that the patient
fully understands what I have explained.

                            _____
                            Physician Signature/ Date
_____ copy given to patient   _____ original placed in chart
initial   initial

Figure 8-2. Informed consent forms. **(A)** For a botulinum toxin type A (Botox cosmetic) procedure.
(B) For a flexible sigmoidoscopy surgical procedure. **(C)** For refusal to consent to treatment.

FLEXIBLE SIGMOIDOSCOPY

Flexible sigmoidoscopy involves passing a lighted flexible tube (sigmoidoscope) through the anus into the lower intestinal tract (colon). This procedure allows the practitioner to examine the inside of the lower two feet of the colon. Sometimes small tissue growths (polyps) are removed during the sigmoidoscopy (polypectomy), as polyps can grow inside the colon and become cancerous. Occasionally biopsies (sampling of small pieces of colon) are performed during the sigmoidoscopy. Bleeding sites may be treated during the sigmoidoscopy by injection of sclerosing material or use of electrocautery. On rare occasions, a narrowing or obstruction may be encountered during the sigmoidoscopy. The narrowing may be stretched (dilated) at the time of sigmoidoscopy.

Patient's
Initials

_____ The details of the procedure have been explained to me in terms I understand.

_____ Alternative methods and their benefits and disadvantages have been explained to me.

_____ I understand and accept possible risks and complications include but are not limited to:

- *bleeding*
- *gassy discomfort/bloating*
- *infection*
- *need for surgery*
- *pain*
- *perforation*

_____ I have informed the doctor of all my known allergies.

_____ I have informed the doctor of all medications I am currently taking, including prescriptions, over-the-counter remedies, herbal therapies and supplements, aspirin, and any other recreational drug or alcohol use.

_____ I have been advised whether I should avoid taking any or all of these medications on the days surrounding the procedure.

_____ I am aware and accept that no guarantees about the results of the procedure have been made.

_____ I have been informed of what to expect postoperatively, including but not limited to: estimated recovery time, anticipated activity level, and the possibility of additional procedures.

_____ I understand that any tissue/specimen removed during the surgery may be sent to pathology for evaluation.

_____ The doctor has answered all of my questions regarding this procedure.

I certify that I have read and understand this treatment agreement and that all blanks were filled in prior to my signature.

I authorize and direct _____ , with associates or
(practitioner's name and title, i.e., M.D., N.P., P.A.)

assistants of his or her choice, to perform a flexible sigmoidoscopy on _____ .
(patient name)

I further authorize the physician(s) and assistants to do any other procedure that in their judgment may be necessary or advisable should unforeseen circumstances arise during the procedure.

_____   _____
Patient or Legal Representative Signature/Date   Relationship to Patient

_____   _____
Print Patient or Legal Representative Name   Witness Signature/Date

I certify that I have explained the nature, purpose, benefits, risks, complications, and alternatives to the proposed procedure to the patient or the patient's legal representative. I have answered all questions fully, and I believe that the *patient/legal representative (circle one)* fully understands what I have explained.

_____
Physician Signature/ Date

_____ copy given to patient   _____ original placed in chart
initial   initial

Figure 8-2.—cont'd

Continued

Refusal to Consent to Treatment

I have been advised by Dr. _____ that the following treatment
_____ should be given to me/the below-named patient
(please type or print): _____

Dr. _____ has fully explained to me the nature and
purposes of the proposed treatment, the possible alternatives thereto and the risks
and consequences of not proceeding.

I nonetheless refuse to consent to the proposed treatment.

I have been given an opportunity to ask questions, and all my questions have
been answered to my satisfaction.

I hereby release Dr. _____
and their employees, students, and medical staff from any liability for any ill effects
that I may suffer from failure to perform the proposed treatment.

I confirm that I have read and fully understand the above and that all the
blank spaces have been completed prior to my signing.

_____   _____
Patient or Legal Guardian Signature   Date

_____   _____
Witness   Relationship

I hereby certify I have explained the nature, purpose, benefits, and alternatives
to the proposed treatment and the risks and consequences of not proceeding,
have offered to answer any questions, and have fully answered all such questions.
I believe that the patient/relative/guardian fully understands what I have explained
and answered.

_____   _____
Physician Signature   Date

Note: This document must be made part of the patient's medical records.

Figure 8-2.—cont'd

that the informed consent process is as patient-friendly as possible. This new program is a great
complement to the success of VA's electronic patient records systems."

SUMMARY

Consent may be quite formal, requiring the signature of the client on a form that includes all the
necessary components for informed consent. It may be very informal and implied, requiring no formal signature, and occurs in the routine activities of health care. What is most important, however,
is that any consent be informed. Clients must understand and give permission for any procedures
or tests to be performed. Any confusion or lack of understanding on the part of the client is an
"open door" for difficulties later. Health-care employees must be particularly sensitive to making
certain clients comprehend what is happening.

 Watch It Now! What is your place in the consent process? at
http://FADavis.com, keyword *Tamparo*.

Questions for Review

SELECT THE BEST ANSWER

1. When a client understands all aspects of a consent and signs a consent form, it is considered
   a. Informed consent.
   b. Uninformed consent.
   c. Informed express consent.
   d. Informed implied consent.
   e. None of the above.

2. An emancipated minor is
   a. Someone who lives at home with his parents but is older than 18 years.
   b. Someone who lives at home and is younger than 18 years.
   c. Someone who is younger than 18 years but is married.
   d. Someone who is living at college but is still under their parent's health insurance and the parents pay for their room and board.
   e. Only c and d above.

3. When creating a consent form, most states require which of the following?
   a. Name of the procedure
   b. The possible risks involved
   c. Any alternative procedures or treatments
   d. All of the above
   e. None of the above

4. In an uninformed consent, the client has done the following:
   a. Read the consent form
   b. Read, understood, and signed the consent form
   c. Read, not understood, but signed the consent form
   d. Only a and c above
   e. Only b and c above

5. With regard to clinical trials or human research, which of the following often occur?
   a. Clients are often desperate to get into a clinical trial and so will consent to anything.
   b. Clients are placed into inappropriate trials where there is a need for more subjects.
   c. Clients are usually coerced into waiving their rights to sue for any damages during the trial.
   d. All of the above.
   e. None of the above.

SHORT ANSWER QUESTIONS

1. Define the following terms: informed consent, uninformed consent, implied consent, and expressed consent.

   _____

   _____

   _____

2. Describe the situations in which a minor could be considered emancipated.

   _____

   _____

   _____

3. What documentation is needed when obtaining informed consent from a client who does not speak English?

_____

_____

_____

4. During an emergency, is it necessary to obtain consent before giving life-saving treatment? Why or why not?

_____

_____

_____

5. What role does the health-care employee have in signing as a witness on the consent form?

_____

_____

_____

CLASSROOM EXERCISES

1. Jerod Hilton has just been informed that he has prostate cancer. His provider says that the only recommended course of treatment is surgery. Jerod has no hesitation in his response and immediately says, "No way doc, you aren't cutting me down there." After further discussion, Jerod's decision is unchanged. What steps, if any, might the doctor take?

2. The parents of a 6-year-old child consented to allow her to undergo "routine cardiac tests." One of the tests performed was a catheter arteriogram in which complications occurred. Questioning of the parents revealed that they did not fully understand the risks involved. What are the legal implications of this consent? Identify potential problems in this situation.

3. A 15-year-old boy enters your clinic requesting treatment for scalds received on his hand while emptying the dishwasher at his place of employment. Although his family receives medical treatment at the clinic, you are uncertain about seeing him without his parents' knowledge. Can he consent to treatment? What are the legal ramifications?

4. How specific should a consent form be? How general? Explain.

5. When you are asked to witness a signature, what does it legally mean?

6. An unmarried pregnant client requests an abortion. Assuming the abortion is legal, what rights, if any, does the father have in consent? Do you agree? Justify your reasoning.

7. After a client signed a consent form and you have witnessed it, he states, "I think this is the right decision." What would you reply? What would you do?

8. Detail what role medical assistants may assume in the consent process.

INTERNET ACTIVITIES

1. Search the website of the American Medical Association (AMA) regarding informed consent.

2. Go to the governmental website of your own state and find the rules and regulations regarding informed consent.

For additional resources please visit
http://FADavis.com, keyword *Tamparo.*

Workplace Issues

CHAPTER 9

Medical Records

"Do not put your faith in what statistics say until you have carefully considered what they do not say."

—William W. Watt; Writer and author

KEY TERMS

continuous positive airway pressure (CPAP) Small electrical pump that delivers pressurized air through a nasal mask. Used to prevent airway from closing while sleeping, leading to sleep apnea.

degauss To demagnetize. A computer reads stored information magnetically. If information is demagnetized (degaussed), the information is scrambled beyond recognition and cannot be read or reconstructed.

electronic health record (EHR) Combination of a client's care from multiple sources (in electronic format).

electronic medical record (EMR) Computerized version of a client's medical chart in a single clinic or facility.

Evaluation and Management (E&M) A set of codes used to identify a clinic visit rendered by a health-care provider.

Health Information Technology for Economic and Clinical Health (HITECH) Act This law extends the Health Insurance Portability and Accountability Act (HIPAA) data privacy and security regulations to support business associates, such as billing companies, accounting firms, and others.

Holter monitor A device worn by a client to monitor the electrical activity or rhythm of the heart over a certain period of time.

Institute of Medicine (IOM) An organization that gives advice regarding government policies that affect public health.

meaningful use Minimum government standards established for electronic health records in 2009 outlining how client data is shared with health-care providers and insurance companies.

microfilm Method of filing data on film using minute images.

Office of the National Coordinator (ONC) of Health Information Technology Supports the adoption of health information technology and promotes nationwide health information exchange; part of the U.S. Department of Health and Human Services.

practice management system Software to assist health-care professionals in recording client demographics, perform billing procedures, generate reports, and schedule appointments.

problem-oriented medical record (POMR) A comprehensive approach for organizing a health record based on client problems.

protected health information (PHI) Individually identifiable health information that is transmitted or maintained in any medium, including oral statements.

purge A cleansing or clearing away; refers to the clearing away of old medical records that are no longer being used.

SOAP/SOAPER A charting method using subjective and objective data for client assessment and planning, education, and response.

source-oriented medical record (SOMR) A conventional approach for organizing health record sources of data, including health-care personnel and medical departments.

telehealth A broad collection of electronic and communication technologies that support health-care delivery and services from a distance.

telemedicine The use of electronic and communication technologies to provide medical care from a distance.

telemonitoring An electronic observance of activity; in medicine, the monitoring of a client's health status.

LEARNING OUTCOMES

Upon successful completion of this chapter, you should be able to:

9.1   Define the key terms.
9.2   List six purposes of medical records in the ambulatory health-care setting.
9.3   Describe two methods of organizing a medical record.
9.4   Describe *SOAP/SOAPER* and its use in medical records.
9.5   Compare/contrast electronic medical records and electronic health records.
9.6   Discuss the use of practice management systems in clinic health care.
9.7   Demonstrate by example how and when to correct an error in medical records.
9.8   Discuss the impact of the Healthcare Insurance Portability and Accountability Act (HIPAA) on medical records.
9.9   Describe at least five guidelines for keeping client information private in medical records.
9.10 Outline the process to follow when a subpoena or court order is received for records.
9.11 Describe guidelines for the use of telecommunications in health-care settings.
9.12 Discuss the impact of telehealth and telemedicine on health-care access and client–provider communication.
9.13 Explain the ownership of medical records.
9.14 Discuss retention and storage of medical records.
9.15 Discuss purging of medical records.
9.16 List the required information needed on a release of information form.

COMPETENCIES

CAAHEP

- Discuss applications of electronic technology in professional communication. (CAAHEP V.C.8)
- Identify methods of organizing the patient's medical record based on problem-oriented medical record and source-oriented medical record. (CAAHEP VI.C.5)
- Differentiate between electronic medical records (EMR) and a practice management system. (CAAHEP VI.C.8)
- Explain meaningful use as it applies to EMR. (CAAHEP VI.C.12)
- Utilize an EMR. (CAAHEP VI.P.6)

ABHES

- Institute federal and state guidelines when releasing medical records or information; and entering orders in and utilizing electronic health records. (ABHES 4.b)
- Navigate electronic health records systems and practice management software (ABHES 7.b)

The creation and care of medical records require careful attention from the health-care staff. Both employees and providers collect and enter data into clients' medical records. Medical records are a part of every person's life, beginning with the birth certificate and ending with the death certificate.

With increased health awareness, clients are more concerned about what goes into their medical records. Clients also care who has access to their records. Are the records legal documents? Are they confidential? What authorization is required to release clients' medical records? Who owns them? HIPAA regulations (see Chapter 4, State and Federal Regulations) and case law provide guidelines for health-care facilities and employees addressing these common questions.

Medical records serve as a central repository for planning client care and documenting communication between the client, the primary care provider (PCP), and other health professionals contributing to that care. A medical record that is accurate, complete, and concise fosters quality and continuity of medical care.

This chapter considers medical records specifically in the clinic setting and discusses the various state statutes that apply to medical records, including access, retention, and destruction.

PURPOSE

The medical record in any health-care setting serves many purposes, including the following:

1. Providing a base for managing client care that includes initiating, diagnosing, implementing, and evaluating
2. Providing interoffice and intraoffice communication of client-related data
3. Documenting total and complete health care from birth to death
4. Allowing patterns to surface that will alert providers of clients' needs
5. Serving as a legal basis for evidence in litigation and to protect the legal interests of clients and providers
6. Providing clinical data for education and research

MEDICAL RECORD DOCUMENTATION AND ORGANIZATION

A medical record is established at the first encounter between a health-care provider and a client. It chronicles each interaction thereafter between the client and any member of the clinic's staff. The organization of the medical record will vary depending on the health-care setting. Specialists who see the client only once may have an abbreviated form of the medical record. By contrast, a health-care provider who has had the same client for 30 years may have the equivalent of three file folders with several hundred pages of medical data on that client. Policies of the clinic may also influence the organization of documentation, but all medical records usually contain the same information (Fig. 9-1).

DOCUMENTATION

Documentation in the medical record facilitates the diagnosis and treatment of clients, ensures client safety, reduces medical errors, promotes clinical coordination and management, and serves as legal documents in risk management issues. Documentation must include the date, time, details of each encounter (in a nonjudgmental manner), and signature of the health-care professional who took part in the encounter. A common documentation style used in most clinic health-care settings is SOAP or SOAPER.

SOAP/SOAPER—subjective, objective, assessment, plan, education, and response—is a common method of documenting within a medical record. The format is as follows.

- *Subjective* includes what the subject or client says, family comments, and hearsay; the client's exact words are recorded.
- *Objective* includes events that are directly observed or measurable, including laboratory tests, radiograph results, and physical examination findings.

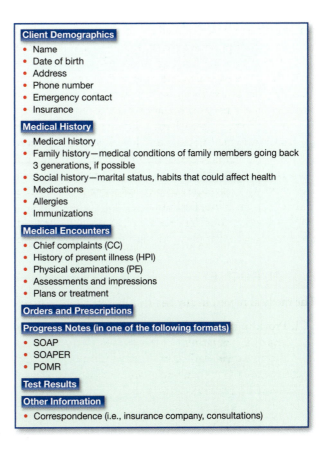

Client Demographics
- Name
- Date of birth
- Address
- Phone number
- Emergency contact
- Insurance

Medical History
- Medical history
- Family history—medical conditions of family members going back 3 generations, if possible
- Social history—marital status, habits that could affect health
- Medications
- Allergies
- Immunizations

Medical Encounters
- Chief complaints (CC)
- History of present illness (HPI)
- Physical examinations (PE)
- Assessments and impressions
- Plans or treatment

Orders and Prescriptions

Progress Notes (in one of the following formats)
- SOAP
- SOAPER
- POMR

Test Results

Other Information
- Correspondence (i.e., insurance company, consultations)

Figure 9-1. Contents of a medical record.

- *Assessment* includes the provider's evaluation based on the subjective and objective data (S + O = A).
- *Plan* includes the treatment(s) prescribed and the actions taken.

Some providers add two additional letters to the SOAP note, thus producing a SOAPER note:

- *Education* includes any health-related teaching or education given to the client.
- *Response* includes the client's understanding of the education and care given.

An example of medical documentation in the SOAP/SOAPER format is shown in Figure 9-2.

Each time the client is seen an entry (regardless of its style) is created by the provider, who either keys the information into the record at the time of the encounter or dictates the information to be transcribed by an employee. Whatever method of documenting is used in medical records, it must be concise, complete, clear, and in chronological order.

ORGANIZATION

There are several methods for organizing the medical record. One common method organizes data by client problems; another uses health-care personnel or sources of documentation to organize the record. This organization can be used in records kept totally on paper or electronically.

The **problem-oriented medical record (POMR)**, developed by Dr. Lawrence L. Weed, is a comprehensive approach to organizing a medical record focused on documenting and accessing client data based on client problems. A client problem is more than a diagnosis. It can be a condition or a behavior that results in physical or emotional distress or interferes with the client's functioning. Examples include pain in the knees and ankles, fear of falling, decreased appetite, and even an inability to pay medical bills. In a paper medical record, the client's problem list is usually numbered and appears early in the record often on the chart face sheet. In an electronic medical record

CALCANEO, Henry. R. 08/18/19--

Date of Onset	Date Recorded	PROBLEM LIST	Date Resolved	INACTIVE PROBLEMS
?	10/08/2---	1. Increased appetite, increased thirst	10/21/2---	
05/28/2---	06/30/2---	2. Dyspnea	07/10/2---	
05/11/2---	08/21/2---	3. Loss of job		

10/08/---

1. Increased appetite, increased thirst

S: "I eat all the time and never gain weight." "I didn't think about it, but yes, I drink water all the time, too."

0: BP 120/88. T-R-P: 98 degrees F--80--18. Color good. Skin turgor adequate. Wt. 5# less than 3 weeks ago. Urine, 4+ sugar. FBS positive.

A: Uncontrolled diabetes; in family history.

P: Dx: Lab workup for diabetes. Tx: Begin on insulin; diabetic diet.

E: Instructed to enroll, attend next diabetic class; taught importance of diet, exercise, insulin injections. Gave our 3 clinic-prepared brochures on diabetes (intro material). Gave 24 hr phone line to call if questions.

R: Seems to understand importance of learning about diabetes, injections, diet, exercise as 2 in family have disease. Asked good questions. **MHL**

7/10/---

2. Dyspnea

S: "I can't seem to get my breath. I'm weak all the time. It's worse when I lay down."

0: BP 180/98. T-R-P: 99 degrees F--88--26. Chest x-ray negative. States he "awakens from sleep with respiratory distress." Cough; slight edema.

A: Congestive heart failure, left sided. History of hypertension and diabetes.

P: Hospitalize for cardiac workup.

E: Explain necessity of hospitalization.

R: States "I really don't want to go but if it'll help me breathe better, I'll do anything! I can't take this much more. It scares me." **MHL**

7/10/---

3. Loss of Job

S: "What can I do now? I'm not trained for anything but construction, and with this heart problem and diabetes, I'll never get back my old job."

0: Heart condition improved; wt. gain 30#; brittle diabetic.

A: Is most upset that current job is not available as it's THE only job he wants. Money apparently not the issue. Off diabetic diet.

P: Return to diabetic classes w/spouse and son. Refer to Social Worker to discuss job situation.

E: Reviewed possible complications if unsuccessful in managing his diabetes. Talked about wt gain and what it means for diabetes.

R: Good interaction w/pt; willing to attend classes w/family; concerned about complications and said he wanted to prevent any, especially since one diabetic in family is nearly blind. **MHL**

Figure 9-2. Example of problem-oriented medical record (POMR) charting in the SOAPER format.

(EMR), problems serve as a filter to connect documentation from various health-care profession-als and problem-specific data from physical examinations, medical history, diagnostic tests, and a client's subjective information.

POMRs are especially beneficial when caring for clients with complex and chronic medical issues and illnesses requiring multiple treatment methods adjusted over time. This organizational system allows the PCP to make clinical decisions based on easily accessible and pertinent data related to a problem. The POMR in an electronic record integrates links to current research or evidence focused on identified problems. This quick literature access is a valuable asset to providers in making informed decisions about a client's health problems.

A **source-oriented medical record (SOMR)** is organized by the individuals and departments involved in the client's care. Individual sources of client data may come from physicians, medi-cal assistants and nurses, other health-care professionals, and department sources frequently include laboratory, radiology, and other specialties. Client data from each source are maintained in separate sections of the medical record.

This conventional and often cumbersome method of organizing a medical record expedites filing of loose reports in a paper medical record where all documents are placed in chronologi-cal order within the respective department or provider section. It provides the PCP with access to department-specific data such as laboratory results when making clinical decisions. Within EMRs, organization by source frequently integrates problem-oriented results to improve clinical decisions. For example, when a health-care professional reviews a specific source in the medical record, the computer program may highlight a relationship between that data and data from other sources.

Whether paper or electronic, all medical records must be organized so that client data and docu-mentation from various providers can be used to evaluate a client's condition, design an appropriate treatment plan, and evaluate outcomes from therapies. The method used to organize the medical record may vary, but all records must be accurate and easily accessible to health-care professionals involved in the client's care.

ELECTRONIC MEDICAL AND HEALTH RECORDS

Computerized records contain the same information found in a paper medical record, except in a digitalized format. These medical records include both the electronic medical record and the elec-tronic health record. The **electronic medical record (EMR)** is a computerized version of a client's medical chart from a single clinic or facility. EMRs contain information collected by and for the providers in the clinic and are used for diagnosis and treatment.

The **electronic health record (EHR)** is inclusive of client data and treatment plans from multiple sources, such as a primary care clinic, hospital, pharmacy, and rehabilitation facility. EHRs con-tain information from all health-care providers involved in the client's care and allows all author-ized health-care professionals to access information from other providers in the provision of the client's care so long as the software systems from the various providers are able to communicate. Any provider seeing a client maintains a medical record. If the clinic is associated with a larger health system, the clinic's EMR often becomes part of an EHR when services from other sources, such as radiology, laboratory, pharmacy, and specialists, are incorporated.

By the early 2000s, converting medical documents to electronic records was accepted nationally and the **Office of the National Coordinator (ONC) of Health Information Technology** was created. The goals focused on improving public safety, reducing medical errors, increasing access to vital client data, providing point-of-care alerts to improve care decisions, and enhancing clients' access to their **protected health information (PHI)** and medical record. The **Institute of Medicine (IOM)** Committee on Data Standards for Patient Safety published in 2003 essential functions of an EMR to improve the quality of care and client safety. Functions were developed as guidelines to standard-ized EMR functionality. The suggested functions are as follows:

1. Health information and data—complete client demographics and past medical history, includ-ing medications and allergies. This information should be arranged in a user-friendly display.

2. Order management—capability of ordering tests and prescriptions. This will eliminate lost orders, handwriting discrepancies, and other ordering mistakes.

3. Result management—all testing is computerized and more readily available to the provider. This quick return of results allows the provider to quickly treat the client, if needed, for abnormal test results.

4. Decision support—information should be accessible to aid providers in their decision making. Some examples of topics covered in this area are drug interactions, allergies, and management of diseases and symptoms.

5. Client support—instruction sheets and treatment plans are readily available for clients. This area also includes **telemonitoring** that could include such information as monitoring a client's electrocardiogram while the client is wearing a **Holter monitor**.

6. Administrative processes and reporting—scheduling, billing, referrals, authorizations, and other administrative tasks need to interact with the medical record so that payment can be realized.

7. Electronic communication and connectivity—information would be accessible between all providers including PCPs, specialists, hospitals, and pharmacies. This type of information is an area that has not been perfected. (Further initiatives have been put into place to address this functionality and are introduced later in this chapter.)

8. Reporting and population health—this function would automate mandatory reporting to governmental agencies.

IN THE NEWS

The Department of Veterans Affairs (VA) was quick to implement EHRs. In 1994, a health information system was deployed across all veteran care sites in the United States. The Veterans Health Information Systems and Technology Architecture (VISTA) currently provides clinical, administrative, and financial functions for over 1,700 VA hospitals and clinics to service nearly 9 million veterans by 180,000 health-care professionals.

The path to full and successful implementation was difficult, however. For decades, the VA and Department of Defense (DOD) struggled to achieve interoperability and seamless sharing of medical record and PHI between health systems. After a complex development process and multiple delays, the VA's new EHR system, Electronic Health Record Modernization (EHRM), is currently being implemented. The 10-year period of this full transition is to end in 2028. The system uses a cloud-based server to interface with and unify all VA and DOD facilities. EHRM will provide veterans and clinicians with a full medical history of any service member receiving care as an active member and/or any care received as a veteran at VA facilities.

In 2009, the **Health Information Technology for Economic and Clinical Health (HITECH) Act** provided funding to health-care providers who implemented EHRs that met "meaningful use" criteria. **Meaningful use** was defined by the U.S. government as the use of a certified, digital health record in a meaningful manner that provided for the electronic exchange of health information to improve the quality of care. The focus was on technology that

- Improved the quality, safety, and efficiency of health care
- Reduced health disparities
- Engaged clients and families in health-care decisions
- Improved care coordination
- Improved population and public health
- Maintained privacy and security protection for PHI

More than $30 billion in subsidies were granted to medical clinics and hospitals nationwide to assist with the implementation of electronic records. By 2010, more than 50% of office/clinic-based providers had implemented an EMR. Members of the American Medical Informatics Association (AMIA) began evaluating the consequences of rolling out new health-care technology so quickly and proposed a national database to track reports of deaths, injuries, and near misses linked to issues with new electronic record software and technologies. Unfortunately, the national database did not occur and in 2011 reports of serious problems with EHR systems began to surface. Thousands of deaths, injuries, and near misses tied to software glitches, user errors, and other system flaws were reported.

IN THE NEWS

Annette Monachelli, a 47-year-old woman in Vermont, experienced pain that radiated from the top of her head and got worse when she moved. She saw her PCP twice about the problem in November 2012 but received no relief. Two months later she was dead from a brain aneurysm, a condition not tested for or diagnosed until she arrived at the emergency department days before her death. Although her medical record indicated that the PCP had considered an aneurysm and had ordered a head scan through the clinic's software system, the test was never done because the order never transmitted. The scan might have caught the bleeding in Monachelli's brain early enough for treatment.

Federal Investigation

This incident led to a federal investigation in 2015 that identified several errors in the EHR system made by eClinicalWorks (eCW). This software offered multiple ways to order a laboratory test or diagnostic image, but not all options functioned properly and alerts for potential complications did not work with any provider's customized order. Additionally, the eCW system failed to use standardized drug, laboratory, and diagnostic codes, which created confusion for health-care professionals and limited the transmission of data.

In May 2017, eCW paid a $155 million settlement instead of going to court. Despite the settlement, the company denies any wrongdoing, and is still selling EMR and EHR software to medical clinics in the United States, with 850,000 health-care professionals currently using the system. This situation is not unique to eCW, but is just one example of the many deaths, injuries, and near misses caused by software errors associated with various electronic software manufacturers.

Over the past decade, manufactures of EHRs/EMRs, health-care providers, federal health-care policy experts, and congressional members have fought over regulations. Arguments, including how to collect EHR-related injury data, who has the power to require data reporting, who should pay for it, and whether findings should be made public, have been the forefront of expert commissions, federal information technology (IT) panels, and medical association reports. Future regulations and case law changes will have an impact on the functionality and use of EHRs/EMRs. Regulations and new electronic records will also affect the practices of health-care professionals and the policies and procedures of clinics and hospitals that use computerized client records.

ADVANTAGES OF THE EMR AND EHR

Standards for EMR and EHR software programs and certification requirements help health-care providers purchase well-constructed, functional, and secure software programs. Records that meet meaningful use and certification requirements improve continuity of care, enhance disease surveillance, promote advancements in medical treatments, and reduce health-care costs. Additional advantages of electronic records include the following:

- *Updated information and accessibility:* The medical record is available at the client point of care and tests or diagnostic results are directly electronically imported, allowing the provider easy access to up-to-date client data.

- *Safety for the client:* Prescription errors are reduced significantly by e-prescribing, which alerts providers of any allergies or interactions. All medical information is organized and easily located. Chart notes are easily read because they are now typed and not handwritten. Health maintenance screenings can be prompted for appropriate age and gender and are easily tracked.
- *Better client care:* EMRs provide alerts and notices to better practice guidelines, allowing professionals to provide the most current standard of client care. Appropriate client instruction sheets can be generated either by print or e-mail. Drug recalls can be easily processed and clients quickly notified.
- *Efficiency and savings:* Electronic messaging systems within the EHR make communication between the PCP and other health-care professionals (clinic staff, consultants, pharmacies, and insurance carriers) an easy and efficient task. Savings are realized using templates for clinic visits that reduce the time needed for any medical scribes or transcriptionists. At the completion of the visit, the EMR generates an appropriate suggestion of an **Evaluation and Management (E&M)** code based on the documentation. EMRs encourage more detailed documentation leading to more accurate and often higher coding and reimbursement levels.

VIGNETTE

A Day in the Life of the Electronic Health Record

You are a 65-year-old woman going to a large multicare health setting for an annual physical examination. When your appointment was made, it was noted that your PCP prescribed fasting laboratory tests, a mammogram, and dermatology screening. You explain that you also need a follow-up visit at the sleep clinic. All appointments are scheduled for 1 day. When you arrive, you go first to the laboratory for the blood draw and urinalysis. Then you have time for breakfast in the clinic's café before you see your PCP.

When you are in the examination room, the PCP reviews your laboratory results from that morning on the computer. The computer is turned toward you so you are able to see today's results on a spreadsheet with the last 2 years' results for comparison. Discussion follows. Your next stop is for a mammogram. The results of that test will be mailed to you. You hasten on to the sleep center, where the specialist discusses your **continuous positive airway pressure (CPAP)** registry that shows on his computer how many hours a night you have successfully used the breathing apparatus. He comments that your PCP indicates in today's documented notes that you are using a new mask and nasal pillow system that you purchased on the Internet.

The final day's visit is to dermatology, where you receive a full body screening for any changes in your freckles, moles, and aging spots. A suspicious mole on your lower cheek causes the dermatologist concern. The mole is removed and a biopsy taken, and you will be notified of the results. The dermatologist says, "I looked at your medical record; you've had a long day! Are you ready to go home now?"

Although the health-care system remains a disconnected patchwork of electronic health data instead of the envisioned integrated network of health information, EMRs and EHRs are present in over 96% of health-care facilities today. All professionals using an electronic record have several opportunities to ensure that the PHI remains accurate, secure, and readily available to manage client health needs:

- *First, do not assume the EHR is working properly.* Take appropriate steps to validate data, ensure timely follow-up on tests that are ordered, and inquire directly about services or products that appear delayed. If client data are missing in the EHR, tell the health-care provider and assist in finding the data.
- *Second, avoid "workaround."* Finding a process that eliminates steps may seem more efficient, but workarounds override potentially life-saving medical alerts. Use the EHR as designed,

implement clear plans when updates are required or the system will be down temporarily, improve EHR training, and promote error reporting.

- *Finally, remember that the EHR does not replace clinical judgment.* Any health-care professional is tasked with multiple responsibilities. Do not allow the computer to make you complacent. Data and information that raises an eyebrow should be verified or rechecked, and reported to the PCP.

PRACTICE MANAGEMENT SYSTEMS

In addition to the EMR and EHR, there is computer software used to manage health-care practices. A medical **practice management system** is health-care software to manage day-to-day operations of a clinic such as appointment scheduling, billing, and other administrative tasks. This management system may contain demographic information, client health histories, and billing content, but it is *not* part of the medical record.

A practice management system enhances clinic staff efficiency. When scheduling appointments, the electronic software keeps multiple health-care provider schedules up-to-date so that client appointments can be easily scheduled around other activities and responsibilities. The system can also send automated e-mail and text messaging appointment reminders to minimize cancellations and no-show appointments. Practice management systems may also assist with organizing client data, billing and claims processing, and reporting data pertinent to the clinic. Comprehensive data reporting may include how often a client does not show for an appointment, how long staff spend on particular tasks, how quickly payers reimburse claims, and how the clinic performs against meaningful use and interoperability objectives.

Similar to the EMR and EHR, a practice management system can assist health-care professionals in improving efficiency and quality health care to clients, but it is only a software system. Therefore, you must be diligent to ensure that data are accurate and secure, and any errors are identified, corrected, and reported appropriately.

LEGAL ASPECTS OF THE MEDICAL RECORD

Medical records, whether paper or electronic, are legal documents containing PHI and are subjected to state and federal regulations related to confidentiality and release of information. Records may also be a vital piece of evidence in a malpractice case. Medical records that are relevant, accurate, legible, timely, informative, and complete protect the rights of the client as well as the health-care professionals employed in the clinic.

CONFIDENTIALITY

As seen in Chapter 4, HIPAA and other state regulations require all health-care professionals managing records to protect the privacy of clients unless otherwise mandated by law. PHI must be kept private by both clinic employees and nonclinic personnel who have access to the electronic record.

The HITECH Act extends HIPAA data privacy and security regulations to business associates, such as billing companies, accounting firms, and others. HITECH allows states to prosecute any individuals who have access to PHI whether or not they are in the health-care setting. HITECH established that these "business associates" would face the same penalties as health-care providers.

EMR and EHR platforms provide a secure, care-focused system to maintain PHI, but individuals using the system must be compliant with HIPAA regulations. The following computer guidelines to ensure confidentiality are important when instituting electronic records and fall under HIPAA guidelines:

- Computer hardware, servers, and network hubs are to be kept secure from intrusion.
- A list of users approved to access medical information must be identified and regularly updated.
- Robust firewalls and antivirus measures must be in place. Blocking of unauthorized intrusion must be a high priority.

- Passwords are to be changed at least every 90 days and created so that they are not easily guessed.
- Passwords are hidden when entered and are securely stored. They are not to be shared with anyone.
- The computer station should limit the number of invalid attempts to access information.
- Computer screens are to be out of view of the public and unauthorized staff.
- Screen savers should be used to prevent unwanted viewers' access.

Ideally, any time a computer workstation is vacated, even for a short period, the user should close out of the document, allowing the screen saver to activate. Upon returning, the user will again need to enter the protected password for access to the medical information.

RELEASE OF INFORMATION

Under HIPAA, clients must grant written consent or permission to provide or disclose their PHI (electronic or paper format) for any reason. A *release of information* signed by the client gives the provider the authority required to release certain medical information. Most clinics have created their own release of information form that a client must sign.

A release form includes the client's name, date of birth, and other demographic information. It authorizes the provider or clinic (specifically named) to release the medical record to a specific entity, which may be a clinic, provider, lawyer, or other specified individual. The form must include a portion that asks specifically if the client wants information to be released concerning the following topics: substance misuse, psychiatric or mental health issues, or HIV/AIDS testing and counseling. The client signs and dates the form that is then signed by a witness and placed into the medical record. To be legal, a clinic should have a form with an original signature; no faxes or e-mailed copies should be accepted. The medical record is then reviewed by providers, and upon their approval, the staff may release only the information specified in the request (Fig. 9-3).

Laws regulate who may sign a release of information form for clients who are underage or unable to sign for themselves:

- If the client is a minor, the parent or legal guardian may sign.
- If the parents are legally separated or divorced, the parent who has legal custody of the minor must sign all release forms.
- If the client is incompetent, the court-appointed guardian signs the release form.
- If the client is deceased, the legal representative of the estate signs the release form.

ERRORS IN MEDICAL RECORDS

If an error is made in a medical record, it must be properly corrected. Handwritten errors discovered later should be corrected by the following method: draw a line through the error using a red pen, write "correction" or "error," sign your initials, indicate the date, and write in the correction. When making a correction in an electronic entry, the original entry is not deleted. Instead the correction is entered with the current date and time, reason for making the change, and the individual making the change identified. If a hard copy of the EMR was printed, the hard copy must be corrected using the handwritten error correction process.

For both paper and electronic records, the original and the corrected data must be legible. When erasures or obliterations occur, confusion and suspicion may result. Poor or altered records can be detrimental to the provider's defense in court.

Health-care professionals will also want to remember that the medical record might be as valuable for what it does not say as for what it does say. "An act not recorded is generally considered an act not performed" by most courts of law. The necessity of using a medical record in a court emphasizes the importance of accurate records that honestly reflect the client's course of treatment. Some clinics do periodic audits of their charts to ensure good charting practices.

AUTHORIZATION TO RELEASE INFORMATION

Please Print Clearly

Name _____
           (Last)   (First)   (M.I.)

Address _____
           (Street)   (City)   (State)

Phone _____ Date of Birth _____ Medical Record# _____

I authorize _____ to release medical information from my medical record to

Name of Doctor, Hospital, etc. _____

Address _____

City/State/Zip Code _____

for the purpose of review/examination. I further authorize you to provide such copies thereof as may be requested. The foregoing is subject to such limitation as indicated below:

☐ Entire record

☐ Specific information: _____

☐ Old records from previous physicians: _____

I give special permission to release any information regarding: (initial on applicable line(s) below)

_____ Substance Abuse _____ Psychiatric/Mental Health Information _____ HIV information

Reason for request _____

This authorization will automatically expire 90 days from the date signed. I understand that I may revoke this content at any time except to the extent that action has been taken in reliance thereon.

Signed _____ Date _____

Witness _____ Date _____

FOR OFFICE USE ONLY

Received _____ Completed By _____

Completed _____ Fee Paid _____

Amount Billed $ _____ Amount Due _____

Disclosure Consisted Of _____
_____
_____
_____

Name

Date: _____

Re: _____

Record #/Date of Birth _____

This is a multiple action form letter with only those items indicated by an "X" being applicable.

IN ANSWER TO YOUR REQUEST FOR MEDICAL INFORMATION

Please see attached medical record copies. NOTE: Request for copies of the entire record will include only the last 2 years of lab work. The attached medical information is CONFIDENTIAL. Subsequent disclosure is not authorized without the specific consent of the patient.

REQUEST FOR ADDITIONAL INFORMATION

☐ Your request is being returned for the following reason(s):

    ☐ We are unable to locate a record of treatment for this individual. Please provide additional information, such as full name of patient at time of treatment, date of birth, record #, or verification of spelling of name.

    ☐ No record on file for specified dates.

    ☐ Medical information is confidential and can be released only on written consent of patient/patient's legally authorized representative. Have the patient complete and return this form.

    ☐ Authorization date is over 6 months. Return your request with a more recently dated authorization signed by the patient/patient's legally authorized representative.

    ☐ The authorization received contained insufficient information for release of the information requested.

☐ Our charge for releasing records directly to the patient/patient's representative is $ _____ . If you provide us with the name and address of your new physician, we will send the copies there instead, thereby eliminating the charge. Otherwise, make check payable to _____, put patient's name on the check, and return a copy of this letter with check.

☐ Please remit _____, which is our fee for processing your request and photocopying the requested record. Make check payable to _____ , reference the patient's name on the check, and return a copy of this letter with check.

☐ Other: _____
_____
_____

Figure 9-3. Example of an authorization to release information form.

SUBPOENAS

At times during the course of medical practice, a court order or a subpoena may be received requesting a client's medical chart and/or specific information from the chart. If a health-care professional and the record are subpoenaed, it is called a *subpoena duces tecum* (see Chapter 6, Law for Health Professionals). Always notify the client before releasing the record in accordance with the subpoena. In some states, the attorney who subpoenas the medical record must notify in writing both the provider and the client and allow 14 days for a response. A certified printout or photocopy of the medical record should be made for the courts. Documents printed from an electronic record should have a watermark designating them as original prints from the facility. The person or agency issuing the subpoena usually covers the cost of preparing the copied record.

The medical record often becomes the center of a malpractice action wherein both attorneys involved bring in forensic document examiners to investigate the reliability of the record and clinical experts to evaluate the client care provided. Inaccurate data, documentation that has been altered or tampered, and space left for missing documentation are suspicious. All of these problems can be avoided by having a compliance plan for documentation within the medical record. (Refer to Chapter 5, Professional Liability.)

Case Study

The medical assistant is catching up on the completeness of the practice's medical records and notes that the provider wanted a transcript of two telephone calls that had not been previously recorded. The medical assistant now records them, posts the dates when the calls were made, and signs the entry.

Discuss.

A well-informed client discusses her marital problems with the provider and says, "Please do not put this in my record."

Discuss.

TELECOMMUNICATIONS

Electronic communication is a useful tool for the health-care setting. The use of email, text messaging, and live video tools improves communication among providers and their employees, and between provider and client. Information can be shared more efficiently and can contain links to education and other data that promote a client's health. Health-care professionals must remember that these electronic tools frequently do not provide a private or confidential means of communication and content is discoverable even after deleting. Messaging through a secure electronic system that requires a password to retrieve messages may assist with privacy, but content remains vulnerable to cyber-attacks and hackers. Health-care facilities must implement specific guidelines to minimize the risk. These guidelines may include the following:

- Use secure communication services that encrypt messages and monitor for security breaches.
- Limit access to telecommunication tools and client correspondence records and monitoring activity of health-care professionals that require the communication for direct client care.
- Require that access passwords be changed frequently.
- Establish specific procedures for personal digital assistant devices, especially if they provide access to PHI or are used to communicate health data.
- Have staff sign confidentiality contracts.
- Publish client information on the privacy risks of using telecommunication.
- Require informed consent from a client to communicate electronically.
- Record and secure all electronic communications; correspondence with a client must be included.

FAX MACHINES

The facsimile (fax) machine may still be used by some facilities, especially those that continue to use paper medical records or when sending client information to a health-care facility that is not associated with the same EHR system. Careful attention to confidentiality must be considered when using a fax transmission for client medical records. Health-care facilities that fax health-care records must establish policies that ensure the security of PHI.

Figure 9-4 illustrates a sample confidentiality notice to accompany any e-mail or fax.

Case Study

A client e-mails her internist requesting permission to begin a water therapy class at the local YMCA that requires a provider's release. The internist responds to the e-mail within 24 hours and says, "Sounds like a good plan. Fax me the release form." The client faxes the release form to the provider's clinic. It is completed and faxed directly to the therapist at the YMCA.

Discuss the advantages of this activity to the client and to the internist. Does it raise any problems?

TELEHEALTH AND TELEMEDICINE

Telehealth refers to the use of electronic information and communication technologies to support health-care delivery and services from distant locations. Telehealth technologies promote long-distance clinical health care, client and provider communications, health-related education, public health, and health administration. Although telehealth technologies have greatly expanded in the past 20 years, the use of telecommunications for health-care services began in the early 1900s with doctors attending to clients via radio calls. Today, telehealth incorporates synchronous health services such as virtual visits with health-care providers via video conferencing; asynchronous health services including communications between clients and health-care providers using a secure messaging portal; and remote monitoring of clients in both community and hospital settings.

Telemedicine, a subset of telehealth, refers to the use of technology to deliver medical care at a distance. A variety of types of medical care are considered telemedicine, but three virtual services are recognized by the Centers for Medicare and Medicaid Services: telehealth visits, virtual check-ins, and e-visits. Telehealth visits use communication technologies for clinic, hospital, and other medical services the generally occur in person. This service greatly increased during the Covid-19 pandemic where health-care providers used interactive audio and video conferencing to engage in real-time communications from a distance with clients in their homes. Telehealth visits are similar to in-person visits and deliver quality medical care to clients in rural communities, clients who are

Confidentiality Notice: This message and any attachments may contain confidential and privileged communications or information. The information contained in this e-mail/fax is transmitted for the sole use of the intended recipient(s). The authorized recipient of this e-mail/fax is prohibited from disclosing this information to any other party. If you are not the intended recipient or designated agent of the recipient of such information, you are hereby notified that any use, dissemination, copying or retention of this e-mail/fax or the information contained herein is strictly prohibited. If you received this e-mail/fax in error, please notify the sender immediately and permanently delete this e-mail/fax.

Figure 9-4. Confidentiality notice.

too vulnerable to leave their homes, and hospitalized clients who may benefit from a specialist at a different location.

Virtual check-ins are generally initiated by the client and involve a brief communication with the health-care provider. They are for clients who have an established relationship with a provider and simply need to clarify a medication, ask a medical question, or receive a new prescription. E-visits are considered asynchronous communications between the client and the health-care provider. These communications occur within a secured online portal and may include the client asking for a referral or the provider supplying health education resources.

There are many benefits to telehealth and telemedicine, but the primary benefit is increased access to care. It removes geographic barriers to health care and provides health-care services to medically underserved communities and rural locations where health-care provider shortages exist. Telehealth services can also be used to screen clients who may have infectious diseases, provide coaching and support in the management of chronic health conditions, monitor clinical signs of certain medical conditions, facilitate a hybrid approach to physical therapy and occupational therapy, and provide nonemergent care to clients within their homes. As chronic medical disorders become more prevalent and the risk of new infections more likely, telehealth and telemedicine may have a large role to play in our future health-care delivery system.

IN THE NEWS

During the 2020-2021 Covid-19 pandemic, the Centers for Medicare and Medicaid Services broadened access to telehealth services through a temporary waiver within the Coronavirus Preparedness and Response Supplemental Appropriations Act. Under the waiver, Medicare agreed to pay for office, hospital, and other health-care visits via telecommunications, and a variety of health-care professionals were approved to offer telehealth services, including doctors, nurse practitioners, clinical psychologists, and licensed clinical social workers. This alternative health-care delivery option allowed clients who needed routine care, as well as those with Covid-19 symptoms, to be cared for within their homes. Telehealth services during the pandemic reduced exposure of health-care professionals to sick clients, preserved personal protective equipment, minimized overwhelming surges on health-care facilities, and ensured that medical services were available to all Americans, particularly those who were most vulnerable.

Although the waiver for the expansion of telehealth services was only temporary, the widespread use of telehealth visits, virtual check-ins, and electronic medical visits delivered an excellent trial for future telemedicine services. Positive client outcomes and decreased health-care costs during the pandemic may lead to a greater use of telehealth services with ongoing Medicare funding.

OWNERSHIP OF MEDICAL RECORDS

The accepted rule is that medical records are the property of the person creating them and entering the data in them. Health-care providers are considered the owners of the medical records they have written. However, clients have access to the information in their medical records. Clients may be expected to make an appointment to obtain that copy. Access should be withheld only when the law prohibits such access or when, in the health-care provider's opinion, great harm would be done to the client.

Clients who request that their medical records be transferred to another health-care provider must do so in writing. The original record is retained in the clinic while the request is honored with a photocopy of the complete record or the health-care provider's summary. The continuance of medical records is important in our mobile society. This continuity can be accomplished only with cooperation from health-care providers. The important factor is to release the record promptly so that the client can receive proper care from the new provider.

Case Study

The use of "smart cards" has been suggested as a remedy for protecting clients' medical information. The smart card encoded with a computer chip contains a person's medical record, and only that person releases the information contained therein by sharing a personally chosen password. Although the idea of smart cards has been discussed for many years, they still are not well known or implemented throughout the U.S. health-care system.

Discuss the advantages/disadvantages of such a system.

STORAGE OF MEDICAL RECORDS

In today's computerized society, medical records are stored electronically and do not pose a physical storage problem. However, most practices have a vast collection of stored medical records in a variety of media. All stored records are to be protected as carefully as active files.

Not all medical records need to be kept in the same location. Active records should be readily available to providers. Closed or inactive files usually include records of clients who are no longer being seen by the provider, who may have moved away, or who have died. These files may be kept in a storage area separate from current and active files. The clinic may have storage space or may rent storage space in another location. Some older medical files may be stored on **microfilm** and, if so, require a reader to access the information.

EMRs are backed up daily. The EMR software used determines the backup process and storage requirements. Some software is accessed through a cloud-based Internet server, and thus a backup record is constantly being generated at the point of origin. If the EMR is installed on the clinic's server, a backup record is generated nightly. This record should be removed from the clinic to protect it from fire or other destruction.

RETENTION OF MEDICAL RECORDS

The question of how long to retain medical records is not easily answered. One guideline indicates that records should be retained until the statute of limitations for any act of medical malpractice has expired so that records are available for any possible litigation. This guideline may require a pediatrician to keep the record for as long as 7 to 10 years beyond the age of maturity. Most states have statutes that set retention guidelines for medical records. When a state has no statute regarding retention of medical records, state medical associations and insurance carriers are the best resources for this information. Hospital medical records and provider medical records have different retention time limits. Health-care professionals should know the limits for the state in which they are employed.

DESTRUCTION OF MEDICAL RECORDS

Once records have reached the limits of retention, follow procedures to **purge** aged data. Whether the medical records are paper based or electronic, their destruction should follow specific guidelines suggested by the American Health Information Management Association (AHIMA) and the Healthcare Information and Management Systems Society.

A destruction log is developed to keep track of all destroyed medical records. It includes the client's name, date of birth, and date of last encounter. The log should also include the date and method of destruction, a statement that the records were destroyed in the normal course of business, and the signatures of the individuals supervising and witnessing the destruction. These records are to be kept permanently.

One method of destruction for paper medical records is to have them picked up by a company specializing in record destruction. After completion of the task, a signed certificate is returned to the clinic indicating the contents and date of the destruction.

Depending on the amount of material to be destroyed, another method involves on-site destruction. A large truck that is fitted with an industrial shredder arrives at the clinic, and the records are placed into the shredder and destroyed. For some clinics this is a preferable method because a health-care employee can observe the actual destruction. Thus, the records are destroyed before they are removed from the property.

AHIMA suggests that the preferred method of destroying computerized data is to **degauss** the data. This is a technique that alters the way data align in the magnetic storage field and renders the previous data unrecoverable and impossible to reconstruct. To keep current on the latest medical record destruction methods, AHIMA recommends reassessing the process annually based on current technology, accepted practices, and availability of timely and cost-effective destruction services.

SUMMARY

Medical records carry pertinent client information and data that, in part, determine the care given. Medical records have very sensitive information and must be kept private and confidential; any information released must be done so only with the consent of the client and/or on a "medical need to know" basis. Health-care professionals must always remember that medical records may become a critical document in litigation of what was or was not performed. Careful documentation in medical records that is complete, organized, sequential, and kept confidential and private tells a story of meticulous client care.

 Watch It Now! How do you protect the medical record and its contents? at http://FADavis.com, keyword *Tamparo*.

Questions for Review

SELECT THE BEST ANSWER

1. Who owns the medical record?
   a. The client
   b. The hospital where the provider is associated
   c. The clinic
   d. The health-care provider
   e. The insurance carrier

2. What is the difference between an electronic medical record (EMR) and an electronic health record (EHR)?
   a. The EHR contains information about health behaviors and the EMR contains information about medications.
   b. The EHR contains protected health information from a single clinic or facility.
   c. The EMR contains a client's health-care information from multiple sources.
   d. The EMR is started by a primary provider and becomes part of an EHR when results from other services are added.
   e. The EMR allows for multiple provider access whereas the EHR is a single-user system.

3. Which are purposes of the medical record?
   a. Serves as a legal basis for litigation
   b. Documents total health care from birth to death
   c. Provides communication between health-care providers
   d. Supports the management and continuity of quality care
   e. All of the above

4. What are the purposes of a practice management system?
   a. Capture client demographics
   b. Schedule appointments
   c. Perform billing tasks
   d. All of above
   e. Only a and c above

5. POMR is an acronym that stands for
   a. Policies On Medical Records
   b. Protected Office Medical Records
   c. Problem-Oriented Medical Record
   d. Private Office Management Report
   e. Practice Office Management Report

SHORT ANSWER QUESTIONS

1. What federal and state guidelines must be followed when releasing medical records and protected health information?

   _____

   _____

   _____

2. Identify each word of the SOAPER acronym and provide an example of client health information that would be included in each section of the charting format.

   _____

   _____

   _____

3. What does it mean when an EMR or EHR meets meaningful use requirements?

   _____

   _____

   _____

4. Discuss how and when to correct an error in a paper medical record and an electronic medical record.

   _____

   _____

   _____

5. Describe five guidelines to keep protected health information secure when using telecommunication tools.

   _____

   _____

   _____

CLASSROOM EXERCISES

1. A fax was received in a private home where no fax was expected. The fax has come from a nearby long-term care facility, is addressed to a health-care provider, has personal information about a resident of the facility, and requests a medication change. What should the homeowner do? What responsibility and action does the long-term facility have?

2. The following report was phoned in and charted: "05/14/2- Urinalysis reveals RBC too numerous to count." When the written report is received, you note it as WBC, not RBC. How would you make this correction in a paper record? How would it be made in an EMR?

3. You are preparing a medical record after it has been subpoenaed. Describe the procedures you would follow. What do you do with medical information from a referring health-care provider?

4. A client becomes angry when refused permission to hand-carry medical records when moving out of state. What alternatives can an employee suggest?

5. Describe what might be done when there is simply no room for any more medical records in the clinic.

6. Refer to the vignette "A Day in the Life of the Medical Record." As a client, how did the availability of the electronic medical record facilitate the care received? As a health-care provider, what are the advantages of having up-to-the-minute information on the client? Discuss the legal implications of a medical record used in this manner.

INTERNET ACTIVITIES

1. The health-care provider that you work for has announced his retirement. Go to the American Medical Association's website and find out what steps need to be taken with regard to medical records.

2. Go to your state's Department of Health website. What is the law regarding retention of medical records?

3. Go to: https://www.reliasmedia.com/articles/142669-legal-case-shows-risk-of-improper-patient-info-disclosure. Identify the errors that caused this litigation.

For additional resources please visit
http://FADavis.com, keyword *Tamparo*.

CHAPTER 10

Reimbursement and Collection Practices

"Even if you're on the right track, you'll get run over if you just sit there."—Will Rogers (1879–1935); American cowboy, humorist, social commentator, actor

KEY TERMS

capitation Providers are paid a fixed monthly amount for each health maintenance organization (HMO) member in their care.

co-payment An amount that a member of an insurance plan must pay for certain medical procedures and provider visits.

COBRA Consolidated Omnibus Budget Reconciliation Act of 1985; mandates that continuation of group insurance coverage be offered to covered persons who lose health or dental coverage due to a qualifying event.

coordination of benefits An agreement between insurance carriers that if a client has two insurance plans, neither the provider nor the subscriber will receive more than 100% of the covered charges.

deductible A cost-sharing arrangement in which the member pays a set amount toward covered services before the insurer begins to make any payments.

Evaluation and Management (E&M) codes A section of the *Current Procedural Terminology, 4th Edition* (CPT-4) manual that lists codes for office visits. Each level of visit dictates how much is charged by the provider and paid by the insurance carrier.

medical savings (or spending) account (MSA) A method for companies with 50 or fewer employees, self-employed persons, and uninsured individuals to purchase medical insurance by making tax-free deposits to an MSA.

TRICARE Federal insurance plan that covers military personnel and retirees and their families.

usual, customary, and reasonable fee (UCR) Describes how providers are reimbursed for their services; is widely accepted by insurance carriers.

LEARNING OUTCOMES

Upon successful completion of this chapter, you should be able to:

10.1 Define the key terms.
10.2 Explain, in a short paragraph, the importance of appropriate reimbursement and collections.
10.3 List at least five guidelines related to reimbursement.
10.4 Recall the laws that have an impact on reimbursement.
10.5 Describe five government insurance programs.

10.6 Discuss the suggestions that help clients be financially responsible for their health care.
10.7 List at least five items to be covered in a collection policy.
10.8 Identify the appropriate procedures to follow when collecting a bill by telephone or by mail.
10.9 Identify the seven "collection don'ts" established by the Federal Trade Commission.
10.10 Discuss solutions to collection problems.
10.11 Explain the one important procedure to follow if a client is denied credit because of a poor credit rating.
10.12 List steps to follow in selecting a collection agency.
10.13 Discuss ethical implications regarding reimbursement and collections.

COMPETENCIES

CAAHEP
- Explain patient financial obligations for services rendered. (CAAHEP VII.C.6)
- Obtain accurate patient billing information. (CAAHEP VII.P 3)
- Inform a patient of financial obligations for services rendered. (CAAHEP VII.C.4)
- Identify types of third party plans. (CAAHEP VIII.C.1.a)

ABHES
- Perform risk management procedures. (ABHES 4.e)
- Perform billing and collection procedures. (ABHES 7.c)

VIGNETTE

Can You Afford This?

A general surgeon practicing in a metropolitan area loves his work. He spends only 1 day of the week in the clinic and performs about six operations a week. He no longer covers night emergencies. Early in his career, he determined that insurance carriers were totally dictating his compensation, so he stopped accepting any insurance. To see this general surgeon, clients must pay cash. If clients want to file for reimbursement from their insurer, it is up to them. His fees are based on what the market will bear. His net income for at least a decade has been nearly $1.2 million per year.

What does this practice say about the state of health care in the United States?

Billing, reimbursement, and collections are sensitive areas for many clients and health-care professionals. The best way to manage finances within a clinic is to have set policies and procedures in place within a compliance plan and to be sure that both clients and employees understand those policies. Policies and procedures related to finances that are both legal and client-oriented will lead to client and employee satisfaction. A major task within a clinic is the appropriate billing and collecting for services performed. It is also a major concern for clients who may not seek medical attention if they feel they cannot afford to pay.

COMPLIANCE PLAN

Compliance plans (see Chapter 5, Professional Liability) are an excellent way to avoid litigation and to help prevent problems from arising in the delivery of health care. When a compliance plan for billing and reimbursement is in place and used appropriately, areas of concern will be noted that the accounts manager (the compliance officer for a billing and reimbursement plan) can correct before they become a major problem. When an insurance carrier audits a clinic's activities in the billing area, it looks for intentional fraud. With a written compliance plan and proof that the compliance plan has been adhered to, a clinic can show that it is making a good faith effort to avoid fraud. This action will work in the clinic's favor.

MEDICAL DEBT

The leading cause of bankruptcy in the United States is medical debt. CNBC reported in early 2019 that 66.5% of bankruptcies are related to medical issues either because of inadequate insurance, no insurance coverage, or being out of work. It is noteworthy that the Affordable Care Act (ACA) has not had an impact on the bankruptcy rate. Most families simply cannot afford a medical emergency. Physicians for a National Health plan are advocating for "Medicare for All," a primary topic in the 2020 election, in the hopes of making medical insurance available for all. The medical reimbursement system in the United States changed with the passage of the ACA. This bill, passed in 2010, is still meeting opposition and likely will face a number of changes throughout its progression toward its goal to reform the health-care system. The ultimate goal of this health-care reform is for all Americans to have health insurance.

HOW PROVIDERS ARE PAID

Health-care providers will receive reimbursement for their services from many different sources. Successful practice management, billing, and collections require knowledgeable personnel who understand the complex characteristics of how reimbursement is made.

Recall from Chapter 2, Medical Practice Management, that 70 years ago, clients expected to pay physicians the full fee for services at the time they were rendered. Out of courtesy, some physicians would send a statement at the end of the month. Insurance of any kind was rare. Today, providers receive reimbursement in any number of ways. Payment may be made by (1) funds received through a client's insurance plan, probably receiving only a percentage of allowable charges; (2) funds from a client in the form of cash, check, or credit or debit card; (3) a set fee for a client's services in a **capitation** arrangement regardless of the costs (not very popular); (4) a bonus if providers perform well in giving service across a spectrum of quality measures in a pay-for-performance (P4P) method; or (5) bundled or episode payments that reimburse providers on the basis of expected costs for clinically defined episodes of care.

PRIVATE PAY

Private pay may come from clients who have no work-related medical insurance, have insufficient medical insurance, or do not qualify for government health-care coverage. These clients may be working only part-time, never having enough working hours to qualify for insurance benefits, or they may choose a medical service that is not covered by insurance. Payment is usually made at the time of service unless other arrangements are made.

THIRD-PARTY PAYERS

Usual, customary, and reasonable fee (UCR) describes how providers are reimbursed for their services from third-party payers and is very much like the bundled or episodic payments just described.

- The usual fee is a provider's average fee for a service or what is usually charged for a procedure.
- The customary fee is the average of fees within a geographic area for a described service or procedure and performed by the same kind of provider.
- The reasonable fee is what is normally acceptable for services that are unusually difficult or complicated.

The UCR is widely accepted across the country by insurance carriers and provides a basis for reimbursement to providers. Diagnostic (ICD-10), procedural (CPT), and DRG code sets also help determine the amount of reimbursement by a third-party payer.

Insurance funds for medical expenses may come from more than one source:

- *Individual policies* are a kind of personal insurance in which clients often must submit to a physical examination and give a detailed medical history to qualify. Premiums are generally expensive, and benefits may be less than with other plans.

- *Group policies* are designed for a group of individuals covered under a master contract issued to their employer. Both employers and employees pay a percentage of the premiums. Deductions may be made from salaries to help pay the costs of group plans. Premiums are less costly than individual policies, and benefits are greater. A physical examination is not normally required.

Government plans include the following:

- **TRICARE** (formerly known as the Civilian Health and Medical Program of the Uniformed Services [CHAMPUS]). This program was formed in 1956 to provide medical treatment to authorized dependents of military personnel and has been known as TRICARE since 1994. TRICARE covers active-duty personnel and their families and military retirees and their families; former spouses are covered if they have not remarried; and children, if unmarried, continue to be covered. The program is managed by the Defense Health Agency under the leadership of the Assistant Secretary of Defense. The Civilian Health and Medical Program of the Department of Veterans Affairs (CHAMPVA) was formed in 1973 to provide benefits to veterans and their dependents.
- *Medicaid,* in 1965, made agreements with states to provide health care to the medically indigent. The federal government provides funds to the states, which, in turn, decide how to use those funds in providing medical care. Thus, Medicaid is funded by both the federal and state governments. There is great variation among the 50 states regarding coverage under the ACA. As of 2020, there were still 14 states not expanding their programs under the ACA. Medicaid also covers certain individuals receiving federal and state aid, persons who receive supplemental Social Security payments, and recipients of Aid to Families with Dependent Children. Medicaid pays Medicare premiums for some low-income elderly persons and provides **COBRA** coverage for some low-income persons who lose employer health insurance benefits. In most states, a provider must accept the Medicaid payment as payment in full. The client cannot be billed for any remaining balance.
- *Medicare* is a federal insurance program established in 1966 for people ages 65 years and older, for individuals who are blind or disabled, and for people on kidney dialysis or who have had a kidney transplant. There are several parts to this plan: Part A is hospital insurance and is mandatory for all individuals who receive Social Security. Premiums are paid from the client's monthly Social Security check. Part B is medical insurance that will help to cover ambulatory care and requires a larger monthly premium. Part C, now known as Medicare Advantage, offers health maintenance organization (HMO) plans to augment Medicare payments. This part also requires additional premiums. Part D provides everyone with Medicare access to prescription drug coverage with a range of different plans, all requiring a premium to be paid by recipients. Only part A is mandatory; the others are optional additions to the Medicare coverage. Medicare is what is known as an 80/20 plan. Medicare will pay 80% of the allowed amount for a service, and the client is responsible for the other 20% unless the client has Medicare Advantage or another supplemental plan, in which case the HMO will cover most of the remaining charges. There is little information at this point as to how Medicare would change should the "Medicare for All" plan be instituted.
- *Workers' compensation* programs were established in all states to cover the cost of medical care resulting from accident or illness related to a person's employment. Loss of income benefits is also included. The provider of services must accept the workers' compensation as payment in full and cannot bill the client.
- *The Health Maintenance Organization Act of 1973* defined the characteristics of managed care. Managed care insurance plans attempt to reduce costs by limiting where and from whom clients can receive medical services. Some plans limit any type of specialty care. Managed care plans provide health care within a network of providers for a predetermined and set fee.

In some instances, a client may have more than one health insurance plan. Through **coordination of benefits**, an agreement is made between insurance carriers that if a client has two insurance plans, neither the provider nor the subscriber will receive more than 100% of the covered charges.

OTHER PAYERS

Providers may receive reimbursement by other methods as well. Clients who have long-term care insurance may be able to use a portion of those benefits to pay medical bills, especially if they have a life-threatening illness. Some life insurance policies allow clients to draw from the policy benefit to pay medical indebtedness. Disability insurance, whether or not work related, can be used to pay for related medical expenses. **Medical savings (or spending) accounts (MSAs)** provide a method for companies with 50 or fewer employees, self-employed persons, and the uninsured to purchase medical insurance by making tax-free deposits to an MSA. Clients can use the funds in their MSA to pay for routine medical expenses. Any money in the account at the end of the year earns tax-free interest.

The complexity of medical reimbursement has created a bookkeeping and accounting nightmare for health-care providers. The most successful facilities in the arena of reimbursement likely have at least one individual, or several individuals in a large clinic, whose sole responsibility is payment and collections. They have computerized their billing and spend several hours weekly in seeking approval for certain services, appealing denied insurance claims, and collecting outstanding balances.

CLIENTS' RESPONSIBILITY FOR REIMBURSEMENT

With or without the involvement of an insurance plan for health-care costs, clients are still responsible for the payment of their medical bills. There are several guidelines to keep in mind related to client reimbursement, some of which may be a part of the compliance plan. They include, but are not limited to, the following:

- If there is no insurance, expect payment at the time of service, and offer installment payments if necessary.
- Request payment for any coinsurance, **deductibles**, or exclusions at the time of service. Consider offering debit or credit card payment for services provided. Remember that you cannot charge clients the fees the facility pays for the use of debit or credit cards.
- Help clients understand their medical services and how much they cost.
- Clearly identify what clients are expected to pay and when. You cannot expect payment up front if clients have not been provided this information.
- Expect to explain to clients at least the basic principles of insurance reimbursement according to their individual plan.
- Never bill for a service that is not clearly identified and appropriately charted.
- Carefully adhere to all laws pertaining to reimbursement and collections.
- Establish a reimbursement and collection policy and then follow a compliance plan with regard to billing, reimbursement, and collections.
- Treat all clients equitably and fairly.
- If clients are to be denied services because of inability to pay, offer and discuss alternatives.

No matter how billing and collection is accomplished, there are numerous legal aspects to consider. A brief presentation of applicable laws for reimbursement and collections is given. Ethical concerns are addressed later in this chapter.

LAWS FOR REIMBURSEMENT AND COLLECTIONS

TRUTH IN LENDING ACT

Regulation Z of the Consumer Protection Act of 1968 is also known as the Truth in Lending Act. This act is enforced by the Federal Trade Commission and, when applied to the health-care setting, deals with collection of clients' payments.

Briefly, the regulation requires that an agreement by providers and their clients for payment of medical bills in more than four installments must be in writing and must provide information regarding finance charges. Even if no finance charge is involved, the agreement must be in writing and stipulate no finance charge.

If consumers decide to pay their bills by installments unilaterally with no established agreement with providers, Regulation Z is not applicable as long as the provider continues to bill for the full amount.

Situations in which the Truth in Lending Act is often used include arrangements for surgery, prenatal or delivery care for fee-for-service plans, or other medical services not covered by insurance. The amount owed by the client is often more than a client can pay in one installment or is more than is covered by medical insurance. Health-care employees then can discuss with the client appropriate installment payments, put the agreement in writing, and provide a copy for the client. Few providers will charge a finance fee in this situation, although to do so is both legal and ethical. If bilateral installment agreements are common or if computer billing automatically includes a finance charge after a certain period, the wording should be approved by a legal representative.

EQUAL CREDIT OPPORTUNITY ACT

The Equal Credit Opportunity Act ensures that all consumers are given an equal chance to obtain credit so that when providers extend credit for one client, all clients must be offered the same opportunity. The act prohibits credit discrimination because of race, color, religion, national origin, sex, marital status, age, or because you receive public assistance. Providers may deny credit to clients based on their inability to pay and inform their clients that credit has been denied. Clients then have 60 days to request the rationale for the denial in writing.

FAIR CREDIT BILLING ACT

The Fair Credit Billing Act states that clients have 60 days to complain about any error in their billing. The health-care employee must document, acknowledge the complaint, and respond within 90 days to the complaint. The response may be to correct any error or to explain to the client why the bill was accurate.

FAIR DEBT COLLECTIONS PRACTICES ACT

The Fair Debt Collections Practices Act, a federal law governed by the Federal Trade Commission, addresses the communication that occurs when collecting debts in the manner a collections agency might. According to the law, its purpose is to eliminate abusive debt collection practices by debt collectors, to ensure that those debt collectors who refrain from using abusive debt collection practices are not competitively disadvantaged, and to promote consistent state action to protect consumers against debt collection abuses. This act is discussed in detail later in the chapter.

FEDERAL WAGE GARNISHMENT LAW

Garnishment of salary is one method that can be used to collect a fairly large delinquent account. The Federal Wage Garnishment Law addresses payment of debts using employee salaries. Garnishment means to attach a person's property or wages by court order to pay debts. The law limits the amount of money that can be garnished and protects an employee from being dismissed because of garnishment. In most cases federal benefits such as Social Security cannot be garnished. Some state laws may differ from the federal law, so it is best for the health-care professional to contact either the Department of Labor or legal counsel for clarification.

STARK I, II, AND III REGULATIONS

Stark I and II Regulations prohibit a physician or provider from referring a Medicare or Medicaid client for services to an entity with which the provider or an immediate family member has a financial relationship through ownership or compensation, unless the referral is protected by one or more exceptions provided in the law. The third phase of the Stark Law went into effect in 2007. It further specified and clarified the rules for referrals and tightened restrictions.

DEFICIT REDUCTION ACT

The Deficit Reduction Act was enacted in 2005 to tighten and regulate Medicare and Medicaid reimbursement. The Act identifies remedies for false claims and statements as well as civil or criminal penalty for the same. It also protects whistleblowers from employer discrimination.

CIVIL MONETARY PENALTIES LAW

The Civil Monetary Penalties Law addresses Medicare and Medicaid fraud. It allows the Secretary of Health and Human Resources to impose monetary penalties for physicians or providers who falsely bill clients' services or incorrectly code services. Employers can be held liable for their own negligence and the negligence of their employees. The penalty can be very costly.

Hence, health-care employees must be current in Medicare and Medicaid policies and be diligent in honestly performing coding and billing procedures.

IN THE NEWS

Since its inception, the Medicare Fraud Strike Force under the Department of Health and Human Services has expanded and continues to file charges against defendants for alleged false Medicare billing. In 2020 the Department of Justice recovered more than 2.2 billion dollars from fraud and false claims and 1.8 billion dollars related to the health-care industry. This amount includes only federal losses. In many cases, the department was instrumental in recovering tens of millions of dollars for state Medicaid programs. The Office of the Inspector General of Health and Human Services posts up-to-date statistics on their website at https://oig.hhs.gov/fraud/enforcement/criminal/.

COLLECTION GUIDELINES

Collection procedures may be necessary to obtain full payment of services provided to clients. Collection procedures must be firm but temperate enough not to irritate otherwise satisfied consumers who intend to pay. If they feel comfortable doing so, providers should not hesitate to discuss directly with consumers the fees for their services.

Medical managers must establish an appropriate collection policy for employees to follow (Fig. 10-1). Clients should be informed in writing of the policy. That policy will state how insurance claims are managed. Will the clinic file claims for all insurance carriers, or only a certain few? Does the client in a managed care plan ever receive a bill; if so, under what circumstances? The policy should state how and when **co-payments** and deductibles are collected. The policy will detail whether and at what point collection letters will be sent. Will there be a minimum payment schedule? Will the collection letter be different for every account? Are collection telephone calls to be made; if so, by whom? How many? When? What procedures will be followed? Will delinquent accounts ever be turned over to a collection agency or pursued through the local courts? A clearly defined or stated policy gives employees the support necessary for successful collections.

It is important to build a professional and cooperative relationship with insurers to prevent billing problems and delayed or inaccurate reimbursements. Medical personnel should meet periodically with insurance representatives to learn their rules and billing processes. When specific problems arise, discuss them with the representatives and pose possible solutions. Gather and analyze these computerized payment records and identify those insurers who are chronically late with payments. Use these data with the insurer to negotiate a better reimbursement timeline. Clinics have a right to reimbursement within 90 days on accurately submitted bills.

MULTIPLE INSURERS

There are a number of individuals whose medical insurance is provided by more than one source; for example, Medicare and private insurance or a primary insurance and any supplemental insurance. Medicare is billed first and sets the parameters for any additional insurance reimbursement. In this case, especially in the managed care sector, the client sometimes does not see the bill. Cost of services provided is revealed only when receiving statements from both insurances, but often

Establishing procedures for collecting fees to eliminate headaches later

- Establish fees
- Discuss fees
- Have a written policy for fees and collections
- Expect at least some payment at time of service, especially any co-payment
- Provide accurate, itemized statements
- Provide addressed envelope for payment
- Have a follow-up policy

Figure 10-1. Collecting fees.

include just procedure codes for which the client has no comprehension. Only the most industrious client goes the extra step of researching the codes via the Internet or questioning any services provided. Unfortunately, providers in these managed care facilities also do not always discuss the potential out-of-pocket cost for their clients simply because they have little, if any, knowledge of the vast insurance reimbursement policies. In this case, checks and balances can, for all practical purposes, be lost to clients.

COLLECTION DO'S

The following guidelines are provided to suggest possible procedures for collections in the health-care setting, quite possibly identified in the compliance plan:

- Discuss fees with clients the first time they present themselves or call for treatment. A written payment policy is essential. Explain to consumers their responsibilities in a managed care plan.
- Provide clients with a clinic brochure that gives them information about hours, emergency contacts, the providers' services, how billing is managed, and whom to call if there is a question about a bill. Identify the insurances accepted by the providers.
- Provide an opportunity for the client to pay co-payments, deductibles, or even full pay before leaving the clinic. The encounter form is an ideal way for the provider to indicate charges and services as well as proper coding and the diagnoses. This form is then presented to the client, who is asked to stop at the bookkeeper's desk on the way out. A risk in many HMO facilities is that the client never sees an encounter form. If/when there are services not covered by their plan, the client has nothing in which to check for accuracy and correctness before paying the balance due. When billing by mail provide addressed envelopes in which to mail the fee.
- Have an established practice for mailing statements and follow that practice. Statements should be itemized, accurate, and easy to understand. Statements must provide a description of the service as well as the procedural code. Make sure all credits have been posted up to the closing date. Statements should be mailed to arrive close to the first of the month. Statements that include envelopes, especially colored ones, are paid faster.
- When your collection policy dictates that an unpaid bill should be followed with a letter or a telephone call, do it. Be consistent, pleasant, and firm. The sooner you follow through on a delinquent account, the more likely it will be collected.
- Employees responsible for collections should have certain phrases and the wording of possible letters at their fingertips for quick and easy referral. They also need the authority to carry the collection process to its completion.
- Suggested procedures for mail or telephone collections include the following: (1) Introduce yourself. (2) Establish that you are speaking to the proper person, if it is a telephone call, or address the letter to the proper person. (3) State the reason for the call or the letter. ("Your account is past due.") (4) Be pleasant but be firm. ("You are generally prompt with your payments; we wondered if this has been overlooked.") (5) Get a commitment. Make it specific.

("May we expect $150 from you by next Monday?") Then mark that commitment in your tickler file and follow up next Monday if there has been no response. (6) End the contact graciously. Do not get pulled into all the financial problems of the client. (7) Be prepared to offer a payment plan that is suitable to both the client and the clinic.

- Have a clearly established practice of when, if ever, to turn the account over to a collection agency or to collect the balance due in small claims court.

 ## COLLECTION DON'TS

The Fair Debt Collection Practices Act is a federal law that governs the actions of parties acting as debt collectors for personal debts. The Federal Trade Commission has specific regulations for debt collection. They include the following:

- Do not misrepresent who you are or why you are contacting a person.
- Do not send postcards; rather, mail a collection letter.
- Do not use deception in any form in your contact.
- Do not telephone at odd hours or make repeated calls or calls to the debtor's friends, relatives, neighbors, employers, or children. Acceptable hours to call are 8 a.m. to 9 p.m.
- Do not use obscene, profane, or abusive language.
- Do not make calls or send letters demanding payment for amounts not owed.
- If a contact must be made to the debtor's place of business, do not reveal to a third party the reason for the contact. All calls to a workplace must be stopped if so requested (written or verbal) by the client. The client's privacy and reputation must be protected.

If your clinic denies credit to a client because of an adverse credit report from a credit bureau or similar agency, you must tell the client the name and address of the agency providing the information, even if you are not asked. Failure to do so could result in legal action. Let clients know that it is their right to obtain a copy of their credit report to see if all the information is correct. A form letter should be available in your clinic that courteously informs the client that credit has been denied, leaving blanks for the name and address of the agency that supplied the credit information. Mail a copy to the client and keep a copy for your records.

COLLECTION PROBLEMS

An up-front, matter-of-fact approach to collections will increase the cash flow in the medical setting and make collections easier for everyone. However, every clinic has slow payers, hardship cases, skips, and a few who never intend to pay. Move slow payers to a cash basis as soon and as often as possible and yet maintain good public relations.

Hardship cases pose another problem. Anyone might have a time when the payment of a medical bill is nearly impossible. Take care to be understanding at all times. Try to establish payment plans with clients so that they, too, may take pride in themselves and their ability to pay. Social agencies may be suggested if necessary.

There will always be a small percentage of clients who never intend to pay their bills. Some of these individuals leave the area, "skipping" out on their financial responsibilities. All possible resources should be exhausted to find the skips and to seek reimbursement. If the client has not skipped but still does not intend to pay, consider action in small claims court. Providers often withdraw themselves formally from these cases and encourage the clients to seek treatment elsewhere.

Chapter 6, Law for Health Professionals, gives information about the procedures to follow for collecting a bill in probate court from the estate of a client who has died. Chapter 6 also provides an explanation of the steps to follow for taking a client to small claims court. Both situations are uncomplicated and will produce results worth the effort if employees are consistent and conscientious in these dealings.

Another problem can occur in reimbursement when insurance claims are denied for one reason or another. Successful medical practice management suggests that spending a couple of hours a week appealing denied claims is well worth the effort.

Case Study

Jenna works as an insurance biller for a large clinic and is often responsible for collections. She delays calling the responsible party of a large family whose members are clients of the clinic because she knows she will become involved in a complex "hard luck" story that probably is true.

What are Jenna's options in this case? Discuss.

COLLECTION AGENCIES

If you have diligently followed billing and collection procedures and conclude that the client is not going to pay, you can refer the account to a collection agency. Obviously, this decision must be consistent with clinic policy. Collection agencies generally are employed as a last resort. Most people, including clients and those who work in clinics, tend to have a negative attitude toward collection agencies. However, the agency can be valuable to those who choose to use such professional services.

Selection of an appropriate agency should be made as carefully as one would choose a bank. Considerations should include the following:

1. Does it handle medical and dental accounts exclusively?
2. What methods does it use to collect?
3. What is the agency's financial responsibility?
4. What percentage will the medical clinic receive?
5. How promptly does it settle accounts?
6. Does the agency have a good bank reference?
7. How much cost versus goodwill will the clinic incur by using this agency?
8. Will it provide you with a list of satisfied customers or references?
9. Will you be able to end the agency's collection efforts?

Check with the Better Business Bureau or the local medical association for possible recommendations. An agency that is a member of the American Association of Credit and Collections Professionals will generally adhere to high ethical standards.

Once the agency is selected, all delinquent accounts are turned over to it, including any useful nonclinical data. A record should be kept of accounts given to the agency, as well as a running account of the agency's progress. Any contact with the client regarding these bills, whether in person, by phone, or by letter, must cease once the account has been turned over to the collection agency. If the client sends payment to the clinic, report it immediately to the agency. If the client calls regarding the account, courteously refer the client to the agency.

The collection agency represents the clinic. Employees should work with the agency to collect the accounts.

REIMBURSEMENT ATTITUDES

Reimbursement for providers in the medical setting is in constant transition and is increasingly complex. Although a large portion of today's society is covered by some form of health plan, often in managed care, many clients are covered by no plan at all. Often these clients will not seek health care or will request detailed information about your clinic's billing practices. Payment plans may need to be established. Also, providers serving in any number of managed care plans will find some plans struggling to find a better method of curbing health-care costs. Medicare is constantly being explored to lower reimbursement rates to providers.

Regardless of the reimbursement plan, financial status has no bearing on the kind of treatment clients should receive. The Medicare or Medicaid client should receive the same care as the client who pays cash. Providers and employees will want to be careful of their attitudes toward those clients who have difficulty paying their bills, for whatever reason. Actions often speak louder than words, and clients easily perceive their true meanings.

 ## ETHICAL IMPLICATIONS

 ### ETHICS CHECK

Reimbursement and collection issues bring to the forefront ethical implications for discussion. Consider the following questions. None has a simple or easy answer.

- Is health care a right or privilege?
- Should providers be able to deny care to anyone?
- What is the driving force behind increasing costs of medical care?
- Who pays for medical insurance and why is it so costly?
- What role does government have in providing health care?
- Who controls client health care—the client, the insurance carrier, the primary care provider, or the government?

Ethics in medicine has received attention in regard to the recent Medicare changes. Medicare no longer pays for consultations, forcing the specialists to charge **Evaluation and Management (E&M)** codes (from the CPT-4 manual) for visits. These codes receive much lower reimbursement than the consultation codes. This was done by Medicare as a cost-saving measure. As a result, some specialists refuse to see Medicare clients. Where will this leave our elderly population? Can this be perceived as discrimination? Will specialists be sacrificing their financial security and their reputation in the long run? This is an area to watch carefully. Many insurance carriers usually follow behind Medicare in making policy changes. If all insurance carriers refuse to pay for consultations, how will a specialist be paid? Will specialists now refuse to see anyone with Medicare insurance?

Case Study

Often, employees in health care believe they have more client contact when performing clinical procedures. After reading and understanding the complexity of this chapter, discuss the importance of client contact when helping clients understand reimbursement and how that relates to overall client satisfaction.

SUMMARY

Providers and health-care professionals receive payment for their services through numerous means. There are more than 100 different insurance plans to cover clients' costs. The complexity of reimbursement challenges both the health professional and the client. Education is paramount for the client; however, there also are numerous laws related to reimbursement and collections that medical professionals must understand.

 ## PERSONAL NOTE

Of all the chapters in this text, this one is most likely to be outdated in a few areas depending on the political changes resulting from the 2020 election and the major changes expected in health care. The Covid-19 Pandemic has made substantial changes as well. It is still uncertain how/when providers will be reimbursed for Covid-19 testing and treatment of their clients. Although some of the information may become obsolete, what will always remain is the client's right to make decisions regarding health care, a client's responsibility for payment of services rendered in one manner or another, and a provider's right to be reimbursed for those services. Health care has changed radically in the last several decades, some for the better, some not so much so. What must always remain, however, is the goal to provide appropriate health care to all.

 Watch It Now! Can you be successful in collections? at http://FADavis.com, keyword *Tamparo*.

Questions for Review

SELECT THE BEST ANSWER

1. The _____ prohibits a provider from referring Medicare clients for services to a laboratory in which the provider has a financial interest.
   a. Truth in Lending Act
   b. Equal Credit Opportunity Act
   c. Deficit Reduction Act
   d. Stark Laws
   e. Civil Monetary Penalties Law

2. This regulation requires that any payment plan that is for more than four installments must be in writing.
   a. Truth in Lending Act
   b. Equal Credit Opportunity Act
   c. Deficit Reduction Act
   d. Stark Laws
   e. Fair Credit Opportunity Act

3. A CPT manual contains which of the following information?
   a. Diagnostic codes
   b. Procedure codes
   c. HCPCS codes
   d. Reimbursement by third-party payers
   e. b and d above

4. Co-payments should be expected
   a. Within 30 days of the visit.
   b. At the time of service.
   c. After primary insurance has paid its portion.
   d. Only after any follow-up visit.
   e. Only after supplemental insurance has paid.

5. A provider may receive reimbursement in which of the following ways?
   a. By a client
   b. By an insurance carrier
   c. According to the UCR
   d. Capitation
   e. All of the above

SHORT ANSWER

1. Briefly describe a compliance plan.

_____

_____

_____

2. When services have been denied by insurance, what steps are taken to collect payment?

_____

_____

_____

3. As an employee, you note that your provider/employer is suggesting a higher service CPT code than the medical record indicates. What will you do?

_____

_____

_____

4. Research the Internet for the cost of an uncomplicated appendectomy on a 34-year-old in three different locations in the United States. What do you find?

_____

_____

_____

5. What circumstances might prevent a clinic from seeking reimbursement through collections?

_____

_____

_____

CLASSROOM EXERCISES

1. As a newly employed medical clinic manager, you discover that one of the providers in the clinic does not follow the written collections policies and is more lenient about clients paying their bills. What problem does this create for you and the other providers? What action might be warranted?

2. A provider overhears the receptionist say to a client, "Well, you know, we can take only so many welfare clients." How can the client now be put at ease? How will you counsel the receptionist?

3. Correct the following telephone conversation:
   BOOKKEEPER (BK): "Hi, this is Dr. Erythro's office. Who's this?"
   CLIENT (CL): "This is Laura Phagocyte."
   BK: "You owe us $46.25. Can you pay us $10 today?"
   CL: "Yeah, I'll put it in the mail."
   BK: "Will it be check or money order?"
   CL: "Check."
   BK: "Fine, I'll expect it in a few days. Thank you. Good-bye."

4. You are a bookkeeper for a very busy two-provider clinic. Managing client accounts that are covered under a myriad of insurance plans providing differing reimbursement rates is taking an increasing amount of time and energy. The providers have already determined not to take any more Medicare or Medicaid clients and are discussing dropping other insurance plans. What are the legal and ethical implications?

5. You have been asked to do the collection calls in your large medical clinic. Although you work in insurance coding and billing, you are not sure you have the skills to do so. This assignment will also include appealing denied insurance claims. What must you do to be prepared and to be successful?

INTERNET ACTIVITIES

1. Research the Internet to determine what impact the Affordable Care Act has on reimbursement for medical providers. Describe what you find.

For additional resources please visit
http://FADavis.com, keyword *Tamparo.*

CHAPTER 11

Employment Practices

"To be successful, the first thing to do is fall in love with your work."—Sister Mary Lauretta; American nun and science teacher

KEY TERMS

Americans With Disabilities Act (ADA) Prohibits discrimination of individuals with physical or mental disabilities from accessing public services and employment.

Family Medical Leave Act (FMLA) Requires public employers and private employers of 50 or more employees to provide up to 12 weeks of job-protected unpaid leave for such family-related issues as birth or adoption, care of a seriously ill family member, or serious illness of employee.

Occupational Safety and Health Act (OSHA) A 1970 act with the goal to ensure a safe and healthy workplace environment; a division of the U.S. Department of Labor. Important components include the following:

Bloodborne Pathogen Standard and Personal Protective Equipment Require employers to protect workers from occupational exposure to infectious agents. This includes needlestick injuries.

Chemical hygiene plan (CHP) Regulation that addresses training, information requirements, and provisions to be implemented for chemical exposure in the ambulatory health-care setting.

Protecting America's Workers Act Updates OSHA to protect all state and local public employees, federal workers, and millions of other workers inadequately covered by other laws; increased civil and criminal penalties for job safety violations.

quid pro quo The plan to get something of value in return for giving something of value.

LEARNING OUTCOMES

Upon successful completion of this chapter, you should be able to:

11.1 Define the key terms.
11.2 Discuss the importance of policy manuals.
11.3 Describe the information in personnel policies.
11.4 Explain, in your own words, the importance of correct hiring practices.
11.5 List at least four necessary components of personnel policies.
11.6 Identify the three necessary elements of job descriptions.
11.7 Discuss clinic hours, workweek schedule, benefits, and salaries.
11.8 Explain where and how to locate prospective employees.
11.9 List eight techniques for effective interviews.

11.10   Identify five potential discrimination problems to consider when hiring.
11.11   Describe sexual harassment.
11.12   Explain the four parts of the Occupational Safety and Health Act.
11.13   Discuss the importance of the Americans With Disabilities Act for employer and employee.
11.14   Outline the Family Medical Leave Act and its use in the medical practice.
11.15   Recall procedures for selecting the right employee.
11.16   Recognize steps that encourage employee longevity.

COMPETENCIES

CAAHEP

- Identify personal safety precautions as established by the Occupational Safety and Health Administration (OSHA). (CAAHEP XII.C.2)
- Identify how the American With Disabilities Act (ADA) applies to the medical assisting profession. (CAAHEP X.C.10.c)
- List and discuss legal and illegal interview questions. (CAAHEP X.C.9)
- Complete an incident report. (CAAHEP X.P.7)

ABHES

- Define scope of practice for the medical assistant and comprehend the conditions for practice within the state that the medical assistant is employed. (ABHES 4.f.1)
- Perform the essential requirements for employment such as resume writing, effective interviewing, dressing professionally, and following up appropriately. (ABHES 10.a)

VIGNETTE

Susan has been an exemplary employee of a growing medical practice that has recently expanded into medical grade aesthetics. Several years ago, she started with Dr. Testa as a registered medical assistant (RMA) and quickly stepped into the role of office manager. She developed the policy and procedure manual as well as personnel policies as the practice grew. She enjoyed assisting clients with everything from scheduling appointments to dealing with insurance companies. She also assisted with hiring and dismissing employees. She maintained detailed records for each employee, making sure that licenses and certifications were kept current. Susan decided to enroll in business classes at the local community college and mentioned it in passing to Dr. Testa. Susan soon graduated with a degree in business management and turned in her resignation to Dr. Testa. He was shocked as he heavily relied on Susan to keep his practice running smoothly.

When asked why she was leaving, Susan stated, "I have been employed by you for several years and have never had a formal evaluation or a raise during that time even though my responsibilities have greatly increased. I now have an Associate's Degree in business management and would like to enroll in a 4-year program, but I can't afford one." Dr. Testa was dumbfounded and stated, "You run this practice so well that I assumed you were also taking care of yourself along with everyone else." Dr. Testa asked Susan to meet with him the next day before making any decisions.

During the meeting, Dr. Testa apologized to Susan for the lack of communication and feedback over the years. It was obvious his informal praise was not enough. He provided Susan a formal evaluation with a raise and a large bonus to reimburse her tuition and missed cost of living raises. He could not imagine the practice without her! He also asked Susan to develop a tuition reimbursement plan for the practice to assist staff members who enrolled in courses that would assist them at the practice. They also set up a yearly schedule for future evaluations.

HIRING EMPLOYEES

Providers do not function alone in the health-care setting. Even providers who are just starting their practice hire an assistant as soon as possible. Selecting appropriate personnel is an important business task. As a practice grows, a clinic manager, in cooperation with the clinic providers, is usually the one responsible for hiring personnel. Current employees commonly are influential in the process of obtaining additional employees. Hiring and preparing employees to function in specific roles are both expensive and time-consuming tasks. Therefore, it is important to perform the tasks effectively the first time. For example, a new doctor arrives in a small town and hires a certified medical assistant (CMA) as a first-hire because the CMA can perform both administrative and clinical responsibilities in the clinic. In just a short time, the practice has grown and more staff is needed. The likely candidate to become the clinic manager to oversee the staff is the CMA who has been there from the beginning. It is important to understand, in some situations, that you might become a manager within a short time after being hired.

There are a number of important areas of consideration and tasks to perform before successful and effective hiring takes place. They include the following:

1. Creating a policy manual
2. Establishing personnel policies
3. Determining job descriptions for each position
4. Locating the best employee for the position
5. Conducting effective interviews
6. Selecting candidates to fulfill the practice's needs
7. Evaluating employees on a predetermined and regular basis
8. Keeping employees for the long term

POLICY AND PROCEDURE MANUALS

Policy manuals identify the policies of the practice. This manual sets the tone for the practice and expresses the philosophy of the providers regarding client care. Policy manuals will identify the scope of client services, providers' specialty areas, clinic hours and workweek schedule, insurances accepted and processed, and biographical and educational information about each provider and staff member. The biographical and educational information often becomes part of a clinic brochure that is made available for clients. Many brochures of this nature only identify the specifics of each provider. However, including background information about each staff member not only heightens the level of importance of each staff member, but it helps clients to identify those individuals with whom they have a great deal of contact during their care.

The policies should be updated from time to time to reflect any changes in the clinic, but they should always be in writing and available to employees. Computerizing the policy manual makes changes and updates quite easy to accomplish.

A *procedure manual* details (usually in steps) how to perform certain procedures, both in the administrative and clinical areas. It is much different from a policy manual but is equally important to a safe and efficient medical clinic. Procedure manuals often need updating more frequently than policy manuals.

Once policy and procedure manuals are established, they should be used as references, especially for new practice hires. The directives contained within are a guide for the practice of employees.

PERSONNEL POLICIES

Personnel policies are established to identify and address concerns of employees and state the desires of management. Without established personnel policies, providers soon lose control of the management of their own practices when or if they begin to make decisions in an arbitrary and inconsistent manner. Larger clinics will have personnel policy manuals, often called employee handbooks. Smaller practices most likely include personnel policies in a separate location of the policy manual.

Personnel policies will identify workweek schedule and hours, salary and benefits, overtime reimbursement, sick leave and vacation policies, employee and client safety, employee conduct and discipline, and employee evaluation and salary review. A most critical personnel piece relates to total confidentiality of all client information. Figure 11-1 gives an example of a policy statement regarding a confidentiality and nondisclosure agreement that employees may be asked to sign. Such a document should be reviewed with employees yearly.

Before a person is hired, staff needs are determined and job descriptions written. Determine in advance if employees are to be generalists or specialists in their skills, or if employees with a combination of these skills will be more effective. It is important, too, to decide if employees will be cross-trained and, if so, for what specific positions.

CLINIC HOURS AND WORKWEEK SCHEDULE

Clinic hours and the workweek schedule are fairly easy to establish. Hours may be determined by the medical specialty and the dictates of the community. The long and often inconsistent hours of a medical practice should be addressed; for example, will every employee stay late, will hours be staggered, and will overtime be compensated? Will the workweek schedule be the same as or longer than clinic hours? How will a policy be established that provides for the needs of clients, is fair to employees, and allows all tasks to be performed?

Employees become unhappy if they are told on hiring that the workweek schedule will be 40 hours and it turns out to be closer to 50 to 60 hours. Planning for overtime is essential. Being honest with employees is a must. Employees are expected to plan for their nonwork responsibilities so that they do not interfere with their employment and also to achieve a work-life balance. Therefore, firm policies on overtime make accommodating for day care, family needs, and nonwork responsibilities easier.

JOB DESCRIPTIONS

Job descriptions indicate minimum qualifications required, a description of the job to be performed, and to whom the employee is responsible. Job descriptions must be developed for each position in the clinic. These job descriptions are often shared with candidates at the time of interviews.

The established health-care clinic will find its employees to be the best resources when writing job descriptions by having the employees put in writing descriptions of the tasks they perform in a normal workday. This exercise becomes the basis for the job descriptions.

CONFIDENTIALITY AND NONDISCLOSURE AGREEMENT

I, _____, do affirm that I will not divulge
_____[PRACTICE NAME]_____ DATA TO ANY UNAUTHORIZED PERSON FOR ANY REASON.
Neither will I directly use, or allow the use of, _____[PRACTICE NAME]_____ DATA for any
purpose other than that directly associated with my official assigned duties.
I understand ALL CLIENT INFORMATION, including financial data, is strictly confidential.

Furthermore, I will not, either by direct action or by counsel, discuss, recommend, or suggest to
any unauthorized person the nature or content of any _____[PRACTICE NAME]_____ information.

Violation of confidentiality is cause for disciplinary action, including immediate dismissal.

I understand that signing this document does not preclude me from reporting instances
of breach of confidentiality.

Signed _____ Date _____

Figure 11-1. Example of a confidentiality and nondisclosure agreement.

When developing a specific job description, education and training requirements must be included. Equally important, job descriptions should also contain any specific physical requirements necessary for the job. The frequency with which each physical requirement is used should be established. *Rarely, frequently,* and *regularly* are terms that may be used. For example, an application for a position in a sports medicine clinic might indicate: "Assistance with ambulation is regularly required," and "lifting up to 50 pounds is frequently required" in many health-care settings. This practice helps ensure that the Americans With Disabilities Act (ADA) is followed and that the right employee is hired to do a specific job.

BENEFITS AND COMPENSATION

Benefits and compensation are of concern to both employees and employers. Providers will want to pay a salary that is commensurate with the responsibilities of the task to be performed and that reflects the education, training, credentialing, and experience of the employees. Another consideration can be the prevailing wage of the community. The Internet is a valuable resource that can aid in the benchmarking of specific salaries per region. It is important to have a method of evaluating salaries yearly. Some tie salary to performance reviews; others review salaries at the end of each calendar year.

Often, benefits are as important to employees as salary. Benefits to consider include medical insurance, sick leave, vacations, holidays, retirement, and profit-sharing plans. Other incentives may include payment of approved educational courses, seminars, professional memberships, a uniform allowance, and possibly a gas allowance. An important benefit, especially in the city, may be free parking or bus passes.

An important consideration for vacation time often occurs when the provider is a sole proprietor. It may be preferable to have an assistant working to direct clients to another source for their care and to provide some catch-up time for administrative tasks such as billing and collecting while the provider vacations. Other clinics, however, will give staff members leave whenever the provider takes leave. The difficulty with this plan is that the provider's vacation leave may not be the best time for the assistant's vacation to occur. If the assistant's vacation period is different from that of the provider, a temporary MA can be hired. However the issue is resolved, it is important for an honest discussion that includes problem-solving from both provider and staff to occur.

Once the employee is hired and the onboarding or orientation process begins, it is important to review the terms of employment and the benefits that are offered with new personnel. New personnel should sign paperwork that states that a review was made with comprehension of all policies to avoid any future issues or misunderstandings.

THE EMPLOYMENT PROCESS

LOCATING EMPLOYEES

A valuable resource for clinics seeking employees may be the county medical society. Some sponsor a medical employment agency. Schools in the community that have accredited education programs for MAs, medical secretaries, or other professionals often have names of graduates seeking employment. Social media is often used for job contacts. Websites such as LinkedIn.com, ZipRecruiter. com, Glassdoor.com, and Monster.com are useful tools in the search for new talent. Some companies will even offer to prescreen candidates, and any fee imposed may be worth the time and energy saved for current employees.

Professional national organizations for MAs, such as the American Association of Medical Assistants and the American Medical Technologists Association, may have local chapters in geographic areas that are able to provide possible candidates for employment.

Other providers and their employees often know of potential candidates. Employment agencies specializing in medical and dental employment can be a resource. Newspaper advertising may also be successful but should specifically identify that a résumé be sent as the first step.

In an established medical practice, the initial screening of candidates is likely performed by a clinic manager or a specific person other than the provider.

INTERVIEWING CANDIDATES

With a printed job description and a list of possible candidates, the interview process can begin. The interview is a time to meet with each candidate personally. A job application is often completed at this point.

 Commonsense techniques to make the interview more effective and satisfy any legal concerns include the following steps for the interviewer to keep in mind:

1. Identify the purpose of the interview and describe the position being filled.
2. Avoid interruptions during the interview. Do not rush; however, it is prudent to inform the interviewee that you have a set amount of time for the interview.
3. Use effective communication skills and listen carefully to the candidate.
4. Match the candidate to the position. Look at the total qualifications of the candidate. Do not pick a "clone" similar to yourself. Look for diversity.
5. Observe nonverbal behavior including neatness of attire and grooming.
6. Ask each candidate for a position the same questions. This is important and makes the comparison of more than one candidate as fair and unbiased as possible (Fig. 11-2).
7. Remain objective.
8. Maintain control of the interview.
9. Present possible scenarios requiring a solution to help determine skill level and communication style.
10. End on a positive note; summarize, allow for questions from the candidate, and provide the candidate with a possible date for a decision. ●

Once the interview has ended, time should be taken to make notes that will serve as a reminder later when considering all the candidates. Inform applicants that you will be taking notes during the interview; otherwise, they may be concerned.

 IN THE NEWS

The American Association of Medical Assistants (AAMA) states that medical assisting is one of the nation's careers growing much faster than average for all occupations. Much of the reason for this rapid growth is the predicted surge in outpatient care facilities, technological advancements, and the growing number of elderly Americans who need medical treatment.

Questions may include:

A. What are your qualifications?
B. Why are you leaving your present position?
C. When can you begin work?
D. What salary do you expect?
E. What do you expect to be doing in 1 year? In 5 years?
F. Why do you want to work here?
G. Do you foresee any difficulties that may prevent you from doing a good job?
H. How did you become interested in the medical field?
I. What is your major strength?
J. What is your major weakness?
K. Describe a difficult situation that you were involved in and the outcome. Could there have been a different outcome?

Figure 11-2. Possible questions to ask potential employees.

SELECTING EMPLOYEES

After completion of the interview process, make a careful study of all candidates and their responses to your questions. Contact references listed on the employment applications. Talking with former employers and individuals named as references is an important part of the decision-making process. Ask permission from any prospective employee before checking references or include a permission request on the job application form. Possible reference check questions follow:

1. Can you share information about this applicant?
2. Our applicant has listed a position with you as _____. Is this correct?
3. Does the applicant work best as a member of a team or alone?
4. Can you give an example of this applicant's exemplary performance?
5. How does the applicant perform under stress?
6. Would you rehire this person? Why or why not?
7. Would you recommend the applicant for this specific position?
8. Is there anything else we should know about this applicant?

How each candidate will function with other staff members is to be considered. If candidates have been asked to perform any skill functions, check the tests for accuracy. Candidates may be asked to do some keyboarding, take a spelling test (medical and nonmedical words), or perform a clinical function. Telephone candidates or ask them to call the clinic at a later time to screen their telephone personalities. The manner in which candidates handle the telephone is important because the client's first contact with the provider's clinic is often made via the telephone.

Many employers also conduct background checks and preemployment drug screening. If the practice includes treating minors and/or vulnerable adults, a child-abuse clearance check will be needed as well.

Once a decision is made, contact the chosen candidate to offer the position. Once the position has been filled, *all* candidates should be informed. This courtesy is often overlooked. Set a start date for employment and establish a probationary period for the new employee; 3 months is usually adequate time to determine whether the working relationship is a good one. At the end of this period, either employee or employer should be free to end the employment agreement. Salary paid during the probationary period may be less than that offered for permanent employment.

Case Study

An applicant who is morbidly obese is interviewed for a position as a security guard in a hospital. The division unit clerk states, "Who are they going to be able to chase down?"

What effect, if any, does the obesity of this candidate have on likelihood of being hired?
What legal ramifications must be kept in mind? What is your reaction to the unit clerk's comment?

EVALUATING EMPLOYEES

Evaluation of employees is an ongoing task throughout the individual's employment. Probably the biggest mistake in health-care employment is not making evaluation a formal process. A clearly established and written evaluation policy and form should be developed and carefully explained to employees, with a copy given to each. At regular intervals during the course of employment, evaluations should be conducted. New employees should be evaluated at 3 months, thus ending the probationary period. Another evaluation is conducted 6 months later. Thereafter, yearly evaluations on the date of original hire are conducted. If problems surface or an employee is assigned a new major responsibility, evaluations may change and increase in frequency. Strengths and weaknesses should be documented. The evaluation then becomes part of the employee's personnel file after it has been reviewed and discussed with the employee. Also, the employee and supervisor should both sign and date the document.

An adequate evaluation enables employees to improve job performance and serves as a tool for employers to discuss salary increases, provides background for any necessary dismissal, and establishes a record for future referral. Samples of employee evaluation forms may be available through the American Medical Association and resources provided by the Medical Group Management Association. One is provided for you on the F. A. Davis website, keyword *Tamparo*.

Although the evaluation records may assist a manager in determining salary increases, a change in salary is best made at the end of each year and discussed with each employee. Salary changes and evaluations should be kept separate. Salary raises attached to evaluations tend to make the whole process a punitive one. When evaluations are separate from salary increases, the whole intent of the evaluation is to make the employee a better one, to praise what has been done well, and to challenge the employee to learn more. When salary raises are given at the end of the year, they encourage management to consider how well the business has done and what profits have been made. Also, less friction occurs among employees when personnel receive a percentage raise related to their base salary. Also, when the economy is in a slump and salary increases may not be possible, that statement to everyone at the end of the year is better than giving no raises at the time of performance evaluations. However, a wise manager recognizes the value of an excellent employee and will make the salary reimbursement or other benefits an encouragement for the employee to remain with the practice.

Case Study Continued

In the vignette at the beginning of the chapter, identify steps that might have been taken by Susan and Dr. Testa to prevent the situation.

EMPLOYEE DISMISSAL

When evaluating employees, the decision may be made to dismiss an employee. Dismissal is a difficult, unpleasant situation, but steps must be taken to protect the clinic while minimizing the stress for the employee who is dismissed.

If the evaluation process has been effective, documentation exists in the employee's personnel file detailing the problem behaviors. The file should include dates the problems were discussed with the employee and specific actions discussed for correction of the problems. You must have the employee sign the documents to ensure that the employee has been informed and understands the problem areas and what specific actions are required for correction. Such written documentation will be essential should the terminated employee later seek litigation.

The employee's progress or lack of progress should be evident in the personnel file. Dismissal should take place during the probationary period if possible. Warnings (both verbal and written) to the employee help ward off surprise when dismissal is made. During the dismissal conference, it is best to be brief, to the point, and honest without degrading the employee.

There are likely three reasons requiring immediate dismissal of employment: (1) breach of client confidentiality, (2) disregard for client safety, and (3) fraudulent or criminal actions. The clinic's policy and/or personnel manual must clearly identify and define these reasons for immediate dismissal. Also, it may be best to take any dismissal action late on a Friday afternoon so that disruption is minimized and there is no opportunity for the employee to compromise the medical clinic. Larger clinics with a personnel department will also have the dismissed employee escorted from the building and will make sure to receive any keys, codes, or clinic property that the dismissed employee may have. Computer passcodes are immediately changed.

Managers can learn from the dismissal experience. Was the job description clear and accurate? Was the probationary period long enough? Was the evaluation process fair, clear, and well documented? How and when were the problem areas communicated to the employee? However unfortunate dismissal is to both the employee and employer, it is best to use good human relation skills, express empathy, and communicate clearly all expectations to employees in both written and verbal formats. All matters regarding the dismissal are confidential.

WHEN EMPLOYEES CHOOSE TO LEAVE

There is any number of reasons for employees to leave a practice. They may find a better job, move, have a change in family responsibilities, or retire. An exit interview should be conducted. This is a time to gather specific information about closing the employment relationship. It is also a time for both employer and employee to evaluate the position and identify any potential changes. Some of the questions to ask of the employee who is leaving include the following:

1. What did you like best about your job?
2. What did you like least?
3. What would you change about your position?
4. Did you receive the support that you needed to do your job?
5. What would improve the workplace for someone in your position?
6. Did you receive the feedback you needed?
7. Was your supervisor's management style a key to your leaving?
8. Is there anything else you would like to comment on?

These questions can help to formulate any changes in the job description when seeking a replacement for the position.

RETAINING EMPLOYEES

Retaining employees is as important as selecting them. Salaries that are commensurate with work performance and the qualifications of employees are a must. Salary is not a place to try to cut clinic expenses. The old adage "You get what you pay for" is especially true in employment. Replacing an employee can cost as much as three to four times a monthly salary.

Salary is very important to employees but so is feeling appreciated and valued as a member of the team. The simple "thank you" and "well done" are compliments that foster goodwill and motivate employees to greater effectiveness. Finding what each staff member likes to do best and allowing him or her to perform that task will enhance employee satisfaction. Good employees merit trust and increased responsibilities. Encourage employees to improve their education and knowledge and provide incentives for them to do so.

If employees are to be corrected or disciplined, never do so in front of other employees or clients. Most will accept tactful criticism well. Few will forget if they are embarrassed before their peers or the clients. Remembering birthdays and employment anniversaries with simple gifts or cards takes little effort but does much for employee morale.

Employees in the health-care setting can make or break a medical clinic. It is a good idea to take the time and effort to ensure that the staff functions as a team to create an atmosphere conducive to good provider-client relationships.

Individuals involved in the hiring process must be knowledgeable of state and federal work and employment regulations. The U.S. Department of Labor, Wage, and Hour Division will answer questions regarding minimum wages, overtime pay, use of child labor, and length of workday. A state's human rights commission can answer questions on possible discrimination in the interview or hiring process. ●

Case Law

Ellen Harris, registered nurse (RN), experienced bullying, harassment, and unfair treatment from coworkers at The Queen's Medical Center in Honolulu, Hawaii. She worked in the intensive care unit from 2006 to 2011. She reported an unsafe coworker who was also allegedly stealing narcotics. Ms. Harris stated that the harassment became worse after she made the report. At one point, she found a racial note in her mailbox and later found a picture of a noose on her locker. Ms. Harris alleged that Queen's Medical Center never said the racial discrimination and retaliation were wrong or offered an apology. On February 28, 2018, a jury awarded her $630,000 in damages and $3.2 million in punitive damages.

Harris v. The Queen's Medical Center, et al. First Circuit Court of Hawaii, Case No. 1CC131001737.

EMPLOYMENT LAW

Title VII of the Civil Rights Act of 1964 is a federal law that states an employer of 15 or more people must not discriminate on any form of application for employment. The discrimination includes age, sex, race, creed, marital status, national origin, color, or disabilities (sensory, mental, or physical). Many states have adopted laws that are more strict than federal law. For example, in the State of Washington, an employer of eight or more cannot discriminate. Massachusetts, however, goes several steps beyond the federal guidelines, stating that employers with six or more employees are prohibited from discriminating against employees based on race, color, religious creed, national origin, ancestry, sex, age, criminal record (applications only), handicap (disability), mental illness, retaliation, sexual harassment, sexual orientation, and genetics. Note that not all states are as specific as Massachusetts in prohibiting discrimination against LGBTQIA community members who find it difficult to be employed if/when their sexual orientation is identified. In addition, employers in some states have an affirmative responsibility to provide maternity leave to biological and adoptive parents even though it is not mandated by federal law.

IN THE NEWS
In April of 2019, the U.S. Supreme Court announced it would hear the following three cases to determine whether protection for LGBTQIA people under Title VII of the Civil Rights Act would be reversed:
1. *Altitude Express v. Zarda:* Don Zarda was fired once he revealed his sexual orientation to a customer at the skydiving business where he worked.
2. *Bostock v. Clayton County, GA:* Gerald Bostock was fired from his position as a child welfare services coordinator when his employer learned he was gay.
3. *R.G. & G.R. Harris Funeral Homes v. EEOC and Aimee Stephens:* When Aimee Stephens, a funeral director, informed her employer she is transgender and would come to work as a woman consistent with that identity, the funeral home told her that was unacceptable and fired her. *(Author's note: On May 12, 2020, Aimee Stephens died at age 59, the result of complications from kidney disease. She died in her home in Detroit with her wife at her side. ACLU lawyer Chase Strangio said, "Our country owes her a debt of gratitude for her commitment to justice for all people and her dedication to the transgender community.")*

You can research these three cases on the Internet for more information. The Court heard oral arguments on October 8, 2019, and in June 2020, it ruled that the decision was made that the landmark civil rights law barred sex discrimination in the workplace to gay, lesbian, and transgender employees, making it illegal to do so. Unfortunately, Aimee Stephens did not live long enough to see this ruling.

Nothing in either the federal or state discrimination laws is intended to prevent the employer from hiring only the most qualified person. Obviously, to protect this right, a well-written job description is essential, followed by impeccable attention to personnel issues.

Potential discrimination problem areas include the following:

- *Age*—Any inquiry implies a preference and is prohibited.
- *Marital status*—No inquiries are permitted.
- *Race or color*—No inquiry concerning race or color of skin, hair, eyes, and so forth is permitted.
- *Sex or sexual orientation*—No inquiry is permitted.
- *Disabilities*—No inquiry is permitted if disabilities or health problems are not related to job performance. If the employer needs to take a special need or handicap into account in determining job placement or fitness to perform, an inquiry can be made.

Most laws permit employers to talk about the position, its duties, and its responsibilities but prohibit any questions unrelated to the position. For example, it is not job related to note that the applicant has children, but it is job related to note whether the applicant indicated problems getting to work or working overtime. Managers preparing for an interview who bring a structured outline of subjects to cover with all applicants and who treat the candidates alike in all respects will have greater success in the hiring process and will prevent legal repercussions.

Even though some health-care settings may not have 15, or even 6, employees, it is best to follow the state and federal requirements, not only for protection but also for ethical reasons and for good public relations. See Figure 11-3 for valid reasons for declining applicants.

FAMILY AND MEDICAL LEAVE ACT

Another law that may affect medical clinics is the **Family and Medical Leave Act (FMLA)** of 1993. The law applies to organizations with 50 or more employees and will most likely be seen in large medical centers, hospitals, and hospital-affiliated clinics. The act provides employees up to 12 weeks of job protection and unpaid leave for family and medical reasons. The reasons include (1) birth and care of a child, as well as adoption or care of a foster child; (2) care of an immediate family member who is seriously ill; and (3) care of an employee's own serious health condition. Employees must have been employed at least 12 months and worked at least 1,250 hours during the 12 months before the FMLA leave begins.

SEXUAL HARASSMENT

Title VII of the Civil Rights Act of 1964 protects employees from sexual harassment that may occur on the job. The guidelines from the Office of Equal Opportunity at the U.S. Equal Employment Opportunity Commission make the employer strictly liable for the acts of supervisory employees as well as for some acts of harassment by coworkers and clients of the company. A written policy on sexual harassment, detailing inappropriate behavior and stating specific steps to be taken to correct an inappropriate situation, should be established. Such a statement can be placed in the policy manual and referred to in personnel policies.

The traditional form of harassment is the scenario in which sexual favors are implicit and demanded of an employee by a supervisor in exchange for job advancement. This is known in legal terms as *quid pro quo*, which means "this for that." For example, the provider says to an employee, "You know, there's a promotion available if you spend the weekend with me." A second, probably more common form of harassment, a hostile work environment, occurs when the work environment

Valid reasons for declining employment applicants:

- There is a health problem that would preclude the applicant from safe and efficient job performance.
- Applicant is not available for the required work schedule for the particular job (observance of religious holidays not included).
- Applicant lacks sufficient skills, training, or experience to perform the required duties of the job.
- Another applicant is better qualified.

Figure 11-3. Valid reasons for declining employment applicants.

interferes with the employee's work performance. The conduct must be severe or pervasive and may take the form of a series of sexual questions, comments, jokes, inappropriate touching by coworkers, or verbal belittling and teasing (refer to Case Law in Chapter 1). For example, a male MA is always making comments in the front office about "my girls," teasing them about premenstrual syndrome (PMS), and letting them know that they are inferior to men. When the harassment is commonplace and the supervisor or employer does not correct the situation, the employer and the clinic manager are liable under Title VII.

Generally, the easiest way to end harassment is to tell the harasser to stop the behavior. This works in some cases. Telling a supervisor or a designated person if the harassment does not stop is the best course of action. Ignoring the offensive behavior does not work, and it is illegal not to take corrective action. If the harassment continues, employers must make it easy and safe for those being harassed to seek help, and the harassment must stop.

The policy on harassment should include at least the following:
1. A statement that sexual harassment of employees and a hostile work environment will not be tolerated.
2. A statement that an employee who feels harassed needs to bring the matter to the immediate attention of a person designated in the policy.
3. A statement about the confidentiality of any incidents and specific disciplinary action against the harasser.
4. The procedure to follow when harassment occurs. ●

OCCUPATIONAL SAFETY AND HEALTH ACT

Congress passed the **Occupational Safety and Health Act (OSHA)** to prevent workplace disease and injuries. This statute applies to virtually every U.S. employer. The general purpose of the act is to require all employers to ensure employee safety and health.

Occupational Safety and Health Administration (OSHA) mandates that employers do all of the following:

- Encourage employers and employees to reduce workplace hazards and to implement new and improved health programs.
- Establish "separate but dependent responsibilities and rights" for employers and employees for the achievement of better safety and health conditions.
- Maintain a record-keeping system to monitor job-related injuries and illnesses.
- Develop mandatory job safety and health standards and enforce them effectively.

OSHA representatives may make unannounced visits to the workplace and may issue citations or penalties per violation to an employer who does not provide a safe environment.

Penalty rates changed in 2020. The maximum penalty for a serious violation is $13,494 per violation. Failure to abate is $13,494 per day beyond the abatement date, and willful or repeated incidents are $134,937 per violation. Amendments to the **Protecting America's Workers Act** (H.R. 1074) were introduced to Congress on February 7, 2019. It was referred to the House Committee on Education and Labor. No further updates are presently available for this bill. Contained in the OSHA are two regulations especially important in the health-care setting: the **Bloodborne Pathogen Standard and Personal Protective Equipment** and the Occupational Exposure to Hazardous Chemicals Standard or the **chemical hygiene plan (CHP)**.

The Bloodborne Pathogen Standard became effective in 1992. Its primary goal is to reduce occupational-related cases of HIV/AIDS and hepatitis B and C infections among health-care workers. The procedure or policy manual should carefully detail the following steps addressed in the Bloodborne Pathogen Standard and identify early updates and employee education:

1. Exposure control plans
2. Universal precautions
3. Engineering and work practice controls

   4. Personal protective equipment
   5. Laboratories
   6. Hepatitis B vaccination
   7. Postexposure follow-up
   8. Housekeeping
   9. Hazard communication and training
  10. Record-keeping

In 2001, in response to the Needlestick Safety and Prevention Act of 2000, OSHA revised the Bloodborne Pathogens Standard. The revised standard clarifies the need for employers to select safer needle devices and to involve employees in identifying and choosing these devices. The updated standard also requires employers to maintain a log of injuries from contaminated sharps.

The chemical hygiene plan addresses training, information requirements, and provisions that must be implemented for chemical exposure in the ambulatory health-care setting. Chemical inventories must be taken, a material safety data sheet (MSDS) manual has to be assembled or maintained online, and employers are required to provide a hazard communication education program to employees within 30 days of hire.

The Occupational Exposure to Hazardous Chemicals Standard requires the following tasks to be performed by employers:

  1. Inventory any and all hazardous chemicals regarding quantity, manufacturer's name, address, and chemical hazard classification.
  2. Assemble MSDSs from manufacturers. The MSDS can be easily stored online. This format makes updating the manual more efficient and allows greater accessibility. MSDS manuals were previously kept as hard copies. Should the need to keep a hard copy of the manual arise, the sheets should be reviewed regularly. Label the chemicals using the National Fire Protection Association's color and number method.
  3. Provide educational training to all employees who handle any hazardous chemicals within 30 days of employment and before an employee is allowed to handle the chemicals.
  4. Develop and evaluate a chemical hygiene plan to address how to handle any spills or exposures.

For the safety of employees and all clients, carefully following and monitoring these regulations is essential. Job descriptions should identify any position that may cause exposure to hazardous chemicals, bloodborne pathogens, and needlesticks.

AMERICANS WITH DISABILITIES ACT

The **Americans With Disabilities Act (ADA)** was passed in Congress in 1990 to eliminate discrimination in employment against a qualified individual with a disability. The statute applies to all persons with substantial impairment that significantly limits a major function. This includes hearing, seeing, speaking, walking, breathing, performing manual tasks, caring for oneself, learning, and working. It also protects persons with a history of cancer in remission, persons with a history of mental illness, and persons with AIDS or who are HIV positive.

Also, ADA covers individuals with a substance misuse addiction who are currently in a drug rehabilitation program or have successfully completed rehabilitation and have not used illegal substances for some time. However, an employer may be able to dismiss or refuse to hire a person with a recent history of illegal drug use, even if the person no longer misuses substances, in such specific occupations as law enforcement or public transportation when an employer can show that this policy is job related and consistent with business necessity. This exemption may apply to a health-care setting if controlled substances are regularly kept in the facility. For the most part, however, except in the case of such health-care settings as surgery centers, pain clinics, and oncology centers, very few clinics keep controlled substances on site.

The ADA Amendments Act (ADAAA) of 2008 was in response to a number of Supreme Court decisions regarding the original ADA. Definitions of "disability" were frequently narrowed so much

3. Identify the causes for immediate termination.

_____

_____

_____

4. Summarize what topics are off limits during an interview.

_____

_____

_____

5. Summarize the provisions and importance of the Family Medical Leave Act.

_____

_____

_____

CLASSROOM EXERCISES

1. In the case study about the morbidly obese candidate, identify the conversation that might be held between the clinic manager and the unit clerk. Describe what might happen if the applicant overhears the conversation.

2. The provider says to the assistant in the hall, "I'm tired of telling you how to do things and having you mess it up during an examination. Pick up your check at the end of the week and don't come back." How could this situation be prevented by using wise employment practices? What are the implications of how this was handled?

3. Under what conditions might clinic hours and an employee's actual workweek be different? Why?

4. Your supervisor makes lewd remarks and obvious sexual advances toward you. What will you do?

5. You have the "perfect" employee and want to show your appreciation. What might you do?

6. As a potential employee, answer the candidate questions listed in number 6 under the section "Interviewing Candidates" found earlier in the chapter.

7. You find the right candidate for the job who is wheelchair dependent. What will you do?

8. For the position of clinical medical assistant, identify standards related to hazardous chemicals, bloodborne pathogens, and needlesticks that must be in place.

INTERNET ACTIVITIES

1. Search the Internet for your state's law regarding discrimination related to employment. Is your state more or less restrictive than the federal law? If you live in a city or large metropolitan area, you might also research antidiscrimination laws in that area.

2. Check the Internet to determine whether the three cases before the U.S. Supreme Court regarding Title VII and the LGBTQIA allowed monetary compensation to the complainants.

3. This chapter identifies ADA and ADAAA regulations in employment. Search the Internet to determine what kind of accommodations a medical clinic must have to be in compliance with AD and ADAAA.

REFERENCE

Harris, D. M.: *Contemporary Issues in Healthcare Law and Ethics, 4th Edition*. Chicago: Health Administration Press, 2014.

For additional resources please visit
http://FADavis.com, keyword *Tamparo*.

CHAPTER 12

A Cultural Perspective for Health Professionals

"As different as we are from one another, as unique as each one of us is, we are much more the same than we are different. That may be the most essential message of all, as we help our children grow toward being caring, compassionate, and charitable adults."

—Fred Rogers; American educator, Presbyterian minister, songwriter, and television host

KEY TERMS

ageism Discrimination on the grounds of a person's age.

bias Prejudice in favor or against one thing, person, or group compared with another, usually in a way considered unfair.

culture The customs, arts, social institutions, and achievements of a particular nation, people, or other social group.

cultural competency The ability to communicate and collaborate effectively with individuals from different cultures.

ethnicity Pertaining to a group of people who share a common national or cultural tradition.

gender identity A person's perception of having a particular gender such as male, female, transgender, gender neutral, nonbinary, or something else.

health disparities Differences in health and health care between groups that are linked by social, economic, and/or environmental disadvantage.

invisible illnesses Any medical condition that is not easily visible to others.

prejudice Opinions that are not based on knowledge, reason, or actual experience.

race Major divisions of humankind based on behavioral and biological attributes that are biologically inherent.

sexual orientation A person's identity in relation to the sex of those to whom the person is sexually attracted.

socioeconomic status The social standing or class of an individual or group.

social determinants of health The conditions in the places where people live, learn, work, and play that affect health risks and outcomes.

values A person's principles or standards of behaviors.

LEARNING OUTCOMES

Upon successful completion of this chapter, you should be able to:

12.1 Define the key terms.
12.2 Discuss the impact of culture on health care.
12.3 Identify steps to achieve cultural competency.
12.4 Identify the many components of cultural diversity.
12.5 Discuss examples of cultural diversity.
12.6 Examine the concept of a new culture in health care.
12.7 Evaluate self as related to cultural competency.
12.8 Identify any personal prejudice or bias and determine a strategy to address it.
12.9 Facilitate cross-cultural communication.

COMPETENCIES

CAAHEP
- Discuss examples of diversity including cultural, social and ethnic. (CAAHEP V.C.18)
- Demonstrate respect for individual diversity. (CAAHEP V.A.3)

ABHES
- Analyze the effect of hereditary, cultural, and environmental influences. (ABHES 5.g)
- Demonstrate cultural awareness. (ABHES 5.i)

 ## UNDERSTANDING CULTURAL DIVERSITY

In today's increasingly mobile society, clients with diverse backgrounds, cultures, and values seek health-care services within our communities. **Culture** refers to the shared knowledge, beliefs, values, attitudes, customs, roles, relationships, cuisine, music, and art of individuals within a group. Individuals may identify with one culture or many cultures (Fig 12-1). **Values** are morals or standards that are acceptable and practical in a culture. Values are determined by ethnicity, family, religious beliefs, school, friends, and mentors. They are shaped by life experiences and are one way in which to identify culture. Sometimes cultural variances are obvious by color, dress, stature, or action. However, cultural differences may also be obscure.

As a health-care professional, you will have the opportunity to provide services to diverse individuals who may or may not look, act, and think like you. Being aware of individual and cultural differences is necessary for you and all professionals to perform legally, ethically, and therapeutically in today's health-care system. To provide culturally sensitive health care, you do not need to be an expert in every culture or know the values that each culture holds. Instead, you must be aware of your own culture and beliefs; have an open attitude toward cultural differences; seek opportunities to learn about different cultural practices and values; and cultivate skills to effectively interact with individuals from various cultures.

Cultural competency is the ability to collaborate effectively with individuals from different cultures. Research shows that health-care professionals who have cultural competency improve experiences and health outcomes for clients. Throughout the chapter, various facets that create culture will be presented so that you can begin to develop your cultural competency. Remember to stop after each section and reflect on your own culture, your attitude toward other cultures, and your opportunities to provide culturally competent health-care services.

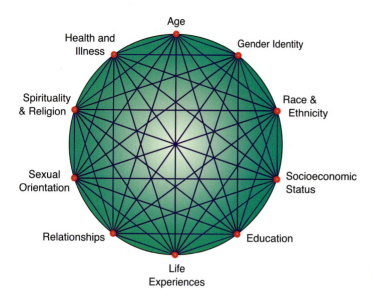

Figure 12-1. Cultural differences that make us unique.

 ## COMPONENTS OF CULTURAL DIVERSITY

Refer to Figure 12-1 throughout this section.

AGE

Ageism is any form of **prejudice**, **bias**, or discrimination that negatively targets the person on the basis of age. The term *ageism* was first used by Robert N. Butter, a gerontologist, to describe discrimination against older adults. Today, the term is applied to any type of age-based discrimination. This includes prejudice against children, teenagers, adults, and senior citizens. Ageism can take many forms, including prejudicial attitudes, discriminatory practices or policies, and actions that perpetuate stereotypical beliefs. Ageism is *not* about a person's age. It is about the meaning we assign to individuals based on their age or the way they look. For example, someone thinks an individual with gray hair and wrinkles probably is hard of hearing, forgetful, and set in their ways. Therefore, this individual should retire and could not possibly change careers or achieve a promotion. These assumptions about an older adult demonstrate ageism and are inappropriate and show bias and prejudice.

In health-care settings, ageism can cause disorders and diseases to be overlooked or mistakenly categorized as "normal" based on the client's age. Examples include dismissing dementia based on the assumption that it is a natural effect of aging, and misdiagnosing a sexually transmitted disease due to stereotypical beliefs that young adolescents and elderly adults are not sexually active. Ageism diminishes trust between clients and health-care providers, which results in ineffective medical care. The importance of age and how differently it is viewed varies among cultures.

Case Study

The Wang family is elderly. They are Chinese. Mrs. Wang has difficulty walking and has severe kyphosis. Mr. Wang loves his garden but has circulatory problems. He finds it increasingly difficult to cultivate his vegetables and help his wife. The Wang children are moving their mother and father into the home of the eldest son, who has already prepared his house for the two of them.

Next door to the Wang family is another elderly couple. Mr. and Mrs. Johnson are struggling to stay in their home. The house is too large, the yard work is getting away from them, and they have stairs to climb. Their children are pressing them to enter an assisted living facility where their meals will be prepared for them, there is no yard work, and someone will make sure they take their medications. Mr. Johnson worries that he will have to give up his car.

How do these examples show a variation on the ideas of care for elderly people? Explain.

GENDER/GENDER IDENTITY

Gender can be difficult to understand. It is complex and people are defining themselves in new and different ways as we gain a deeper understanding of identities. Gender is a social and legal status and a set of society's expectations about behaviors and thoughts. **Gender identity** is a person's perception of having a particular gender. It is the person's sense of oneself as male, female, transgender, gender neutral, nonbinary, or something else. Gender resides within the individual but can also be influenced by societal structures, cultural expectations, and personal interactions. It is essential to understand that the individual alone decides how to identify and how to express gender. As a health-care professional, you must ask the client how they would like to be identified, and show respect and support no matter what gender is identified.

SEXUAL ORIENTATION

Sexual orientation is the term used to refer to a person's emotional, romantic, and/or sexual attraction to a particular gender. LGBTQ is an acronym which stands for lesbian, gay, bisexual, transgender and queer or questioning. Additional letters are frequently added including an "I" for intersex and an "A" for ally or asexual. A plus sign (LGBTQ+) may also be used to demonstration inclusion of all genders and sexual orientations including pansexual, omnisexual, Two Spirit, gender-fluid, gender-non-conforming, non-binary, and other identities. While there are many variations of the acronym and disagreements on which letters should be included, research by Community Marketing Insight shows that "LGBTQ" is most widely accepted in the U.S. and around the world.

Although the definitions focus on the acronym, LGBTQ stands for much more than the individual terms. It describes a culture of individuals who do not identify with binary genders or heterosexual orientation. LGBTQ people have been publicly advocating for equal rights and responsibilities with heterosexuals within the U.S. since the late 1960s. Progress has been made on some issues, including marriage equality, same-sex adoption, and workplace discrimination protections, but many challenges still remain. Today, positive representations of LGBTQ people and issues are increasingly visible within mainstream media and popular culture. The civil rights movement continues to drive forward in pursuits of political, legal and social freedom and equality for the entire LGBTQ community. The health-care community has been particularly slow in adapting care and attention to the special needs of these individuals.

To achieve cultural competency, you must reflect on your own gender identity and sexual orientation. Seek opportunities to learn about individuals who differ from you. You also will want to be aware of circumstances in which differences based on gender and sexual orientation are significant and be able to act in promoting equitable outcomes. For example, health-care professionals should question medical treatments and therapies based on research conducted only on male clients. Women and/or members of the LGBTQ community are not similar enough to the male client to ensure the safety of these treatments. Medical studies in the United States are beginning to be more inclusive, but more research is needed to ensure that medical therapies are safe and effective for all people.

Case Law

1. Title VII of the Civil Rights Act of 1964 prohibits employment discrimination based on race, religion, national origin, and sex. In June 2020, the U.S. Supreme Court determined that "discrimination based on sex" applies to sexual orientation and gender identity, and therefore protects homosexual and transgender workers from workplace discrimination. Before this ruling, it was legal in more than 50% of states to discriminate based on sexual orientation

and gender identity, and to fire workers for being homosexual, bisexual, or transgender. The 6-to-3 ruling extended workplace protections to millions of people across the nation and encouraged LGBTQ activists with a potentially new era for civil rights.

2. During the same week, in the middle of June 2020, the Trump administration finalized a regulation that removed protections for transgender clients against discrimination by doctors, hospitals, and health insurance companies. This regulation narrowed the legal definition of sex discrimination to exclude transgender people, and reversed civil rights protections implemented in the Affordable Care Act by eliminating requirements for health-care providers and insurers to provide and cover medically appropriate treatment for transgender patients. The U.S. Department of Health and Human Services claimed that sex discrimination language in the Affordable Care Act did not explicitly refer to the legal status of transgender people.

National, state, and local organizations continue to fight for the civil rights of *all* people regardless of gender identity or sexual orientation. Future regulations and court rulings should be followed closely.

Update: President Joseph Biden restored health-care protection for transgender clients in May 2021.

Describe differences in the definitions of gender and sex discrimination from these two cases. How do these regulations affect your role as a health-care professional and your interactions with clients?

RACE AND ETHNICITY

The difference between race and ethnicity is complicated and continues to be debated. Today, **race** is generally understood as a mixture of behavioral and biological attributes. Race is often perceived as something that is inherent in our biology and therefore is passed from generation to generation. The U.S. Census offers several options for race: white, Black or African American, Asian, American Indian and Alaska Native, Native Hawaiian, and Other Pacific Islander.

Alternatively, **ethnicity** is usually understood as something acquired based on where we live or the culture we share with others. Ethnicity is the way in which an individual identifies learned aspects of themselves, including nationality, language, and culture. Examples of ethnicity include being Jewish, Indian, or Asian, regardless of race. An individual born to Korean parents in San Francisco may racially be considered an Asian, but ethnically as Korean, Asian American, Korean American, or just American. Individuals may self-identify with one ethnicity or multiple ethnicities

In 2020, almost 60% of the U.S. population was white. It is projected that people of color will account for the majority of the population by 2050, with the largest growth occurring among Hispanics. As our communities become more culturally diverse, ethnic and racial disparities become more apparent. The health-care system must adapt to meet the unique needs of our population and address the many challenges that cultural diversity creates. As a health-care professional, you will be challenged by language and communication barriers as well as health beliefs and values that are new and different from your own.

Case Study

A 15-month-old Puerto Rican child enters the urgent care center with a history of persistent, productive cough, fever, sleeplessness, and congestion. The child is diagnosed with pneumonia and is to be hospitalized. The child is wearing a delicate bracelet with black and red stone beads. The mother explains that this bracelet is what protects the infant from the evil eye. Two hours later, a hospital nurse removes the bracelet.

Were the actions of the nurse culturally sensitive? Might there be a reason for needing to remove the bracelet? Discuss the implication of this situation.

SOCIOECONOMIC STATUS

Socioeconomic status refers to a group of people with similar characteristics based on wealth. Multiple factors are associated with socioeconomic status, including income, employment, education, and available resources. According to the U.S. government, health is determined by access to economic and social opportunities. This means that the health of individuals is affected by resources and supports available in our homes, neighborhoods, and communities; the quality of our schools and educational opportunities; the safety of our workplaces; and the cleanliness of our water, food, and air. These factors are frequently called social determinants of health and are the conditions in which people live and work. Understanding how socioeconomic status affects your clients' health status and access to health-care services will assist you in your journey toward cultural competency.

Recent studies have shown significant health disparities for lower socioeconomic communities. Lower-income individuals are more likely to be uninsured, have higher rates of obesity, and to exhibit unhealthy lifestyle habits. Lower-income neighborhoods also have greater access to fast-food restaurants and convenience stores that offer food sources that promote unhealthy eating, whereas higher-income neighborhoods have more access to foods that support healthy eating patterns. Additionally, barriers to adequate health-care services for lower-income families include health illiteracy, distrust of health-care providers, and fewer health-care providers available in their communities.

Case Study

A young mother works for a community service agency. She receives a small amount of child support from her former husband. She has no health insurance other than Medicaid. She has an abscessed tooth. The dentist says she needs a root canal. She has no funds for the antibiotics to treat the abscess or to have the root canal. The dentist can only pull the tooth.

Why is adequate dental care not accessible to this mother?

Rene Helbling is a wealthy philanthropist. She has been on the kidney transplant list for some time. In her desperation, she turns to India in search of a kidney match and the surgery. Money is not an issue, and she has decided not to tell her nephrologist of her plans until after she returns from India.

Why is this client seeking health-care services in another country?

Reflect on both situations. How do socioeconomic factors affect these situations? Explain your answer.

IN THE NEWS

In May 2020, Covid-19 demographic data were collected from 48 states and Washington, D.C., through the COVID Racial Data Tracker. This information showed that nonwhite persons accounted for about 50% of all Covid-19 cases and 90% of Covid-19 deaths. Analysis of the data demonstrated that African American deaths are two times greater than expected based on population; confirmed cases for Hispanic/Latino persons are up to four times greater than expected; and white deaths are lower than their share of the population in 37 states. Racial and ethnic disparities related to Covid-19 are similar to prepandemic health disparities for minority populations and lower socioeconomic communities. Health disparities result from limited access to health-care services, higher rates of underlying conditions such as diabetes and heart disease, crowded neighborhoods and living conditions, and limited access to low-risk employment options.

With these data, public health officials are tailoring medical services, public health messages about Covid, and resources to provide basic needs including food, wage support, and temporary housing for people who get sick or are exposed to the virus. Public health responses will continue to be challenged by widespread mistrust of government and health officials within these minority and low socioeconomic communities. Understanding the culture, community values, and unique health barriers of residents is essential to overcome this mistrust and provide necessary health and economic resources.

EDUCATION

Educational preparation is a person's formal education, such as kindergarten through high school; some cultures provide children with only 4 or 5 years of formal education and educate only the males. In other cultures, privately funded education is the norm. Such differences may include private, public, or parochial education or home schooling. People moving to the United States may come with a high level of skill and education that is recognized in their country but are forced to take low-paying, menial jobs because of language barriers or lack of recognition for their level of accomplishment. An example of this is seen when doctors coming from another country must reeducate themselves in the United States before taking the licensing examination. Others may come with limited education and are able to reap benefits from the U.S. education system.

Case Study

Two expectant mothers come to the women's clinic for their prenatal care. One woman of Appalachian heritage has limited educational preparation. The other woman holds a Ph.D. from the nursing department in the local university. Each is having her first child.

What are the implications for each of these women and/or for the health-care professional?

LIFE EXPERIENCES

Life experiences shape how individuals adjust to life's challenges and perceive health and illness. These experiences may be related to specific events such as a family member's death, the adoption of a child, a rape or other traumatic event, a military tour during war, or homelessness. Abuse, neglect, and drug addiction are unfortunately common life experiences that significantly affect not only the individuals involved but also family, friends, and others associated with the individuals. The Covid-19 pandemic is definitely a life experience that has affected individuals around the world in a variety of ways. Sickness and death; unemployment and disrupted schooling; fear and anxiety; isolation and depression have all been experienced. Your experience with Covid-19 may be very different from someone else's experience. It is essential that health-care professionals try to understand how life experiences affect individual clients so that effective care can be provided.

Case Study

Jared was 18 when he went into the military. He wanted nothing more than to serve his country. He had his wish. He spent time in Croatia, Bosnia, and Afghanistan. Few can imagine the violence and devastation that Jared saw and experienced while helping to retrieve bodies from the war zone. He returned home after two tours of service, disillusioned with the entire military experience. He felt his future was in question and found it difficult to integrate back into society. His former friends were strangers to him. He was diagnosed with posttraumatic stress disorder.

How does the health-care professional relate to this client?

RELATIONSHIPS

Every relationship is unique. There are family relationships, friendships, friends related to employment, acquaintances, and romantic relationships. Some relationships are healthy, with effective communication, boundaries, and respect; others are not. As a health-care professional, you need to understand each client's relationships without judgment or prejudice. There may be relationships that you do not agree with or do not understand, but that does not mean the relationship is wrong or that the individuals involved are unsafe. Learning about modern families and romantic relationships will assist you in developing your cultural competency.

A family can be conceptualized in numerous ways, including individuals who share a household or live together; people who share common ancestors; a unit consisting of parents and their children; and a collection of individuals sharing biological kinship or related by marriage, adoption, partnership, or friendship. Families, no matter the defining characteristics, have an impact on who we are and how we relate to others. They frequently provide a foundation on how future relationships are built. Today's families may include three or four generations living within the same household with young adults not leaving home until late into their 30s, families of two mothers or two fathers and families with a step-parent. Today's families often are more influenced by economics than culture or religion, and family members are assuming nontraditional roles and responsibilities that change relationships among members. Understanding each client's unique experiences with family may assist the health-care provider to identify support services and establish attainable goals.

Romantic relationships are also unique to the individuals involved. Usually romantic relationships involve intimacy and sexual activity. Sexual orientation, as discussed earlier in the chapter, is a person's sexual identity in relation to the sex of those to whom the person is sexually attracted. A person may be sexually attracted to male partners, female partners, both, or none. Sexuality can change based on experiences, situations, and time. A person's sexual or romantic partner at any moment in time should not define the individual. Identifying or labeling a client based on sexual orientation feeds biases, stereotypes, and discrimination. Health-care providers must develop safe and trusting relationships with clients to provide effective sexual health care and education.

SPIRITUALITY AND RELIGION

Spiritual influences may include any of the major religions or no specific religion. A person's belief system may be a separate and unique spiritual support system. Religion and spirituality often have a significant impact on values and beliefs about health and illness, medical treatments and therapies, and experiences of dying and death. Some clients may seem more prepared for illness or surgery, and some may accept death more easily due to religious beliefs. Other clients may not seek medical treatment or might view illness or disease as a "punishment." Each client's spiritual beliefs must be respected by health-care professionals even when those beliefs are different from their own.

Case Study

The Reverend Jesse Morris is a retired clergyman. His faith has been strong for more than 70 years. He has a serious illness that will take his life in a short period of time. His nurse has tears in her eyes as she gives him a shot for pain. Reverend Morris says, "It is okay. I am fine. I am ready. God has a better place for me where there is no pain."

Joseph Rutherford is a Jehovah's Witness who needs a hip replacement. After being told that this type of surgery commonly requires a blood transfusion during or immediately after, Mr. Rutherford refuses to sign the surgical consent. He says, "God is the giver of life. I can endure pain and disability in obedience to God but will not take blood which is the life."

Is there a place for spirituality in health care? Justify your response.

HEALTH AND ILLNESS

The World Health Organization defines health as a state of physical, mental, and social well-being, not merely the absence of disease or injury. Health perceptions are affected by individual health status and experiences with diseases and/or injuries. People with chronic illnesses may perceive themselves in good health, whereas people with no evidences of illness may consider themselves in poor health. Some individuals are intensively private about their health issues; others broadcast them to anyone who will listen. Clients may also choose to ignore their health challenges altogether. The way a person reacts to health and illness is an attitude and judgment that encompasses all of the other cultural components from this chapter.

There are several disabilities and illnesses that are easy to identify due to physical deformities and medical aids, but there are many others that are not immediately apparent. Ninety-six percent of people with chronic medical conditions live with an illness that is invisible. **Invisible illnesses** include various mental health disorders as well as chronic physical conditions such as arthritis, diabetes, celiac disease, fibromyalgia, and renal failure. These clients may look healthy while experiencing significant pain or other internal symptoms that impair their ability to perform normal activities of daily living. Clients with invisible illnesses often experience discrimination and may be accused of faking or imagining their disabilities.

Case Study

Ron Harrison is a 68-year-old man. He is active and slender; he plays golf and eats very healthy food. No one knows that he is a walking time bomb with a cholesterol level of 385.

Bess Thor is 53. She parks in a handicap parking place and has a handicap license, but she walks into the grocery store with ease and without aid. The shopper who sneers at her and points to the disabled parking sign cannot know that Bess has chronic obstructive pulmonary disease (COPD) that will limit her shopping time to only 10 minutes before she will have to return to her car to rest.

What do these examples tell us about assumptions we sometimes make?

ESTABLISHING A NEW CULTURE IN HEALTH CARE

Every exchange with a client is a cross-cultural one. Each person brings to that exchange a diverse background, experience, education, age, gender, race, ethnicity, physical ability, religious belief, and sexual orientation. Developing a new culture, if that is what it might be called, where there is mutual respect, acceptance, and an environment conducive to teamwork among clients, health-care providers, and other health-care professionals, must be the goal. Health-care professionals must recognize that the failure to accept such diversity among clients and each other or the inability to embrace one's own differences becomes a barrier to quality health care.

Entering into a new culture of mutual respect, acceptance, and teamwork does not require total agreement with another person's differences; it merely requires acceptance of those persons for who they are and what they believe. It also gives them the right to their beliefs and values. A compassionate and thoughtful health professional must become nonjudgmental, put aside prejudices and biases, and always be aware of others' cultures. We do not have to alter or change our personal cultural experiences in order to respect and accept someone of a cultural experience. We must be able to see each person as a unique and special human being who has a right to culturally sensitive treatment.

EVALUATING SELF

Cultural competence begins with the honest desire to treat everyone with respect regardless of their cultural heritage. This requires an honest assessment of positive and negative assumptions about others. This is not easy because no one wants to admit cultural ignorance or negative prejudices. Examine each bias or prejudice you hold. On what assumptions is it based? Do those assumptions have any merit? Ask someone whose judgment you value to assist you in this examination. Recall someone with whom you have great differences. Can you foster the kind of respect and acceptance of that person to enable you to see a human being with equal merit rather than as a person with whom you disagree?

 ## CROSS-CULTURAL COMMUNICATION

Facilitating cross-cultural communication requires sensitivity to differences, attentive listening, and a respectful, nonjudgmental attitude. However, conflicts will arise. To deal with cultural conflicts, pay close attention to body language and tone of voice. When negative emotions expressed during a cultural conflict are yours, it is a good idea to step back, breathe deeply, and control your own emotions first. Then ask clients to express their experiences and feelings, if possible, and acknowledge them. Help clients find options suitable to them, and compromise over treatment goals and modalities whenever possible.

When language is a barrier, the use of a translator who is not a family member may prove to be beneficial. When interpreting, family members frequently leave out, add to, or change health-care content due to concerns about upsetting the client or feeling uncomfortable with the disorder or treatments being discussed. It is the responsibility of health-care providers to make certain that a professional interpreter is available when necessary to ensure the client's full understanding of procedures and treatment.

SUMMARY

Cultural diversity has been examined in this chapter, and personal feelings were explored in order to recognize the importance of cultural diversity in every client interaction. Continue to evaluate your behavior so that your actions reflect an automatic sensitivity to cultural differences. In the next section on bioethical issues, your culture and your belief system will be challenged. In each situation, strive to remain as free from bias and prejudice as much as possible, thus allowing open examination of all sides of an issue.

Consider the following quotes:

"The real act of discovery consists not in finding new lands, but in seeing with new eyes." —Marcel Proust, French novelist and critic.

"A new idea is first condemned as ridiculous and then dismissed as trivial, until finally, it becomes what everybody knows." —William James, American psychologist and philosopher.

 Watch It Now! Are you sensitive to other cultures? at http://FADavis.com, keyword *Tamparo.*

Questions for Review

SELECT THE BEST ANSWER

1. Ethnicity refers to
   a. Those who are gays and lesbians.
   b. National heritage, race, tribe.
   c. Language, geography.
   d. None of the above.
   e. Only b and c above.

2. Which statement(s) is (are) an example of ageism?
   a. "You roller skate well for a child who is only 6 year old."
   b. "It is normal to forget things at your age."
   c. "You need a pneumococcal vaccine since you are 78 years old."
   d. "Adolescents are at high risk for sports injuries."
   e. a, b, and c above

3. Gender identity
   a. Is a client's biological sex.
   b. Determines sexual preference.
   c. Is based on genitalia.
   d. Is defined by the client.
   e. Is unimportant in today's health-care climate.

4. To provide culturally sensitive health care, the health-care professional must
   a. Become an expert in every client's culture.
   b. Be aware of personal beliefs, values, and biases.
   c. Develop cross-cultural communication skills.
   d. All of above.
   e. Only b and c above.

5. Factors of socioeconomic status include
   a. Income.
   b. Employment.
   c. Education.
   d. All of above.
   e. None of above.

SHORT ANSWER QUESTIONS

1. A client who does not speak English is scheduled for an appointment. What steps will you take to ensure that the client receives culturally sensitive health care?

   _____

   _____

   _____

2. What does it mean to you to be nonjudgmental?

   _____

   _____

   _____

3. What is required of health-care professionals to enter into a new culture of health care?

   _____

   _____

   _____

4. What invisible illnesses have you encountered in your personal or professional life? How will your interactions with these clients change based on your new understanding of invisible illnesses?

_____

_____

_____

5. Identify a personal bias or prejudice. Develop a plan to ensure that this bias does not negatively affect your health-care career and professional interactions with clients.

_____

_____

_____

CLASSROOM EXERCISES

1. In each of the case studies given in the chapter, what would be your response? Is your response accepting and nonjudgmental?

2. Interview two persons who are of a different culture than your own. Ask them how they access health care. What is the influence of the family unit? Who makes health-care decisions?

3. Recall a time when you personally have been discriminated against in the health-care setting or some other setting because of your culture.

4. Identify a prominent cultural issue in the news today. How might this issue affect the health of your clients? How might this issue affect your role as a health-care professional?

5. Identify the largest ethnic minority in your geographic location. How are the health needs of this group addressed?

INTERNET ACTIVITIES

1. What are the laws in your state addressing discriminatory actions related to sexual orientation?

2. Related to Classroom Exercise number 5, search the Internet to determine as much about that culture as you can. Identify its customs and traditions. How do people of that culture celebrate births, birthdays, and weddings? What kind of custom is followed on the death of a loved one?

REFERENCES

Artiga, S., Orgera, K., & Pham, O. (2020). Disparities in health and health care: Five key questions and answers. Kaiser Family Foundation. https://www.kff.org/disparities-policy/issue-brief/disparities-in-health-and-health-care-five-key-questions-and-answers/

Centers for Disease Control and Prevention. (2018). Social determinants of health: Know what affects health. https://www.cdc.gov/socialdeterminants/index.htm

Disability World. (2019). Invisible disabilities: List and general information. https://www.disabled-world.com/disability/types/invisible/

Godoy, M., & Wood, D. (2020). What do coronavirus racial disparities look like state by state. NPR, May 30, 2020. https://www.npr.org/sections/health-shots/2020/05/30/865413079/what-do-coronavirus-racial-disparities-look-like-state-by-state

Liptak, A. (2020). Civil rights law protects gay and transgender workers, Supreme Court rules. *The New York Times,* June 16, 2020. https://www.nytimes.com/2020/06/15/us/gay-transgender-workers-supreme-court.html

Sanger-Katz, M., & Weiland, N. (2020). Trump administration erases transgender civil rights protections in healthcare. *The New York Times,* June 12, 2020. https://www.nytimes.com/2020/06/12/us/politics/trump-transgender-rights.html

World Health Organization. (2020). Ageing and life-course. https://www.who.int/ageing/ageism/en/

For additional resources please visit
http://FADavis.com, keyword *Tamparo*.

Bioethical Issues

CHAPTER 13

Allocation of Scarce Medical Resources

"Due to budget cuts, the light at the end of the tunnel will be out."—Bumper sticker on car

KEY TERMS

Apgar score System of scoring a newborn's physical condition 1 minute and 5 minutes after birth. Heart rate, respiration, muscle tone, response to stimuli, and skin color are measured. Maximum score is 10; those with low scores require immediate attention if they are to survive.

"concierge" medical service Medical care that provides "over and above" medical services to clients for a fee.

diagnosis-related groups (DRGs) Categorization of hospital medical services to standardize prospective medical care.

macroallocation System in which distribution decisions are made by large bodies of individuals, usually Congress, health systems agencies, state legislatures, and health insurance carriers.

microallocation System in which distribution decisions are made by small groups or individuals, such as hospital staff and physicians.

LEARNING OUTCOMES

Upon successful completion of this chapter, you should be able to:

13.1 Define the key terms.

13.2 Compare/contrast allocation of and access to health care.

13.3 Describe how "defensive medicine" occurs.

13.4 Explain "concierge" medical coverage.

13.5 Provide examples of how politics, economics, and ethics influence allocation of scarce medical recourses.

13.6 Explain the phrase *microallocation and macroallocation of scarce resources*.

13.7 Describe how decisions are made at the microallocation and macroallocation level.

13.8 Outline both systems of selection.

13.9 Formulate a personal understanding of the impact scarce medical resources has on clients.

COMPETENCIES

CAAHEP
• Identify the effect personal morals on professional performance. (CAAHEP XI.C.3)
ABHES
• Display compliance with the Code of Ethics of the profession. (ABHES 4.g)

VIGNETTE

Who Decides?

You are employed by a team of transplant surgeons in a major city when a call comes from a hospital that donor organs are available. The wheels move quickly to determine proper matches among the clinic's clients. Your surgeons discover that two equally needy clients are waiting for the donor liver. One is an 18-month-old infant whose first liver transplant is being rejected. The other possible recipient is a 7-year-old recently diagnosed with liver failure.

Allocation of scarce medical resources and access to medical care are major bioethical concerns today. *Allocation* refers to the distribution of available health-care resources. *Access* refers to whether people who should have health care are able to receive that care. Winners in the arena of access to health care are most likely healthy and well-insured individuals with good corporate coverage. Losers in this dilemma are often children, persons of color, and those who are poor and powerless. It is reported that in 2020 more than 30 million Americans were living without health insurance. Many more are underinsured. During the Covid-19 Pandemic many more millions lost their health insurance when their jobs were lost.

ALLOCATION AND ACCESS IN TODAY'S HEALTH-CARE ENVIRONMENT

Many examples of allocation and access concerns can be found in today's health-care environment. More than 28% of all children younger than 18 years are without adequate health care. Prenatal care is an unaffordable luxury for most of the uninsured. Often, adequate care is unavailable even after infants are born. There are a number of individuals working full-time and part-time jobs who "fall through the cracks" for coverage with medical insurance. Elderly people are increasingly having difficulties obtaining adequate health care and paying for their prescription medications. Medicare, with its increasing costs and decreasing coverage, is inadequate. Without a quality Medicare supplement program, elderly persons, like many of the nation's children, will go without. About 6 million Medicare recipients had no supplemental insurance in 2020.

The Affordable Care Act (ACA) of 2010 expanded Medicaid and subsidized coverage for nearly 20 million Americans without health insurance. As of January 2020, 14 states still had not expanded their Medicaid programs under the ACA. The ACA has met much controversy from politicians opposed to the bill and survived many attempts to overturn it in the courts. It still stands today but will continue to face additional challenges related to the political arena.

ETHICS CHECK

Access to and allocation of heath care often relate to geography. There are vast rural areas in many parts of the United States with few providers of health care and/or hospitals in which to provide necessary services. During the Covid-19 Pandemic, we learned of rural areas of the country that had no hospital or only one small hospital without the equipment or supplies to properly and safely treat those infected with Covid-19. In some cases, individuals were left in hallways or in ambulances lined up outside waiting for a bed. Many rural communities had difficulties acquiring the Covid-19 vaccine. Some clients were driving more than 100 miles to reach medical care that is clustered in cities and suburban areas. The ethical question has to be, What value is placed on human life in America when basic health care is not available to those in need? ●

Case Study

A young boy in a rural area of Maine dies in a small hospital after an automobile accident. The family practice physician, on emergency call at the hospital when the ambulance brings in the boy, works feverishly for more than an hour to save him, but the boy dies. The next morning the doctor shares with you the feeling of hopelessness knowing the boy's life might have been saved if a neurosurgeon and more sophisticated equipment had been accessible to the hospital.

How did geographic location dictate who lives and who dies?
Is there anything that might have made a difference in this young boy's treatment?

With the ever-changing health-care climate, health professionals in all facets of the industry are required to do more with less, forcing hospitals and acute care centers to radically alter their health-care delivery system. For example, a surgical nurse with 10 years of experience may be moved to the role of circulating nurse while a surgical technician with only 9 months of recent training steps in to assist the surgeon. The circulating nurse is removed from the actual operation yet is ultimately responsible for the supplies and equipment in the room and must document any incidents that might occur. Responsibility and accountability issues in all areas of health care are shifting toward cost containment.

The hospital has become a massive business entity whose financing comes from government programs, private insurers, bond issues, loans, donations, and the personal pockets of clients. Medical supply houses and pharmaceutical manufacturers develop new devices and drugs, market aggressively to the public, and gain a stronger foothold in the total health-care climate. Legal regulations abound, and malpractice is a continued concern. This threat tends to lead providers into practicing "defensive medicine" by ordering tests and procedures that normally might be considered unnecessary—just to make certain that all bases are adequately covered.

All clients are directly affected by increased health-care costs, and some must make difficult choices about what to eliminate from their health. Will they pay $1200 a month for necessary medication or pay the rent? One person reports a required medicine for cancer treatment totals $13,058 for a 3-week dose *with* good insurance coverage. Those who are older often lose the option to move closer to family when the only available providers do not take new Medicare clients and turn away all Medicaid recipients because of inadequate reimbursement. At the same time, well-insured and financially successful clients are able to purchase nearly any kind of health care they desire. This has been proved by the numbers of individuals who readily purchased **"concierge" medical service** or "premier" medical service as soon as it was made available by their medical providers. Such services provide guaranteed access to their provider, telephone and e-mail contact, hospital-stay coordination, and prompt follow-through on any ordered tests. Most concierge services even provide house calls to their clients. Major medical clinics such as Mayo, Virginia Mason, and Scripps offer concierge options. It is interesting to note that in the 1940s and 1950s, with the exception of e-mail access, this type of service was generally provided to all clients by physicians.

Continual innovation in medical technology has made it possible to replace body parts; create new drugs for mental distress; refine diagnostic procedures to quickly determine fractures, tumors, or infections; and supply complex pharmaceutical regimens for many chronic illnesses. Nonessential reconstructive surgery, assisted reproduction, and experimental therapies are available, whereas the less fortunate are either denied access or are given no choice in their health-care treatment. The result is there are medical luxuries for a few, but others do without.

POLITICS, ECONOMICS, AND ETHICS INFLUENCE HEALTH CARE

Inadequate access to health care is a complex problem. It is a political issue; it is an economic enigma; it is an ethical dilemma. Each has a profound influence on today's health care. This influence leads to a number of questions.

The political questions are, Who will pay for basic health care? Who decides what kind of benefit package everyone should receive? and How can I maintain status quo in the political arena?

The economic questions are, How can scarce medical resources be allocated in light of the necessary costs and human needs or desires? How can costs be curtailed? and Is the ACA a step toward a solution or an economic disaster still to be solved?

The ethical questions are, Is medical care a right or a privilege? and How will these scarce resources be justly and fairly distributed? The current president believes that medical care is a right for all persons but how to make that possible is a political quandary.

HEALTH-CARE LEGISLATION

In an attempt to make health care more accessible and more affordable, states entered into the political arena hoping to answer these questions.

 In 1999, Oregon passed the first program for rationing health care in the United States. The Oregon legislature created the Health Services Commission, which presented a prioritized list of health services they believed warranted diagnosis and treatment. Illnesses below a certain number were not covered because it was believed that either the persons would get well on their own or treatment would be futile.

Maine passed a similar law in 2003 to expand health care to its underserved population. In 2006, Massachusetts lawmakers required all of its 500,000 uninsured citizens to have some form of health insurance. Every citizen earning $9500 or less yearly is covered at no cost. Businesses that do not offer health insurance pay a $295 annual fee per employee. Other states with similar actions include Tennessee and Minnesota.

The Healthcare Reform Bill of 2010, finally enacted after decades of debate and a great deal of opposition, further identifies and mandates health-care services for many of the underserved and altered some of the states' plans. To say that the health-care reform legislation was political is an understatement. The vote taken followed strict Republican and Democratic party lines with just a few exceptions and passed only because the Democrats controlled Congress. There have been more than five votes taken since that time to overturn the ACA; all failed.

Key provisions of the ACA expand access to medical insurance, add protection to consumers, emphasize prevention and wellness, and curb rising health-care costs. The 900-page document identifies parameters for carrying out the mandate.

Some say such legislation was long overdue; others see these plans as examples of government controlling health care. In any instance, the plans provide for treatable health-care coverage, however limited, to increased numbers of residents. Only time will address how care will continue or be expanded in the ACA.

Whenever health-care access and allocation decisions are made, improving health care is a basic and primary goal. Health professionals, researchers, and members of nearly all academic disciplines have been formally debating such issues for many years. To set guidelines for discussion, it is easier to define the problem in terms of macroallocation and microallocation of scarce resources.

MACROALLOCATION AND MICROALLOCATION

Allocation decisions deal with how much shall be expended for medical resources and how these resources are to be distributed (Fig. 13-1).

Macroallocation decisions are made by larger bodies, such as Congress, health systems agencies, state legislatures, health organizations, private foundations, and health insurance carriers. For example, Congress determined that Medicare should provide medical care for clients with chronic renal disease, yet no other chronic disease is specifically named in the Medicare program. Macroallocation decisions also are evident when determinations are made regarding funding of medical research. How much should be allotted for cancer research, for preventive medicine, or for technological advances in medical equipment? The health insurance industry largely determines the "reasonable and customary" fees in medical care and therefore what will and will not be covered by health insurance premiums.

In addition, Congress instituted a Medicare prospective payment system in 1983 that reflects macroallocation called **diagnosis-related groups (DRGs)**, used in hospitals to categorize clients' conditions by number. Payment is made on the basis of a predetermined rate or average cost. The intended effect of the DRGs was to encourage facilities to be better stewards of their time and resources in treating individuals in the hospital and to equalize Medicare payments made to facilities and providers. The prospective payment system has inadvertently encouraged providers to be more specific in documenting their services so that their coders find no gaps in documentation for the correct and most appropriate diagnoses and procedures.

Case Study

The family at 913 Twelfth Street will be saved from financial ruin because Medicare will help defray the costs of their young son's kidney dialysis. The family at 909 Twelfth Street may suffer great financial stress because of increasing medical bills for the treatment of their daughter's juvenile-onset diabetes mellitus, which has left her blind and nephrotic.

How does the government determine that one medical problem warrants financial assistance and another does not?

Microallocation decisions concerning who shall obtain the resources available are made on an individual basis, usually by local hospital policy and providers. Decisions at the microallocation level cut deeper into the conscience, because of their personal closeness to everyday living. Examples of questions requiring these decisions include the following: Who is allowed to occupy that one available bed in intensive care? Who receives the ventilator when there are only two remaining and six patients likely will die without one? Does the Medicaid client receive the same care as the local VIP? Does a 60-year-old Medicaid client have an equal chance at the kidney transplant as the foreign visitor who has cash to pay for the procedure? Who gets the shingles vaccination when there is not enough vaccine for all those at risk?

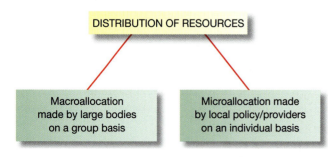

Figure 13-1. A brief description of how resources are allocated.

Case Study

Review the vignette at the beginning of the chapter.

How will the decision be made regarding the available liver?
Who makes the decision?
How much time might be available before a choice is made?

IN THE NEWS

The Covid-19 pandemic made allocation of scarce medical resources a reality for millions of individuals. The pandemic reached more than 124 countries and territories. None were fully prepared for the demands that would be made by those ill with the virus. The United States quickly discovered that there were not enough masks or personal protective equipment (PPE) to protect health-care workers. Soon, many were reusing masks and wearing the same PPE from one infected patient to another. Residents in skilled nursing facilities were especially vulnerable, and many lives were lost even before the cause was understood and steps taken toward prevention. Physicians in Italy directed that crucial resources such as intensive care unit beds and ventilators be reserved for those who could benefit the most. In South Korea, some individuals died while waiting for hospital admission. Like the United States, the United Kingdom was also forced to relax some of their PPE requirements. The result is that many health-care workers became infected and some died of the virus. For quite some time there were insufficient test kits to really determine when and how quarantines and stay-at-home orders were necessary.

SYSTEMS FOR DECISION-MAKING

How are the criteria established that attempt to answer such questions of allocation? Two prominent systems have arisen. The first system identifies three possible selection processes. The second system identifies five principles for a fair selection process. An outline of the two systems follows.

SYSTEM I

1. *Combination criteria system.* Those who satisfy the most criteria ought to receive treatment. Such criteria might include the following:
   a. Capacity to benefit from treatment without complications
   b. Ability to contribute financially or experimentally as a research subject
   c. Age and life expectancy
   d. Past and potential future contributions of the client to society
2. *Random selection system.* This system is more like "first come, first served," or a simple chance selection or drawing of lots.
3. *No-treatment system.* This system is based on the premise that if all cannot be treated, treatment should be given to none.

SYSTEM II

Decisions should be made on the following basis:

1. To everyone an equal share
2. To everyone according to their individual needs
3. To everyone according to their individual efforts
4. To everyone according to their contributions to society
5. To everyone according to their abilities and merits

A summary of the American Medical Association's Council on Ethical and Judicial Affairs suggests that, when making allocation decisions of scarce resources, the only ethically appropriate criteria to consider are quality of life, benefit and duration of benefit, and urgency of need. Such factors as age, ability to pay, client contribution to illness, or social worth should not be considered. If the allocation decision poses little disparity among clients who will receive treatment, practitioners should use the "first come, first served" approach.

There has been much debate about whether individuals with unhealthy lifestyles (defined as smoking, obesity, and not exercising) should pay more for their health insurance premiums than healthy individuals. There is a strong belief that it is fair to require higher premiums in much the same manner as car insurance premiums increase or are canceled after a certain number of motor vehicle crashes. In addition, is it fair to seek higher co-payments and deductibles from unhealthy individuals? Insurance carriers are making offers to subscribers to influence good health—partial payment of exercise club memberships and financial bonuses for not smoking or for losing excess pounds. Still others believe that the exclusionary posture of insurance makes it a poor candidate for health care because everyone deserves health care without exclusions.

Case Study

When a 58-year-old employee, Sam, loses his job because his company is downsizing, he is unable to maintain his health insurance premiums for more than 6 months. He also finds it impossible to find employment with similar pay and benefits. His wife, receiving care for cancer, is now uninsured. Sam pays more than $350,000 for his wife's care before her death, which occurred just 3 months after the health-care coverage was lost. Sam is nearly bankrupt.

Case Law

Cheryl Matthews, plaintiff, brought suit against Blue Cross/Blue Shield of Michigan for wrongfully refusing to pay $38,000 in insurance claims stemming from Applied Behavior Analysis (ABA) treatment for her autistic son. Blue Cross defendants argued that ABA therapy was not covered under the policy held by Matthews and filed to dismiss the case.

Judge Prentis Edwards denied the motion, forcing Blue Cross to either settle the claim or go to court. Blue Cross was ordered to pay $125,000 to Matthews based on the fact that Matthews' inability to access ABA therapy for her son will increase his life care costs.

Matthews v Blue Cross, Case No. 09-018750-CK.

 ## HOW WOULD YOU DECIDE?

To appreciate more fully the difficulties in making choices related to the allocation of scarce medical resources and to assist in establishing criteria for selection, the following examples are given for you to ponder.

ALLOCATION OF RESOURCES

Example 1

On the advice of the staff nurse in an assisted living facility, an 82-year-old woman is transported by Medic 1 to the nearest hospital with suspected fractures after a fall in her bathroom at 9:30 p.m. Two miles from the hospital, Medic 1 is advised that the hospital emergency department is overflowing and is on divert. Medic 1 continues to the second hospital, 10 additional minutes away. The second hospital emergency department is so busy that two individuals on hospital beds are placed in the hallway. After x-rays and a long wait for an examination, it is discovered that there are no fractures, only bruises. The doctor sighs, "I'm so glad to send you back to your home. If you needed hospitalization, I'd have to send you to another hospital an hour's drive away. We do not have one empty bed."

Example 2

You have just given birth to a 20-oz infant of 6 months' gestation. The **Apgar score** is –2. The infant cannot suck and has no muscle tone, no gag, and no reflux. There is a need to protect the brain and the nervous center. The attending physician approaches you and the infant's father with the news that the only chance of survival is to transport the infant to a neonatal center in the nearest city, 200 miles away from home.

What is your response? How might the infant's father respond? What problems do you foresee? What are the legal implications of your decision?

Consider this case a second time, only 6 months later and with more facts. The decision was made to send the infant to the neonatal center. After 2 weeks, your medical bill is well over $420,000, and you know you have only enough money to add to your medical insurance to cover a normal labor and delivery. It appears that the infant will be unable to come home for several more weeks, if ever. The infant has now been diagnosed with the following problems: cerebral palsy; blindness; hydrocephalus, which has been alleviated with a shunt in the brain; and seizures.

What choices are available to you and the infant's father now? Who is responsible for the increasing hospital bill and the lifelong care of this infant? Is medical care a right or a privilege under these circumstances? Who makes the decisions involved in this case?

It quickly becomes obvious that no established criteria provide clear-cut solutions to the aforementioned examples. None would be easy to follow. Factors other than those mentioned in the two systems will also influence decisions. They include personal ethics, personal preferences, religious beliefs, geographic location, legal requirements, and the political climate. Many problems and few solutions are evident when considering how and to whom scarce medical resources are to be allocated.

SUMMARY

Many times allocation of and access to scarce medical resources pose more questions than answers. Influences, such as economics, geographic location, availability of health-care professionals, politics, and insurance coverage, determine both allocation of and access to health care. How decisions are made and who decides are critical questions to be asked. As a health-care professional, it is important to help clients recognize what services are available to them and to help them determine where or how to access other services if needed. If time has not been spent thinking through some of these difficult choices, responding ethically becomes a challenge.

 Watch It Now! How do you choose when there really is no choice? at http://FADavis.com, keyword *Tamparo*.

Questions for Review

SELECT THE BEST ANSWER

1. Microallocation
   a. Decisions are made on an individual basis.
   b. Uses the DRGs for decision-making.
   c. Is used by insurance carriers to determine reasonable and customary coverage.
   d. Is determined by state legislatures.
   e. Is determined by insurance plans.

2. The "first come, first served" system for decision-making
    a. Is a combination criteria system.
    b. Identifies the random selection system.
    c. Is not approved by the American Medical Association's (AMA's) Council on Ethical and Judicial Affairs.
    d. Considers capacity to benefit.
    e. Eliminates those with an unhealthy lifestyle.

3. Macroallocation
    a. Decisions are usually made by hospitals.
    b. Determines who gets the flu vaccine when there is a severe shortage.
    c. Helps to determine how much money is spent on medical research.
    d. Gives to everyone an equal share.
    e. Considers age and life expectancy in decision-making.

4. Allocation of scarce medical resources is a bioethical issue because
    a. Health care is available to everyone.
    b. Hospitals have to report their services to the federal government.
    c. Health care is simply too costly for the country.
    d. Guidelines for health-care decisions are essential to fairness.
    e. Otherwise insurance carriers will make decisions for providers.

5. Action by state legislatures making decisions about allocation of medical care is an example of _____ at work.
    a. Microallocation
    b. Bioethics
    c. Economics
    d. Politics
    e. System II

SHORT ANSWER QUESTIONS

1. In your own words, define "access."

_____

_____

_____

2. Compare "concierge" health care to health care under Medicaid.

_____

_____

_____

3. What problems arise under System II decision-making?

_____

_____

_____

4. What do you think about a health-care rationing program such as the one instituted by Oregon in 1999? Explain your decision.

_____

_____

_____

5. How might a "Medicare for All" program be paid for?

_____

_____

_____

CLASSROOM EXERCISES

1. Consider each of the case studies in the chapter and answer the following questions:
   a. At what level (macroallocation or microallocation) is a decision made?
   b. Can one of the selection systems be applied?

2. On what basis do you decide who gets the last open slot of the provider's appointment schedule? What system of selection is followed?

3. Two clients desperately need the use of one remaining hemodialysis machine. One is an elderly Medicaid client. The other is a young college student who has full health insurance benefits. Which client would you choose to treat? Support your answer.

4. What suggestions do you have to make health care available to all? How would your plan be funded?

5. Bioethicist Dan Callahan states that the root of the allocation problem in modern medicine is "our cultural inability to acknowledge limits to life and to face the reality of death." Comment on this statement, describing your personal feelings and giving an example of this philosophy.

INTERNET ACTIVITIES

1. Research the Internet for examples of the high cost of neonatal care for premature infants and how families must cope. Describe your feelings.

2. After reading the article at the following link, what advice would you give to a grandparent? What surprises you most about the article? https://money.usnews.com/money/personal-finance/saving-and-budgeting/articles/2018-04-13/6-ways-to-pay-for-long-term-care-if-you-cant-afford-insurance

REFERENCES

Allocation of scarce resources. https://journalofethics.ama-assn.org/article/ama-code-medical-ethics-opinions-allocating-medical-resources/2011-04

Beauchamp, T. L, & Walters, L.: *Contemporary Issues in Bioethics, 8th Edition*. Belmont, CA: Wadsworth, 2013.

For additional resources please visit
http://FADavis.com, keyword *Tamparo.*

CHAPTER 14

Genetic Modification

"It is not easy to be a pioneer—but oh, it is fascinating! I would not trade one moment, even the worst moment, for all the riches in the world."

—Elizabeth Blackwell (1821–1910); the first female doctor in the United States

KEY TERMS

amniocentesis Method of prenatal diagnosis in which a needle is used to withdraw fluid from the amniotic sac within the uterus of a pregnant woman; the fluid withdrawn is tested for genetic anomalies.

autosomes Non–sex-determining chromosomes; humans have 22 pairs.

blastocyst An outer and inner cell layer from which an embryo develops; the stage at which implantation in the uterus lining occurs.

chorionic villus sampling (CVS) A method of genetic testing whereby a flexible catheter inserted through the vagina and cervix sucks out a tiny piece of chorionic villi tissue on the outermost layer of the amniotic sac.

chromosome A threadlike strand of DNA that carries genetic information.

chronic myeloid leukemia (CML) A cancer of the blood characterized by increased numbers of certain cells; results from the translocation or swapping of genetic material between chromosomes 9 and 22.

deoxyribonucleic acid (DNA) A type of molecule that encodes genetic information.

Down syndrome Genetic disorder causing a moderate to severe mental disability. It is marked by a sloping forehead, short broad hands with a single palmar crease, a flat nose or absent bridge, low-set ears, and generally dwarfed physique. Also called trisomy 21 because individuals have an extra chromosome number 21.

eugenics Improving a species through genetic engineering.

genetic modification The alteration, replacement, or repair of genetic material by artificial means.

genome All the hereditary material possessed by an organism.

genomics The study of genes and their function.

homologous Having similar structure and anatomical position in different organisms suggesting a common ancestry or origin.

Huntington disease A rare inherited disorder that causes part of the brain to degenerate; symptoms usually are not obvious until adulthood. Dementia and death usually occur between ages 25 and 55 years. Also called Huntington chorea.

liposome A synthetic, microscopic globule consisting of layers of lipids to encapsulate certain substances.

pharmacogenomics The study of how variations in the human genome affect the response to medications.

phenylketonuria (PKU) Hereditary disease caused by an enzyme deficiency; requires immediately starting a special diet to prevent complications such as mental retardation.

sickle cell anemia Hereditary, chronic form of anemia, affecting principally people of Mediterranean and African ethnic origins.

spina bifida Neural tube defect involving incomplete development of the brain, spinal cord, and/or their protective coverings caused by failure of the spine to close properly during development.

ultrasound Sound waves of extremely high frequency used to examine structures inside the body for diagnostic purposes; produces an image or photograph of an organ or tissue.

vector In medicine, a carrier; usually an insect; can be a virus.

LEARNING OUTCOMES

Upon successful completion of this chapter, you should be able to:

14.1   Define the key terms.

14.2   Describe the work of the International Human Genome Sequencing Consortium.

14.3   Discuss the implications of genetically informed medicine.

14.4   Name at least six diseases that can be detected by genetic testing.

14.5   Compare voluntary and mandatory genetic screening.

14.6   Explain six reasons for genetic screening/testing.

14.7   Discuss the possible components of genetic counseling.

14.8   Identify uses for gene therapy.

14.9   Compare/contrast the following stem cells: embryonic, adult, umbilical cord, and amniotic fluid.

14.10   Identify the use of stem cell research in treating disease.

14.11   Trace the political conflict of stem cell research.

14.12   Discuss the use of stem cells in creating "new" organs and tissues.

14.13   Discuss the legal and ethical implications of genetic engineering.

14.14   State special considerations for health-care employees concerning any area in genetic engineering.

COMPETENCIES

CAAHEP

- Differentiate between personal and professional ethics. (CAAHEP XI.C.2)
- Identify the effect of personal morals on professional performance. (CAAHEP X1.C.3)
- Develop a plan for separation of personal and professional ethics. (CAAHEP X.P.2)
- Recognize the impact personal ethics and moral have on the delivery of healthcare. (CAAHEP XI.A.1)

ABHES

- Comply with federal, state, and local health laws and regulations as they relate to healthcare settings. (ABHES 4.f)

VIGNETTE

Do You Really Want to Know?

Maryann just turned 70. Every year on her birthday, she identifies goals for the coming year. This birthday is a major milestone. She realizes more than ever, even though her health is quite good, that she has lived the better part of her life. Will she have 10 more years, perhaps 15, or only 5? She recalls her genetic heritage. She is an only child, and both parents are deceased—her father at age 88 and her mother at 85. Maryann worries about

Alzheimer disease. Her mother began showing symptoms in her 70s. By the time of her death, she could not speak and did not recognize anyone. Maryann's aunt on her mother's side died of Alzheimer disease, and a cousin now is afflicted. Two of her dad's brother's had Alzheimer disease before their deaths. Maryann keeps her mind active, but she wonders about being tested to see if she has the genetic trait.

GENETIC ADVANCES

Advances in **genetic modification** raise legal and ethical concerns never before considered. Giant strides have been made in the field of genetics since **deoxyribonucleic acid (DNA)** was first isolated, analyzed, and recognized in the nucleus of the cells in 1869 by Friedrich Miescher. In 1928, experiments showed that DNA carried genetic information, and its role in heredity was confirmed in 1952 by Alfred Hershey and Martha Chase (Fig. 14-1.)

Genes are the pattern for heredity. Each gene directs cells to produce proteins and enzymes. The human **genome** is the complete set of genes present in virtually every body cell that is inherited from parents. Genes are organized in stringlike structures called **chromosomes**. Every individual inherits two sets of 23 chromosomes, one from each parent. There are two sets of 22 **autosomes** and one set of sex chromosomes.

In October 2004, the International Human Genome Sequencing Consortium, led by the United States' National Human Genome Research Institute and Department of Energy, published a scientific description of the human genome sequence. The Consortium confirmed approximately 20,000 human protein-coding genes, which was a significant reduction from the 100,000 genes scientists originally estimated. Scientists also analyzed specific DNA segments. They learned that each human genome is unique and how genes are switched on and off. Outcomes from the Consortium

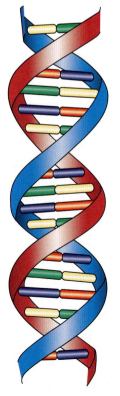

Figure 14-1. DNA strand.

led scientists to explore the use of genetics in the prevention and treatment of some diseases, specifically those caused by gene mutations resulting from environmental factors or the inheritance of harmful genes.

GENETICALLY INFORMED MEDICINE

Genomics enables the targeted treatment of damaged or mutated cells. In other words, it is now possible in some circumstances to learn enough about individual characteristics in a cell's DNA to specifically tailor a client's treatment. Such genetically informed therapy may also use genome markers inherited from parents to determine risks for certain diseases.

Genetic research has made it possible for scientists to identify how genes are damaged by mutations, rejoined, amplified, or inappropriately expressed to play a major role in some cancers. For example, genetically influenced cancer medicine became quite successful in treating **chronic myeloid leukemia (CML)** once scientists learned that the disease is dependent on a single mutation found in more than 95% of clients with that cancer. As a result, the drug Gleevec is one of the main medications now used for treating CML in clients with the mutation.

This type of research has advanced the field of pharmacology and established a new area in science called **pharmacogenomics**, the science of determining how genetics influences a medication's response. Pharmacogenomics is often able to determine whether a client will benefit from a particular drug, suggest the medication dosage, and identify possible effectiveness of the drug.

GENETIC SCREENING AND TESTING

Genetic research accompanies or is quickly followed by decisions related to genetic screening and testing. Approximately 4,000 genetically related disorders have been identified. In some cases, genetic testing is helpful in determining treatment of a client's disorder. In others, no treatment or cure is possible even if genetic testing can detect both the carriers and the sufferers of the disorder.

A genetic disease or disorder is one caused by an abnormality in an individual's genome. The abnormality can range from minuscule to major—from a discrete mutation in a single base in the DNA of a single gene to a gross chromosome abnormality involving the addition or subtraction of an entire chromosome or set of chromosomes. Some genetic disorders are inherited from the parents. Other genetic diseases result from acquired changes or mutations in a preexisting gene or group of genes. Mutations can occur randomly or from some environmental exposure.

A DNA sample for genetic testing can be obtained from any tissue, but blood or a swab from inside the cheek is most often used. Cost of testing can range from about $100 to more than $2,000 depending on the nature and complexity of the test. Health insurance plans may pay for the testing when recommended by a primary care provider (PCP). Genetic tests are used for several reasons and are identified here.

CARRIER SCREENING

Carrier screening is used to identify unaffected individuals (adults) who carry one copy of a gene for a disease requiring two copies for disease expression. Carriers are individuals who have an abnormal gene for a disorder but do not have any symptoms or visible evidence of the disorder. Risk is higher when one or both partners have a family history of certain disorders or have characteristics that increase the risk for having certain diseases. In this case, the screening is often performed to allow couples to make a choice about passing on a genetic abnormality to any offspring.

PREIMPLANTATION GENETIC DIAGNOSIS

Preimplantation genetic diagnosis (PGD) is used to detect genetic abnormalities before in vitro fertilization (see Chapter 15, Reproductive Issues). Developed in the 1980s, PGD is an alternative to prenatal diagnosis. PGD tests a single cell from the **blastocyst** for genetic disorders before implantation in the uterus. Not all genetic disorders can be diagnosed. Therefore, PGD is most often used for couples with repeated pregnancy loss as a result of genetic disorders, couples with one child with a genetic disease who are at high risk for having another, and couples who wish to identify a tissue match for a sick sibling who can be cured with transplanted cells.

PRENATAL DIAGNOSTIC TESTING

Pregnant women often choose some form of prenatal diagnostic testing. **Ultrasound** can identify the size and gestational age as well as examine structures inside the fetus. It can detect some visible fetal anomalies, such as **spina bifida** and heart defects. A sampling of the mother's blood for serum alpha-fetoprotein testing can detect proteins that may indicate neural tube defects or **Down syndrome**. **Chorionic villus sampling (CVS)** is a test used to detect genetic defects as early as the 10th week of gestation. This test can detect chromosomal defects, but cannot test for certain brain and spine birth defects. In **amniocentesis**, a sample of amniotic fluid surrounding the fetus is taken, and cells are studied for genetic defects. The procedure is performed no earlier than at 14 weeks' gestation and is generally done between 16 and 18 weeks' gestation.

NEWBORN GENETIC SCREENING

Genetic testing of newborns is increasingly common, and even required in most states. **Phenylketonuria (PKU)**, a congenital disease resulting in serious neurological deficits in infancy, can be detected when infants are screened within 24 hours of delivery. PKU can be effectively treated with a diet that does not contain phenylalanine (an amino acid) or is low in phenylalanine. *Mandatory* screening of all newborns for PKU began in 1960 and is now required at birth in the United States. Screening of newborns for the sickle cell trait is also required.

IN THE NEWS

In 2010, the National Collegiate Athletic Association (NCAA) Division I announced the requirement that all athletes be screened for sickle cell trait. This action, in response to eight football players who died during intensive training between 2000 and 2009, was intended to help prevent sudden deaths of athletes who carry the trait. Persons with the trait are believed to be at higher risk for death from intensive exercise when their kidneys fail. This is especially critical when the athlete is not hydrated enough and is exercising in hot and humid weather. The ruling has helped to make coaches more aware of how to conduct training sessions with players carrying the trait.

PRESYMPTOM GENETIC TESTING

Presymptom genetic testing is performed to predict adult-onset disorders such as **Huntington disease,** cystic fibrosis, breast cancer, and Alzheimer disease. Diseases linked to a gene mutation are predictable if the mutated gene is inherited from a parent, causing offspring to have a 50% chance of getting the disease. Women who have the breast cancer susceptibility genes (*BRCA1* or *BRCA2*) are about five times more likely to develop breast and/or ovarian cancer than women without the mutation.

FORENSIC IDENTITY GENETIC TESTING

Forensic identity genetic testing is not done to detect disease; it is performed for legal purposes using DNA sequences to identify an individual for legal purposes, for parentage, or in criminal investigations.

GENETIC COUNSELING

Counseling is a major component in any form of genetic testing and screening to determine the following:

- Family members with the disorder identified by the testing
- The cause of death in family members

- The health of all living first-degree relatives (parents, siblings, and children) and in some cases the health of second-degree relatives (aunts, uncles, and grandparents)
- Ethnic background and risk for certain disorders associated with specific ethnic groups

Counselors who specialize in genetic counseling are often members of the National Society of Genetic Counselors (NSGC). These are individuals with knowledge and skills in both counseling and genetics. The NSGC and its members provide the following services:

1. Review family and medical histories
2. Explain how genetic conditions are passed down through families
3. Determine who is at risk for a disease
4. Provide information about genetic conditions
5. Offer guidance to help in making informed choices or life plans
6. Provide information about testing options
7. Assist in finding medical specialists and advocacy and support networks

Genetic counseling can be especially pertinent when a disease detected is debilitating or lethal. Surveillance can be increased when it becomes known that an individual is likely to develop a genetic disorder, hopefully catching a disease early while it may be most treatable. In some cases, such as breast or ovarian cancers, women have chosen prophylactic surgery to remove healthy breasts or ovaries and fallopian tubes to avoid the disease. Certain drugs have also been created to reduce the risk for developing some cancers. One of those, raloxifene (often prescribed for prevention and treatment of osteoporosis), is approved by the U.S. Food and Drug Administration (FDA) for postmenopausal women at higher risk for breast cancer.

ETHICS CHECK

The results of genetic testing often pose difficult decisions. Individuals may choose not to have children when they learn their offspring will suffer a debilitating genetic disease. Pregnancies may be terminated if it is known that the fetus is unhealthy, malformed, or seriously compromised. Often, prospective parents have neither the funds nor the stamina to face such an issue. If the results of the testing are positive but there is no prevention or cure, as in Huntington disease or Alzheimer disease, is there an advantage to be gained by knowing? Some will suggest that there is. Others will argue that not knowing is far less stressful.

Case Study

Bert Schurr is in the clinic of his primary care provider with a health insurance application. Bert has decided it is time to purchase a long-term health insurance policy to help defray expenses of any long-term illness in his later years. As the doctor looks over the application, he makes the comment, "Bert, you know, this might not work for you. Remember when we did the DNA testing for Huntington disease a few years back? You were concerned that if your older brother had it you could have it, too." "Yeah, but the test showed I was OK." "True, but the insurance carrier may still look at you as high risk." "Well, then just take that information out of my medical record."

What, if anything, can the doctor do at this point? Can Bert be discriminated against in this manner?

GENETIC DISCRIMINATION

Individuals seeking genetic screening or testing may be discriminated against when the results of their testing appear in medical records. There is a law to prevent discrimination based on genetic information in relation to health insurance and employment, but the law does *not* cover life, disability, or long-term care insurance. It also does not cover members of the military. The Genetic

Information Nondiscrimination Act (GINA) of 2008 became fully effective in May 2010. However, life, disability, and long-term care insurance providers are skilled at "seeing through the haze" of blood testing reported in a client's health record to be able to determine whether the tests were likely ordered for genetic reasons. Because of this risk, some individuals will choose to pay for genetic testing out of pocket rather than to risk the results affecting their life, disability, or long-term care insurance coverage. Also, clients have the right to ask that providers not include any discussion related to genetic screening or testing in their medical record (see Chapter 9, Medical Records.)

GENE THERAPY

Identifying genetic causes of disease points in one direction—altering the human genome. A number of possibilities exist to change, prevent, and treat potentially harmful genes that put offspring at risk or put people at risk for disease in adult years. When gene mapping leads to any change or manipulation of the identified gene that causes illness or disease, this is known as gene therapy. There are several approaches in gene therapy. It is possible to do the following:

1. Place a normal gene within the genome to replace an abnormal one (the most common technique)
2. Swap an abnormal gene for a normal gene through **homologous** recombination (known as DNA crossover between two homologous DNA molecules)
3. Repair an abnormal gene through reverse mutation to return it to normal function
4. Regulate the degree to which a gene is turned on or off or altered

When a normal gene replaces an abnormal one (number 1 above), a **vector** is used to deliver the therapeutic gene to a client's target cells. Viruses are the most common vectors to date. Viruses have an effective way of encapsulating and delivering their genes to human cells to cause disease. Scientists have been able to manipulate the virus genome to replace the disease-causing genes with therapeutic genes. There are a number of nonviral options for gene delivery, but they require large amounts of DNA, the creation of an artificial **liposome** to transport the therapeutic DNA, or chemically linking the DNA to a molecule that will bind to special cell receptors. Researchers are also experimenting with the creation and introduction of a 47th artificial chromosome into target cells.

Gene therapy is not without concern, however. If genes are to be replaced in the ovum or sperm, the replacement gene is passed on to the next generation. This can be beneficial or harmful. For example, two copies of the gene for sickle cell trait cause sickle cell disease. If you replace the two sickle cell genes with two normal genes, you also eliminate protection from malaria, which is provided by a single copy of the sickle cell.

ETHICS CHECK

With advances in genetic research, ethical and legal dilemmas are raised. Many genetic tests predict the possibility that a person will someday be inflicted with a potentially dreadful and progressive disease. Knowing this information may force decisions by those who want to minimize their risk and parents who do not want to birth a child carrying a gene for a lethal or disabling disease.

There are many questions related to genetic testing that have not been addressed, including "What is normal?" "What is a disability?" and "Who decides?" If genetic testing is done later in life and there is nothing to do to prevent or treat the disease, what has been accomplished? Is gene therapy performed in the adult cells of persons known to have a disease more or less ethical than gene therapy that selectively chooses the "healthiest" blastocyst and eliminates the unhealthy ones? Also, preliminary attempts at gene therapy are very expensive. Who can afford the expense? Who pays?

As research progresses in gene therapy, there is the potential to alter specific characteristics and appearance. Use of new research and technology may conceivably move from genetic therapy for the correction of disease into social engineering for the creation of a "superior" human being. This is known as **eugenics**. Today, the term *eugenics* is an uncommon reference even in clinical research mostly due to the perversion of the doctrine used by the Nazis to create a "master race." Some are so fearful of similar possibilities that they believe all genetic research should be ended now. Others believe that the genetic age will create a society that is healthier and freer from some debilitating illnesses.

 Another question being debated is the use of patent rights to DNA. In fact, about 20% of the human genome is patented by the U.S. Patent and Trademark Office. The U.S. Department of Health and Human Services currently holds a gene patent for the protein the hepatitis A virus uses to attach to cells. About one-half of the genes that affect cancer are patented. A private corporation has patented a gene that plays a key role in early spinal cord development. Governments, private individuals, corporations, and research institutes have rushed to patent certain genes in order to claim ownership for future use and research. Interestingly, more private corporations have gene patents in the United States than public entities. ●

The ethical debate is intense and ethical questions continue to arise. How can someone "own" my genes? Whose right is it to own a gene? Who decides? Can laws keep up with gene technology?

STEM CELL RESEARCH

A major piece of genetic modification relates to stem cell research. Stem cell research strives to cultivate and nurture stem cells, the basic cells of the body, so that they might be reproduced to other specific parts of the body. With the raw material for virtually every kind of human tissue, new treatments for a wide range of human diseases (diabetes, heart disease, some forms of cancer, and Parkinson disease) are now possible (Fig. 14-2). The controversy in stem cell research is not so much related to the method of research as it is to the source of the stem cells.

TYPES OF CELL TISSUES

Terms are defined here to explain some technical concepts presented throughout the following discussion on stem cell research.

- *Stem cells* are single cells that can regenerate and turn themselves into any one of the body's more than 200 cell types. They come from adult tissues (mostly blood and bone marrow), embryonic cells, and umbilical cord blood.
- *Embryonic stem cells* are stem cells derived from embryos that develop from eggs that have been fertilized in vitro. These cells are donated for research purposes with the consent of the donors.
- *Adult stem cells* are found in many body tissues, such as bone marrow, skin, and liver. Scientists more likely use the term *somatic* stem cell instead of *adult* stem cell because somatic refers to body cells rather than to germ cells, sperm, or eggs.

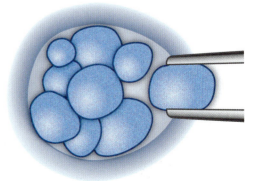

Figure 14-2. Stem cell manipulation.

- *Umbilical cord stem cells* are collected from the umbilical cord at birth and can produce all the blood cells in the body. Studies indicate that cord blood is useful in restoring blood cells to individuals who have undergone chemotherapy to destroy their bone marrow.
- *Amniotic fluid stem cells* are collected from amniotic fluid when an amniocentesis is performed. Scientists believe that cells at the very early stage of prebirth development can be directed to become virtually any cell in the human body.

Many expectant mothers plan to store their umbilical cord blood and/or fluid obtained through amniocentesis for future use in the life of their child should stem cell transplantation be warranted. For example, stem cells from a single placenta are enough to restore the blood and immune system of a child with leukemia. The stem cells in cord blood can also help restore red blood cells in people with **sickle cell anemia**. Human cord blood contains as many stem cells as bone marrow and is much easier and safer to use as a transplant.

Of all these cells, the embryonic cells are the most versatile and the most controversial.

IN THE NEWS

In 2019, the National Institute of Health's clinical research clearinghouse listed over 7,500 clinical studies focused on stem cells. With billions of dollars from government and private sources funding genetic research, many advances have been made. In April 2019, Stanford scientists successfully used the gene-editing system CRISPR-Cas9 to replace mutated genes in mice. Due to the complexity of transferring donor stem cells into a client, the researchers explored correcting genes in a person's own cells. This novel approach of gene editing has the potential of treating "bubble boy," a devastating immune disease caused by mutated genes. Researchers are working on embryonic stem cell therapies to treat type 1 diabetes mellitus. A group of scientists at ViaCyte, Inc., in collaboration with the California Institute for Regenerative Medicine and the International Juvenile Diabetes Research Foundation, have invented a recipe to turn human embryonic stem cells into cells known as "pancreatic progenitor cells." These cells can mature into fully functional, insulin-producing beta cells and replace cells lost in type 1 diabetes. A human clinical trial is currently testing this new therapy at the University of California, San Diego.

FETAL TISSUE RESEARCH

As early as the 1950s, scientists knew that fetal tissue cells held promise for medical research and advances in the treatment of numerous diseases and medical conditions including, but not limited to, Parkinson disease, Alzheimer disease, Huntington disease, spinal cord injury, diabetes, and multiple sclerosis. Fetal tissue research, however, has had a rocky road due to a medical community anxious to move forward on the frontiers of stem cell research and conservative activists with moral and religious objections to any research that tampers with "human life."

Federal funding for such research was severely restricted from the late-1980s to 1993. In 1993, President William Clinton issued an executive order lifting the ban on federal funding for research involving fetal tissue cells, especially those coming from induced abortions. The action was reversed, however, in 2001 when President George W. Bush said there would be no federal funding for stem cell research except for present existing cell lines. There would be no destruction of embryos (even spare frozen embryos, some abandoned and destined for disposal) used for stem cell research or human cloning.

President Bush took additional action in December 2005, in creating a new federal program to collect and store cord blood and expand the current bone marrow registry program to also include cord blood. The Act was known as the Stem Cell Therapeutic and Research Act of 2005.

President Obama cleared the way in 2009 for new government spending on scientific research using embryonic stem cells. In doing so, he overturned the 8-year-old ban on government financing for the research first imposed by President Bush. In June 2019, President Trump implemented new policy creating barriers for federal funding of research that uses fetal tissue following any abortion performed for nonmedical reasons. President Joseph Biden removed the Trump-era restrictions on fetal tissue research in April 2021.

The policy requires an additional ethics review before receiving funding from the federal government. This policy does not affect private or state funds but may deter some scientists from fetal tissue research.

Major conflict still exists, however. ●

Case Law

In August 2010, Royce Lamberth, a federal district judge in Washington, D.C., overturned President Obama's decision to relax funding rules for research using embryonic stem cells and to allow the National Institutes of Health (NIH) to set the boundaries for that research. The judge wrote in his decision that the NIH guidelines, as well as the more restrictive Bush administration policy, violate the 1996 Dickey-Wicker amendment banning federal funds for research that destroys human embryos. In April 2011, a U.S. appeals court reversed the ruling based on an understanding that human embryonic stem cell research is not research in which human embryos are destroyed. Judge Lamberth upheld the court of appeals ruling in July 2011 by dismissing a case that threatened to ban federal funding for all human embryonic stem cell research again.

Several states have enacted legislation related to fetal tissue research. State laws may restrict the use of embryonic stem cells from some or all sources or specifically permit certain activities. The laws vary widely. California, Connecticut, Illinois, Massachusetts, and New York encourage embryonic stem cell research. South Dakota and Nebraska strictly forbid research on embryos regardless of the source.

China, Japan, South Korea, Singapore, Israel, and the United Kingdom receive generous government support for fetal tissue research and have less political controversy than the United States. The conflict in the United States has created a strong trend toward private funding rather than government funding for research. The University of California at San Francisco and Stanford University have received substantial private grants. In addition, millions of dollars have come from the Howard Hughes Medical Institute, the Juvenile Diabetes Foundation, and the Michael J. Fox Foundation.

TISSUE AND ORGAN ENGINEERING

Therapeutic cloning, the use of cells cultivated from human embryonic stem cells to build custom-made organs, is developing but not currently viable for widespread medical application. Somatic cell nuclear transfer (SCNT), or therapeutically cloned tissues, is very effective and more viable in terms of being accepted by a recipient because the tissues themselves can contain the same genetic structure as the recipient. Cloned tissues for organs, known as neo-organs, are already available as synthetic skin and have saved many lives in the United States. It is conceivable that a person with liver failure could soon be implanted with a "neo-organ" made of identical liver cells and plastic fibers, and an insulin-dependent diabetic patient may forego frequent insulin injections because of a semisynthetic pancreas. Research funding for this technology is limited and quite political, but researchers continue to remind us that disease knows no political boundaries.

> ## IN THE NEWS
> Artificially grown human organs for organ transplantation has overcome significant hurdles in 2019. A new technique called SWIFT (sacrificial writing into functional tissue) was created by researchers from Harvard's Wyss Institute for Biologically Inspired Engineering and the John A. Paulson School of Engineering and Applied Sciences. SWIFT provides three-dimensional printing of vascular channels into living matrices composed of stem-cell–derived organ building blocks (OBBs) and produces viable, organ-specific tissues with high cell density and function. By integrating recent advances from stem-cell research with new bioprinting methods, SWIFT has greatly advanced the field of organ engineering and may help more than 113,000 individuals currently on organ transplant lists, including those requiring a heart, liver, kidney, and/or pancreas.

REPRODUCTIVE CLONING

Many said it would never happen. But it did. In February 1997, the first successful mammalian cloning took place in Scotland when a sheep, "Dolly," was cloned. One week later, Oregon successfully produced genetically identical rhesus monkeys through nuclear transfer. To date, cloning has been successful in cattle, rabbits, horses, deer, mice, goats, dogs, and pigs. This is called reproductive cloning. It is interesting to note, however, that the health and longevity of cloned animals is sometimes compromised. "Dolly" died prematurely in 2003 after developing arthritis and cancer, yet she was a mother to six lambs bred the old-fashioned way.

Internationally, cloning is controversial. The General Assembly of the United Nations adopted a measure to prohibit all forms of human cloning in August 2005 even though the vote was not unanimous. The basis for the decision was that human cloning was incompatible with human dignity and the protection of human life.

LEGAL AND ETHICAL IMPLICATIONS OF TISSUE CELL RESEARCH

Scientific developments and advances in technology give rise to moral and social issues of considerable complexity. It is difficult to identify all the legal and ethical implications of tissue research. Often there are more questions than answers.

In some cultures, tissue research and certainly human cloning of any form are forbidden. Other cultures and countries are more eager to step into this arena, always pushing science further into the future. Who monitors fraudulent or false research results? Should there be an international advisory group of scientists and ethicists to help determine how tissue research should move forward? If funding for tissue research comes mostly from private entities, who will claim ownership of the results? Should the political climate and leadership in any country determine whether tissue research advances? If tissue research has the potential for curing even one devastating disease, why would we not run as fast as possible toward a successful result? How can ethical guidelines and legal regulations keep abreast of medical technology? One thing is certain—tissue research is both exciting and frightening.

CONSIDERATIONS FOR HEALTH PROFESSIONALS

Genetic screening, testing, therapy, counseling, and tissue research are delicate topics. Because genetic modification is continually evolving, it is imperative that health professionals remain knowledgeable and up to date on scientific discoveries. For clients to be open and honest about their concerns, all employees involved must demonstrate a professional attitude. Confidentiality must be protected. Informed consent of any procedure or testing is especially important. Employees' personal views on these matters should be fully explored before seeking employment in a facility that actively participates in any procedure related to genetic modification. Also, those personal views should not be made known to clients during or after any decision-making process.

SUMMARY

Genetic modification of any kind stimulates a number of legal and ethical issues. Legal guidelines are still limited; both legal and ethical concerns have difficulty keeping up with the medical technology and scientific research. The topics included in this chapter are very personal, intimate, and sensitive in nature. Privacy and confidentiality are imperative. As technology marches on, *compassion* and *care* are watchwords for health-care professionals.

Watch It Now! Do you have a role in genetic engineering? at http://FADavis.com, keyword *Tamparo*.

Questions for Review

SELECT THE BEST ANSWER

1. The human genome
   a. Is organized in boxlike structures called chromosomes.
   b. Has two sets of 23 chromosomes, one from each parent.
   c. Consists of 300,000 genes.
   d. Includes 12 sets of autosomes.
   e. All of the above.

2. Genetic diseases/disorders
   a. Number about 4,000.
   b. Are caused by abnormalities in an individual's genome.
   c. Can be cured or corrected in most cases.
   d. All of the above.
   e. Only a and b above.

3. The NCAA requires all athletes to be screened for
   a. PKU.
   b. Sickle cell trait.
   c. Enlarged heart syndrome.
   d. Hypertension.
   e. Huntington disease.

4. The cells used in stem cell research that cause the most controversy are
   a. Adult stem cells.
   b. Umbilical cord stem cells.
   c. Embryonic stem cells.
   d. Amniotic fluid stem cells.
   e. Teenage stem cells.

5. Health-care professionals are expected to
   a. Be up to date and knowledgeable related to genetic research.
   b. Protect clients' confidentiality in all genetic-related matters.
   c. Keep their personal views on the subject to themselves.
   d. Be professional while demonstrating compassion and understanding.
   e. All of the above.

SHORT ANSWER QUESTIONS

1. What is the difference between an embryonic stem cell and an adult stem cell?

_____

_____

_____

2. What makes genetic modification so controversial?

_____

_____

_____

3. What is the purpose of genetic counseling?

_____

_____

_____

4. Identify any law in your state related to the use of embryonic stem cells for research.

_____

_____

_____

5. How is stem cell research improving the treatment of diseases?

_____

_____

_____

CLASSROOM EXERCISES

1. Should genetic screening or testing be mandatory for any disease? Support your answer.

2. Professor Joseph Fletcher, bioethicist and noted author, says, "It is unethical and morally wrong to deliberately or knowingly bring a diseased child into the world, or to turn a cold shoulder on prenatal tests. Never bring a baby into the world with anything more than minimally serious defects or disease." Discuss.

3. Paul Ramsey, professor of religion at Princeton University, says, "We cannot begin by bloodying ourselves with the killing of our own kind because they are defective in the womb, without also going into infanticide of similarly defective born infants." Discuss.

4. On a personal level, identify for yourself what is the meaning of the terms "normal" and "disabled."

5. In a small group, debate the question, "Who is responsible for the care of persons with severe disabilities?" Does the debate bring the group closer to or more distant from support of genetic research?

6. If you were Maryann in the vignette at the beginning of the chapter, would you want to know your genetic risk for Alzheimer disease? Research the genetic relationship in Alzheimer disease, comparing early-onset to later-onset disease. Does this information increase or decrease Maryann's risk?

7. Is adult stem cell therapy more or less ethical than embryonic stem cell therapy? Justify your response.

INTERNET ACTIVITIES

1. Access news and the latest information related to gene therapy at MEDLINEPLUS: Genes and Gene Therapy at www.nlm.nih.gov/medlineplus/genesandgenetherapy.html. What new information did you find?

2. Visit www.cancer.gov for the latest information on gene therapy in cancer treatment. Identify the cancers that can benefit from gene therapy.

3. Research www.genetherapynet.com/united-states-of-america.html to determine how gene therapy is regulated; summarize your findings.

For more resources, visit
http://FADavis.com, keyword *Tamparo*.

CHAPTER 15

Reproductive Issues

"I have met brave women who are exploring the outer edge of human possibility, with no history to guide them, and with a courage to make themselves vulnerable that I find moving beyond words."

—Gloria Steinem; American feminist, journalist, social and political activist

KEY TERMS

conceptus General term referring to any product of conception.
heterologous artificial insemination Artificial insemination by donor (AID).
homologous artificial insemination Artificial insemination by husband (AIH).
infanticide A type of homicide consisting of killing the newborn.
mitosis The process by which the cell splits into two new cells, each having the same number of chromosomes as the parent cell.
ovum The female germ cell.
pulmonary surfactant A lipoprotein important in lung expansion in the neonate.
quickening The first perceptible movement of the fetus in the uterus.
spermatozoon The male germ cell.
surrogate A substitute or replacement.
therapeutic abortion Abortion performed to preserve the life or health of the mother.
viable Capable of living, surviving, and developing.
zygote The fertilized ovum; the cell produced by the union of gametes.

LEARNING OUTCOMES

Upon successful completion of this chapter, you should be able to:
15.1 Define the key terms.
15.2 Describe female genital mutilation.
15.3 List the many methods of natural contraception.
15.4 Recall prescription contraception methods.
15.5 Identify sterilization for both male and female.
15.6 Explain AIH, AID, and IVF.
15.7 Discuss the correct use of the terms *abortion* and *miscarriage*.
15.8 Outline the process of fetal development.
15.9 List five theories of when life begins.
15.10 Explain the methods of abortion.
15.11 Discuss the Supreme Court decisions on abortion from 1973 to the present.

15.12   Discuss the "global gag" rule.
15.13   Discuss legal and ethical implications of all reproductive health issues.
15.14   Identify important guidelines for health professionals in all reproductive health services.

COMPETENCIES

CAAHEP
- Identify the effect of personal morals on professional performance. (CAAHEP XI.C.3)
- Develop a plan for separation of personal and professional ethics. (CAAHEP XI.P.1)
- Examine the impact personal ethics and morals may have on the delivery of healthcare. (CAAHEP XI.A.1)

ABHES (NONE)

VIGNETTE

Where Is She Today?

She realized today was her birthday. She wondered what she would be doing. Would she have a party? Would she be traveling? Was she happy and in love with life? Was she as beautiful as she pictured in her mind? Tears filled her eyes. It was difficult to realize that she was not a part of her daughter's special day. It was more difficult to realize that when she was born 20 years ago, she could not have been the mother she wanted to be. The decision to give her child up for adoption had been devastating, but even today she knew it had been right—far better than an abortion.

REPRODUCTIVE ISSUES

There are a number of reproductive issues in today's world. Generally, the issues directly affect the lives of mostly women and cover a full range of reproductive health issues. When women's rights to make choices about their lives are threatened, the legal community is called into action. Whenever there is disagreement related to a woman's right to choose, the bioethical debate begins and includes masterful, thoughtful, and passionate opinions on both sides of the issue. Some reproductive issues include, but are not limited to, female genital mutilation, contraception, sterilization as a form of birth control, abortion, antiabortion terrorism, the global gag rule, assisted reproduction, and access to reproductive health information. Each of the many techniques for these topics will be explored along with their legal and ethical issues.

FEMALE GENITAL MUTILATION

The World Health Organization (WHO) reports that there are nearly 513,000 girls and women in the United States and more than 200 million around the world who have been subjected to female genital mutilation (FGM). Although FGM has been illegal in this country since 1996, the many immigrants from countries where FGM is regularly practiced continue to press legal and ethical boundaries in the United States. The practice is found in several places in Africa, Indonesia, Malaysia, and the Middle East. A mixture of cultural, social, and religious beliefs plays a strong role in the practice.

The WHO identifies four major types of FGM: partial or total removal of the clitoris (female circumcision); partial or total removal of the labia minora and/or labia majora; infibulation (narrowing the vaginal opening by creating a covering seal); and the pricking, piercing, scraping, or cauterizing of the genitals. The rationale given by those performing FGM is to prevent women from engaging in "illicit" sexual practices, thereby preserving the family honor, and to enhance sexual pleasure for men. Meanwhile, the practice severely limits or destroys a woman's capacity for sexual pleasure and can cause serious infections and even death if untreated. The practice causes extreme pain and can cause problems in urination, persistent urinary tract infections, difficulty with menstruation, chronic pelvic infections, infertility, fibrosis, pregnancy complications, and risk of newborn deaths.

As well as being illegal under federal law in the United States, the practice of FGM has been condemned by human rights groups around the world. The WHO details the practice in their genital mutilation fact sheet. The WHO is particularly concerned about the increasing trend for medically trained personnel to perform FGM. In part, medical professionals have become involved, hoping to provide sanitary conditions and sterile instruments for the procedure in order to discourage the use of common knives, sharp stones, or machetes in very unclean environments. The WHO strongly urges health professionals not to perform such procedures or have any part in FGM.

Legal and Ethical Implications

Congress is trying to do more to ensure that the practice is completely eradicated. Two former U.S. Representatives (Mary Bono, Republican from California, and Joseph Cowley, Democrat from New York) introduced in 2010 the Girls' Protection Act that would make it a crime to transport minors outside the United States for the purpose of performing FGM. This act would amend the federal criminal code and impose a fine and/or 5-year prison term. On April 26, 2010, the bill was referred to the House Committee on the Judiciary, then 2 months later to the Subcommittee on Crime, Terrorism, and Homeland Security. The bill evolved to be called the Stop FGM Act, but died without a vote.

Ethically, it seems rather easy to oppose such a practice, even taking into account vast cultural differences in countries. What is more difficult is to provide adequate and professional reproductive health care to the girls and women who are survivors of FGM. Health-care professionals are most likely to see these women only long after the procedure has been performed. They are to be treated with dignity, respect, and compassion with no hint of repulsion. Many may still be living within the family and in the culture that performed the procedure.

CONTRACEPTION

There are more issues related to contraception than one might expect. For centuries, women have sought the means to enjoy sexual intimacy with a partner without the fear of pregnancy. In almost all instances and cultures, because the woman is the one who bears a pregnancy, the woman has been the one most responsible for the contraception. Aside from abstinence, which is 100% effective, there are numerous contraception options: fertility awareness (natural) methods, over-the-counter methods, prescription options, and permanent methods (Table 15-1).

Fertility awareness methods (FAMs) of contraception are neither mechanical nor the result of hormone manipulation. They require that a man and woman abstain from having sexual intercourse during the time when an ovum is most likely to be fertilized by a sperm. FAMs require accurate record-keeping, a regular menstrual cycle, and cooperation of the male partner. The ovum is generally released about 14 days before a woman's menstrual cycle. The ovum survives for as long as 3 to 4 days or as little as 6 to 24 hours after ovulation; the sperm can live as little as 48 to 72 hours or as long as up to 5 days in fertile mucus. Therefore, the actual time during which a woman can become pregnant is measured in days or more than a week. FAMs are often also used by couples desiring to become pregnant because they can reveal when a woman is most likely fertile and receptive to conception.

Over-the-counter contraception methods do not require a prescription. They include condoms for both female and male, sponges, and spermicides. All these methods are a barrier form of protection, either covering the penis or being placed within the vagina, and are often used with spermicides. Spermicides come in the form of jelly, cream, or foam and as tablets or suppositories that dissolve. Some forms of spermicide block the entrance to the uterus; all act to disable or destroy the sperm. Condoms are the only form of contraception that helps protect against sexually transmitted diseases (STDs) when used properly.

Prescription contraception includes birth control pills, patches, rings, the Depo-Provera shot, intrauterine devices (IUDs), diaphragms, cervical caps, and shields.

TABLE 15-1 Contraception Methods and Effectiveness When Properly Used

Fertility Awareness Methods	Over-the-Counter Methods	Prescription Methods
70% to 85% effective	85% effective	90% to 98% effective
Calendar rhythm—counts days until ovulation	Male condoms—cover penis during intercourse	Birth control pill; thickens cervical mucus and/or prevents ovulation
Basal metabolic temperature (BMT)—daily measures of temperature to determine ovulation	Female condoms—reverse barrier pouch placed inside vagina	Patch—releases synthetic estrogen and progestin to prevent ovulation
Mucus inspection—cervical mucus produced before ovulation	Sponge—polyurethane foam placed inside vagina, often used with spermicide	Ring—inserted into vagina; releases synthetic estrogen and progestin to prevent ovulation
Symptothermal method; combines calendar, BMT, and mucus inspection	Spermicides—collect and destroy sperm; most effective when used with sponge or condom	Shot—injectable form of progestin; prevents ovulation
Ovulation prediction kits—measure amount of luteinizing hormone in urine		Intrauterine device (IUD)—T-shaped; inserted into uterus; releases progestin to prevent ovulation
Withdrawal—pulling out before ejaculation		Diaphragm and cervical caps—often used with spermicide; cover the cervix preventing barrier for semen
Lactational method—used for 10 to 12 weeks of breastfeeding		

The birth control pill is by far one of the most common methods of contraception. There are many brands, with the synthetic forms of hormones of both estrogen and progestin or only progestin. They both work by thickening the cervical mucus, making it hard for the sperm to get through, or in the case of the combination pill, preventing ovulation. There are even extended cycle pills that allow women to have fewer periods a year.

The patches, rings, Depo-Provera shot, and IUDs release synthetic estrogen and progestin, preventing ovulation and providing protection against pregnancy. IUDs are small T-shaped flexible plastic devices inserted into the uterus. Some IUDs can be left in place for as long as 10 years.

Diaphragms and cervical caps or shields are barrier forms of contraception inserted before intercourse and removed 6 to 8 hours afterward, most often used with a spermicide. According to the Population Center for Research in Reproduction at the University of Washington, men may soon have a contraceptive pill similar to those available for women. The pill combines two hormone activities in one and is designed to decrease sperm production while preserving libido. The pill passed the first stage of approval by the FDA in early 2019. As of April 2021, it still is not available.

Emergency Contraception

Emergency contraception (EC) is often referred to as the "morning-after pill." It will either prevent or delay ovulation, block fertilization, or keep a fertilized egg from implanting, depending on where a woman is in her menstrual cycle. The EC will not harm or stop a pregnancy that has already taken place, and EC is not the same as RU-486. (RU-486 is a pregnancy hormone drug used to induce abortion.)

Sterilization

Surgical sterilization has become the most popular form of contraception in the world; it is also considered permanent. In certain cases, sterilization can be reversed, but the success of reversal is not guaranteed. For this reason, sterilization is meant for men and women who do not intend to have children now or in the future. Individuals whose genetic testing indicates they are carriers for a serious disease sometimes also consider permanent sterilization.

Sterilization for women is called tubal ligation and involves cutting, tying, cauterizing, or clamping the fallopian tubes so that the ovum will not meet the sperm and pass into the uterus. Tubal ligations are performed abdominally or vaginally. A nonsurgical sterilization method for women is known as *hysteroscopic sterilization*. A flexible microinsert device is placed into each fallopian tube (via a scope), passed through the cervix into the uterus, and into the openings of the fallopian tubes. In a few months tissue grows over the coils, forming a plug that prevents sperm from fertilizing the ova as it travels from the ovaries to the uterus.

Sterilization for men is by vasectomy. The procedure requires a local anesthetic and a small bilateral incision into the scrotum. Each vas deferens is extracted and ligated. It is important to monitor this procedure to ensure that all the sperm have been discharged before sterility occurs. Two consecutive sperm counts must prove negative before any other contraceptive methods are discontinued.

Case Law

Parents of a minor and incompetent girl, K.M., petitioned through counsel to be appointed guardians of her person and her estate. They also wanted authorization to consent to her sterilization. K.M. has an IQ of 40 with a mental age of 6 to 7 years. Her independent functioning is severely limited. K.M.'s neurologist testified that she would never be able to exercise responsible judgment in sexual matters or in caring for a child. K.M. expressed to a counselor that she did not want to have children, but she may have been parroting what she heard her parents say.

The court ruled that K.M. could be sterilized, and her parents were granted authorization. Authorization was withheld, pending appeal.

Outcome: On repeal the decision was reversed and remanded. The court was found in error for not appointing independent counsel for K.M.

Juvenile law, case summaries, re the guardianship of K.M., No. 25941-5-1 (Division one), September 16, 1991.

Legal and Ethical Implications

Contraception is legal in the United States, and most barriers for service have long been lifted. It still is an ethical and bioethical issue in a number of circles, however. The Roman Catholic Church opposes contraception and denies access to it in their hospitals. In the Old-Order Amish tradition, all types of artificial birth control are forbidden, including any variety of natural family planning. Today, however, women in Amish communities are beginning to use contraception, as are many Catholics.

The other issue with contraception comes from the debate, especially in families with teenagers, of the availability of contraception to their sons and daughters. Nearly all parents prefer and support abstinence as the best prevention of unwanted pregnancy. Some parents prefer that contraception not be available to teens; others prefer contraception be used when their sons and daughters become sexually active. The majority do not condone an abortion. Today, many teenagers resort to oral sex as a way to avoid pregnancy, even though it is not a protection against STDs and may even contribute to the increase of STDs.

 ## ASSISTED REPRODUCTION

Recent scientific and technological innovations in assisted reproduction have caused rethinking of the concepts of family, parenthood, and human sexuality. The biological concept of family considers those who are genetically related to be a family. However, this does not include the broader cultural customs and kinships that define family.

Societal laws determine the definition of family. There are laws on adoption, artificial insemination, surrogacy, foster placement, custody arrangements, and removal of children from homes where they are neglected or abused. There are, however, some states without laws related to assisted reproduction. Yet, assisted reproduction raises such complex issues as legal parentage, the right to privacy, the right to make childbearing decisions, the interpretation of any existing statutes that may relate to this issue, and the role of financial compensation in assisted reproduction. All of these issues create a continuing challenge to accept and embrace a broader view of human sexuality and family.

Assisted reproduction choices can strain the family unit, the legal system, the health-care team, and the personal values of all involved. Any health-care professional, whether serving in a medical clinic or a hospital, cannot adequately function without knowledge of these concerns and their legal and ethical implications.

Assisted reproduction is a reality. Artificial insemination, in vitro fertilization, and surrogacy have captured popular attention. The use of semen from either a husband or a donor; the fertilization of the ovum in the laboratory for later transplantation in the uterus, fallopian tube, or peritoneum; the use of frozen sperm and embryos; and the services of a surrogate mother provide alternatives to traditional modes of procreation.

LEGAL AND ETHICAL IMPLICATIONS

As assisted reproduction methods become more common, legal issues have been increasingly resolved. Informed consent guidelines are to be carefully followed. All procedures should be carefully explained, including their effectiveness and any possible problems. Permission to perform the procedures should be in writing, and confidentiality must be ensured. The primary role of the provider is to inform clients of all aspects of the process. Clients should be allowed to make all necessary decisions while providers facilitate the process.

ARTIFICIAL INSEMINATION

Artificial insemination is not a complicated procedure. It is simply the mechanical injection of viable sperm into the vagina, cervical canal, or uterus. This method has been practiced for hundreds of years by animal breeders seeking to enhance their stock. The first successful artificial insemination in humans occurred during the 1950s but was predated by centuries of scientific study and experimentation. Today, the Centers for Disease Control and Prevention (CDC) reports that about 4 million babies are born by artificial insemination each year.

Artificial insemination is described as (1) **homologous artificial insemination** by husband (AIH) or (2) **heterologous artificial insemination** by donor (AID). AIH might be used when a husband's sperm vitality is too low or a wife's cervical mucus is too hostile to achieve conception. Semen collected and concentrated over a few days often can overcome a low sperm count or a sperm vitality problem. AID might be used when the partner is sterile or carries serious genetic defects. It has also been used by women who want to have children but who choose not to have sexual intercourse with men.

Obstetricians and gynecologists are asked about AIH and AID almost daily. These specialists and their employees will want to be able to discuss the topic with intelligence and understanding.

Women are sometimes referred by their primary care providers to fertility clinics found in most major cities.

Legal and Ethical Implications

AID presents problems separate from AIH. Using the semen of a donor raises the issues of the donor's right to the child and the child's right to know its father, screening for infections and genetic diseases, and when, if ever, a formal adoption is recommended. A federal law that has implications for AIH and AID is the 1973 Uniform Parentage Act (UPA) and last updated in 2017. The 2000 and 2002 amendments to the UPA modernized the law for determining the legal parents of children and methods of testing for parentage. California, Delaware, Texas, Vermont, Washington, and Wyoming have adopted versions of the UPA. Other states have introduced similar legislation. In Washington, the UPA updated in 2008 has specific guidelines for physicians who must certify the consent signatures and the date of insemination and file the consent with the registrar of vital statistics, where it is kept confidential and sealed similarly to adoption records. Persons seeking AID might be wise to seek legal counsel regarding the legal protection and parentage of their offspring.

For married couples, counseling likely occurs to ascertain that both the individuals want AID; however, women can and have received AID without spousal or partner consent. The written consent of the donor is required in all cases to release all claims of paternity. Some fertility clinics have a number of donors who can be called to bring semen when asked and usually are paid a fee for their services. Sperm banks provide another alternative for suitable sperm. For more information, research Sperm Bank Directory on the Internet.

Practitioners and clinics using sperm donors must screen them carefully and meticulously. Some considerations include a complete physical and psychological examination, a sperm analysis, a genetic history, and appropriate blood tests, including testing for STDs and HIV/AIDS. Some practitioners prefer only donors who have already fathered healthy children. Careful consideration may be given to selecting a donor who has physical characteristics similar to those of the husband or those desired by the woman.

Using frozen sperm for insemination is more commonly practiced. During a 6-month quarantine, the sperm undergoes extensive testing for disorders and diseases, showing a negative result for testing three times every 2 months. Some practitioners who perform AID recommend that the woman seek another practitioner, if she becomes pregnant, for prenatal care and delivery. This precaution may prevent any unnecessary questions regarding paternity of the newborn and may be prudent in states that have not addressed the issue or whose laws are particularly vague.

According to some religions, AID is adultery. Is the child then illegitimate? What occurs in states where no regulations have been enacted? Who monitors practitioners practicing AID? Does anyone have the ethical responsibility to prevent the potential marriage of people who have the same father through AID?

IN VITRO FERTILIZATION

The development of in vitro fertilization (IVF) (literally, "fertilization in glass") is the process of fertilizing the ovum in a culture dish, allowing it to grow, and then implanting it in the uterus. It is the most well known of assisted reproduction techniques. Successful IVF and embryo transfer in humans were first achieved in 1978. One of the creators of IVF in humans, Robert G. Edwards, won the Nobel Prize for medicine in 2010 for his pioneering work in IVF.

A number of options are available today to assist with IVF, including gamete intrafallopian tube transfer (GIFT), zygote intrafallopian transfer (ZIFT), and intracytoplasmic sperm insertion (ICSI). Some fertility providers transfer more than one embryo in order to improve the pregnancy success rate. This practice, however, can lead to multiple births. Widespread attention was given to Nadya Suleman, the mother of octuplets born in California in 2009, the result of IVF. The birth of Suleman's babies caused increased discussions related to ethics and limits of IVF. In 2020, Suleman's children were all healthy and growing strong.

A test that screens for genetic flaws among embryos fertilized through IVF is called preimplantation genetic diagnosis (PGD). (Refer to Chapter 14, Genetic Modification.) With PGD, DNA samples from embryos are analyzed for gene abnormalities that can cause disorders. These results can be used by fertility specialists to select only mutation-free embryos for implantation into the mother's uterus. Before PGD, the only options individuals had for determining whether there were fetal abnormalities were chorionic villus sampling (CVS) in the first trimester or amniocentesis in the second trimester. If abnormalities were found in either trimester, individuals had to determine whether or not to terminate the pregnancy.

Legal and Ethical Implications

The many ethical and legal concerns for AIH and AID apply to IVF. There is, however, the added dilemma of creating life "outside" the normal realm of reproduction, purposely creating more than one embryo to implant hoping for better success, and what to do with those embryos not implanted.

Aside from the religious communities who oppose any assisted reproduction techniques, the greatest conflict arises over the use of the unused embryos. Generally, they are considered the property of the individuals for whom IVF was intended. They are cryogenically preserved for future use. A few individuals do return for those embryos and have them implanted, resulting in a pregnancy. Others leave them and never return. Some ethicists and scientists say those embryos should be used for stem cell research. That, however, has been denied, generally following political lines. See Chapter 14 for additional discussion on stem cell research. The destruction of frozen embryos after a period of time is viewed the same as abortion for many—it is the destruction of life. For others, it is a fact of scientific technology that occurs every day.

Case Study

A major fertility clinic has a problem. They have a number of frozen embryos stored beyond the recommended 3-year deadline. When the clinic attempted to contact the owners of the embryos, 15% could not be found.

Should the frozen embryos be donated, destroyed, or given for stem cell research?
Who makes these decisions?

Additional specific concerns, more ethical in nature, are to be considered in all forms of assisted reproduction. These procedures are most likely not covered by insurance and thus usually performed only for the affluent. Should these procedures be available to all people whether they can afford it? Many argue that assisted reproduction is unnatural and an attempt to "play God." Who are the legal parents of an infant born of assisted reproduction? Perhaps equally critical, what rights does the conceptus have? Is selective breeding being practiced?

SURROGACY

If a woman's eggs and uterus are nonfunctioning, the sperm of her male partner can be injected into another woman's (**surrogate**) ovum for fertilization. This "surrogate" carries the baby to term. In another scenario, a woman's eggs are retrieved, inseminated by her partner's sperm, and then transferred to the uterus of another woman who is considered to be a gestational surrogate. Also, donor eggs and donor sperm can be used to create an embryo that is placed in the uterus of a gestational surrogate. In a gestational surrogate, none of these individuals is genetically related to the child, and an adoption procedure is recommended for legal parentage.

Legal and Ethical Implications

Historically, surrogacy received national attention in 1987 when a surrogate mother in Newark, New Jersey, chose not to relinquish the infant she bore to the child's biological father and his wife, who had contracted with the surrogate *(Stern v. Whitehead)*. The courts ruled in favor of the biological father and allowed his wife to adopt the infant. The decision was appealed to the New Jersey Supreme Court. In what became known as the "Baby M" case, the New Jersey Supreme Court ruled that the child's father, William Stern, could retain custody of the 22-month-old child but that Mary Beth Whitehead-Grould, the surrogate, maintained her rights as a parent.

In California, Crispina and Mark Calvert hired Anna Johnson to gestate an embryo composed of the Calverts' egg and sperm. The Calverts paid Johnson $10,000 and purchased life insurance for her during pregnancy. During the pregnancy, the Calvert–Johnson relationship soured, and Johnson requested her money earlier than agreed on. Before the delivery of the baby, both the Calverts and Johnson brought suits, each side claiming parental rights. The Orange County Superior Court said that a "three-parent, two–natural mom situation" would confuse the child and "invites financial and emotional extortion." The court concluded that Johnson and "the child are genetic hereditary strangers." The judge compared the contract between the Calverts and Johnson to a common foster care arrangement in that Johnson was "providing care, protection, and nurture during the period of time that the natural mother, Crispina Calvert, was unable to care for the child."

The difficulty in surrogacy often arises when the surrogate must relinquish rights to the infant she bore. Some argue that it is similar to buying and selling babies. Others argue that without fees surrogate mothers would have little reason to offer their services. The New Jersey Supreme Court in the "Baby M" case stated that "baby selling potentially results in the exploitation of all parties involved" and that payment in a surrogacy contract is "illegal and perhaps criminal." Funds do exchange hands, however, and can include such items as maternity clothing allowance; a $100,000 term life insurance policy; a daily allowance for lost wages, child care, and meals; and attorney fees for the surrogate.

Finally, any time there is a contract, mistrust on the part of one or more parties is a possibility. Significant legal issues include whether contractual arrangements between the parties are legally enforceable and what parental rights, if any, the participants have to the child. Some states with legislation on the issue have declared surrogacy contracts invalid. Other states have no statutes. As long as technology advances further and faster than the legal system can address, these developments and ethical dilemmas will continue.

ABORTION

When contraception fails, women (and sometimes, but not always, their partners) can be faced with an unplanned pregnancy. Some couples will adjust their lives and reasons for not wanting a child at that time, embrace their pregnancy, and go on to love and provide for the child born to them. Others will choose a different route. The reasons chosen to terminate a pregnancy are many and varied. They include lack of income to raise a child, lack of a committed relationship, career paths that make a pregnancy particularly difficult, illness or age that is not conducive to childrearing, or even the emotional or physical inability to raise a child.

Abortion, the termination of pregnancy before the fetus is **viable**, is a highly emotional issue that elicits controversy no matter what the setting. Medically, the terms *abortion* and *miscarriage* both refer to the termination of pregnancy before the fetus is capable of survival outside the uterus. Accuracy related to fetal development is an important issue in understanding the dilemma attached to abortion choices.

FETAL DEVELOPMENT

Fertilization occurs when a **spermatozoon** (sperm cell) unites with an **ovum** (egg). Normally, this takes place in the fallopian tubes, after which the fertilized ovum, now called a **zygote**, begins its journey to the uterus (womb). The zygote begins a process of **mitosis** (cell division) during the approximately 3-day journey to the uterus. Mitosis continues while the zygote floats freely in the uterus and begins to attach itself to the uterine lining. The proper term for this attached ball of cells is a *blastocyst*.

The blastocyst continues development and attachment to the uterus until firmly implanted at the end of the second week. Some authorities refer to the period from fertilization to gestational day 14 as the preembryonic period. From the third week until the end of the eighth week, the blastocyst is called an *embryo,* and this time period is referred to as the embryonic period. During this time, organ systems begin to develop, and some features take on a human shape.

At approximately the eighth week, the embryo becomes known as a fetus and is marked by the beginning of brain activity. The term *fetus* is used until the time of birth, usually 9 months after fertilization. Rudimentary formation of all organ systems is complete by gestational week 16. Further maturation of the body systems and organs essential for survival outside the uterus occurs after week 24 when the **pulmonary surfactant** is formed. The 9-month gestational period is generally divided into three segments, or trimesters. The first trimester is from fertilization to 3 months; the second trimester is from 3 to 6 months into the pregnancy; and the third trimester is from 6 to 9 months (Table 15-2).

WHEN DOES LIFE BEGIN?

Five possible considerations of when life begins are commonly identified as (1) at the time of conception; (2) when the brain begins to function, usually at 8 to 12 weeks; (3) at the time of **quickening**, 16 to 18 weeks; (4) at the time of viability, from 20 to 35 weeks; and (5) at the time of birth (Fig. 15-1). A few states currently identify that life begins when a heartbeat is detected—often as early as 5 to 6 weeks.

TABLE 15-2	Fetal Development	
End of Week	**Size and Weight**	**Representative Changes**
4	3/16 in	Eyes, nose, and ears not yet visible. Backbone and vertebral canal form. Small buds that will develop into arms and legs form. Heart forms and starts beating.
8	1¼ in 1/30 oz	Ossification begins. Limbs become distinct as arms and legs. Digits are well formed. Major blood vessels form. Size is like a kidney bean.
12	3 in 1 oz	Eyes almost fully developed, but eyelids still fused; external ears present. Appendages are fully formed. Heartbeat can be detected. Body systems continue to develop. Size is a little more than 3 inches.
16	6½-7 in 4 oz	Head large in proportion to rest of body. Face takes on human features, and hair appears on head. Many bones have ossified, and joints begin to form.
20	10-12 in ½-1 lb	Head is less disproportionate to rest of body. Fine hair covers body. Rapid development of body systems. Eyebrows and lashes appear.
24	11-14 in 1¼-1½ lb	Head becomes even less disproportionate to rest of body. Bone marrow begins to make blood cells. Lungs continue to develop, but do not produce surfactant.
28	13-17 in 2½-3 lb	Head and body are more proportionate. Skin is wrinkled and pink. Rapid brain development.
32	16½-18 in 4½-5 lb	Testes descend into scrotum. Bones of head are soft. Rapid increase in body fat occurs. Body begins storing iron, calcium, and phosphorus.
36	20 in 7-7½ lb	Additional subcutaneous fat accumulates. Nails extend to beyond fingertips. Head hair thickens.

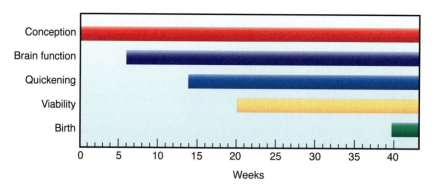

Figure 15-1. When does life begin?

The religious community often weighs in on the life issue. Judaism, Christianity, and Islam use their religious texts, human reasoning, and teaching authorities to make ethical decisions and recommendations. Yet, within these three traditions, there is great variation. Some religious scholars believe that God creates all life and that the embryo is a human being with rights from the moment of conception. Roman Catholics comprise one religious group that claim that life begins at conception because the zygote carries the entire genetic code for a new human being. Abortion is considered a sin against life. Buddhists, who believe in reincarnation, also believe that life begins at conception. This theory is seen in the Chinese and Korean cultures, which count a child as 9 months or 1 year old at the time of birth. A number of religious groups do not take a stand on the status of the fetus and take both the life of the mother and the fetus into account when confronting decisions on abortion.

Another determination for the beginning of life is at the time the brain begins to function. Proponents of this theory believe the fetus cannot be a human without a functioning brain. Because there is strong support for the idea that death occurs when the brain ceases to function, it may be logical to believe that life occurs when the brain begins to function.

Quickening has been determined by some to be the beginning of life. Aristotle believed that before quickening, the human fetus had only a vegetable or animal soul. Another reason for this position perhaps is that women truly feel "life" at the time of quickening.

The idea that life begins when the fetus is viable or can live independently of the uterus is partly based on the premise that if the fetus indeed can live on its own, life has begun. More variation of time is allowed in this theory if you consider that viability may be sometime between 20 and 35 weeks.

Those who believe that life begins only at the time of actual birth believe so because now the being can be seen, can be held, and is perceived as being fully human. Interestingly, the law states that because viability varies so much, each abortion case needs to be considered on its own.

Most definitions of abortion refer to the viability of a fetus. *Viability* means capacity for living and generally refers to a fetus that has reached a certain gestational age and weight and is capable of living outside the uterus. The time of viability is changing. In past years it was rare for an infant to survive if born before 28 weeks of gestation. (A full-term birth is between 37 and 40 weeks of gestation.) Modern technology has made it possible for about a 9.8% survival rate at 22 weeks, 53% at 23 weeks, and 67% at 24 weeks. The term "extreme preemies" is often used to identify those born before 26 weeks of gestation, and these infants often have ongoing neurodevelopment impairment issues.

METHODS OF ABORTION

The method of abortion depends to a great extent on the stage of the pregnancy. Both medicinal and surgical methods are presented.

Mifepristone is a pregnancy hormone drug often referred to as RU-486. It has been available for use in the United States to induce abortion since 2000. When a woman discovers she is pregnant, she may take RU-486 up to 63 days from her last menstrual period. The pill blocks the production of progesterone. Forty-eight hours later, the woman takes misoprostol, a prostaglandin, which makes the cervix dilate and the uterus contract. Mifepristone is often preferred because it is noninvasive, has no risk of infection, requires no anesthesia, and is less expensive. Most woman abort within 24 hours in what seems like a heavy menstrual flow. A follow-up visit to the provider may be made to determine completion of the abortion. This regimen can be used in the early stages of pregnancy and is 95% to 98% effective.

An approved method of abortion when the pregnancy is less than 7 weeks from the last menstruation is called *menstrual aspiration*. In this procedure, a tube with a suction device is inserted through the cervix into the uterus (dilation is usually unnecessary). Within 1 to 2 minutes, the lining of the uterine wall and the **conceptus** are aspirated out. A woman undergoing this procedure may experience cramping, nausea, and faintness. It is commonly performed in the ambulatory health-care setting.

To terminate pregnancy between the 7th and 14th weeks, an aspiration abortion and curettage may be performed. The woman may be sedated or a local anesthetic given while the cervix is dilated to permit suction and scraping of the uterine lining. Cramping, nausea, and vomiting may follow the procedure. The client can go home approximately 2 hours later. These methods of abortion occur in the first trimester up to the end of the 13th week of pregnancy.

A second-trimester abortion, at 14 to 24 weeks, is usually a two-step dilation and evacuation procedure that can take up to 2 days. The cervix is gradually dilated gradually. The procedure is accomplished by using a combination of aspiration, curettage, and manual evacuation of the fetus and placenta. This procedure is more uncomfortable than previous methods identified, often requiring local anesthesia.

In the case of fetal demise in the second trimester, surgical evacuation is most commonly used. The procedure is performed in the operating room by removing the fetus through the cervix while the woman is under anesthesia. Less than 0.5% of pregnancies end as a result of fetal death in the womb.

A procedure known as intact dilation and extraction (D&X) or partial-birth abortion (not a medical term recognized by the American Medical Association [AMA]), a controversial procedure both legally and ethically, was prohibited by law in 2003.

Generally, the later an abortion of any type is performed, the greater the risk. Most abortion providers are obstetricians and gynecologists, but their numbers have decreased, and medical students can opt out of training for the procedure.

For additional information, the CDC maintains statistics in the United States related to abortions under reproductive health. Reporting is optional, but 46 areas have consistently reported since 1996. The reporting areas are the 50 states and the District of Columbia.

Legal and Ethical Implications

In the United States, as states turned away from English common law during the late 18th and early 19th centuries, statutory criminal law began to address abortion. In 1821, Connecticut, and then in 1828, New York, passed abortion laws making postquickening abortion a felony and prequickening abortion a misdemeanor. This process continued through to the 1830s and 1850s, respectively. In the 19th century, abortion regulations tightened. By the late 1860s, throughout most of the United States, abortions were prohibited except to preserve the life of the mother. Those laws and subsequent ones remained in place until the 1960s and 1970s, when many states liberalized their abortion laws.

One of the monumental decisions affecting a change of all abortion laws was the 1973 U.S. Supreme Court *Roe v. Wade* decision. Jane Roe (a pseudonym) was a single, pregnant woman who took action against Henry Wade, the District Attorney of Dallas County, in 1970. Roe pleaded the 14th Amendment and her "right to privacy," claiming that the Texas antiabortion statute was unconstitutional.

As a result, 3 years later, the Supreme Court held that during the first trimester, pregnant women have a constitutional right to abortion, and the state has no vested interest in regulating abortion at that time. During the second trimester, the state may regulate abortion and insist on reasonable standards of medical practice if an abortion is to be performed. During the third trimester, the state interests override pregnant women's rights to abortion, and the state may "proscribe abortion except when necessary to preserve the health or life of the mother."

Although this court decision did "favor" Roe, many unanswered questions resulted, and states began to apply restrictions. In the 1973 *Doe v. Bolton* case, the Supreme Court struck down four preabortion procedural requirements: (1) residency, (2) performance of the abortion in a hospital accredited by the Joint Commission on Accreditation of Healthcare Organizations (JCAHO), (3) approval by a committee of the hospital's medical staff, and (4) consultations. It also had a "conscience clause" stating that physicians and medical employees could refuse to participate in abortions without being discriminated against.

Another U.S. Supreme Court decision in 1976 ruled, on constitutional grounds, that spousal and parental consent is not necessary for an abortion. Currently courts tend not to differentiate between minor and adult pregnant women. A 1978 U.S. Supreme Court decision held that a state may not constitutionally legislate a blanket, unreviewable power of parents to veto their daughter's abortion.

In June 1977, three related cases, *Beal v. Doe, Maher v. Roe,* and *Poelker v. Doe,* resulted in Supreme Court decisions affecting abortion laws. The ruling stated that "the states have neither a constitutional nor a statutory obligation under Medicaid to provide non-therapeutic abortions for indigent women or access to public facilities for the performance of such abortions."

In 1983, the Supreme Court reaffirmed the *Roe v. Wade* decision when it heard *Akron v. Akron Center for Reproductive Health, Inc.* In Akron, Ohio, three physicians and the Center brought suit against the city, challenging the constitutionality of city provisions that regulated abortion performance. The city had passed an ordinance requiring that (1) second-trimester abortions be performed in hospitals, (2) specific information be given by physicians to patients undergoing abortion, (3) there be a 24-hour waiting period between consent and performance of the abortion, and (4) there be specific procedures about how physicians were to dispose of the fetal remains. The case was appealed to the U.S. Supreme Court, which found all provisions unconstitutional except for the hospitalization requirement for second-trimester abortions.

In a similar case in 1986, the U.S. Supreme Court again reaffirmed *Roe v. Wade.* In *Thornburgh v. American College of Obstetricians and Gynecologists,* the Supreme Court ruled against the following issues: informed consent and printed information that would have required a physician to provide information 24 hours before the abortion related to available medical assistance benefits; the father's liability for assistance; a description of alternatives to abortion; possible detrimental effects not foreseeable; and medical risks of the abortion, as well as of carrying the child to full term. In addition, the Supreme Court struck down a ruling that would have required physicians to determine whether the fetus was viable and to report to the State Department of Health specific information normally considered private. This information would have included such items as the woman's age, race, number of pregnancies, marital status, and date of last menses. This information was to be open for public inspection without the woman's name. The Supreme Court ruled against physician involvement in postviability care for the child and the requirement for a second physician at postviability abortions.

In 1991, the U.S. Supreme Court upheld the federal rule that banned abortion counseling at federally funded clinics. This ban affected approximately 4,000 clinics serving more than 4.5 million women, mostly with low incomes. The result was that these clinics could not mention abortion as an option. What became known as the "gag rule" continues to seesaw back and forth in the political world rather than in the courts.

In July 1992, the U.S. Supreme Court, in *Planned Parenthood v. Casey,* ruled that Pennsylvania's requirement that spouses be notified before abortion was an "undue burden." In June 2000, the U.S. Supreme Court ruled on *Stenberg, Attorney General of Nebraska, et al. v. Carhart,* stating that Nebraska's law was unconstitutional. Nebraska law prohibited any "partial-birth abortion" unless that procedure was necessary to save the mother's life. Nebraska held that this was a violation of the law and was a felony. Further related to this issue, however, the Partial-Birth Abortion Ban Act became law in 2003, prohibiting partial-birth abortion. In 2007, the constitutionality of the law was upheld by the U.S. Supreme Court.

In 2003, *Scheidler v. NOW; Operation Rescue v. NOW,* the U.S. Supreme Court dissolved the 10-year permanent injunction prohibiting protesters from demonstrating outside abortion clinics. In 2006, *Ayotte v. Planned Parenthood of Northern New England* challenged the New Hampshire law that requires a parent be notified 48 hours before an abortion is provided to a minor. The Supreme Court held the law unconstitutional because it did not permit an immediate abortion without notifying a parent in medical emergencies that threaten a minor's health.

In March 2010, the Patient Protection and Affordable Care Act (PPACA) was passed. This act now includes the Nelson Amendment, named for its sponsor, Senator Ben Nelson, Democrat from Nebraska. The amendment restricts the means by which insurers can offer insurance coverage for abortion in the state insurance exchanges created in 2014 as part of the National Healthcare Reform Act of 2010.

In the most recent years, there have been challenges to *Roe v. Wade* that would require providers who perform abortions to have hospital admitting privileges at a hospital within 30 miles of their clinic. This restriction caused many clinics providing abortions to close. In 2016, the Texas law instituting this requirement was struck down by the U.S. Supreme Court. Very recently Louisiana passed the same restriction. The Court, however, banned the state from enforcing the law at least until the court decides whether to take up the case in 2020. On October 4, 2019, the Court announced it would hear *June Medical Services LLC v. Gee* in the 2019–2020 session. In a 5-4 decision, the U.S. Supreme Court ruled that the Louisiana law was unconstitutional, reversing the Fifth Circuit's decision. Missouri has hoped to be the first state to ban all abortions by rescinding licenses of all facilities performing abortions, thus forcing them to close their doors. To date there is only one clinic left in Missouri.

The majority of abortion questions arise over the 14th Amendment and the equal protection clause. Every citizen of the United States has "equal protection of the law" and shall not be discriminated against. This includes abortion. The parties are testing the courts on these constitutional issues.

Ethically, there are a number of issues. Is it discriminatory for a woman who has money and insurance coverage to receive an abortion but for a woman who is poor and relies on Medicaid to be denied an abortion? Will this withstand the scrutiny of the court on the issue of discrimination? Another trend in the states is the push to confer personhood status on fertilized eggs through state constitution amendments, via the ballot measure process. The status of the fetus in any abortion procedure is still most controversial. When does the fetus become a person with the same rights as those who are born?

The abortion issue and abortion law are in a state of flux. Radical changes have occurred during the past 100 years. The political climate, moral attitudes, advances in medical technology, and impact of current abortion laws will influence the next 100 years.

Pro-Choice/Pro-Life

An individual who believes there are reasons to justify a legal abortion likely believes a pregnant woman's right to choose is paramount to the rights of the unborn. Proponents of this theory are often referred to as "pro-choice." Individuals who believe the fetus is innocent, weak, and helpless and that its right to life should be protected at all costs are usually referred to as "pro-life." These individuals often believe abortion is murder and that to allow it is to also condone **infanticide**. The rights of the fetus and newborn are paramount to the rights of any others. Most individuals stand somewhere in the middle of these two theories. These are the advocates who believe that abortion is permissible to save the life of the mother (**therapeutic abortion**) or in the case of rape or incest.

One may expect that religion offers a solution to the question of when life begins, but there is no consensus or agreement that settles the issue. A few religious groups propose that abortions be performed only when necessary to save the mother's life. Some religious groups determine a time or establish viability of the fetus for performing abortions. All truly make an attempt to understand the pain and trauma associated with any decision on abortion. Abortion issues are more often based on the following factors: economics, age, health, religion, and culture.

The consideration of how abortions are to be funded is even more complex. The 1977 Supreme Court ruling that said states were not required to fund abortions for indigent women raises the question of fairness and justice in following the law. Essentially, this ruling has the force of denying an abortion to a woman who is unable to pay for one. The right to choose becomes hinged on the ability to pay. This, in effect, denies personal freedom in a free society that has guaranteed equality under the 14th Amendment. The other side of the coin means that opponents of abortion will pay through their taxes in Medicaid funding for those who choose abortion. Persons who object on this basis also must weigh the costs of a funded abortion against the pregnancy, delivery, and welfare costs of the mother and child. One cannot hold that abortions are morally wrong and therefore should not be funded without being an advocate of adequate support that provides for babies born to welfare mothers who will require financial assistance, child care, and health services.

The two highest incidences of "abortions on demand" come from individuals who do not practice birth control because it is not available to them or because it is not convenient. The two groups range in age from 20 to 24 and from 15 to 19, respectively, are white, and are unmarried. There really is no explanation for these statistics other than that sexually active individuals are not using contraception and seek an abortion when they become pregnant. Further data indicate that some of the same women return a second or third time for abortions. It has taken the fear of AIDS to bring this country to the point at which sexuality (and more specifically, contraception) is a topic of national discussion and concern. Yet, for many, this topic is still one of considerable discomfort.

Perhaps the problem has developed because easily accessible abortions have encouraged sexual activity without responsibility. Is sex education, whether in the home or school, adequate? Are parents intentional and realistic about teaching morals? Bringing a new human being into the world is a privilege and a responsibility, and it should not be left to accident as a result of exploitation, fear, or ignorance.

GLOBAL GAG RULE

An example of the power of politics in human rights is acutely demonstrated in the global gag rule. In 1984 President Ronald Reagan established a federal rule that blocked U.S. funds being given to international family-planning groups that offered abortion and abortion counseling even if the money was targeted for a different health-care need. President Bill Clinton ended the gag rule in 1993, but it was reinstated by President George W. Bush in 2001. It was rescinded by President Obama very early in his administration—January 2009. Under the Trump presidency, the gag rule was reinstated and expanded. President Biden once again rescinded the gag rule in 2021.

ANTIABORTION TERRORISM

Reflected in the volatility of the abortion issue is the amount of violence expressed by antiabortionists to individuals who perform abortions and to their clinics. Violent acts include arson, bombings, stabbings, and shootings. Eight providers have been shot to death since 1993, and five more suffered serious injuries from gunshot wounds. Offenders justify their acts on the basis that they are preventing the death of unborn children.

These actions are extreme. Other actions may include carrying banners near abortion clinics; approaching clients and asking if they can pray for them as they enter the clinics; and distributing print material, often inaccurate, in opposition to abortion. Some antiabortion groups practice civil disobedience, attempting to disrupt and block abortion clinic activities. These acts have resulted in a great deal of litigation and added to the complexity of the abortion issue.

In *Schenck v. Pro-Choice Network*, 519 US 357 (1997), the U.S. Supreme Court addressed the question of whether an injunction that places restrictions on demonstrations outside abortion clinics violates the First Amendment. Health-care providers and others wanted to restrict blockades and other disruptive activities in front of abortion clinics. The U.S. District Court created a "fixed-buffer zone," prohibiting demonstrations within 15 feet of entrances into abortion clinics, parking lots, or driveways. The court also created a "floating-buffer zone," prohibiting demonstrators from coming within 15 feet of people or vehicles wishing access to abortion clinics. The U.S. Supreme Court held that the fixed buffer zones were constitutional because they protected the government's right to protect public safety. Floating buffer zones were later found unconstitutional because they imposed a greater burden on free speech (First Amendment).

Legal and Ethical Implications

There is little debate here. Terrorism is a crime. It is illegal. The deaths, injuries, and damages caused by antiabortion criminal acts have weakened the influence of those who oppose abortion. To say that the killing of an abortion provider saves the lives of the unborn is to say, "I commit murder to prevent murder." Few would disagree on how irrational that argument is. Those who believe abortion is murder must struggle with the deaths, supported by their taxes, that occur in military conflicts and war or be able to justify why these deaths are any different.

 ## ACCESS TO REPRODUCTIVE HEALTH SERVICES

Often at issue is the availability of reproductive health services, especially for women. Today, contraception is widely available to any who choose to practice contraception, but that was not always the case. In the not too distant past, condoms and spermicides were kept behind the counter in a pharmacy, and the calendar rhythm method of FAM was not well understood. With the inception of prescription contraception, medical providers became more involved in reproductive health services. Women might have to travel to a larger community where Planned Parenthood clinics could provide a prescription if a country doctor would not.

Sterilization allowed women greater control over their bodies but was originally fraught with much controversy. In some religious communities, sterilization was a far greater sin than the use of contraception. Sterilization was performed by only a few providers, and the written consent of both the woman and her partner was necessary. Tubal ligations, most performed in hospitals, were not allowed in hospitals with religious connections. Today, most sterilization procedures are performed on an outpatient basis, and only the consent of the participant is necessary.

The availability of abortion is just one of many issues of concern. "Conscience clauses" generally allow institutions and providers the right to opt out of providing abortion care. Many providers are employees in group practices, hospitals, and health maintenance organizations that prohibit abortion. Catholic hospitals in the United States are even more restrictive, prohibiting sterilization, contraception, condom distribution, fertility treatment, and some emergency pregnancy terminations.

During the past two decades, Congress has debated the limited circumstances under which federal funding for abortion should be allowed. For a brief period of time, coverage included cases of rape, incest, life endangerment, and physical health damage to the woman. However, beginning in 1979, those services were gradually eroded, leaving the states to determine under what circumstances abortions are to be performed for women on Medicaid. To date, the number of restrictions placed by states permitting abortions for all or most health reasons would take an entire book to detail.

The Guttmacher Institute provides the very latest and up-to-date information on each state's legislation, approval, and enactment of restrictions and/or guidelines in "State Legislation Tracker: Major Developments in Sexual and Reproductive Health" (www.guttmacher.org/state-policy). For more than 40 years, the Hyde Amendment has banned the use of federal Medicaid funds to cover almost all abortions and is often misunderstood by the general public. It does not, however, limit the state's ability to use its funds for abortions, and 15 states have done so. The present version of the Hyde Amendment requires coverage of abortion in cases of rape, incest, and life endangerment.

Yet, several states have passed very restrictive legislation in noncompliance with the Hyde Amendment. They include Alabama, Missouri, Ohio, and South Dakota. The ultimate goal of these states is to overturn *Roe v. Wade*. It seems that the political arena will always have a great impact on women's reproductive health.

The Healthcare Reform bill of 2010 stated that individuals receiving federal subsidy dollars must use their private money to pay for coverage of abortion except in cases of rape, incest, or to save the life of the mother. For the 12% to 15% of couples in the United States who struggle with infertility, the health-care bill also carries no mandates to cover the soaring cost of assisted reproduction procedures such as IVF and egg donation. Very few private insurers pay for assisted reproduction techniques, either. The cost of one round of IVF can be more than $23,000, making it out of the reach of even moderate-income families.

Access to reproductive health care, or any health care for that matter, is even more difficult when the economy is depressed.

 ## PROTOCOL FOR HEALTH PROFESSIONALS

Professionals involved in any of the reproductive health issues will want to be comfortable in any of the circumstances identified in this chapter. Individuals who are solid in their own beliefs yet understanding of those whose choices may be different will be most successful. Treating clients in a professional manner, especially with the recognition that providing reproductive health-care services is not a place for slapstick humor, will alleviate clients' anxieties and encourage open communication. All the issues are truly private and extremely personal. Tact and courtesy are essential at all times, and the confidentiality and privacy of those involved must be carefully protected. Care must be taken to preserve the dignity of all involved. Comments made by staff need to be pertinent, informative, helpful, and nonjudgmental.

With any of the assisted reproduction procedures, health-care professionals will want to remember that both men and women may be uncomfortable with the knowledge that several members of the medical staff know of their reproductive issues and that artificial techniques are being attempted. Health-care professionals may have to ask men to manually produce their semen and to explain to women how that semen will be deposited, usually on more than one occasion, in their cervix in the hope of gaining a pregnancy.

Health-care providers and their employees must decide if they will be employed where reproductive services or abortions may be performed. The conscience clause is designed to protect those who choose not to participate; however, in 2018, a federal judge in New York denied health-care workers this right. Physicians and employees who understand their own feelings on abortion or assisted reproduction will be able to make a decision before becoming personally involved. Generally, employees and physicians cannot be forced to participate in abortions against their wishes. The right to refuse, however, does not authorize the right to judge. Health-care professionals must also remember that it is not their place to impose their personal opinions on anyone considering any reproductive health procedure. Even when asked a question directly, the response should be that such a very personal decision can only be reached by the person making it. It is better to select employment outside the arena of reproductive health care when one's personal views conflict with those of the medical practice.

Physicians and employees who participate in any area of reproductive health-care services are advised to adhere to the following:

1. Participate only within the law, especially the UPA.
2. Provide medical knowledge to clients on all stages of any procedure.
3. Obtain written, informed consent.
4. Provide counseling as indicated by the situation.
5. Refer as necessary.
6. Keep records confidential.
7. Seek legal counsel when indicated.
8. Be understanding and compassionate.

IN THE NEWS

The Covid-19 Pandemic has had an impact on sexual and reproductive health. The pandemic may create shortages of contraceptives, antiretrovirals for HIV/AIDS, and antibiotics to treat sexually transmitted illnesses. China is the second largest exporter of pharmaceutical products and has closed several of its drug-manufacturing plants.

SUMMARY

The beginning of this chapter introduced reproductive health-care issues and the rights of women. The rights of a partner, the unborn, and in some cases a donor are discussed. There is little if any agreement on many of the issues, even when or if law is in place. Abortion laws, especially, are continually in flux and are constantly challenged. Ethical opinions change, and debate moves on. Abortion is one of the longest debated issues and has become increasingly politicized. Resolutions to any of the reproductive health issues will never satisfy everyone. Health-care professionals will find it difficult to hold a neutral stand. The law grants rights that are to be protected, yet health professionals also must embrace their personal ethics.

Watch It Now! Can you be objective and compassionate when you disagree? at http://FADavis.com, keyword *Tamparo*.

Questions for Review

SELECT THE BEST ANSWER

1. FGM
   a. Has been performed on more than 200 million women around the world.
   b. Is illegal when practiced on adult women in the United States.
   c. Is most commonly practiced in South America and Russia.
   d. Enhances both male and female sexual experience.
   e. Makes pregnancy and delivery easier for a woman.

2. Prescription contraception includes
   a. Ovulation prediction kits.
   b. The female condom and sponge.
   c. Pills, patches, rings, IUDs, diaphragms, caps, and shields.
   d. A law preventing dispensing to teenagers.
   e. Coverage by all insurances.

3. The most popular contraception method in the world is
   a. Coitus interruptus.
   b. Surgical sterilization.
   c. Vasectomy.
   d. The pill.
   e. Abstinence.

4. A critical time for the viability of a fetus is
    a. When the brain begins to function.
    b. When the pulmonary surfactant is formed.
    c. The time of birth.
    d. The time of quickening.
    e. The 24th week of pregnancy.

5. Assisted reproduction may include
    a. AIH, AID, IVF, and surrogacy.
    b. PGD analysis.
    c. FAM and WHO.
    d. All the above.
    e. Only b and c above.

SHORT ANSWER QUESTIONS

1. Describe the global gag rule:

    _____

    _____

    _____

2. Compare/contrast AIH and AID and identify at least one advantage/disadvantage of each.

    _____

    _____

    _____

3. Research the circumstances under which a therapeutic abortion may or may not be performed in your state.

    _____

    _____

    _____

4. Does sex education enter into the issue of abortion? Justify your response and possible solution to any issues raised.

    _____

    _____

    _____

5. It might appear that recent action by New York State has put the conscience clause in jeopardy. How would you personally respond to the loss of the conscience clause?

    _____

    _____

    _____

CLASSROOM EXERCISES

1. Sperm bank donors generally expect anonymity when they donate their sperm. With new DNA technology, it is possible to trace ancestry, including sperm donors. How will the courts respond when a child has a genetic health risk or disease and needs to know about his or her genetic medical history? Will the courts respond as they did with adoption? Discuss.

2. Should permission of a spouse or partner be mandatory for sterilization or artificial insemination? Explain and justify your response.

3. A couple comes into a fertility clinic for AID. They have determined that the husband's brother should be the donor and already have made arrangements with him. What counseling might be suggested? Discuss the pros and cons of such an arrangement.

4. Katherine is a surrogate mother for a couple living 15 miles away. Katherine, near term of the pregnancy, decides she does not want to relinquish the baby. What she does not know is that the prospective mother was killed in an auto accident 2 weeks ago. Who has the right to the child? How is a decision made?

5. As an individual *opposed to all abortions,* respond to the following issues:
   a. Pregnancies and resultant births from rape or incest
   b. Unwanted children
   c. Infants with severe birth defects

6. As an individual *supporting all abortions,* respond to the following issues:
   a. Abortion as contraception
   b. A late-term abortion for convenience
   c. The right to life versus the right to freedom

7. Identify where in your community you might refer an individual for the types of reproductive health services discussed in this chapter.

8. Under what conditions is an abortion denied in your state?

INTERNET ACTIVITIES

1. Research Nadya Suleman, the octuplet Mom, on the Internet. Describe your findings. Discuss with a classmate your feelings about Suleman's IVF, identifying both the legal and ethical implications.

2. Research FGM and the Subcommittee on Crime, Terrorism, and Homeland Security to determine the status of the 2010 Girls' Protection Act to determine whether any action has been reinstated. What protection does the law provide?

3. Research your state's laws on abortion and identify key components.

For additional resources please visit
http://FADavis.com, keyword *Tamparo.*

CHAPTER 16

End-of-Life Issues

"Life is not measured by the number of breaths
we take, but by the moments that take our breath
away."—Author unknown

KEY TERMS

advance directive A state's response to the living will; sometimes called the Natural Death Act; often includes all documents related to end-of-life choices.

code blue Medical phrase used to indicate life-or-death emergency.

durable power of attorney An appointed proxy or substitute who makes decisions related to property and finances.

durable power of attorney for health care Sometimes called medical proxy; the legal right to act on another's behalf in making health-care decisions.

euthanasia From the Greek term meaning "good death," willfully allowing death, to keep a person with incurable disease from suffering; more commonly used today to express actively taking one's life.

hospice A lodging, association, or service for those who are terminally ill.

living will Legal document, voluntarily made by an adult, stating what treatment and procedures that person wants done in the event of a terminal illness, especially helpful if the person becomes comatose or incompetent.

Patient Self-Determination Act Federal law requiring institutions giving medical care to inform clients of their option to use such advance directives as living wills and durable powers of attorney for health care.

LEARNING OUTCOMES

Upon successful completion of this chapter, you should be able to:

16.1   Define the key terms.
16.2   Describe the living will, advance directive, and durable power of attorney for health care.
16.3   Appraise components of the Patient Self-Determination Act.
16.4   Restate choices an individual might have in death.
16.5   Describe the importance of medications for dying clients.
16.6   Discuss at least three ethical implications of life-and-death decisions.
16.7   Identify and explain at least five psychological aspects affecting dying clients.
16.8   Differentiate among various legal definitions of death.
16.9   Describe two famous court cases and their impact on prolonging life.
16.10   Express possible legal implications of life-and-death decisions.
16.11   Identify and explain at least five physiological aspects affecting dying clients.
16.12   Discuss the stages of dying as defined by Kübler-Ross.

16.13 Describe the services of hospice for dying clients.

16.14 Differentiate between active euthanasia and physician-assisted death.

16.15 Discuss the Uniform Anatomical Gift Act.

16.16 Describe an autopsy and who may authorize one.

16.17 Define the role of the health professional in dealing with clients and families in life-and-death decisions.

COMPETENCIES

CAAHEP

- Identify the effect personal morals may have on professional performance. (CAAHEP XI.C.3)
- Define:
  - Uniform Anatomical Gift Act (CAAHEP X.C.7.e)
  - Living will/advance directive (CAAHEP X.C.7.f)
  - Medical durable power of attorney (CAAHEP X.C.7.g)
- Develop a plan for separation of personal and professional ethics. (CAAHEP XI.P.1)
- Recognize the impact personal ethics and morals may have on the delivery of healthcare. (CAAHEP XI.A.1)

ABHES

- Use empathy when treating terminally ill patients. (ABHES 5.b.1)
- Identify common stages that terminally ill patients go through and list organizations and support groups that can assist patients and family members of patients struggling with terminal illness. (ABHES 5.b.2)
- Partner with health care teams to obtain optimal patient health outcomes. (ABHES 5.g)
- Display effective interpersonal skills with patients and health care team members. (ABHES 5.h)

VIGNETTE

What Happened to My Plan?

Ted is 76 years old. He is retired and lives with his wife of 44 years and their adult daughter. As a laborer, he spent most of his working years with heavy equipment and cranes on land, tug boats, and ships. From his home, he sees the Puget Sound and watches the passing ships. Ted has been diagnosed with emphysema and suspected asbestosis. More than 7 years after diagnosis, his breathing is now difficult. His sense of humor, his love of family, his care for others, and his knowledge of the passing ships is as keen as ever.

Ted and his internist are friends. They worship in the same church. When Ted sees his doctor, they tell jokes and swap stories before getting down to the serious business of his illness. Ted refuses using oxygen until he can no longer sleep peacefully. Ted and his wife, Ann, discuss a living will; they talk with their children, and meet with their attorney to update their wills and have the Washington State advance directive executed. Ted shares it with his physician, and they agree on his care management.

On a cold and gloomy December day there is rain and even some snow in the Pacific Northwest. Ted is housebound most of the time now. The weather makes his breathing more labored. He is having severe headaches. When Ann suggests Ted visit his doctor, Ted grumbles that there is nothing more the doctor can do. One evening, Ted is unable to wear even his slippers because his feet and legs are so swollen. The water retention makes his feet feel like water pads. In his humor he comments, "I feel like Jesus—walking on water." Early the next morning, Ted cannot breathe. He is suffocating. Ann dials 911. In minutes emergency medical technicians are at the door. In their quick assessment, they comment on the strength of Ted's heart but the weakness of his lungs. Ann explains the emphysema and suspected asbestosis. Ted is transported to the hospital, treated in the emergency department, and moved to intensive care. Ann, their daughter, and their son are at his bedside. Although breathing is stabilized, the medical staff inquires about the use of a respirator and his living will. The family responds positively, and the advance directive is supplied to the hospital that afternoon.

Circumstances in the next few days greatly alter Ted's life. Ted's physician suffers his own tragedy and is called to Denmark for a family death. When attempts to remove Ted's excess fluid are not totally successful, a nephrologist is called who orders the placement of a shunt in Ted's shoulder for dialysis. Neither Ted nor the family is anxious to begin dialysis. Ted had watched a close and dear friend suffer greatly, lose a limb, and eventually die after years of dialysis. Ted believes that dialysis will make a "good death" next to impossible. The nephrologist insists and discusses options with the family. "This is just a 'jump start' to get your kidneys going; we will probably only have to dialyze you twice." Ted and Ann discuss dialysis. There is hesitation, but the decision is finally made to go ahead, and the consent for dialysis is signed. Both Ted and Ann are concerned about all the side effects. A chaplain who visits explains why the form has to list all the possible side effects, even though few if any are likely to occur. Dialysis will begin the next morning.

The family goes home for a night's rest before their return to the hospital early the next morning. The weather, however, intervenes; heavy snow falls during the night. The hills of Seattle are clogged with vehicles going nowhere. Freeways are treacherous. Even the streets to the hospital are impassable. Dialysis technicians and portable dialysis machines are delayed. Their load backs up, and patients more critical than Ted wait long past their dialysis time for treatment. Ted's condition worsens. Fortunately, the weather moderates, and the schedule moves forward for Ted's dialysis to begin. It helps little, however. After two treatments, Ted begins to bleed internally, and his laboratory tests indicate that an emergency exists. A surgeon is called in—another stranger to the family, but the "freshest" one available. It seems every surgeon and every hospital is overburdened this Christmas holiday. Emergency surgery is scheduled for 5:00 p.m. The family is at the bedside, but the operating room is full; a **code blue** in the room Ted is to use delays surgery further. Ted's condition is so critical that the surgeon checks nearby hospitals for an operating room. None is available. Finally, at 1 a.m., Ted goes into surgery. The family is told that there is only a fifty–fifty chance he will survive.

Ted survives 4 hours of surgery but is returned to the intensive care unit (ICU) on a ventilator. There was a bowel perforation, and half his colon was removed. He is critical, but amazingly is able to be weaned from his ventilator in 24 hours. By now Ted is receiving food and hydration, blood, platelets, antibiotics, and pain medication intravenously. He cannot speak but is somewhat alert. He is seriously weakened. Urine output decreases, and the question of dialysis returns. At this point, all persons involved in Ted's care meet to discuss treatment; they meet with the family. Each family member is interviewed separately about their wishes and Ted's wishes regarding extraordinary means. Earlier an ICU nurse told the family that if even one of them has any hesitation about treatment, the hospital will not follow Ted's wishes. After completion of the interviews, it is clear that the family intends to follow Ted's wishes. Dialysis will cease. It is only a matter of time now. The nephrologist, however, has other ideas. When she discovers dialysis has been discontinued, she demands to know why. When the family explains, she says, "I was not present for that consultation. I will have to hear it from Ted himself." She goes to Ted's bedside, asks him if he can understand her, and says, "Ted, do you want dialysis?" Ted, in his hospital bed with head and shoulders elevated 10 to 20 degrees, has his arms immobilized at his side for the drip of numerous intravenous (IV) lines. An oxygen mask covers his nose and mouth. His eyes show lack of rest and sleep, fear about what is happening to him, and concern for his family. Ted shrugs his shoulders and opens his hands palms upward in gesture. The nephrologist is ordering a chest x-ray and dialysis when the family intervenes. An on-call physician and the nephrologist argue outside Ted's room, in earshot of the family. The attending physician indicates that in Ted's condition, dialysis probably will do more harm than good. His body cannot withstand dialysis. The nephrologist disagrees. When there seems no hope and the family is feeling powerless, their family physician returns and intervenes on behalf of the family. The damage has already been done, however. Ted has suffered not just one but all of the possible side effects the family feared. Ted is now bleeding internally from almost every organ of his body. All IV lines are removed except what is needed to keep Ted comfortable. Every breath is the hardest work his body has ever known. Each member of his family says good-bye and tells Ted how much he is loved. Nurses and doctors, so attentive in the previous 25 days, also stop by. The ICU nurses continue to do what they are best known for—attending to the needs of the critically ill. The primary care physician remains close. The end is peaceful. The end is relief—relief from agony and pain, relief from any more difficult decisions, relief from the disappointment that a loved one's wishes were so hard to carry out.

CHOICES IN LIFE

ETHICS CHECK

Throughout the text, many discussions of rights have surfaced both in the legal and the bioethical context. The dialogue continues in this chapter, taking a closer look at the right to die with dignity.

Choices are continually made about the quality of one's life. How is it decided what health care is received? Is there discrimination in care for the elderly? How can vulnerable populations be protected? People living in dire poverty struggle daily with life issues. An elderly person alone with no transportation and no nearby relatives fears the loss of personal control and independence. Some live with the challenge of decreased mental and emotional capabilities. There are those who respond to life's challenges with grace, strength, and a happy disposition no matter what life gives them. Others may only be able to face life's challenges with awkwardness, difficulties, and depression. All health-care professionals are to be reminded of the vulnerabilities and circumstances of their clients. Nowhere has this been truer than during the Covid-19 Pandemic when many of the most ill died in hospitals with no family members at their side. The examples of compassionate and thoughtful health-care employees who stood in for family members with patients during their last moments is both heartbreaking and heartwarming. Understanding and accepting clients and their wishes while providing quality and personalized health care is the challenge, even more specifically when facing death.

Adults have the right to make choices to forego life-sustaining treatments when death is imminent. Life-prolonging technology, however, has pushed death further into the future, and health professionals are often unable to help clients deal with the emotional strain and diminished capacity that often follow. Incompetent adults also need a voice in their choices in dying. These circumstances create an environment for action from the legal community. ●

LIVING WILLS, ADVANCE DIRECTIVES, AND THE PATIENT SELF-DETERMINATION ACT

When health-care professionals found themselves in legal and ethical dilemmas related to end-of-life issues, states began to pass legislation giving clients the specific legal right to forego life-sustaining treatments, nutrition, and hydration. The legislation also provided protection to providers and hospitals carrying out such orders. These directives allow individuals or their appointed agents to make decisions regarding their dying. The importance of these directives was uniquely identified in the opening Vignette.

California and Washington were forerunners in end-of-life legislation. California's document was the living will; Washington's response to the legal dilemma was the physicians' directive, or Natural Death Act. The intent of both documents was to provide an avenue through which individuals could make choices regarding their death before the event, usually while still healthy. A living will is an advance directive stating an individual's wishes regarding whether to be kept alive through the use of artificial means, such as life support, feeding tubes, and artificial ventilation. Advance directives can include the living will as well as powers of attorney and health-care proxies that may be known by other names—medical surrogate, health-care power of attorney, designation of health-care agent, and designation of conservator (guardianship). Each of these documents serves to provide direction and/or name someone to act on an individual's behalf when that individual is unable to convey his or her wishes to others. Today, all 50 states and Washington D.C. have end-of-life legislation (Fig. 16-1). ●

In some states, the living will and advance directive documents or appointments are combined into a single form, often called the advance directive. Each state identifies particular stipulations, but the intent is the same: to direct health-care professionals on decisions that are often made before death—if or when to resuscitate and what if any kind of heroic measures are to be performed. In recent years, each of these documents has grown increasingly specific. Individuals can relate if or under what circumstances artificial feeding or hydration is to begin and at what point only "comfort" measures are started. See Appendix II for examples of both a living will and an advance directive.

Another avenue for clients to express their wishes is becoming more popular. The Physician Orders for Life-Sustaining Treatment (POLST) is designed to improve the quality of care individuals receive at the end of life. Not all states use the POLST form, and each state that participates has designed its own form. Sections are likely to include information about resuscitation instructions, advance directives, and orders for other life-sustaining orders. See www.polst.org/state-programs to see if your state participates and to view a sample form.

In addition, the federal government passed the Patient Self-Determination Act in 1991. This law applies to all health-care institutions receiving payments from Medicare and Medicaid, including hospitals, skilled nursing facilities, hospices, home care programs, and health maintenance organizations. The act requires that all adult persons receiving medical care from such institutions be given written information about their right to accept or refuse medical or surgical treatment. These clients must also be given information about their right to formulate advance directives such as living wills and to designate someone to act on their behalf in making health-care decisions. The Patient Self-Determination Act, however, does not override any state law, allowing a health-care provider to object on the basis of conscience in the implementation of such an advance directive. It is important for clients to discuss their wishes with family members, durable powers of attorney, and health-care providers. Clients should make sure their wishes are understood and can be met.

DURABLE POWER OF ATTORNEY FOR HEALTH CARE

In addition to living wills or advance directives, many individuals choose to create the durable power of attorney and/or the durable power of attorney for health care. The durable power of attorney is a legal form that allows a designated person to act on another's behalf, making decisions related to finances and property. Likewise, the durable power of attorney for health care or the medical proxy allows a designated person to make only health-care decisions for another. A person must be competent to sign a power of attorney. Some states require that signers must be able to manage their own property effectively at the time of signing. Signers keep control over the document as long as the person can manage independently. The signed document can be given to a lawyer or a close friend with instructions

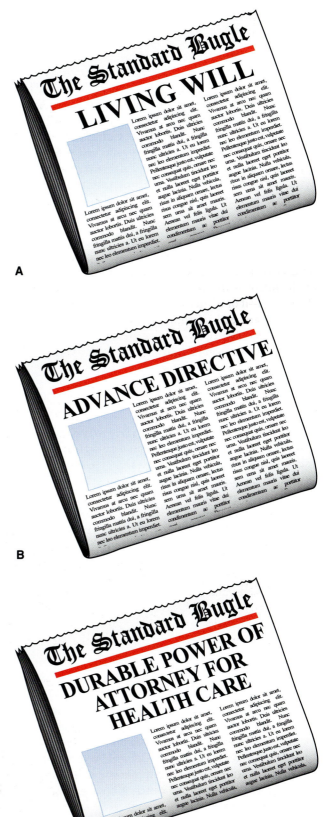

Figure 16-1. Three legal documents allowing clients to express their choices regarding their health care. **(A)** Living will. **(B)** Advance directive. **(C)** Durable power of attorney for health care.

that it is turned over to the attorney-in-fact only if the need arises. Once signed, the document is in effect until it is revoked.

This designated person should know and understand the client's personal wishes to ensure that the person with power of attorney will act on the client's behalf in all instances of health care. This agent is often a spouse, partner, grown child, close friend, other relative, or someone in whom the person has full confidence. Each state has established rules governing the use of the durable power of attorney. Individuals are advised to periodically update and review (usually every 5 years) their durable power of attorney for health care as well as an advance directive. Also, reviewing each state's laws if moving from state to state is necessary. Professional legal advice regarding a given state's stipulations may be advisable, but preprinted forms are readily available. See Appendix II for an example of a durable power of attorney for health care.

NATIONAL REGISTRY

Individuals can register their advance directive with a national registry that will electronically transmit a copy of their document to any health-care provider (hospital, doctor, skilled nursing facility, home health agency, provider of home health care, ambulatory surgery center, and hospice). The registry agrees not to release the personal information to any party other than health-care providers, so information is kept private and confidential. The registry provides labels to affix to an insurance card and driver's license, stating that the individual's advance directive is registered. The registrant is contacted annually by mail to confirm that the advance directive has not been changed or revoked and to update personal and emergency contact information. Health-care providers can contact the registry 24 hours a day to gain access to advance directives. See www.uslivingwillregistry.com for more information.

CHOICES IN DYING

No one escapes death. From the moment of birth, each day of life moves a person closer to death. Some die peacefully during sleep. Some die suddenly as a result of an accident or as a victim of crime. Some die slowly and gradually, with bodies that deteriorate and organs that cease to function. Some die with little or no pain or discomfort. Others suffer a great deal. Most want to live, but, when faced with death, desire to go quickly, painlessly, and with dignity. However, not all are so fortunate.

In dying, there are choices that can be made. Some face a life-threatening illness and take action to direct their wishes for the time when death is imminent. Others create advance directives when making their last will and testament. There are also a large group of individuals who refuse to think of death, make no plans of any kind, and may leave loved ones to make decisions with a great deal of anguish. Still others live in a culture where discussing or planning for death is forbidden or frowned on.

Personal attitudes and public opinion have changed through the years regarding death. In 1938 the Euthanasia Society of America was founded. It was a national, nonprofit organization dedicated to fostering communication about complex end-of-life decisions among individuals. The organization invented the living will in 1967. The premise of the organization was to create an atmosphere in which one could take measures to end life, creating a "good death," when threatened with a terminal condition. Euthanasia was identified as passive (allowing death to come naturally, taking no measures to prevent it) or active (the intentional taking of one's life). Now euthanasia is more commonly defined as the latter. Today there are numerous organizations dedicated to choices in dying, such as Compassion in Choices (www.compassionandchoices.org); the National Hospice and Palliative Care Organization (www.nhpco.org); the World Federation of Right to Die Societies (www.worldrtd.net); and the Death With Dignity National Center (www.deathwithdignity.org).

Although individuals increasingly seek control over their choices in dying, the almost coercive power of medical technology and medicine to preserve and prolong life may cause many to suffer debility, pain, and perhaps a lesser quality of life. The desire to have choices in dying comes from fears and concerns related to prolonged dying as the result of technological interventions. Most desire the right to be able to refuse treatment or hospitalization. A few might choose assisted death. Generally, individuals do not want to be a burden to significant others. They fear losing their independence and control and want to choose their quality of both life and death.

Every day, medical personnel confront complex issues regarding the meanings of life and death. There is a fine line between helping a person to live and allowing that person to die. When is it appropriate to use extraordinary means to prolong life? What are extraordinary means? What are the legal implications if treatment is withheld or withdrawn? Technological or mechanical intervention has saved the lives of many. Medical technology offers insulin to control diabetes, a cardiac pacemaker or mechanical heart valves for a weak or diseased heart, renal dialysis for kidney failure, angioplasty for blocked arteries, even antibiotics for pneumonia.

Consider the following example from Donald M. Hayes writing in *Between Doctor and Patient:* "Mr. Baker had terminal kidney failure and was comatose. Several tubes came from various places in his body. He was receiving both blood and glucose into his veins. One night he went into cardiac arrest. A team of nurses and physicians responded to a code blue and worked vigorously to resuscitate. The attempt was futile, and Mr. Baker died. The memory of Mr. Baker's death was lasting to Mr. Rogers, the recently admitted patient in the same room. He said to his physician, 'Please don't ever let that happen to me. I've tried all my life to live like a man; I want to die like one.' Mr. Rogers underwent surgery that revealed inoperable, widespread cancer. He did not respond well, and a few days later he had a tube in his stomach, a catheter in his bladder, a tube through his nose, and intravenous tubes in both arms. When he suffered respiratory failure, a tracheotomy was performed to save his life. He was given a slate to write on, since a tracheotomy precludes speech. Later that evening, before he managed to switch off this respirator so that he might die peacefully, he wrote on the slate, 'Doctor, remember; the enemy is not death. The enemy is inhumanity.'"

Few turn their backs on the medical technology that has added years of life for so many. Such advances in medicine are heralded by the public and the media; however, if not used judiciously, technology can disturb the quality of life. At some time, every individual is apt to face the issue of how much medical technology to use to prolong life, and hopes, at the same time, for a "good death." Whether or not to prolong life can be a serious problem when the decision is made with little forethought or adequate planning. When the cardiologist tells a loved one that a pacemaker is necessary to regulate the heartbeat, the general response is, "When can it be done?"

The decision is more complex, however, when a loved one is hospitalized with a heart condition that is rapidly deteriorating and little can be done. The questions of how much intervention to use and when to intervene are much more serious. When the heart monitor indicates with a buzzing sound and a continuous monotone sound that the heart has ceased to beat, somewhere, someone is going to ask, "Do we resuscitate?" It is at this point that the decisions declared in a living will or advance directive become significant.

SUFFERING IN DYING

It is the fear of suffering more than the actual death that concerns the majority of individuals. Suffering can be short or long term. Short-term suffering presents a set of problems different from those of long-term suffering. Consider the following:

Case Studies

Example 1: A 35-year-old teacher was diagnosed with acute myelogenous leukemia (AML). A bone marrow transplant was offered as treatment. A donor was found after a fund raiser in her honor. Hospitalization and induction followed, with severe side effects and pain. She died 2 months later when remission attempts failed and an overwhelming infection developed.

Example 2: A 45-year-old plumber was diagnosed with colorectal cancer. Surgery was recommended, and he received a permanent colostomy. Postoperatively, he did fairly well and returned to work part-time during chemotherapy. Within a year, the cancer metastasized with complications. Oncology, surgery, and pain management consultations recommended only symptomatic treatment. Large doses of narcotics and sedatives were required to keep him comfortable for the remaining 6 months. The plumber remained home until about 6 weeks before death when inpatient hospice was requested by himself and the family.

Consider the variables of time, cost, and dependency in the two examples. Who suffered the most? Where are the greatest costs? Who is most dependent?

The amount of suffering often influences care decisions. Are antibiotics prescribed when a hospitalized person suffering from the last stages of pancreatic cancer contracts pneumonia? Under what circumstances are "do not resuscitate" orders placed in clients' charts? Consider an individual being kept alive by a ventilator who has no recognition and no awareness of surroundings. Is the person suffering? Is life being prolonged beyond its natural course of events or is recovery possible?

How much pain medication is prescribed to ease the suffering? When sufficient pain medication is prescribed to keep those close to death comfortable, health professionals know the medication provided for pain relief may depress breathing in some clients already so fragile and debilitated that death is hastened. Is this action seen as an act of euthanasia? Many see it as an act of compassion that allows the person to die with dignity and as close to pain-free as possible.

USE OF MEDICATIONS

Medications are used to ease suffering and pain, but are also given for many other reasons, including sedatives for sleep and specific medications for the particular disease condition. Antidepressants and antianxiety medications also may be prescribed. Medications are to be respected for their intended action and the client's needs. The greatest difficulty arises with pain medications, especially in long-term suffering.

Problems arise when family members, friends, and even health professionals circumvent or question medication orders. This can be problematic for the client; therefore, it is helpful for all persons close to the client to understand the medication orders. Unless everyone understands that the medication amount is needed to keep the level of pain bearable, the medication amount is often withheld or reduced. Medications may be given in different dosages, frequencies, and combinations for each individual. Age, weight, illness (whether chronic or acute), and the client's threshold for pain all influence a medication choice.

Sometimes health professionals are reluctant to prescribe or administer the known safe dosage of pain medications. In fact, in some cases health professionals will administer less than the prescribed dose because they believe what was prescribed was too much. Some fear the client will become addicted. The client or family members may push to use less medication than the amount prescribed because of the belief it is too harmful. Clients often wait too long to ask for pain medication, thinking they "can handle it." If there is a history of substance misuse, a client may attempt to forego opioids. All these circumstances have the potential of working against the client's comfort. The idea that a dying person who is in pain would have medications withheld to prevent addiction is indefensible.

PSYCHOLOGICAL ASPECTS OF DYING

Dying clients differ in their psychological experiences. Although basic personalities remain the same, changes occur. A person normally calm and loving may have periods of violence and hostility. A happy person may become severely depressed. An individual who usually is able to accept medical facts may totally deny a life-threatening illness. In fact, a person who is nearly comatose or close to death may be unaware of his or her responses to questions or be unable to make any decisions.

Relationships change. The dying person may reject any close contact or relationships. Some individuals are incapable of continuing a close relationship with a person who is dying. Closest friends may become aloof and distant. Some may fear touching the dying person. The opposite may also be true. A stronger bond of friendship can develop, and new friendships will be made, possibly from individuals in similar circumstances. Broken relationships may be healed.

Relationships are important because they provide strength and support that may not be available through any other source. The depth of relationships during this time and the degree of acceptance by dying clients may depend on their self-image. When a person is ill, is in pain, lives in a deteriorating body, and possibly is unable to perform the activities of daily living, self-image is fragile. When self-image is lacking, hope is lost; dying clients feel useless, think they are burdens, and have difficulties accepting help. The psychological effect of a poor self-image may even hasten death. Those who are dying worry that they are not fulfilling their usual role in the family and worry about their lack of control.

Personal goals are altered, dropped, or identified. There may be the goal to see a son or daughter graduate or a grandchild born; however, some goals will seem unrealistic to the dying because of limited time. The dying person either gives up or strives to live until a certain event takes place. The total loss of personal goals, no matter how insignificant they may appear, can be devastating to everyone. Indecision is often a psychological dilemma that accompanies lack of personal goals. Individuals close to the dying may be able to recommend goals and provide offers of help in the decision-making process.

Communication may become difficult. Aside from any physiological problems precluding speech or communication, what dying clients are unable to understand or hear may depend on what they choose to hear or are ready to understand. Communication may be complicated further if the client's condition has not been honestly addressed. Of course, the opposite may be true. Some dying clients express the ability to communicate with greater depth because of the urgency of their circumstances.

There is often the question of whether dying clients should be told of their terminal condition. How much information should they be given? Some believe that all clients need to be told the medical facts and treated openly and honestly by all health professionals. They believe informed clients are better able to face death and are less afraid of the truth. Others believe no clients should be told they are dying, or that only those clients who give some verbal or nonverbal indication that they want to know should be told.

Case Study

Ethel, a 74-year-old woman, had required home oxygen for many years but was experiencing worsening respiratory complications. When the diagnosis was lung cancer, her four sons decided it was better not to tell her. Her health continued to decline and a permanent feeding tube was considered. When just a daughter-in-law was in the room, Ethel grabbed her hand and said, "Don't lie to me, am I dying, do I have cancer?" Although her daughter-in-law did not agree with the decision to withhold information from Ethel, she was still hesitant to answer her. Ethel pleaded with her until finally, with tears in her eyes, she gave a small nod. Ethel stated, "Thank you. No feeding tube." Ethel did not reveal that she knew the truth and died several days later surrounded by her family.

Do you think it was right to keep the diagnosis from Ethel? Why or why not?
Do you think that Ethel's daughter-in-law was right in telling her the truth?
What would you do in this situation?

In some cultures, only family members rather than the client are told of impending death. There is the belief that once they are told some clients may refuse to set goals, give up hope, and wait impatiently for death. Fear is often a traumatic psychological aspect of dying. There is fear of pain, fear of long suffering, fear of losing independence, fear of financial ruin, and fear of death itself. The client's fears are to be recognized and alleviated, if possible. To recognize these fears requires active and passive listening on the part of all people close to the dying individual and a willingness on the part of this individual to express those fears.

Much fear can be lessened if people close to the dying anticipate the fear and provide possible solutions and appropriate resources. Outside help may be sought, if necessary. Social workers, psychologists, pain management specialists, home health aides, clergy, and other health professionals can be valuable resources. Clients' fears should be taken seriously, and reference to their supposed unimportance should be avoided.

The psychological aspects of death are difficult for everyone because they generally are less understood than the physiological aspects of death, but to care for the physical and ignore the psychological is to treat only half the client. As Norman Cousins said, "Death is not the greatest loss in life. The greatest loss is what dies inside us while we live."

PHYSIOLOGICAL ASPECTS OF DYING

Medicine has numerous treatments for some of the physiological problems of suffering and pain experienced in the dying process. Sometimes the treatments are sufficient; at other times, they barely address the problem. Untreated or undiagnosed physiological problems can cause or enhance psychological difficulties. Separating the psychological from the physiological is difficult. For example, pain and suffering, if untreated by therapy or medicinal means, may prove to be a psychological barrier for clients, their families, and health professionals.

Loss of communication skills as seen in the aphasic or the comatose client may be frustrating and unbearable. If clients are indecisive or suffer from dementia because of physiological changes, they may not be able to participate in the decision-making process of their life-threatening illness. Family members then may need to assume greater roles in talking for clients and making decisions.

Other common physiological problems encountered include loss of bodily functions; inability to move or ambulate; inability to eat or drink; and inability to tolerate medications, treatments, light, or sound. In some settings, these symptoms may be treated without much difficulty. However, if clients choose to die at home, professional help or training may become necessary. If clients become severely disabled physically, they may be reluctant to go anywhere, even to their own medical clinic. Family members may become exhausted caring for their loved ones and may be unable to administer some of their treatments. The more severe these physiological problems, the more difficult daily existence becomes.

Physiological difficulties may hinder sexual identity and involvement, altering sexual expression. The physiological and psychological aspects of sexuality are so intertwined that cause and effect are difficult to determine. It may be difficult or impossible to have sexual intercourse, so other ways to express love, caring, or the relief of sexual tension are sought. A discussion of the expression of sexuality and related client problems should be initiated by the health professional but rarely is.

HOSPICE

The first **hospice**, lodging for the dying, was formed by Cecily Saunders in London in 1965. Hospice provides care for the terminally ill at home, in a hospital, in a skilled nursing facility, or in a special hospice facility. The main objective of care is to make clients comfortable, "at home," and close to family. Treatments, such as cardiopulmonary resuscitation, intravenous therapy, nasogastric tubes, and antibiotics, are discouraged. Treatments are given in light of the client's personal and social circumstances.

Death is seen as "all right." A balance is kept between human needs and medical needs. Children are encouraged in hospice as a reminder that life is an ongoing process. Clients might share a cup of tea with staff and each other rather than receiving an intravenous solution during their last hours.

An advantage hospice offers is that death is managed with dignity, and experienced staff members want to care for the dying. The expense is generally less than acute care costs and is often covered by insurance, including Medicare. In a special hospice facility, the dying client is not isolated behind curtains but rather is surrounded by others. In addition, survivors are helped to deal with the death. If the hospice care is at home, clients are in familiar surroundings, may have their favorite foods, and are close to loved ones.

STAGES OF GRIEF

Elisabeth Kübler-Ross defines five stages of grief or responses to dying. There is no set period for any one stage, nor will every dying person go through every stage. Some believe that no real grief work begins until passing through all five stages. Some may stay in denial until death; others may manage denial and bargaining and stumble in depression. Still others may move back and forth from one stage to another. Some may move through some or all of the stages several times. There is no set or acceptable pattern. However, these stages do offer information on how to relate to clients and their families who will experience similar stages.

Elisabeth Kübler-Ross defines five stages of dying and death: (1) denial, (2) anger, (3) bargaining, (4) depression, and (5) acceptance.

DENIAL

Clients deny their life-threatening or terminal illness or go through periods of disbelief. Clients commonly say, "This is not happening to me" or "I'll go for another opinion." Denial generally is a temporary defense and offers therapeutic meaning to clients. Health professionals should listen to clients during this stage. Trying to contradict clients or force them to believe what is happening to them will be to no avail. Encourage clients to talk about death. Listen, listen, and listen.

ANGER

Clients suddenly realize, "It is me. This is happening to me. Why me?" They may become "problem clients" and are envious and resentful. Anger may be dispersed in all directions, at people and toward the environment. Rage and temper tantrums can occur. Professionals and family members will want to remember that the anger is truly not directed toward them and will want to be understanding no matter how angry the client becomes. Listening to clients is important, allowing them to vent their own feelings.

BARGAINING

During this stage, clients try to make deals with their provider, God or a higher being, or family, usually for more time or for a period of comfort without pain. Clients tend to be more cooperative and congenial. Common responses include the following: "Please let me see my homeland again." "Dear God, I'll never . . . if you make me well." Health professionals can listen to dying clients' requests, but are not to become a party to the bargain. Some bargaining is associated with guilt. Bargaining can give the client the hope and stamina to reach a desired goal. It is OK to mourn and cry. Allow for silences.

DEPRESSION

The dying client's body is deteriorating, sometimes rapidly; financial burdens are likely increasing; pain is unbearable; and relationships are severed. All can lead to depression. The dying are losing everything and everyone they love. Dying may be a time of tears, and crying may allow relief. Professionals who appear happy, loud, and reassuring will not provide much help to depressed clients. Clients may need to express their sorrow to someone or merely have someone close. They may have little need for words at this stage. Simple tasks may be impossible. Helplessness is real.

ACCEPTANCE

The final but perhaps not last stage is when clients are accepting of their fate. They usually are tired, weak, and able to sleep. They are not necessarily happy, but rather at peace. Professionals will be aware that clients may prefer to be left alone and not bothered with world events or family problems. Family members usually require more help, understanding, and support than clients in this stage. Touching and the use of silence may prove helpful.

Case Study

Relate the five stages identified to any death or grieving experience you have had. Did you pass through all the stages? Did you circle back to a previous stage? What was/is most difficult for you?

Following a death or the experience of loss, there will come a time when friends and neighbors stop calling, "closure" has occurred, and everything slowly gets back to normal. Some say this is when the real and the very difficult grief work begins. A common definition of grief work is summarized by the acronym TEAR.

T = To accept the reality of the loss
E = Experience the pain of the loss
A = Adjust to the environment of what was lost
R = Reinvest in the new reality

LEGAL DEFINITIONS OF DEATH

An early legal definition of death was the cessation of the heart to beat and the lungs to breathe. The two are so interrelated that the cessation of one leads to the cessation of the other, followed by the cessation of all cognitive activity, all other brain functions, and all general responsiveness. The cessation of the heart to beat and of breathing has been the simplest to identify and the easiest test of life, and it became the acceptable definition of death. Today, the majority of deaths in the United States are still determined by this traditional definition of death. ●

With medical technological advances, resuscitative devices, increased complexities of life, and the increased demand for organ transplants, the heart–lung definition of death was found insufficient in some cases. Death is a continuum, and different parts of the body die at different times. As long as there is a heartbeat to pump oxygenated blood to tissues, cells thrive. Even when an irreparable brain injury does not support life and life support is removed, the heart continues to beat for a short time. However, when the blood it pumps is no longer oxygenated, tissues and cells die. Approximately 3 to 4 minutes pass before there is irreparable brain death. Once the brain dies, all the other body organs die at various intervals.

Subsequently, the concept of brain death was presented by the Harvard Ad-Hoc Committee, chaired by Henry Beecher. The criteria follow: An individual appears to be in a deep coma. The condition can be satisfactorily diagnosed by the following points: (1) unreceptivity and unresponsivity, (2) no movements or breathing, (3) no reflexes, and (4) a flat electroencephalogram. Each of these tests is to be repeated at least 24 hours later with no change. This definition of brain death does not cover cases such as Karen Ann Quinlan, who was in a persistent vegetative state, or people who are in comas but do not meet other accepted criteria. ●

In 1983, President Ronald Reagan formed a commission to discuss the ethical implications of dying and death. The commission recommended that all U.S. jurisdictions accept the Uniform Determination of Death Act developed with the guidance of three organizations: the American Bar

Association, the American Medical Association, and the National Conference of Commissioners on Uniform State Laws. The act "established that the irreversible cessation of all circulatory and respiratory functions, or irreversible cessation of all functions of the entire brain, including the brain stem" is the criterion of death.

Some believe that this higher brain death definition addresses all purposes. Whatever the state's legal definition of death, the declaration of death will be made by medical standards as defined in the Uniform Determination of Death Act. This means that as technology changes and medicine advances, laws will not necessarily change; rather, good medical practices will determine what counts as good evidence that the legal definition of death has occurred.

 ## LEGAL IMPLICATIONS

Most legal rulings on life and death center on "Who makes the decisions?" Prolonging life by artificial means usually poses few legal problems. Federal laws state that clients with failing kidneys have the right to funding and the use of kidney dialysis machines. Some means of prolonging life artificially, such as insulin administration, are so easy, inexpensive, and widely practiced that there is no controversy about their use. On the other hand, some procedures, such as dialysis, are so expensive that federal legislation was necessary to ensure that every citizen has the right to such treatments. If questions arise in any health-care facility, consider a referral to an ethics committee when one is available.

Choices in dying, however, are complex and controversial. Consider landmark case law in the following two circumstances. In seeking greater choice in the process of dying, the courts appear to be regulating in a more restrictive manner. The fear of litigation is the reason in some cases why health-care professionals and institutions are hesitant to abide by clients' choices in dying.

Case Law

Karen Ann Quinlan: The litigation over the case of Karen Ann Quinlan was widely publicized. Karen was a New Jersey woman who, at age 21, was taken to the hospital in a comatose state by friends after a birthday party. No one is sure exactly what happened to Karen on Tuesday, April 14, 1975, but the world soon began to follow her life closely. Her case was a newsworthy first. Karen's condition deteriorated. On July 31, her parents asked her physicians to take Karen off the ventilator and signed a letter to that effect. The physicians disagreed with the decision on moral grounds and refused to take Karen off of the ventilator. Legal action ensued. On September 12, the attorney for Joseph Quinlan, Karen's father, filed a plea with the superior court on three constitutional grounds: (1) the right to privacy, (2) religious freedom, and (3) cruel and unusual punishment.

Judge Robert Muir ruled against Joseph Quinlan, who then appealed the decision to the New Jersey Supreme Court. The court's decision was in Joseph Quinlan's favor and set aside any criminal liability for removing the ventilator. It further recommended that Karen's physicians consult the hospital ethics committee to concur with their prognosis for Karen. Weeks later Karen was weaned from the machine. She lived until 1986.

Theresa (Terri) Schiavo: Terri Schiavo suffered cardiac arrest in February 1990, probably due to an eating disorder that may have caused a serious electrolyte imbalance diagnosed when she was admitted to the hospital. She was without oxygen 5 to 7 minutes longer than medical experts believe is possible without irreversible brain damage. Her husband, Michael, insisted she be intubated, given a tracheotomy to breathe, and placed on a ventilator. Without these actions, she would have died. Terri lived in a coma for 2 months and then was repeatedly diagnosed as in a persistent vegetative state. She was removed from the ventilator and kept functioning with an artificial feeding and hydration tube. She could breathe and swallow her saliva, but could not drink or eat. What happened in the next 15 years is almost unimaginable.

Terri's husband and her parents struggled for a few years, but conflict arose when Michael and her parents disagreed about removing the feeding tube so that Terri could die peacefully. Terri had no living will. Twice courts ordered the feeding tube to be removed, but Terri's parents fought to have it reinserted. The Florida legislature passed a law known as "Terri's Law" to give the governor the prerogative of reinserting the feeding tube and required a special guardian ad litem be appointed. Later, the Florida Supreme Court ruled Terri's Law unconstitutional, and the U.S. Supreme Court refused to overturn that decision. Just a week before Terri's death, the U.S. Congress passed legislation to move the case from Florida to the federal courts. The Florida Federal District Court, the 11th Circuit Court of Appeals, and the U.S. Supreme Court refused to review the findings of the lower courts.

By this time and through all the court battles, Michael and Terri's parents were estranged and could no longer be civil toward each other. In testimony, Terri's parents said that even if Terri had a living will, they would have fought to have it voided. Michael became even more determined to carry out the wishes he believed Terri would have had. In the last few days of Terri's life, private citizens, religious leaders, and news media lined up on both sides of the issue outside the hospital to witness a most public death. Michael's wishes finally prevailed, and Terri died March 31, 2005, 14 days after the feeding tube was removed and 15 years after her cardiac arrest.

Both cases provoked discussions about end-of-life issues and medicine's limitations. Both Quinlan and Schiavo were alive when their cases were brought before the courts. The question in both cases was whether each woman should be kept alive, one by use of a ventilator, the other by artificial hydration and nutrition. It was not whether they were legally dead. There are questions to be asked. Should the two women have been allowed to die earlier? Is vegetative existence better than death? What impact does medical technology have on these decisions? Who pays for the high costs incurred in these cases? Who should decide? Is it more difficult to remove hydration and nutrition than a ventilator?

ETHICAL CONSIDERATIONS

ETHICS CHECK

Life-and-death choices are numerous. The many factors to consider include the following: Who makes the decision? What role do politicians and the courts play in making decisions? What is the influence of economics? Do circumstances influence decisions? What is considered ordinary and extraordinary treatment? ●

The burden of such decisions is heavy. If a decision is required in an emergency life-and-death matter, those in closest proximity to the client will decide. In health-care facilities, the law may determine who decides. If there is any question, consideration is given to the wishes of the client, the wishes of the family, the recommendations of the provider, and perhaps the recommendations of a professional team of individuals (ethics committee) whose purpose it is to make a decision—not necessarily in that order.

The problem arises over whose right is paramount in a decision. At times it is obvious. If a client is unable to decide, others are involved. The family has an influence, but the cases of Karen Ann Quinlan and Theresa Schiavo demonstrated that the influence of family is not decisive. In the case of Theresa Schiavo, the governor of Florida, the 11th Circuit Court of Appeals, the Florida Supreme Court, the President of the United States, Congress, and the U.S. Supreme Court were all involved.

The same often is true of a client's wishes. Even if clients are able to express their wishes to physicians and health-care providers, circumstances may override them, as was so clearly demonstrated in the vignette at the beginning of the chapter.

Many circumstances influence decisions. Age is a factor. Resuscitation may be started on a 16-year-old and not on an 89-year-old. Cost is also a factor. Triple cardiac bypass surgery may be performed for someone of substantial means more readily than for the indigent derelict. Health is a factor. A pacemaker may be inserted for the elderly client whose general health is good, but it may not be used if the client's health is poor and other severe physical difficulties exist. The availability of resources is a factor. With only one kidney and four needy persons, three will have to do without. The Covid-19 pandemic of 2020 put all these factors into consideration. Many facilities worldwide and in the United States experienced a shortage of much-needed resources such as personal protective equipment, medications, and ventilators. Decisions on whom to treat first were made by medical personnel, and in some cases by political appointees.

Other factors include region, personal philosophy of life, the amount of pain one can endure, whether a client is comatose, and what the client's feelings are about a good life versus a good death. Yet, all these factors are relative. Some are old at age 55; others are young at 90. Some can endure great pain, and others have a low threshold for pain. What is poor health to one person may seem to be good health to another. The relativity of the factors complicates the decision and mandates that each decision be considered individually on its own merits.

 ## CULTURAL VIEWS

Cultures view life and death differently. For example, people of Jewish heritage strive to appreciate each day and live it as though it is their last. Death is seen as a part of the life cycle. Mexicans also view death as a natural part of life and the will of God. In the Filipino culture, planning one's death is taboo; hence, discussing advance directives and living wills is difficult. Many Chinese believe their spirits do not rest unless living descendants care for the grave and worship the memory of the dead. In the Japanese culture, family members want to be by the dying person's bedside, and traditionally the eldest son has decision-making responsibility at this time. There is, however, a taboo against the discussion of serious illness and death. Cultural and religious differences exist in cases of organ and tissue donation. For example, many Hmong immigrants from Southeast Asia believe that organ donation prevents the person from experiencing reincarnation; for this reason, the Hmong also resist autopsies. Many Native Americans often oppose organ donation because of their enormous reverence for the body, which is considered both the residence and the manifestation of a person's essence.

Health-care professionals will want to be sensitive to, understand, and appreciate cultural preferences. Being aware of a client's cultural perspective and asking questions related to his or her wishes is better than assuming everyone thinks and believes alike.

 ## ASSISTED DEATH

Some people believe that assisted death weakens morality in the country and may have far-reaching consequences. If death is justified for one individual to prevent further suffering, why not for infants with severe disabilities who have no possibility of a "normal" life? Consider the circumstances of an infant born with severe congenital defects and no possible chance of survival. The parents may choose not to begin measures to preserve the infant's life. This can mean watching a tiny infant gradually deteriorate over a period of days. The ordeal can be terrible. Parents may be somewhat protected from this experience if the infant remains in the hospital, but the medical staff is not. Many physicians and health professionals ask, "Would it not be more merciful to inject the infant with a lethal dose of medication that would hasten death and prevent the suffering?"

Perhaps even more personal and difficult questions are raised related to death. "How do I want to die?" "What kind of lifesaving measures do I want?" "Might I choose assisted death?" "Can I stand to suffer?" "Do I have any control over my own death?" "What do I want health professionals to do for me?"

Questions arise about whether assisted death or euthanasia should be endorsed. It is considered assisted death when the physician provides a dying individual with a lethal dose of medication to be self-administered; it is considered active euthanasia when a physician administers a lethal dose to the client. In physician-assisted death, the client acts last, whereas in active euthanasia, the physician acts last.

Just as California and Washington were forerunners with their living wills and natural death laws, they were forerunners in legislation to give people the option to seek "aid in dying from physicians to end life in a dignified, painless, and humane manner." These laws are much broader in their scope than any living will or advance directive. In 1994, Oregon passed the Death With Dignity measure that was later challenged by the courts. In 1997, the act was reaffirmed by the Oregon voters. Oregon became the nation's first state to allow a physician to prescribe a lethal dose of medication when asked by a terminally ill client. The four safeguards in this measure are as follows: (1) The attending physician must truly convey informed consent, which must include all feasible opportunities, such as pain management, hospice, and palliative care. (2) The attending physician's diagnosis and prognosis must be confirmed by a consulting physician. The latter physician must verify that the client has made a voluntary and informed decision. (3) If either physician thinks the client might have depression that might impair judgment, a counseling session must be attended. (4) The client making the request must do so both orally and in writing. The law details specific timelines and a waiting period for the client before receiving the lethal medication. The request must be witnessed by at least two people who can verify the client's capacity to decide and that the decision is voluntary. Oregon's Death with Dignity 2019 Annual Report indicated that 112 Oregon physicians wrote 290 prescriptions to qualified dying Oregonians with the resultant deaths of 188 individuals. In the 22 years since the passage of the law, patients consistently gave three main reasons for making their choice. Loss of autonomy, decreased ability to remain active in daily life, and loss of dignity were their main factors for making this end-of-life choice. Since the law took effect in 1998, 2,518 individuals have received the prescription and 1,657 have died from ingesting the medications.

In fall 2001, U.S. Attorney General Ashcroft determined that the government would step in to revoke the licenses of any physician who prescribed controlled substances to clients seeking physician-assisted death in Oregon. By a 6-to-3 vote the U.S. Supreme Court ruled that Ashcroft exceeded his authority when he tried to block the Oregon law to help terminally ill clients die. The Supreme Court decision opened the door for other states to legalize physician-assisted death.

In 1997, the U.S. Senate passed a bill barring the federal government from financing physician-assisted death. The vote was 99 to 0. The same measure previously cleared the House of Representatives by a vote of 398 to 16. Medicare and Medicaid are prohibited from funding physician-assisted death. In June 1997, all nine Supreme Court justices refused to grant assisted death as a fundamental liberty for the terminally ill.

On November 4, 2008, the state of Washington passed Initiative 1000, the state's Death With Dignity Act, which became law on March 5, 2009. This act allows terminally ill adults seeking to end their life to request lethal doses of medication from medical and osteopathic physicians. These individuals must be Washington residents who have less than 6 months to live. Details of the Washington Death with Dignity Act can be found at www.doh.wa.gov/dwda. In 2018, 267 individuals received the medication to assist in their deaths, and 203 died following the ingestion. The others died without having taken the medication.

IN THE NEWS

As of 2021, the following 11 jurisdictions had passed the Death with Dignity law: California, Colorado, District of Columbia, Hawaii, Montana, Maine, New Jersey, Oregon, Vermont, New Mexico, and Washington. At least 16 other states have been actively considering Death With Dignity legislation. The Covid-19 pandemic of 2020 caused many states to publicly encourage individuals to establish their end-of-life decisions as it became more critical when family members did not have access to their loved ones.

Legislation on physician-assisted death continues to be controversial, contradictory, confusing, and as emotional as legalization of abortion has been in the United States. In fact, many right-to-life organizations oppose assisted death legislation based on the principle that abortion and assisted death are the same as murder.

UNIFORM ANATOMICAL GIFT ACT

The legal definition of death identified earlier is particularly important in the area of organ transplantation. All 50 states and the District of Columbia have some form of the Uniform Anatomical Gift Act. Persons 18 years or older and of sound mind may make a gift of all or any part of their body to the following persons for the following purposes:

1. To any hospital, surgeon, or physician for medical or dental education, research, advancement of medical or dental science, therapy, or transplantation
2. To any accredited medical or dental school, college, or university for education, research, advancement of medical or dental science, or therapy
3. To any organ bank or storage facility for medical or dental education, research, advancement of medical or dental science, therapy, or transplantation
4. To any specified individual for therapy or transplantation needed by him or her

The gift may be made by a provision in a will or by signing, in the presence of two witnesses, a card. The card is generally carried with the person at all times. The card method may be the best because advance directives may not be readily available until it is too late for donation of organs or tissues. Donated organs include heart, lung, kidney, pancreas, liver, and intestine; tissue includes eyes, skin, bone, heart valves, veins, and tendons. There is no cost to the donors or their families. See Figure 16-2 for the steps followed in organ donation.

It is illegal to sell body parts in this country; however, the practice is common in some developing countries. It is becoming increasingly popular to find compatible donors for transplant organs on the Internet. Many clients needing a transplant organ are telling their life stories on their own websites, making electronic pleas for willing donors. An example tells of an individual on a waiting list for a kidney for 5 years who paid monthly fees to have his profile posted on www.matching-donors.com. He received 500 offers for a donation, found a match, and paid his donor $5,000 in transportation costs and other expenses incurred. Currently more than 108,000 Americans are on lists for organs, mostly kidneys and livers. A person is added to the national transplant waiting list every 10 minutes. About 20 people die every day waiting for a phone call that an organ has been found for them. Bartering for organs is apt to continue.

Persons may place conditions on their organ donation, and donors are carefully screened before their body parts are used. The physician and hospital may be found negligent, so there are strict

Steps to organ donation:

1. Irreparable brain damage occurs; life support is to be suspended. Individual's signed donor agreement is presented; family agrees.
2. Transplant surgical team is notified; ethics dictate that transplant surgeons not be present when life support is removed.
3. Life support is removed (usually a ventilator); heart continues to beat and pump deoxygenated blood to tissues and cells.
4. If heart continues to beat more than 1 hour, organs are unfit for transplant due to the lack of oxygen; transplant is called off; if the heart ceases to beat in less than an hour, transplant moves forward.
5. Transplant team must wait 120 seconds to make sure heart does not start to beat again; if it does, the team waits—back to step 4.
6. Once heart has stopped for the 2 minutes, death is announced; transplant team arrives to harvest donor organs for waiting recipients.

Figure 16-2. Steps taken before organ donation.

standards for donor screening. HIV does not necessarily rule out a donor as the organs may be used in an HIV-positive patient.

The Gift of Life organization provides helpful information on facing end-of-life situations. Once notified, a representative from the Gift of Life will approach the family to discuss organ donation. Physicians and hospital personnel do not have to make first contact with families; however, in most cases they do.

AUTOPSY

An autopsy is an examination of a dead body to determine the cause of death. Statutes generally state who can authorize an autopsy and under what circumstances. Coroners or medical examiners may give such authorization. Others include, in order of priority, the following:

PRIORITY AUTHORIZATION FOR AUTOPSY

1. The surviving spouse
2. Any child of the deceased who is 18 years of age or older
3. A parent of the deceased
4. An adult sibling of the deceased

Autopsies may be complete or partial. In other words, a pathologist may perform an autopsy on the entire body and examine every part and organ or do an autopsy only of the thoracic cavity or the brain. The extremities rarely are involved unless indicated by trauma, prior surgical procedure, or vessel involvement. No parts of the body can be retained for any reason without family consent. If the autopsy is done properly and in a professional manner, the body can be viewed by survivors or at a death ritual.

Some circumstances require an autopsy to investigate the cause of a suspicious death. Autopsies also offer valuable information for medical science and research. Knowledge gained from an autopsy may prevent another person from suffering similar circumstances. Refer to Chapter 7, Public Duties, for further information on autopsy.

ROLE OF HEALTH PROFESSIONALS

Health-care employees will make life-and-death decisions in personal relationships with their families and friends, but rarely in any professional capacity. They often, however, may be involved in conversations with clients or their families who are struggling with the question. They also may be sounding boards to providers involved in the decision-making process. Certainly the law should be followed, religious and cultural practices considered, and the clients' rights protected when possible, but no clearly established guideline is available.

Clients who willingly and openly discuss their beliefs and wishes concerning their own deaths should be encouraged to complete living wills, advance directives, and durable power of attorney documents. Legal counsel should be recommended to people if appropriate. Clients should not be made to feel ashamed or guilty because of their feelings about death, no matter how much they differ from your personal feelings.

Understanding and compassion are important. Every attempt must be made to respect the feelings of clients and their families. Families should be allowed to express any guilt they may feel in making decisions. A clear picture of the circumstances, explained by the provider in words clients can comprehend, can alleviate much of that problem. Clients who have strong feelings about having their lives prolonged should be encouraged to make their wishes known.

When health professionals are confronted with situations or questions they cannot handle, consultations and referrals should be sought. Attorneys may be called, and medical societies may offer assistance. Hospital ethics committees may be valuable. Hospital chaplains, staff psychiatrists, and social workers are specially trained to help others with these personal issues and processes involved.

SUMMARY

Choices about dying are best made while living whenever possible. Legal documents should be executed and shared with loved ones, family members, and health professionals to ensure that personal wishes are followed. These choices are not easily made unless there is a willingness to discuss the issue of death and what measures are to be taken when dying. If death can be viewed as another stage in life, even if the final one, it will be easier to have this discussion. Health professionals are bound to abide by the wishes of their clients within legal parameters.

 Watch It Now! Are you familiar with end-of-life issues? at http://FADavis.com, keyword *Tamparo*.

Questions for Review

SELECT THE BEST ANSWER

1. An advance directive
    a. Is quite different from the living will.
    b. Is a release made by parents for children.
    c. Expresses end-of-life issues.
    d. Replaces the Patient Self-Determination Act.
    e. None of the above.

2. Durable power of attorney for health care
    a. Appoints an agent to act on the behalf of another.
    b. Makes decisions related to finances and property.
    c. Is executed at the time of death.
    d. Must be recorded in the National Registry.
    e. Only a, b, and d above.

3. Euthanasia
    a. Is defined as murder.
    b. Means bad death.
    c. Is a term not often used today.
    d. Literally means "good death."
    e. Only c and d above.

4. Assisted death
    a. Is illegal.
    b. Is supported by the American Medical Association.
    c. Was legal in 10 jurisdictions as of 2020.
    d. Is under consideration in a number of other states.
    e. Only c and d above.

5. The five stages of grief
    a. Are identified by Kübler-Ross.
    b. Spell the acronym TEARS.
    c. Are passed through in sequence.
    d. Apply only to the dying.
    e. Only a and c above.

SHORT ANSWER QUESTIONS

1. Identify the common definition of grief work using the acronym TEAR.

_____

_____

_____

2. Explain the difference between durable power of attorney and durable power of attorney for health care.

_____

_____

_____

3. Identify Kübler-Ross' five stages of death.

_____

_____

_____

4. Compare two legal definitions of death.

_____

_____

_____

5. Define living will.

_____

_____

_____

CLASSROOM EXERCISES

1. If you knew you would be put in the same situation as Karen Ann Quinlan or Terri Schiavo, what would you wish? Why?

2. Identify procedures that prolong life that you would be willing to have. Identify those you would not choose and justify your responses.

3. A family member comes to the medical clinic. She is angry because the hospital "won't stop the endless testing" and "keeps trying the impossible with my husband." What is your response?

4. In the case of Ted in the opening Vignette and the conflicts that arose among Ted, the family, and the medical professionals, who held the power? Was the comment made by the ICU nurse regarding the advance directive dilemma appropriate? Explain your answer. Discuss your personal reaction to Ted's case. What went right and what went wrong?

INTERNET ACTIVITIES

1. Research the following website: https://www.deathwithdignity.org/assisted-dying-chronology/. What is your reaction? What surprises you the most?

2. Research the living will and/or advance directive appropriate for the state in which you live. Print the form and fill it out. What difficulty do you have in doing so? Discuss with a family member or a loved one.

3. Research artificial feeding and artificial hydration. Describe the difference. What makes the choice a critical one in the death process?

4. Research the Internet to determine the criteria necessary to be placed on a list for a donor kidney.

5. After Internet research, identify the requirements for an autopsy in your particular state.

REFERENCES

Hayes, D. M.: *Between Doctor and Patient*. Valley Forge, PA: Judson Press, 1977, pp. 9–11.

Munson, R.: *Intervention and Reflection: Basic Issues in Medical Ethics*. Belmont, CA: Wadsworth, 1992, p. 147.

For additional resources please visit
http://FADavis.com, keyword *Tamparo*.

Have a Care

AUTHOR'S NOTE

"Have a Care" appeared in the first edition of this text. It was then and remains now a moving story of one individual's life and struggle with chronic illness and the sometimes seemingly cruel management by health-care teams. The story's goal is to express how important—even essential—compassion, understanding, and empathy are to the care of individuals in need.

We share another poignant story with you here.

EILEEN

Eileen came into my life shortly after she moved with her husband to a continuing care retirement community (CCRC) in a fishing village on the Puget Sound. I first noticed her infectious smile and warm greeting, and then her motorized scooter.

Eileen's medical issues probably began when she was 15. She was diagnosed with a severe case of mononucleosis, which kept her out of school for a semester. Eileen grew into adulthood, spent years in and out of college, and would later earn a master's degree in clinical psychology. She spent years as a "wandering hippie," as she called herself. She became immersed in a spiritual journey seeking God. She spent time in India and lived in an ashram for 2 years in the 1970s, where she learned meditation and found quiet and peace, but not God.

She worked as a private therapist as well as a contract therapist for at-risk students. She found her work as the school therapist stressful because it brought her close to students who were enraged, extremely frustrated, and challenging to manage. On occasion Eileen would suffer bouts of severe exhaustion that would make it difficult for her to keep up with her responsibilities. She loved her work, however, and maintained an active life outside of work—especially hiking and swimming. She was always on the go.

While living in California, she joined a spiritual psychology group, where she met her soul mate and the man who would become her husband. The two married in 1990 and moved to Maui, Hawaii, in 1996. Eileen again opened a private practice as well as counseling at-risk students. The stress was extreme, but her husband, her love of the ocean, and her enjoyment of all the wonders of the island made her happy.

The happiness wouldn't last. Only a few months after beginning work in Maui, Eileen experienced the first symptom of a disease that took 3 years and many physician visits before finally being diagnosed as multiple sclerosis. **Multiple sclerosis** (MS) is a potentially disabling disease of the brain and spinal cord. In MS, the immune system attacks myelin, the protective sheath that covers nerve fibers. Any interruption in the myelin covering can cause communication problems between the brain and the rest of the body.

One night Eileen was awakened by what felt like an "electric shock" starting in the right side of her neck and moving down her right side, all the way to her foot. Such a symptom is known as **Lhermitte's sign** or **Lhermitte's phenomenon**. Also called the "barber chair phenomenon," this shocklike sensation typically occurs when the neck flexes, as when a barber cuts hair on the back of the neck. The sensation radiates down the spine, often into the legs, arms, and sometimes also into the trunk. Lhermitte's sign is caused by a stretching of highly excitable demyelinated nerves in the spinal cord, particularly those in the cervical region. This stretching results in the shocklike sensation. Eileen would continue to have Lhermitte's phenomenon throughout her care.

She visited her primary care provider (PCP), who ordered tests. Multiple tests were run, but showed no definitive solution or diagnosis, and her PCP dismissed her again and again with only the words, "You are really a strange one." Physical therapy was recommended.

The anxiety and fear of the unknown increased and added to her stress. Eileen was increasingly frustrated and requested a magnetic resonance imaging (MRI) scan. The wait for the MRI took 4 months. In the meantime, sometimes Eileen's right leg would buckle, often when she was in the shower. Her fatigue increased, and she experienced a tingling sensation in her neck and leg.

Between the initial event that took her to her PCP and a definitive diagnosis, Eileen would experience many encounters with her health-care team in the largest health maintenance organization (HMO) in Hawaii. Her first realization was that referrals did not come easily, and time never seemed to be in her favor.

*****

From 1996 to 1999, Eileen would see 11 different providers, make 2 trips to the emergency department, have more than 6 MRIs of the neck and/or brain, and receive a spinal tap. MRI referrals took anywhere from 6 weeks to 4 months to be approved. Providers did not agree on the MRI results. It could be MS; it could just be anxiety; the spot on the film is just an artifact; you should exercise more, do stomach crunches, and take muscle relaxants; gingko biloba will help; you might be having a stroke.

During this time Eileen experienced foot drop, leg spasms and weakness, and loss of strength to stand; could no longer drive safely or go to work; was confined to home; and needed assistance with daily living. She continued to suffer the Lhermitte's phenomenon, loss of weight, muscle cramping, and severe headaches. She was often dizzy and felt like her head was a fishbowl and she was a fish swimming around in it.

*****

While Eileen and her husband were doing massive research on MS, they were becoming increasingly frustrated with the system and a lack of a definitive diagnosis and treatment plan. They sought treatment with a specialist outside the HMO. This specialist reviewed the medical record and all the films. After an examination he told them, "This is not anxiety. There are spots at C2 and C3 of the cervical spine and two spots in the brain." He also recommended that they go to the mainland where there are specialists who see many individuals with MS-like symptoms for a more definitive diagnosis and treatment plan.

A friend of Eileen and her husband suggested they go to the Mayo Clinic. The HMO balked at the idea of the referral, but finally approved, agreeing to pay for *only* any tests they would run and only after prior approval. An appointment was made, and in December 1999 they made the trip, at their own expense. Flight arrangements were a nightmare—Eileen needed both a walker and a wheelchair—but they persevered.

On arrival and check-in at Mayo, they had 3 days of tests and numerous visits with specialists all trying to rule out MS. The "relapsing-remitting" form of MS, or RRMS, however, was the final diagnosis. Their intake physician told them there were three disease-modifying drugs that could help. The data showed that the drugs could slow the progression of the disease by approximately 30%, but they were extremely expensive and might not be covered by her insurance. He told them to go home, research the medications, and work with their neurologist to determine a course of treatment. They went back to the hotel dismayed and discouraged by the final diagnosis, knowing the disease would get worse and had no cure.

They reached out to their close friend to give her the news. She told them not to get on the plane and to wait for a call. Shortly a call came from Mayo Clinic instructing them to come to the clinic at 9 in the morning where they would be seeing Dr. Noseworthy, the head of the neurology department of some 60 physicians. (It seems the friend's father had strong connections to Mayo Clinic.)

On arriving at Mayo for the appointment with Dr. Noseworthy, his first words were, "Who do you know that would cause me to cancel a full schedule of all my morning appointments?" When given the name, Dr. Noseworthy smiled, but quickly calmed. He then reviewed all the records, discussed them with Eileen and her husband, and agreed with the assessment of the intake physician. He confirmed the recommended medications, adding his own advice that Eileen should take the most powerful one she could tolerate, because if she did not, she probably would become totally paralyzed. That information dashed all hopes of any recovery.

Back in Hawaii, now armed with a definitive diagnosis, her HMO finally referred her to a neurologist on Oahu, a specialist in MS. Dr. Chu made an immediate impression on Eileen when she walked into the examination room with braces on both legs. The doctor got up close to Eileen, took her hand, and just listened as she revealed her 3-year saga. They went home saying, "Had we had Dr. Chu in the first place, we would have had a solution much quicker, started the disease-modifying medication sooner, and maybe slowed the progression of MS."

Eileen and her husband moved to the Mainland in 2007 and immediately chose health care outside their HMO. They settled into an apartment in the CCRC decorated with lovely things from their lives. Today Eileen's activities are limited due to constant fatigue and sensitivity to heat. She is most uncomfortable when the temperature is above 68 degrees. She wears "ice pack" vests that she has made to wear when she is in public. She uses a motorized scooter. Loud noises and bright lights bother her. She is sensing some neurological facial issues. She leads a contemplative life reading, meditating, and looking out at the trees and sky from her chaise lounge.

During the writing of this piece she had several bouts of severe muscle twitching caused by the overactive nerves that would keep her from sleeping. This was the worse episode she'd had, and it took several days to find the best medication solution in order to find the calm to sleep.

*****

It is my privilege and honor to be Eileen's neighbor and friend. What is so special about Eileen? She is a determined participant of her health-care plan. She has tremendous support from her husband. She finally accepted what she could not control or change. She has an infectious smile and positive outlook. She knows the road ahead has many bumps, uncomfortable happenings, maybe even an unpleasant end, but her hope is that this story will encourage each of you to be better able to share your compassion

"Remember to be loving, gracious, human, and able to put yourself in the place of your clients. Remember that the client is someone with an illness or an injury. Clients are people with responsibilities, families, and personal and emotional needs."

Please, throughout your career as a health professional: "Have a Care."*

*****

Codes of Ethics

1. Hippocratic Oath, Classical and Modern Versions
2. American Association of Medical Assistants (AMAA)
3. Principles of Medical Ethics: American Medical Association

1. HIPPOCRATIC OATH, CLASSICAL VERSION*

I swear by Apollo Physician and Asclepius and Hygieia and Panaceia and all the gods and goddesses, making them my witnesses, that I will fulfil according to my ability and judgment this oath and this covenant:

To hold him who has taught me this art as equal to my parents and to live my life in partnership with him, and if he is in need of money to give him a share of mine, and to regard his offspring as equal to my brothers in male lineage and to teach them this art if they desire to learn it without fee and covenant; to give a share of precepts and oral instruction and all the other learning to my sons and to the sons of him who has instructed me and to pupils who have signed the covenant and have taken an oath according to the medical law, but to no one else.

I will apply dietetic measures for the benefit of the sick according to my ability and judgment; I will keep them from harm and injustice.

I will neither give a deadly drug to anybody if asked for it, nor will I make a suggestion to this effect. Similarly I will not give to a woman an abortive remedy. In purity and holiness I will guard my life and my art.

I will not use the knife, not even on sufferers from stone, but will withdraw in favor of such men as are engaged in this work.

Whatever houses I may visit, I will come for the benefit of the sick, remaining free of all intentional injustice, of all mischief and in particular of sexual relations with both female and male persons, be they free or slaves.

What I may see or hear in the course of the treatment or even outside of the treatment in regard to the life of men, which on no account one must spread abroad, I will keep to myself holding such things shameful to be spoken about.

*From Ludwig, E.: *The Hippocratic Oath.* Baltimore: Johns Hopkins University Press, 1943; and Lasagna, L.: *A modern version of the Hippocratic Oath.* Tufts University Medical School, 1964. Available at www.medterms.com

If I fulfil this oath and do not violate it, may it be granted to me to enjoy life and art, being honored with fame among all men for all time to come; if I transgress it and swear falsely, may the opposite of all this be my lot.

HIPPOCRATIC OATH, MODERN VERSION

I swear to fulfill, to the best of my ability and judgment, this covenant:

I will respect the hard-won scientific gains of those physicians in whose steps I walk, and gladly share such knowledge as is mine with those who are to follow.

I will apply, for the benefit of the sick, all measures which are required, avoiding those twin traps of overtreatment and therapeutic nihilism.

I will remember that there is art to medicine as well as science, and that warmth, sympathy, and understanding may outweigh the surgeon's knife or the chemist's drug.

I will not be ashamed to say "I know not," nor will I fail to call in my colleagues when the skills of another are needed for a patient's recovery.

I will respect the privacy of my patients, for their problems are not disclosed to me that the world may know. Most especially must I tread with care in matters of life and death. If it is given me to save a life, all thanks. But it may also be within my power to take a life; this awesome responsibility must be faced with great humbleness and awareness of my own frailty. Above all, I must not play at God.

I will remember that I do not treat a fever chart, a cancerous growth, but a sick human being, whose illness may affect the person's family and economic stability. My responsibility includes these related problems, if I am to care adequately for the sick.

I will prevent disease whenever I can, for prevention is preferable to cure.

I will remember that I remain a member of society, with special obligations to all my fellow human beings, those sound of mind and body as well as the infirm.

If I do not violate this oath, may I enjoy life and art, respected while I live and remembered with affection thereafter. May I always act so as to preserve the finest traditions of my calling and may I long experience the joy of healing those who seek my help.

2. AMERICAN ASSOCIATION OF MEDICAL ASSISTANTS (AAMA)[†]

AAMA CODE OF ETHICS FOR MEDICAL ASSISTANTS

The Code of Ethics of the AAMA sets forth principles of ethical and moral conduct as they relate to the medical profession and the particular practice of medical assisting.

Members of AAMA dedicated to the conscientious pursuit of their profession, and thus desiring to merit the high regard of the entire medical profession and the respect of the general public which they serve, do pledge themselves to strive always to:

A. Render service with full respect for the dignity of humanity.
B. Respect confidential information obtained through employment unless legally authorized or required by responsible performance of duty to divulge such information.
C. Uphold the honor and high principles of the profession and accept its disciplines.
D. Seek to continually improve the knowledge and skills of medical assistants for the benefit of patients and professional colleagues.
E. Participate in additional service activities aimed toward improving the health and well-being of the community.

[†]American Association of Medical Assistants, Chicago, IL, 1996–2020. Reprinted with permission.

MEDICAL ASSISTING CREED

The Medical Assisting Creed of the AAMA sets forth medical assisting statements of belief:

I believe in the principles and purposes of the profession of medical assisting.
I endeavor to be more effective.
I aspire to render greater service.
I protect the confidence entrusted to me.
I am dedicated to the care and well-being of all people.
I am loyal to my employer.
I am true to the ethics of my profession.
I am strengthened by compassion, courage, and faith.

3. PRINCIPLES OF MEDICAL ETHICS: AMERICAN MEDICAL ASSOCIATION‡

PREAMBLE

The medical profession has long subscribed to a body of ethical statements developed primarily for the benefit of the patient. As a member of this profession, a physician must recognize responsibility to patients first and foremost, as well as to society, to other health professionals, and to self. The following Principles adopted by the American Medical Association are not laws, but standards of conduct that define the essentials of honorable behavior for the physician.

PRINCIPLES OF MEDICAL ETHICS

    I. A physician shall be dedicated to providing competent medical care, with compassion and respect for human dignity and rights.

    II. A physician shall uphold the standards of professionalism, be honest in all professional interactions, and strive to report physicians deficient in character or competence, or engaging in fraud or deception, to appropriate entities.

    III. A physician shall respect the law and also recognize a responsibility to seek changes in those requirements which are contrary to the best interests of the patient.

    IV. A physician shall respect the rights of patients, colleagues, and other health professionals, and shall safeguard patient confidences and privacy within the constraints of the law.

    V. A physician shall continue to study, apply, and advance scientific knowledge, maintain a commitment to medical education, make relevant information available to patients, colleagues, and the public, obtain consultation, and use the talents of other health professionals when indicated.

    VI. A physician shall, in the provision of appropriate patient care, except in emergencies, be free to choose whom to serve, with whom to associate, and the environment in which to provide medical care.

    VII. A physician shall recognize a responsibility to participate in activities contributing to the improvement of the community and the betterment of public health.

    VIII. A physician shall, while caring for a patient, regard responsibility to the patient as paramount.

    IX. A physician shall support access to medical care for all people.

‡From the American Medical Association, adopted by the American Medical Association's House of Delegates, June 17, 2001. Reprinted with permission from American Medical Association, Code of Medical Ethics, Copyright 2001.

Sample Documents for Choices About Health Care, Life, and Death

DURABLE POWER OF ATTORNEY FOR HEALTH CARE AND HEALTH

DURABLE POWER OF ATTORNEY FOR HEALTH CARE

Notice to Person Executing This Document

This is an important legal document. Before executing this document you should know these facts:

- This document gives the person you designate as your Health Care Agent the power to make <u>MOST</u> health care decisions for you if you lose the capability to make informed health care decisions for yourself. This power is effective only when you lose the capacity to make informed health care decisions for yourself. As long as you have the capacity to make informed health care decisions for yourself, you retain the right to make all medical and other health care decisions.

- Your Health Care Agent should be someone you trust to make health care decisions on your behalf. Your Health Care Agent may be any adult, including relatives such as your spouse, state registered domestic partner, father, mother, adult child, or adult brother or sister. Unless they are one of the relatives listed above, your Health Care Agent may not be any of your physicians or your physicians' employees, or the owners, administrators or employees of a health care facility or long-term facility (as defined by RCW 43.190.020) where you reside or receive care.

- You may include specific limitations in this document on the authority of the Health Care Agent to make health care decisions for you.

- Subject to any specific limitations you include in this document, if you do lose the capacity to make an informed decision on a health care matter, the Health Care Agent GENERALLY will be authorized by this document to make health care decisions for you to the same extent as you could make those decisions yourself, if you had the capacity to do so. The authority of the Health Care Agent to make health care decisions for you GENERALLY will include the authority to give informed consent, to refuse to give informed consent, or to withdraw informed consent to any care, treatment, service, or procedure to maintain, diagnose, or treat a physical condition. You can limit that right in this document.

- When exercising authority to make health care decisions for you on your behalf, the Health Care Agent will have to act consistent with your wishes, or if they are unknown, in your best interest. You may make your wishes known to the Health Care Agent by including them in this document or in another manner.

- When acting under this document the Health Care Agent GENERALLY will have the same rights that you have to receive information about proposed health care, to review health care records, and to consent to the disclosure of health care records.

1. Creation of Durable Power of Attorney for Health Care

I intend to create a power of attorney (Health Care Agent) by appointing the person or persons designated herein to make health care decisions for me to the same extent that I could make such decisions for myself if I was capable of doing so, as recognized by Washington law. This power of attorney shall become effective when I become disabled and I cannot make health care decisions for myself as determined by my attending physician or designee, such as if I am unconscious, or if I am otherwise temporarily or permanently incapable of making health care decisions. The Health Care Agent's power shall cease if and when I regain my capacity to make health care decisions.

2. Designation of Health Care Agent and Alternate Agents

If my attending physician or his or her designee determines that I am not capable of giving informed consent to health care, I _____, designate and appoint:

Name _____ Address _____

City _____ State _____ Zip _____ Phone _____

as my attorney-in-fact (Health Care Agent) by granting him or her the Durable Power of Attorney for Health Care recognized in Washington law and authorize her or him to consult with my physicians about the possibility of my regaining the capacity to make treatment decisions and to accept, plan, stop, and refuse treatment on my behalf with the treating physicians and health personnel.

In the event that _____ is unable or unwilling to serve, I grant these powers to

Name _____ Address _____

City _____ State _____ Zip _____ Phone _____

In the event that both _____ and _____
are unable or unwilling to serve, I grant these powers to

Name _____ Address _____

City _____ State _____ Zip _____ Phone _____

DURABLE POWER OF ATTORNEY FOR HEALTH CARE

3. General Statement of Authority Granted

My Health Care Agent is specifically authorized to give informed consent for health care treatment when I am not capable of doing so. This includes but is not limited to consent to initiate, continue, discontinue, or forgo medical care and treatment including artificially supplied nutrition and hydration, following and interpreting my instructions for the provision, withholding, or withdrawing of life-sustaining treatment, which are contained in any Health Care Directive or other form of "living will" I may have executed or elsewhere, and to receive and consent to the release of medical information. When the Health Care Agent does not have any stated desires or instructions from me to follow, he or she shall act in my best interest in making health care decisions.

The above authorization to make health care decisions does not include the following absent a court order:

(1) Therapy or other procedure given for the purpose of inducing convulsion;

(2) Surgery solely for the purpose of psychosurgery;

(3) Commitment to or placement in a treatment facility for the mentally ill, except pursuant to the provisions of Chapter 71.05 RCW;

(4) Sterilization.

I hereby revoke any prior grants of durable power of attorney for health care.

4. Special Provisions

_____

_____

_____

DATED this_____day of _____, _____.

  (year)

GRANTOR _____ GRANTOR'S SIGNATURE_____

NOTE: Washington State requires this directive to be witnessed by two people or acknowledged by a notary public.

WITNESS REQUIREMENTS: The witnesses to this document must be competent and must NOT be:

- Related to you or your health care agent by blood, marriage, or state registered domestic partnership.
- Your home care provider or a care provider at an adult family home or long-term care facility where you live.
- Your designated health care agent(s).

WITNESS_____   WITNESS_____

STATE OF WASHINGTON   )
)
(COUNTY _____)

This record was acknowledged before me on this _____ day of _____ _____, _____.

by _____ .
      (Name of individual)

                                    _____
                                         (Signature of notary public)

        (Stamp)   _____
                                         (Title of office)

                                    My commission expires _____

HEALTH CARE DIRECTIVE

Directive made this _____ day of _____, _____.

(year)

I, _____ being of sound mind, willfully, and voluntarily make known my desire that my dying shall not be artificially prolonged under the circumstances set forth below, and do hereby declare that:

(A) If at any time I should have an incurable and irreversible condition certified to be a terminal condition by my attending physician, and where the application of life-sustaining treatment would serve only to artificially prolong the process of my dying, I direct that such treatment be withheld or withdrawn, and that I be permitted to die naturally. I understand "terminal condition" means an incurable and irreversible condition caused by injury, disease, or illness that would, within reasonable medical judgment, cause death within a reasonable period of time in accordance with accepted medical standards.

(B) If I should be in an irreversible coma or persistent vegetative state, or other permanent unconscious condition as certified by two physicians, and from which those physicians believe that I have no reasonable probability of recovery, I direct that life-sustaining treatment be withheld or withdrawn.

(C) If I am diagnosed to be in a terminal or permanent unconscious condition, [*Choose one*]
I want _____ do not want _____
artificially administered nutrition and hydration to be withdrawn or withheld the same as other forms of life-sustaining treatment. I understand artificially administered nutrition and hydration is a form of life-sustaining treatment in certain circumstances. I request all health care providers who care for me to honor this directive.

(D) In the absence of my ability to give directions regarding the use of such life-sustaining procedures, it is my intention that this directive shall be honored by my family, physicians, and other health care providers as the final expression of my fundamental right to refuse medical or surgical treatment, and also honored by any person appointed to make these decisions for me, whether by durable power of attorney or otherwise. I accept the consequences of such refusal.

(E) If I have been diagnosed as pregnant and that diagnosis is known to my physician, this directive shall have no force or effect during the course of my pregnancy.

(F) I understand the full import of this directive and I am emotionally and mentally competent to make this directive. I also understand that I may amend or revoke this directive at any time.

(G) I make the following additional directions regarding my care:

_____

_____

_____

_____

WITNESS_____   WITNESS_____

STATE OF WASHINGTON   )
)
(COUNTY _____)

This record was acknowledged before me on this _____ day of _____ _____, _____.

by _____ .
         (Name of individual)

_____
(Signature of notary public)

(Stamp)   _____
                                       (Title of office)

                                       My commission expires _____

What To Do With These Forms

The attached Health Care Directive and Durable Power of Attorney for Health Care forms are all legal documents once they are completely filled out and signed with the appropriate signatures. Signed copies of the completed directives should be included in your medical record, given to any person to whom you give your durable power of attorney—including any alternate people you may have named—and to your personal attorney. Originals should be kept by someone you trust and who can obtain them in an emergency.

For Further Information

These forms have been provided as a public service by the Washington State Medical Association. You are encouraged to discuss the directives with your physician. Any legal questions you may have about the use and effect of these directives may be answered by an attorney.

CARE DIRECTIVE FORMS

Available at https://wsma.org/advance-directives; free download available.

ORGAN DONATION FORM

The top portion of the card (printed upside-down) reads:

of
_____
(Print or type name of donor)

In the hope that I may help others, I hereby make this anatomical gift,
if medically acceptable, to take effect upon my death. The word and
marks below indicate my desires.

I give: (a) ____ any needed organs or parts,
          (b) ____ only the following organs or parts
_____
(specify the organs or parts)

for the purpose of transplantation, therapy, medical research,
or education.
Limitations or special wishes, if any:

UNIFORM DONOR CARD

- - - - - - - - - FOLD HERE - - - - - - - - -

UNIFORM DONOR CARD

Signed by the donor and the following two witnesses
in the presence of each other

_____   _____
Signature of Donor   Date of Birth

_____   _____
City and State   Date Signed

_____   _____
Witness   Witness

This a legal document under the Uniform Anatomical Gift Act
or similar laws. For further information, contact the New England
Organ Bank **1 800 446-NEOB** or the Center for Donation and
Transplant **1 800 803-6667.**

ORGAN DONATION CARD

Available at https://www.organdonor.gov/register.html; choose a state for registering; donor cards
not necessary with registration.

INDEX

Note: Page numbers followed by *f* refer to figures; those followed by *t* refer to tables.